State Ocean Jurisdiction

Proposing a systematic analytical framework which assists in understanding and applying the international law regime governing State ocean jurisdiction with a view to improved ocean governance for sustainable development, this book distinguishes between, and focuses on, the form, the ground, the scope and the purpose of State ocean jurisdiction. Defining jurisdiction as the international-law authority of a State to be involved in a factual matter on the basis of a valid legal ground to perform authoritative acts impacting on that matter, it disaggregates the concept the complexity of which often leads to States failing to make full use of their existing ocean jurisdictions. In the process, it identifies when and to what extent there are gaps and overlaps of jurisdictions. Bringing clarity on an inevitably complex and often misunderstood framework that is aimed at striking a universally accepted balance of competing interests, the book lays the foundation for future research, contextualising the position of State ocean jurisdiction not only in terms of ocean governance, but in the whole of public international law. With an original systematic focus on State ocean jurisdiction, the book will be of interest to academics, students and practitioners working in the areas of international law of the sea, ocean governance, human rights and environmental law.

Patrick Vrancken is the incumbent of the South African Research Chair in the Law of the Sea and Development in Africa, which is funded by the South African National Research Foundation and hosted at Nelson Mandela University, where he is professor in the Department of Public Law.

Routledge Research on the Law of the Sea

Available titles in this series include:

The International Court of Justice in Maritime Disputes
The Case of Chile and Peru
Julio Faundez

Freedoms of Navigation in the Asia-Pacific Region
Strategic, Political and Legal Factors
Sam Bateman

Maritime Claims and Boundary Delimitation
Tensions and Trends in the Eastern Mediterranean Sea
Nicholas A. Ioannides

Freedom of Navigation and the Law of the Sea
Warships, States and the Use of Force
Cameron Moore

Due Diligence and the High Seas
Tony Cabus

The Law of the Sea
Normative Context and Interactions with other Legal Regimes
Edited by Nele Matz-Lück, Øystein Jensen and Elise Johansen

Law of the Sea and Maritime Delimitation
State Practice and Case Law in Latin America and the Caribbean
Angel Horna

Maritime Salvage Operations and Environmental Protection
Durand M Cupido

Peaceful Management of Maritime Disputes
James Kraska and Hee Cheol Yang

State Ocean Jurisdiction

Patrick Vrancken

Routledge
Taylor & Francis Group
LONDON AND NEW YORK

First published 2023
by Routledge
4 Park Square, Milton Park, Abingdon, Oxon OX14 4RN

and by Routledge
605 Third Avenue, New York, NY 10158

Routledge is an imprint of the Taylor & Francis Group, an informa business

British Library Cataloguing-in-Publication Data
A catalogue record for this book is available from the British Library

ISBN: 978-1-032-46137-3 (hbk)
ISBN: 978-1-032-46937-9 (pbk)
ISBN: 978-1-003-38387-1 (ebk)

DOI: 10.4324/9781003383871

Typeset in Times New Roman
by Deanta Global Publishing Services, Chennai, India

Contents

Preface

I started reflecting almost compulsively on State ocean jurisdiction at the beginning of my tenure as the incumbent of the South African Research in the Law of the Sea and Development in Africa. At that time, I became involved, among others, in efforts to raise awareness among States about the many, sometimes egregious, forms of criminal behaviour sometimes associated with fishing activities, and to support States in taking legal and practical steps to combat that behaviour, thereby reducing its impact both on the natural environment and on all those among us who are either directly or indirectly affected by it. I realised that one of the factors complicating the identification and taking of those steps is the fact that the State ocean jurisdiction framework is much more complex than the related framework applicable on land. That complexity creates opportunities for (often international) criminal syndicates, who take advantage of existing or perceived areas of uncertainty. At the same time, that complexity paralyses organs of State responsible for law enforcement, who are not given the legal authority that they need and/or decide not to exercise that authority, in case of doubt, for fear of acting ultra vires.

As I grappled with the intricacies of the State ocean jurisdiction framework, I became convinced that the limited, but excellent work on State jurisdiction, from a primarily land perspective, does not offer the best foundation on which to disaggregate its ocean component. I also became convinced that the main reason is probably the emphasis on territoriality (and extraterritoriality) that finds limited support at sea and that leads to a one-size-fits-all approach that does not accord well with the variegated nature of State ocean jurisdiction. This work will have reached its goal if it brings greater clarity to all ocean stakeholders on an inevitably complex and often misunderstood framework that is aimed at striking a universally accepted balance of competing interests and, as a result, if it injects renewed analytical rigour into research and advocacy related to the wide range of urgent ocean-governance challenges with which humankind is confronted.

As I already pointed out a decade ago, academic life in a so-called developing State has both advantages and disadvantages, which are combined in a unique way in a State like South Africa. Once again, making the most of the former while overcoming the latter would have been impossible without funding from the South African National Research Foundation (grant number: UID 85714) which, among others, made it possible for this work to be available on an open-access basis. In addition, I gratefully acknowledge the financial and material assistance of the research support structures at Nelson Mandela University (NMU) as well as the financial support of the UK Research and Innovation's GCRF One Ocean Hub project (grant reference: NE/S008950/1). I am very grateful for the managerial support of Prof Avinash Govindjee (the Dean of the NMU Faculty of Law before he rose to the Bench of the High Court) and Dr Lynn Biggs (who has acted as the Dean since then). Among the many individuals who provided invaluable assistance, I must single out Prof Derry Devine, emeritus professor in the Faculty of Law at the University of Cape Town who, without hesitation, accepted to peruse the draft of this longer-than-average manuscript and to give me the benefit of his always extremely meticulous comments. I also thank Dr Tajudeen Sanni and Ms Miche-Lee Van Schalkwyk, my research and editorial assistants. Moreover, I am indebted to Ms Siobhán Poole, Mr Sanjo Puthumana and their colleagues at Routledge for their utmost professionalism. Finally, I am, as always, by far the most indebted to my spouse, Maria, and my two daughters, Ashley and Candysse, for their countless sacrifices as well as their unremitting love and support.

Patrick Vrancken
Nelson Mandela Bay
October 2022

Abbreviations

AFDI	Annuaire français de droit international
AIDI	Annuaire de l'Institut de droit international
AJIL	American Journal of International Law
ATS	Australian Treaty Series
BYIL	British Yearbook of International Law
CBD	1992 Convention on Biological Diversity
CCNH	1972 Convention for the Protection of the World Cultural and Natural Heritage
CCNL	1930 Hague Convention on Certain Questions Relating to the Conflict of Nationality Laws
CHS	1958 Convention on the High Seas
CLCS	Commission on the Limits of the Continental Shelf
CLRHS	1958 Convention on Fishing and Conservation of the Living Resources of the High Seas
CPJC	1952 Convention on Penal Jurisdiction in Matters of Collision
CPUCH	2001 Convention on the Protection of the Underwater Cultural Heritage
Cs jurisdiction	continental shelf jurisdiction
CsA jurisdiction	adjudicative continental shelf jurisdiction
CsE jurisdiction	executive continental shelf jurisdiction
CsL jurisdiction	legislative continental shelf jurisdiction
CTS	Consolidated Treaty Series
CTSCZ	1958 Convention on the Territorial Sea and Contiguous Zone
CWILJ	California Western International Law Journal
Cz jurisdiction	contiguous zone jurisdiction
CzE jurisdiction	executive contiguous zone jurisdiction
CzL jurisdiction	legislative contiguous zone jurisdiction
D jurisdiction	delegated jurisdiction
DOALOS	United Nations Division for Ocean Affairs and the Law of the Sea
ECHR	1950 Convention for the Protection of Human Rights and Fundamental Freedoms
ECtHR	European Court of Human Rights
ECJ	European Court of Justice

ECN	1997 European Convention on Nationality
EEZ	exclusive economic zone
Eez jurisdiction	exclusive economic zone jurisdiction
EezA jurisdiction	adjudicative exclusive economic zone jurisdiction
EezE jurisdiction	executive exclusive economic zone jurisdiction
EezL jurisdiction	legislative exclusive economic zone jurisdiction
EIF	entry into force
EJIL	European Journal of International Law
EU	European Union
F jurisdiction	flag State jurisdiction
FA jurisdiction	adjudicative flag State jurisdiction
FAO	Food and Agriculture Organisation
FCCC	1992 United Nations Framework Convention on Climate Change
FE jurisdiction	executive flag State jurisdiction
Fish Stocks Agreement	1995 Agreement for the Implementation of the Provisions of the United Nations Convention on the Law of the Sea of 10 December 1982 Relating to the Conservation and Management of Straddling Fish Stocks and Highly Migratory Fish Stocks
FL jurisdiction	legislative flag State jurisdiction
Fo jurisdiction	objective flag State jurisdiction
FoA jurisdiction	adjudicative objective flag State jurisdiction
FoE jurisdiction	executive objective flag State jurisdiction
FoL jurisdiction	legislative objective flag State jurisdiction
Fs jurisdiction	subjective flag State jurisdiction
FsA jurisdiction	adjudicative subjective flag State jurisdiction
FsE jurisdiction	executive subjective flag State jurisdiction
FsL jurisdiction	legislative subjective flag State jurisdiction
GYIL	German Yearbook of International Law
ICCPR	1966 International Covenant on Civil and Political Rights
ICESCR	1966 International Covenant on Economic, Social and Cultural Rights
ICJ	International Court of Justice
ICLQ	International and Comparative Law Quarterly
ICNT	1977 Informal Composite Negotiating Text
ICRW	2007 Nairobi International Convention on the Removal of Wrecks
IDI	Institute of International Law
IJMCL	International Journal of Marine and Coastal Law
ILA	International Law Association
ILC	International Law Commission
ILM	International Legal Materials
ILO	International Labour Organisation

ILR	International Law Reports
IMO	International Maritime Organization
ISA	International Seabed Authority
ISNT	1975 Informal Single Negotiating Text
ITLOS	International Tribunal for the Law of the Sea
IUU	illegal, unreported and unregulated
JHIL	Journal of the History of International Law
JICJ	Journal of International Criminal Justice
JMLC	Journal of Maritime Law and Commerce
JOLGA	Journal of Ocean Law and Governance in Africa
LC 1972	1972 Convention on the Prevention of Marine Pollution by Dumping of Wastes and Other Matter
LCP	Law and Contemporary Problems
LNTS	League of Nations Treaty Series
LOSB	Law of the Sea Bulletin
LOSC	1982 United Nations Convention on the Law of the Sea
MARPOL	1973 International Convention for the Prevention of Pollution from Ships, as amended by its 1978 Protocol
MP	Marine Policy
MPA	marine protected area
MPEPIL	Max Planck Encyclopedia of Public International Law
NJIL	Nordic Journal of International Law
NM	nautical miles
NSA	non-State actor
ODAS	ocean data acquisition system
ODIL	Ocean Development and International Law
OY	Ocean Yearbook
P jurisdiction	personal jurisdiction
PA jurisdiction	adjudicative personal jurisdiction
Part XI Agreement	1994 Agreement Relating to the Implementation of Part XI of the United Nations Convention on the Law of the Sea of 10 December 1982
PCA	Permanent Court of Arbitration
PCIJ	Permanent Court of International Justice
PE jurisdiction	executive personal jurisdiction
Pe jurisdiction	protective jurisdiction exercised for economic purposes
PeA jurisdiction	adjudicative protective jurisdiction exercised for economic purposes
PeE jurisdiction	executive protective jurisdiction exercised for economic purposes
PeL jurisdiction	legislative protective jurisdiction exercised for economic purposes
Pi jurisdiction	piracy jurisdiction
PiA jurisdiction	adjudicative piracy jurisdiction
PiE jurisdiction	executive piracy jurisdiction

PiL jurisdiction	legislative piracy jurisdiction
PL jurisdiction	legislative personal jurisdiction
Po jurisdiction	objective personal jurisdiction
Pp jurisdiction	passive personal jurisdiction
PRLPJ	Pacific Rim Law & Policy Journal
Ps jurisdiction	protective jurisdiction exercised for State security purposes
PsA jurisdiction	adjudicative protective jurisdiction exercised for State security purposes
PsE jurisdiction	executive protective jurisdiction exercised for State security purposes
PsL jurisdiction	legislative protective jurisdiction exercised for State security purposes
PSM	2000 Protocol against the Smuggling of Migrants by Land, Sea and Air, Supplementing the 2000 United Nations Convention against Transnational Organised Crime
PSMA	2009 Agreement on Port State Measures to Prevent, Deter and Eliminate Illegal, Unreported and Unregulated Fishing
Pt jurisdiction	port State jurisdiction
PtA jurisdiction	adjudicative port State jurisdiction
PtE jurisdiction	executive port State jurisdiction
PtL jurisdiction	legislative port State jurisdiction
RCADI	Recueil des cours de l'Académie de droit international
RGDIP	Revue générale de droit international public
RSNT	1976 Revised Single Negotiating Text
SAYIL	South African Yearbook of International Law
SCAS	1956 Supplementary Convention on the Abolition of Slavery, the Slave Trade, and Institutions and Practices Similar to Slavery
Sl jurisdiction	slave trade jurisdiction
SlE jurisdiction	executive slave trade jurisdiction
SPLOS	Meeting of States parties to the LOSC
St jurisdiction	statelessness jurisdiction
StA jurisdiction	adjudicative statelessness jurisdiction
StE jurisdiction	executive statelessness jurisdiction
StL jurisdiction	legislative statelessness jurisdiction
SUA	1988 Convention for the Suppression of Unlawful Acts against the Safety of Maritime Navigation
SUA PROT	1988 Protocol for the Suppression of Unlawful Acts against the Safety of Fixed Platforms Located on the Continental Shelf to the SUA
T jurisdiction	territorial jurisdiction
TA jurisdiction	adjudicative territorial jurisdiction
TE jurisdiction	executive territorial jurisdiction
TILJ	Texas International Law Journal
TL jurisdiction	legislative territorial jurisdiction

To jurisdiction objective territorial jurisdiction
Ts jurisdiction subjective territorial jurisdiction
UDHR 1948 Universal Declaration of Human Rights
UKTS United Kingdom Treaty Series
UN United Nations
UNC 1945 Charter of the United Nations
UNCLOS I First United Nations Conference on the Law of the Sea
UNCLOS III Third United Nations Conference on the Law of the Sea
UNCTAD United Nations Conference on Trade and Development
UNGA General Assembly of the United Nations
UNICPOLOS United Nations Open-Ended Informal Consultative Process on Oceans and the Law of the Sea
UNEP United Nations Environment Programme
UNSC Security Council of the United Nations
UNTS United Nations Treaty Series
VCLT 1969 Vienna Convention on the Law of Treaties
VOC United East India Company
YILC Yearbook of the International Law Commission

Table of Cases

PERMANENT COURT OF INTERNATIONAL JUSTICE

INTERNATIONAL COURT OF JUSTICE

PERMANENT COURT OF ARBITRATION

INTERNATIONAL TRIBUNAL FOR THE LAW OF THE SEA

EUROPEAN COURT OF JUSTICE

EUROPEAN COURT OF HUMAN RIGHTS

AUSTRALIAN CASE

BRITISH CASES

CANADIAN CASES

FRENCH CASES

GHANAIAN CASE

PAPUA NEW GUINEAN CASE

SINGAPOREAN CASE

TONGAN CASE

UNITED STATES CASES

Table of International Instruments

1 Introduction

1.1 Introduction

The first rules governing relations between independent human groups are probably forever forgotten in the deep recesses of humankind's prehistory.[1] We will also probably never know when, and under what circumstances, humans first interacted with the ocean environment. What we know, however, is that the scale of human activities at sea increased considerably during the last two centuries.[2] Today, that has resulted in a great number and complexity of conflicts between stakeholders in marine spaces as well as an ever-increasing negative impact on the marine environment. For those reasons, an appropriate normative regime to govern the oceans has never been, early in the twenty-first century of the present era, so crucial to our survival as a species.[3] At the same time, States are the polities claiming primary normative powers and the exclusive right to use force at sea.[4] As a result, a thorough understanding of the attribution and exercise of State authority in ocean matters is essential if humankind is to have any chance of overcoming the challenges ahead. At the beginning of this book, which aims to make a contribution to that understanding, this chapter outlines humankind's uses of the ocean environment, identifies the various stakeholders at sea and interrogates the concept of "jurisdiction", before it sketches the analytical framework described in depth in the following chapters.

1.2 Maritime uses

The oceans and their resources have been part of the natural resources used by coastal communities for at least 150,000 years.[5] In due course, technology and

1 See e.g., A Altman "Tracing the earliest recorded concepts of international law. The early dynastic period in southern Mesopotamia" (2004) 6 JHIL 153–172 at 153.

2 See e.g., L Lucchini & M Voelckel *Droit de la Mer* (1990) I 18.

3 See e.g., M Vœlckel *Rien que la Mer* (1981) 132.

4 See e.g., D Guilfoyle "Article 107" in A Proelss (ed) *United Nations Convention on the Law of the Sea – A Commentary* (2017) 755–759.

5 See e.g., B M Holt "Anatomically modern *Homo sapiens*" in M P Muehlenbein (ed) *Basics in Human Evolution* (2015) 177–192 at 186; K Kyriacou, JE Parkington, AD Marais & DR Braun "Nutrition, modernity and the archaeological record: Coastal resources and nutrition among Middle Stone Age hunter-gatherers on the western Cape coast of South Africa" (2014) 77 *Journal of Human Evolution* 64–73, on evidence found on several sites along the southern and south-western coasts of South Africa; RC Walter *et al.* "Early human occupation of the Red Sea coast of Eritrea during the last interglacial" (2000) 405 *Nature* 65–69.

DOI: 10.4324/9781003383871-1

knowledge of the marine environment improved to such an extent that migration took place across the Indonesian archipelago into Australasia at least 40,000 years ago.[6] Further developments made it possible for the Sumerians, 4,000 years ago, to be engaged in maritime trade with their neighbours around the Persian Gulf and beyond.[7] At the same time, the Minoans, and later the Phoenicians, were trading across the Mediterranean,[8] sometimes venturing beyond the Strait of Gibraltar,[9] probably up to the British Isles[10] and down the coast of West Africa,[11] while the Egyptians plied the waters of the Red Sea up to the Horn of Africa[12] and ventured even further. Herodotus relates the three-year journey around what was then referred to as "Libya", undertaken about 2,600 years ago by a crew of Phoenicians sent by the Egyptian pharaoh Neco.[13] If the journey did indeed take place, one of the most striking phenomena the crew experienced and duly reported – so we are told – must have been seeing the noon sun moving from the back to the right and then to the front as they rounded the southern African coast from east to west.[14] When the Romans asserted their authority over the Mediterranean, 2,000 years ago, they had developed the means to control that body of water in such a way that they were able to claim it as *mare nostrum*,[15] from which they regularly sailed to India after crossing the land bridge between Africa and Asia.[16] In fact, the Mediterranean was integrally linked to the Indian Ocean[17] which, in contrast, was "free of state

6 See e.g., WF McNeil *Visitors to Ancient America: The Evidence for European and Asian Presence in America Prior to Columbus* (2004) 18; D Salesa "The Pacific in indigenous time" in D Armitage & A Bashford (eds) *Pacific Histories* (2014) 31–52 at 33–34. See further e.g., P Johnstone & S McGrail *The Sea-Craft of Prehistory* (1988) 3–16.

7 See e.g., ECL During Caspers "New archaeological evidence for maritime trace in the Persian Gulf during the late protoliterate period" (1971) 21 *East and West* 21–44.

8 See e.g., AB Knapp "Thalassocracies in Bronze Age eastern Mediterranean trade: Making and breaking a myth" (1993) 24(3) *World Archaeology* 332–347. See also e.g., P Horden & N Purcell "The Mediterranean and 'the New Thalassology'" (2006) 111 (3) *American Historical Review* 722–740.

9 See e.g., A Brody "From the Hills of Adonis through the Pillars of Hercules: Recent advances in the archaeology of Canaan and Phoenicia" (2002) 65(1) *Near Eastern Archaeology* 69–80.

10 See e.g., M Denny *How the Oceans Work* (2012) 4.

11 See e.g., DB Harden "The Phoenicians on the West Coast of Africa" (1948) 22 *Antiquity* 141–150.

12 See e.g., J Phillips "Punt and Aksum: Egypt and the Horn of Africa" (1997) 38(3) *Journal of African History* 423–457 at 445–449.

13 Herodotus *The Histories* (1997) IV 42.

14 R Knox-Johnston *The Cape of Good Hope: A Maritime History* (1989) 20–26.

15 See e.g., DJ Bederman "The sea" in D Fassbender *et al.* (eds) *The Oxford Handbook of the History of International Law* (2012) 359–379 at 363. See further Chapter 5 section 5.3.

16 See e.g., RP Anand *Origin and Development of the Law of the Sea* (1982) 14–16; MP Fitzpatrick "Provincializing Rome: The Indian Ocean trade network and Roman imperialism" (2011) 22(1) *Journal of World History* 27–54.

17 See e.g., P Beaujard "The Indian Ocean in Eurasian and African World-Systems before the Sixteenth Century" (2005) 16(4) *Journal of World History* 411–465 at 412. See further e.g., EA Alpers *The Indian Ocean in World History* (2014).

power".[18] At that time, "the Malay peoples were already intrepid sailors, travelling long distances",[19] sometimes up to the east coast of Africa.[20] During the ensuing centuries, African, Arab, Chinese and Indian vessels turned the region into the world's main maritime trade area[21] while, further east, Polynesian peoples crossed hundreds of miles of open sea to settle and trade between the Pacific islands.[22]

The fifteenth century witnessed an extraordinary outburst of maritime activity. In the East, "Zheng He commanded a series of voyages which extended over three decades and involved the deployment of great fleets and tens of thousands of soldiers and officials on journeys that lasted for years and which eventually took the Chinese as far as the Red Sea and the coast of Africa".[23] In the West, besides maritime trade which had thrived in the Baltic Sea and the North Sea during the whole period of the Middle Ages,[24] the focus shifted towards south-western Europe. Indeed, the until-then-peripheral Iberian nations of Portugal and Spain found a competitive advantage by establishing permanent links with the Americas across the Atlantic as well as with sub-Saharan Africa and south-east Asia around the Cape of Good Hope.[25] Although other European nations very quickly started trading along the same routes,[26] the scale of shipping remained limited[27] until the nineteenth century when, in the Pacific, Europeans slowly supplanted the Polynesians,[28] at the same time that industrialisation progressively turned maritime transportation into the major globalised industry that it is today.[29]

The development of sailing techniques and knowledge not only had an impact on the nature and scale of navigation and maritime trade, but also on fishing. While the contribution of small-scale fishing to the GDP remains largely underestimated

18 T Andrade "Was the European sailing ship a key technology of European extension? Evidence from East Asia" (2011) 23(2) *International Journal of Maritime History* 17–40 at 18. See also e.g., Anand (n. 16) 20; *Award of the Arbitral Tribunal in the Second Stage of the Proceedings (Maritime Delimitation) (Eritrea v. Yemen)*, award of 17 December 1999, XXII RIAA 335 § 85.

19 LN Shaffer *Maritime Southeast Asia to 1500* (1996) 11.

20 *Ibid.* 16.

21 Beaujard (n. 17) 411–465. C Bouchard & W Crumplin "Neglected no longer: The Indian Ocean at the forefront of world geopolitics and global geostrategy" (2010) 6(1) *Journal of the Indian Ocean Region* 26–51 at 27.

22 See e.g., Denny (n. 10) 4.

23 C Wake "The myth of Zheng He's great treasure ships" (2004) 16(1) *International Journal of Maritime History* 59–75 at 59.

24 See e.g., N Hybel "The grain trade in Northern Europe before 1350" (2002) 55(2) *Economic History Review* 219–247.

25 K Zemanek "Was Hugo Grotius really in favour of the freedom of the seas?" (1999) 1 JHIL 48–60 at 48.

26 See e.g., RP Anand "Maritime practice in South-East Asia until 1600 AD and the modern law of the sea" (1981) 30(2) ICLQ 440–454 at 441.

27 See e.g., AP Usher "The growth of English shipping 1572–1922" (1928) 42(3) *Quarterly Journal of Economics* 465–478.

28 See e.g., N Thomas "The age of empire in the Pacific" in Armitage & Bashford (n. 6) 75–96.

29 See e.g., UNCTAD *Review of Maritime Transport 2019* (2019).

today,[30] that maritime activity has made a vital contribution to the life of coastal communities for millennia is undisputed.[31] Indeed, there is evidence of fishing in the Arctic Ocean, the North Sea and the Persian Gulf, as well as along the Chinese and southern African coasts, at least 5,000 years ago.[32] As far as they are concerned, the Romans were efficiently harvesting species such as the Bluefin tuna, something which was only possible by means of "large scale fishing operations requiring the support of an association of fishermen or investments from wealthy businessmen to supply expensive nets, boats, and lookouts".[33] However, "the people of the Roman Empire never developed the technology to over-exploit sea resources and threaten the fish stock of the Mediterranean".[34] One would have to wait for "[t]he invention of machinery at the beginning of the industrial era [to see] revolutionary developments and […] a complete change to the structure of fisheries".[35] Today, overfishing,[36] fisheries crime[37] and environmental pressures,[38] including climate change,[39] make ever more urgent the adoption of the necessary measures to ensure sustainable fisheries and aquaculture for the sake of better food security and nutrition.[40]

As far as it is concerned, the exploitation of non-living resources remained, until recently, affected by severe technical constraints. "The first known instance of undersea mining occurred 2,000 years ago when the Greeks dug lead and zinc ores out of the Mediterranean".[41] But it is only late into the nineteenth century that, as a result of the considerable increase in world energy demand, huge oil and gas resources were discovered and the technology necessary for their exploitation was developed.[42] Since then, exploitation has been taking place on an increasingly

30 See e.g., D Zeller, S Booth & D Pauly "Fisheries contributions to the gross domestic product: Underestimating small-scale fisheries in the Pacific" (2006) 21(4) *Marine Resources Economics* 355–374.
31 See e.g., KM Stewart "Early hominid utilization of fish resources and implications for seasonality and behaviour" (1994) 27(13) *Journal of Human Evolution* 229–245.
32 See D Sahrhage & J Lundbeck *A History of Fishing* (1992) 12–41.
33 AJ Papalas "Review of A Marzano *Harvesting the Sea: The Exploitation of Marine Resources in the Roman Mediterranean* (2014)" (2015) 27(1) *Journal of Maritime History* 158–159 at 158.
34 *Ibid.*
35 See Sahrhage & Lundbeck (n. 32) 103.
36 See e.g., AN Honniball "Engaging Asian States on combatting IUU fishing: The curious case of the State of nationality in EU regulation and practice" (2021) 10 *Transnational Environmental Law* 543–569.
37 See e.g., E de Coning & E Witbooi "Towards a new 'fisheries crime' paradigm: South Africa as an illustrative example' (2015) 60 MP 208–215; P Vrancken, E Witbooi & J Glazewski "Introduction and overview: Transnational organised fisheries crime" (2019) 105 MP 116–122.
38 See e.g., E Hey "The Anthropocene, five discourses and frontier space" in R Barnes & R Long (eds) *Frontiers in International Environmental Law: Oceans and Climate Challenges* (2021) 515–532.
39 See e.g., D Bodansky "The ocean and climate change law" in Barnes & Long (n. 38) 316–336; S Lee & L Bautista "Climate change and sea level rise" in Barnes & Long (n. 38) 194–214.
40 See e.g., FAO *Sustainable Fisheries and Aquaculture for Better Food Security and Nutrition* (2014).
41 RF Marx *The History of Underwater Exploration* (1990) 163.
42 MW Mouton "The impact of science on international law" (1966) 119 RCADI 183–258 at 197–198.

wider scale,[43] at greater and greater depths[44] and in more and more challenging locations, such as the Arctic.[45]

The above are not the only uses of the ocean environment made by humankind. For instance, pearls have been harvested for hundreds of years in the Indian Ocean (primarily in the Gulf of Mannar, between India and Sri Lanka,[46] and around Bahrain Island)[47] as well as in lower California[48] and southern China.[49] Much more recently, the first submarine cable was laid between Calais and Dover in 1851[50] and a treaty to protect submarine cables was adopted as early as 1884.[51] Today, the global economy and international communication are heavily dependent on the vast network of cables that crisscross the oceans.[52] The technology to exploit ocean renewable energy is constantly improving,[53] marine tourism has become a major segment of the tourism industry[54] and marine genetic resources are the object of increasing interest.[55] In short, while the oceans continue to play a crucial role in geo-strategic terms,[56] they are now seen as a challenge and priority for sustainable development at the national,[57] regional[58] and global levels,[59] something which is

43 See e.g., S Managi *et al.* "Forecasting energy supply and pollution from the offshore oil and gas industry" (2004) 19(3) *Marine Resource Economics* 307–332.
44 See e.g., JG Speight *Handbook of Offshore Oil and Gas Operations* (2015) 161–167.
45 See e.g., T Koivurova "Framing the problem in Arctic offshore hydrocarbon exploitation" in C Pelaudeix & EM Basse (eds) *Governance of Arctic Offshore Oil and Gas* (2018) 19–30.
46 See CJB Hurst "Whose is the bed of the sea? Sedentary fisheries outside the three-mile limit" (1923/1924) 4 BYIL 34–43 at 41.
47 See RL Bowen "The pearl fisheries of the Persian Gulf" (1951) 5(2) *Middle East Journal* 161–180 at 161.
48 See SA Mosk "Capitalistic development in the Lower California pearl fisheries" (1941) 10(4) *Pacific Historical Review* 461–468.
49 See EH Schafer "The pearl fisheries of Ho-P'u" (1952) 72(4) *Journal of the American Oriental Society* 155–168.
50 M-R Simonnet *La Convention sur la Haute Mer* (1966) 135.
51 The International Convention for the Protection of Submarine Cables (163 CTS 391; adopted: 14 March 1884; EIF: 1 May 1888).
52 See e.g., S Ash "The development of submarine cables" in DR Burnett, RC Beckman & TM Davenport (eds) *Submarine Cables – The Handbook of Law and Policy* (2014) 19–30.
53 See e.g., SP Neill & MR Hashemi *Fundamentals of Ocean Renewable Energy* (2018).
54 See e.g., M Lück (ed) *The Encyclopedia of Tourism and Recreation in Marine Environments* (2008).
55 See e.g., B Guilloux *Marine Genetic Resources, R&D and the Law 1: Complex Objects of Use* (2018).
56 See e.g., N Klein *Maritime Security and the Law of the Sea* (2011); MD Evans & S Galani (eds) *Maritime Security and the Law of the Sea: Help or Hindrance?* (2020); L Otto (ed) *Global Challenges in Maritime Security* (2020).
57 See e.g., MS Schutter & CC Hicks "Networking the blue economy in Seychelles: Pioneers, resistance, and the power of influence" (2019) 26 *Journal of Political Ecology* 425–447.
58 See e.g., K Vella "International ocean governance – An EU agenda for the future of our oceans" in DJ Attard (ed) *The IMLI Treatise on Global Ocean Governance* (2018) I 199–215.
59 See, especially, sustainable development goal 14 of the 2030 Sustainable Development Agenda (UNGA "Transforming our World: The 2030 Agenda for Sustainable Development" UN Doc. A/RES/70/1 of 25 September 2015) and the proclamation of the years from 2021 to 2030 as the United Nations Decade of Ocean Science for Sustainable Development (UNGA "Oceans and the law of the sea" UN Doc. A/RES/72/73 of 4 January 2018 § 292). See further M Ntona & E Morgera "Connecting SDG 14 with the other sustainable development goals through marine spatial planning" (2018) 93 MP 214–222.

hardly surprising in the light of their significant contribution to economic output and employment.[60]

1.3 Maritime stakeholders

The variety and scale of the maritime uses explain the great number of individuals and entities having a stake in the oceans.[61] Among the individuals whose interests are too easily overlooked are those who belong to the coastal communities and who have relied on fishing for their subsistence from time immemorial and are today often among the most impoverished sections of the populations of coastal States.[62] Other stakeholders are the individuals who actually work at sea and whose working conditions are so at odds with those of workers in other sectors that organising and protecting maritime labour present many distinct challenges.[63] To those individuals must be added the array of highly specialised land-based professions which support human ventures at sea.[64] It would be a mistake, however, to overlook the fact that the economic health of the population of whole villages, towns and cities has in the past, and continues today, to depend on the oceans.[65] In fact, every single individual on the planet today – and humankind as a whole[66] – has a clear stake in the oceans, be it because of their influence on the climate, the resources which they contribute to the global economy, the routes which they make available to the great majority of international trade or the support they give to the main channels of international communication.[67]

60 See e.g., OECD *The Ocean Economy in 2030* (2016).

61 See e.g., Lucchini & Voelckel (n. 2) I 98–125.

62 See e.g., *Maritime Delimitation in the Red Sea (Eritrea v. Yemen)* (n. 18) § 106; *In the Matter of the South China Sea Arbitration (Philippines v. China)*, award of 12 July 2016, XXXIII RIAA 153 §§ 794 and 805; AM di Lieto "Le rôle des peuples autochtones dans la gestion de l'environnement marin" in G Andreone, A Caligiuri & G Cataldi (eds) *Law of the Sea and Environmental Emergencies* (2012) 387–399; U Udo, T Prior & SL Seck "Human rights at the ocean-climate nexus: Opening doors for the participation of indigenous peoples, children and youth, and gender diversity" (2022) 36 OY 95–138. The Global Programme on Fisheries (PROFISH) of the World Bank focuses "on the welfare of the poor in fisheries and fish farming communities in the developing world" (World Bank "Global Programme on Fisheries (PROFISH)" at <http://www.worldbank.org/en/topic/environment/brief/global-program-on-fisheries-profish>).

63 See e.g., L Fink *Sweatshops at Sea: Merchant Seamen in the World's First Globalized Industry, from 1812 to the Present* (2011).

64 On the challenges confronted by women in maritime professions, see e.g., M Kitada, E Williams & LL Froholdt (eds) *Maritime Women: Global Leadership* (2015).

65 See e.g., FW Knight & PK Liss (eds) *Atlantic Cities: Economy, Culture and Society in the Atlantic World, 1650–1850* (1991).

66 See e.g., PB Payoyo *Cries of the Sea: World Inequality, Sustainable Development and the Common Heritage of Humanity* (1997); R Kelly *et al.* "Foresighting future oceans: Considerations and opportunities" (2022) 140 MP 105021 at 1.

67 The International Ocean Institute is one of the non-governmental bodies attempting to advance the interests of global civil society in ocean affairs. See e.g., E Mann Borgese 'The International Ocean Institute story' (1993) 10 OY 1–12.

As the sophistication of maritime uses increased, necessity and opportunities drove entrepreneurial individuals to associate. In Europe, for instance, large-scale fishing in the Roman Empire could, as indicated above, only have taken place through complex business arrangements. Such arrangements existed also for the purpose of maritime trade and, by the end of the European Middle Ages, a continent-wide network[68] had developed with its own normative regime – the *lex maritima* – which the rulers of the polities in existence at the time widely endorsed.[69] The progressive coalescence of those polities into the modern States did not result in a markedly reduced role of the private sector in maritime affairs. On the contrary, in their cut-throat competition with each other, some of the new European States relied heavily on very sophisticated and powerful business organisations to pursue their maritime ambitions.[70] It is only during the nineteenth century that several States were able to consistently backup their claims to exclusive normative and enforcement authority on the oceans,[71] after which a number of them ventured into shipping themselves.[72] Nevertheless, the maritime sector remains overwhelmingly dominated by organised non-State actors,[73] which continue to assert their regulatory role[74] while being increasingly aware of their contribution to humankind's efforts to use the marine environment responsibly.[75]

68 Lucchini & Voelckel (n. 2) 99 speak of a "société de la mer".

69 See e.g., W Tetley "Maritime transportation" (1986) XII *International Encyclopedia of Comparative Law* 12 at 3–8.

70 See e.g., R Parthesius *Dutch Ships in Tropical Waters: The Development of the Dutch East India Company (VOC) Shipping Network in Asia 1595-1660* (2010).

71 Nevertheless, private actors are still expected, in times of emergency, to support States in overcoming their capacity shortfalls. See e.g., E Chadwick "Merchant ship conversion in warfare, the Falklands (Malvinas) conflict and the requisition of the QE2" (2010) 12 JHIL 71–99. "[T]he larger geopolitical ambitions of maritime nations" provoked "a transformation of scientific perspective" regarding the oceans (MS Reidy & HM Rozwadowski "The spaces in between: Science, ocean, empire" (2014) 105(2) *Isis* 338–351).

72 See e.g., HJ Dooley "The great leap outward: China's maritime renaissance" (2012) 26(1) *Journal of East Asian Affairs* 53–76; P Hanson "The Soviet Union and world shipping" (1970) 22(1) *Soviet Studies* 44-60; WL McNair "Legal aspects of State shipping" (1948) 34 *Transactions of the Grotius Society* 31–61; B Walker "Western Australia's coastal shipping: Government versus private enterprise. Part one: 1863-1908" (2008) 30(1) *The Great Circle* 18–40; B Walker "Western Australia's coastal shipping: Government versus private enterprise. Part two: 1908-1914" (2008) 30(2) *The Great Circle* 77–101.

73 That is reflected, for instance, in the role to be played by private operators in the exploration and exploitation of the resources of the International Seabed Area. See e.g., J Dingwall "Commercial mining activities in the deep seabed beyond national jurisdiction: The international legal framework" in C Banet (ed) *The Law of the Seabed – Access, Uses, and Protection of Seabed Resources* (2020) 139–162.

74 One of the fora used for that purpose is the Comité maritime international, "a non-governmental not-for-profit international organization established in Antwerp in 1897, the object of which is to contribute by all appropriate means and activities to the unification of maritime law in all its aspects" (CMI "Welcome to CMI" at <http://comitemaritime.org>).

75 The World Ocean Council is a structure established for that purpose.

The States themselves have, during the last century, put in place a number of institutions, mechanisms and structures to facilitate their involvement in ocean affairs. Those include, for instance, the Arctic Council,[76] the Commission for the Conservation of Antarctic Marine Living Resources,[77] the International Hydrographic Organisation,[78] the International Maritime Organization (IMO),[79] the Meeting of States Parties (SPLOS)[80] to the 1982 UN Convention on the Law of the Sea ("the LOSC"),[81] the International Seabed Authority (ISA),[82] the International Tribunal for the Law of the Sea (ITLOS),[83] the Commission on the Limits of the Continental Shelf (CLCS),[84] the UN Division for Ocean Affairs and the Law of the Sea (DOALOS)[85] and the UN Open-Ended Informal Consultative Process on Oceans and the Law of the Sea (UNICPOLOS).[86] In addition, organisations such as the Food and Agriculture Organisation (FAO),[87] the International Labour Organisation (ILO)[88] and the UN Environment

76 Established by § 1 of the 1996 Ottawa Declaration on the Establishment of the Arctic Council (adopted: 19 September 1996; <https://oaarchive.arctic-council.org/bitstream/handle/11374/85/EDOCS-1752-v2-ACMMCA00_Ottawa_1996_Founding_Declaration.PDF?sequence=5&isAllowed=y>). See e.g., V Golitsyn "The legal regime of the Arctic" in DJ Attard (ed) *The IMLI Manual on International Maritime Law* (2014) I 462–483 at 480–483.

77 Established by article VII(1) of the 1980 Convention on the Conservation of Antarctic Marine Living Resources (1329 UNTS 47, (1980) 19 ILM 837; adopted: 20 May 1980; EIF: 7 April 1982).

78 The Organisation was established in 1921 as the International Hydrographic Bureau (G Gidel *Le Droit international public de la mer* (1932) I 14–16). Today, the Organisation is governed in terms of the 1967 Convention on the International Hydrographic Organisation (751 UNTS 41; adopted: 3 May 1967; EIF: 22 September 1970).

79 The organisation was established by the 1948 Convention on the Intergovernmental Maritime Consultative Organisation (289 UNTS 48; adopted: 6 March 1948; EIF: 17 March 1958). Its name was changed by IMO Assembly resolutions A.358(IX) and A.371(X) of 1975 and 1977 respectively. See e.g., G Librando "The International Maritime Organisation and the law of the sea" in Attard (n. 76) I 577–605.

80 See e.g., T Treves "The General Assembly and the Meeting of States Parties in the implementation of the LOS Convention" in AG Oude Elferink (ed) *Stability and Change in the Law of the Sea: The Role of the LOS Convention* (2005) 55–74.

81 1834 UNTS 397, 21 ILM 1245. Adopted: 10 December 1982; EIF: 16 November 1994.

82 Established by article 156(1) of the LOSC.

83 Established by article 1(1) of Annex VI of the LOSC.

84 Established by article 1 of Annex II of the LOSC.

85 See e.g., DOALOS "The United Nations Division for Ocean Affairs and the Law of the Sea" in Attard (n. 76) I 606–617.

86 See UNGA "Results of the review by the Commission on Sustainable Development of the sectoral theme of 'Oceans and seas': International coordination and cooperation" (UN Doc. A/RES/54/33 of 18 January 2000) § 2.

87 See e.g., DR Rothwell & T Stephens *The International Law of the Sea* (2016) 339–340.

88 The more than 50 ILO instruments having an impact on workers at sea were consolidated in the 2006 Maritime Labour Convention (2952 UNTS 3, (2014) 53 ILM 937; adopted: 23 February 2006; EIF: 20 August 2013). See e.g., PB Payoyo "The contribution of the 2006 ILO Maritime Labour Convention to global governance" in A Chircop *et al.* (eds) *The Future of Ocean Regime-Building* (2009) 385–408. See also the 2007 Convention (No. 188) Concerning Work in the Fishing Sector (adopted: 14 June 2007; EIF: 16 November 2017; available at < https://treaties.un.org/doc/Publication/UNTS/No%20Volume/54755/Part/I-54755-080000028005f62c.pdf>).

Programme (UNEP)[89] also play major roles in oceans affairs. While the above make their own contributions within the scope of their respective jurisdictions, this book focuses on the jurisdiction of States and it is to an interrogation of that concept that one must now turn.

1.4 The concept of "State jurisdiction"

It is not necessary to attempt here to define the word "State" because such an attempt is "either unnecessary as being self-evident, or indeed too controversial".[90] Instead, it is important to stress that the meaning of the word "State" is wider than the meaning of the term "States parties" as it is used in the LOSC because there is a small number of States that are not parties to the Convention.[91] In addition, it must be pointed out that the status of those States is not always undisputed. That is the case of Taiwan (Chinese Taipei), which undoubtedly meets the requirements of article 1 of the 1933 Montevideo Convention on the Rights and Duties of States,[92] but is not recognised by the majority of States.[93] As far as those States are concerned, Taiwan is not a State and, therefore, it does not have any State ocean jurisdiction. At the same time, as far as the States that recognise Taiwan are concerned, the latter is a State and, therefore, it has State ocean jurisdiction like any other State.[94]

The meaning of the word "jurisdiction" is difficult to grasp.[95] Indeed, "[w]hile international lawyers often employ the term 'jurisdiction', and most of them have an inkling of what it means, defining jurisdiction is hardly self-evident".[96] Almost

89 See, especially, the UNEP Regional Seas Programme.

90 M Craven & R Parfitt "Statehood, self-determination, and recognition" in MD Evans (ed) *International Law* (2018) 177–226 at 194.

91 In terms of article 1(2)(1) of the LOSC, the term "States parties" means "States which have consented to be bound by th[e] Convention and for which th[e] Convention is in force". See further E Franckx & M Benatar "Article 305" in Proelss (n. 4) 1968–1979 at 1974–1975.

92 165 LNTS 19; adopted: 26 December 1933; EIF: 26 December 1934. See also Arbitration Commission of the Conference on Yugoslavia "Opinion 1 of 29 November 1991" 92 ILR 162 at 165.

93 See e.g., TS Rich "Status for sale: Taiwan and the competition for diplomatic recognition" (2009) 45(4) *Issues and Studies* 159–188.

94 See Craven & Parfitt (n. 90) 207–208.

95 This is probably a contributing factor to the fact that "[n]o broad-based multilateral treaty governing jurisdiction currently exists. Instead, jurisdiction under international law is primarily regulated by customary international law [...]" (§ 1 comment (a) *Restatement of the Law (Fourth): The Foreign Relations Law of the United States* (2018)). See further e.g., B Simma & AT Müller "Exercise and limits of jurisdiction" in J Crawford & M Koskenniemi (eds) *The Cambridge Companion to International Law* (2012) 134–157 at 134; I Papanicolopulu "A missing part of the Law of the Sea Convention: Addressing issues of State jurisdiction over persons at sea" in C Schofield, S Lee & M-S Kwon (eds) *The Limits of Maritime Jurisdiction* (2014) 387–404 at 390; R Geiß & CJ Tams "Non-flag States as guardians of the maritime order: Creeping jurisdiction of a different kind?" in H Ringbom (ed) *Jurisdiction over Ships* (2015) 19–49 at 49.

96 C Ryngaert *Jurisdiction in International Law* (2015) 5. See also e.g., M Akehurst "Jurisdiction in International Law" (1972–1973) 46 BYIL 145–217 at 145; S Allen *et al.* "Defining State jurisdiction and jurisdiction in international law" in S Allen *et al.* (eds) *The Oxford Handbook of Jurisdiction in International Law* (2019) 3–22 at 4, quoting *United Phosphorus, Ltd v Angus Chemical Co.*, 322 F 3d 942, 948 (7th Cir. 2003).

every court and writer who attempted to do so arrived at a different formulation.[97] The problem can be explained by the fact that "a number of concepts hide themselves behind this single word, 'jurisdiction'",[98] a state of affairs confirmed by the fact that the word, widely used in international instruments applicable in the ocean environment, does not have a consistent meaning in those instruments.

The word "jurisdiction" is an element of the term "national jurisdiction" used in the LOSC as well as the 1994 Agreement Relating to the Implementation of Part XI of the United Nations Convention on the Law of the Sea of 10 December 1982 ("the Part XI Agreement"),[99] the 1995 Agreement for the Implementation of the Provisions of the United Nations Convention on the Law of the Sea of 10 December 1982 Relating to the Conservation and Management of Straddling Fish Stocks and Highly Migratory Fish Stocks ("the Fish Stocks Agreement")[100] and several other law-of-the-sea instruments.[101]

97 See e.g., JH Beale "The jurisdiction of a sovereign State" (1923) 36 *Harvard Law Review* 241–262 at 241 (the "power of a sovereign to affect the rights of persons, whether by legislation, by executive decree, or by the judgment of a court", a definition adopted by B Marten *Port State Jurisdiction and the Regulation of International Shipping* (2014) 7); R Jennings & A Watts (eds) *Oppenheim's International Law* (1992) 456 ("State jurisdiction concerns essentially the extent of each state's right to regulate conduct or the consequences of events"); R O'Keefe "Universal jurisdiction: clarifying the basic concept" (2004) 2 JICJ 735–760 at 736 ("[a] state's 'jurisdiction' [...] refers to its authority under international law to regulate the conduct of persons, natural and legal, and to regulate property in accordance with its municipal law"); C Staker "Jurisdiction" in Evans (n. 90) 289–315 at 289 ("the term that describes the limits of the legal competence of a State [...] to make, apply, and enforce rules of conduct upon persons"); BH Oxman "Jurisdiction of States" 2007 MPEPIL § 1 ("In its broadest sense, the jurisdiction of a State [...] refer[s] to its lawful power to act and hence to its power to decide whether and, if so, how to act, whether by legislative, executive, or judicial means"); AT Gallagher & F David *The International Law of Migrant Smuggling* (2014) 211 ("jurisdiction, literally the *juris dictum* or the speaking of the law, refers to the parameters of a State's ability to create and regulate its particular public order through any exercise of State powers"); Papanicolopulu (n. 95) 390 ("[j]urisdiction may [...] be defined as the power of States to create and apply rules").

98 M Milanovic "From compromise to principle: Clarifying the concept of State jurisdiction in human rights treaties" (2008) 8 *Human Rights Law Review* 411–448 at 412. See also e.g., R Liivoja "The criminal jurisdiction of States" (2010) 7 *No Foundations: Journal of Extreme Legal Positivism* 25–58 at 25–26.

99 1836 UNTS 3, (1994) 33 ILM 1309; adopted: 28 July 1994; EIF: 28 July 1996.

100 2167 UNTS 88, (1995) 34 ILM 1542, (1995) 29 LOSB 25; adopted: 4 December 1995; EIF: 11 December 2001.

101 See e.g., articles 1(1)(1), 142(1)–(2) and 161(1)(c) of the LOSC; articles 3(1)–(2), 11(f), 16(1), 18(3)(b)(iv) and 21(14) of the Fish Stocks Agreement; article 1(c) of the 2001 Convention on the Conservation and Management of Fishery Resources in the South East Atlantic Ocean (2221 UNTS 189, (2002) 41 ILM 257; adopted: 20 April 2001; EIF: 13 April 2003)); article 3(1) of the 2006 Southern Indian Ocean Fisheries Agreement (2835 UNTS 409; adopted: 7 July 2006; EIF: 21 June 2012); article 4(6) of the 1986 Convention for the Protection of the Natural Resources and Environment of the South Pacific Region (1982 UNTS 4; adopted: 24 November 1986; EIF: 22 August 1990)); and article 11(2) of the 1995 Protocol Concerning Specially Protected Areas and Biological Diversity in the Mediterranean to the 1995 Barcelona Convention for the Protection of the Marine Environment and the Coastal Region of the Mediterranean (2102 UNTS 181; adopted: 10 June 1995; EIF: 12 December 1999).

By contrast, the term "national jurisdiction" was not used in the four 1958 Geneva Conventions.[102]

To ascertain what the term means, one must turn to the first operative provision of the LOSC in which the term is used. That provision is article 1(1)(1), which defines the word "Area".[103] The provision corresponds to the first part of the first operative paragraph of the Declaration of Principles Governing the Sea-Bed and the Ocean Floor, and the Subsoil Thereof, beyond the Limits of National Jurisdiction, adopted by the UN General Assembly in its Resolution 2749 (XXV) of 17 December 1970. The term "national jurisdiction" had earlier appeared in the title of the new item introduced by Arvid Pardo, the then Permanent Representative of Malta, during the 22nd session of the General Assembly in August 1967,[104] an item which is widely seen as having sparked the events leading to the Third United Nations Conference on the Law of the Sea (UNCLOS III).[105] The term[106] was used in the phrase "beyond the limits of present national jurisdiction", which referred to "[t]he sea-bed and ocean floor, underlying the seas outside [the] territorial waters and/or the continental shelves [which were] the only areas of our planet which ha[d] not yet been appropriated for national use".[107] The term "national jurisdiction" was therefore a misnomer in that it did not refer to a form of jurisdiction. The

102 The Convention on the Continental Shelf (499 UNTS 311; adopted: 29 April 1958; EIF: 10 June 1964), the Convention on Fishing and Conservation of the Living Resources of the High Seas (599 UNTS 285; adopted: 29 April 1958; EIF: 20 March 1966), the Convention on the High Seas (CHS; 450 UNTS 11; adopted: 29 April 1958; EIF: 30 September 1962) and the Convention on the Territorial Sea and the Contiguous Zone (CTSCZ; 516 UNTS 205; adopted: 29 April 1958; EIF: 10 September 1964).

103 The term appears also earlier in the sixth paragraph of the preamble to the LOSC.

104 "Declaration and treaty concerning the reservation exclusively for peaceful purposes of the sea-bed and of the ocean floor underlying the seas beyond the limits of present national jurisdiction, and the use of their resources in the interests of mankind" (UN Doc. A/6695 of 18 August 1967 reproduced in the Official Records of the UN General Assembly, annexes (XXII) 92 (1967)). See further the address of A Pardo in "Panel: Whose is the bed of the sea?" (1968) 62 *Proceedings of the American Society of International Law* 216–229).

105 J Barkenbus *Deep Seabed Resources* (1979) 32 refers to the initiative as a "legal catalyst". The need for the internationalisation of the seabed already had a long history by then, reaching back to at least 1832 (see A Bello *Principes de Derecho Internacional* (1832) 35. In 1966, LB Johnson, then President of the United States, had declared that "under no circumstances, we believe, must we ever allow the prospects of rich harvest and mineral wealth to create a new form of colonial competition among the maritime nations. We must be careful to avoid a race to grab and to hold lands under the high seas. We must ensure that the deep seas and the ocean bottoms are, and remain, the legacy of all human beings" (quoted in J Van Dyke & C Yuen "'Common heritage' v 'freedom of the high seas': Which governs the seabed?" (1982) 19 *San Diego Law Review* 526–527). A few months later, the General Assembly did adopt Resolution 2172 (XXI) of 6 December 1966 on the resources of the sea, in the first operative paragraph of which the Assembly endorsed the UN "Economic and Social Council Resolution 1112 (XL) of 7 March 1966 requesting the Secretary-General to make a survey of the present state of knowledge of the resources of the seabed beyond the continental shelf, excluding fish, and of the techniques for exploiting these resources".

106 Which appears also in the titles and operative paragraphs of Resolutions 2340 (XXII) of 18 December 1967, 2467 (XXIII) of 21 December 1968 and 2574 (XXIV) of 15 December 1969.

107 Paragraph 1 of the explanatory memorandum.

term actually referred to marine *spaces* over which States have either sovereignty or sovereign rights. In other words, the term referred only indirectly to the forms of jurisdiction that coastal States may or must exercise on the basis of their sovereignty or sovereign rights.

Nevertheless, the term continues to be used today to refer both to marine spaces "*under* national jurisdiction" (that is to say, more accurately, the marine spaces over which coastal States have sovereignty or sovereign rights and, on that basis, extensive jurisdiction) and to marine spaces "*beyond* national jurisdiction" (that is to say, more accurately, the marine spaces over which coastal States do not have sovereignty or sovereign rights and, for that reason, only very limited jurisdiction).[108] The problem is that this distinction is misleading because "[j]urisdiction is not coextensive with state sovereignty"[109] or sovereign rights.[110] Indeed, while there are marine spaces that are not subject to the sovereignty or sovereign rights of coastal States, there is no space "beyond national jurisdiction" in the sense that the space is not subject to the jurisdiction of States in any form.[111] Indeed, all marine spaces are under at least one or another form of State (or national) jurisdiction.

It must be pointed out that the word "jurisdiction" is sometimes used on its own to refer to spaces to which the term "national jurisdiction" more frequently refers. That is the case, for instance, in article 111(7) of the LOSC, which provides that

> [t]he release of a ship arrested within the jurisdiction of a State and escorted to a port of that State for the purposes of an inquiry before the competent authorities may not be claimed solely on the ground that the ship, in the course of its voyage, was escorted across a portion of the exclusive economic zone or the high seas, if the circumstances rendered this necessary.

Although this paragraph is part of the article of the LOSC dealing with the right of hot pursuit,[112] it does not address an aspect of that right. Instead, the paragraph deals with cases where foreign ships are arrested within the coastal States' territorial seas.[113] In this light, the phrase "arrested within the jurisdiction of a State" must be read to mean "arrested within a maritime zone over which the State has

108 See e.g., Y Tanaka *The International Law of the Sea* (2019) 7–11. See further Chapter 3.
109 Jennings & Watts (n. 97) 457.
110 See e.g., I Shearer "The limits of maritime jurisdiction" in Schofield, Lee & Kwon (n. 95) 51–63.
111 For an illustration of the misconceptions in this regard, see *Medvedyev and Others v France*, ECHR Application No 3394/03, judgment of 29 March 2010 § 81. See also *Hirsi Jamaa and Others v. Italy*, ECHR Application No 27765/09, judgment of 23 February 2012 [GC] § 178, where the statement was repeated.
112 An earlier version is to be found in article 23(6) of the CHS.
113 This was confirmed by the International Law Commission (Report of the International Law Commission covering the work of its eighth session, 23 April to 4 July 1956, to the General Assembly, UN Doc. A/3159 (1956) reproduced in (1956) II YILC 285). See further MH Nordquist (ed) *United Nations Convention on the Law of the Sea 1982: A Commentary* (2002) III 259 § 111.9(h).

sovereignty".[114] Another example is the 2012 Convention on the Determination of the Minimal Conditions for Access and Exploitation of Marine Resources within the Maritime Areas under Jurisdiction of the Member States of the Sub-Regional Fisheries Commission.[115] In its *Sub-Regional Fisheries Commission Advisory Opinion*,[116] ITLOS confirmed that the areas under "jurisdiction" for the purposes of the Convention include not only the zones over which the coastal State has sovereignty, but also the exclusive economic zones (EEZs).[117]

While the word "jurisdiction" is used in the LOSC (either on its own or in the term "national jurisdiction") to refer to marine spaces where the coastal State has either sovereignty or sovereign rights, the Convention makes it clear that the word "jurisdiction" and the term "sovereign rights" do not have the same meaning. Indeed, the LOSC stresses, in article 246(8), that marine scientific research in an EEZ or on a continental shelf by, or under the authority of, a foreign State must not unjustifiably interfere with the activities undertaken by the coastal State in the exercise of its "sovereign rights and jurisdiction" provided for in articles 56 and 77 of the Convention.[118] The distinction is also made in articles 297(1)[119] and 298(1)(b).[120] Likewise, the LOSC confirms that the words "jurisdiction" and "sovereignty" have different meanings when it uses the phrase "sovereignty or jurisdiction" in article 34. Here, the purpose of the distinction is to cover "the situation in which the territorial seas of the States bordering a strait do not extend to the full breadth of the strait",[121] in which case "there will be a corridor through the

114 It does not matter whether the foreign ship is arrested within the territorial sea, the internal waters or the archipelagic waters.

115 (2017) 2 JOLGA 160; adopted: 8 June 2012; EIF: 16 September 2012 (in terms of article 41 of the Convention, the latter repeals and replaces the 1993 Convention on the Determination of Conditions for Access and Exploitation of Marine Resources off the Coasts of the SRFC Member States). See § 9 of the preamble to the Convention and articles 1(2), 2(4)(1), 2(11), 3(1), 5, 8(2), 10(1), 11, 12(1), 14(1)–(2), 15, 17(1), 18, 25(3), 29(2), 30, 31(1) and 32(1).

116 Advisory opinion of 2 April 2015, 2015 ITLOS Reports 4.

117 Paragraph 87.

118 See Nordquist (n. 113) (2002) IV 517 § 246.17(a). On the distinction between "sovereign rights" and "jurisdiction" in article 56, see further below.

119 "Disputes concerning the interpretation or application of this Convention with regard to the exercise by a coastal State of its sovereign rights or jurisdiction provided for in this Convention shall be subject to the procedures provided for in section 2 in the following cases [...]". See Nordquist (n. 113) (1989) V 105 § 297.19.

120 "When signing, ratifying or acceding to this Convention or at any time thereafter, a State may, without prejudice to the obligations arising under section 1, declare in writing that it does not accept any one or more of the procedures provided for in section 2 with respect to [...] disputes concerning military activities, including military activities by government vessels and aircraft engaged in non-commercial service, and disputes concerning law enforcement activities in regard to the exercise of sovereign rights or jurisdiction excluded from the jurisdiction of a court or tribunal under article 297, paragraph 2 or 3". See Nordquist (n. 113) (1989) V 135–137 §§ 298.33–298.38.

121 Nordquist (n. 113) (2002) II 299 § 34.8(c).

strait that could be subject to the jurisdiction but not the sovereignty of one or more of the States bordering the strait".[122]

Although this distinction ought indeed to be made, the formulation is problematical in that it suggests that a coastal State bordering a strait has either sovereignty or jurisdiction over a specific location in that strait, with the implication that, where sovereignty is exercised, jurisdiction is not, and vice versa. This is misleading because sovereignty and jurisdiction are not mutually exclusive. On the contrary, "sovereignty" refers to the largest extent of jurisdiction which a State can have.[123] In that light, the phrase "sovereignty or jurisdiction" used in article 34 actually means: "the all-encompassing jurisdiction of the bordering State within its territory or its more limited jurisdiction outside that territory".[124] At the same time, the LOSC appears to suggest that the words "jurisdiction" and "sovereignty" are synonymous when the phrase "place outside the jurisdiction of any State" is used in some of the provisions relating to piracy.[125] It has been pointed out above that the phrase cannot be read literally to refer to a place where no State exercises jurisdiction, because no such place exists.

To understand what the phrase actually means, one needs to recall that the piracy provisions of the LOSC find their origin in provisions of the 1956 Draft Articles Concerning the Law of the Sea of the International Law Commission (ILC),[126] which found their way into the 1958 Convention on the High Seas (CHS).[127] The Commission did itself rely on the 1932 Harvard Draft Convention on Piracy.[128] The latter's drafters made it clear that the document dealt with acts committed "beyond the state's ordinary jurisdiction",[129] that is to say beyond the State's "territorial jurisdiction", which does not extend further than the State's "dominion".[130] This was confirmed by the Commission in its commentary on article 39 when it explained that "[p]iracy can be committed only on the high seas or in a place situated outside the territorial jurisdiction of any State, and cannot be committed within the territory of a State or in its territorial sea".[131] On this basis, the phrase "place outside the jurisdiction of any State" should actually read "place outside the sovereignty of any State" or, more accurately, "place where no State has all-encompassing jurisdiction, because it is outside the territory of any State".[132] Article 58(2) of the LOSC confirms this interpretation when it states that articles 100–107 (which

122 Nordquist (n. 113) (2002) II 299 § 34.8(c). See also e.g., B Jia "Article 34" in Proelss (n. 4) 272–275 at 274.

123 See further Chapter 5.

124 See also article 242(1), which refers to "the principle of respect for sovereignty and jurisdiction".

125 See articles 100, 101(a)(ii) and 105.

126 See articles 38, 39(1)(b) and 43 (Report of the International Law Commission (n. 113) 260–261).

127 See n. 102 and articles 14, 15(1)(b) and 19.

128 See JW Bingham "Piracy" (1932) 26 AJIL Supplement 743–747.

129 Harvard Research in International Law "Draft Convention on Piracy with comments" (1932) 26 AJIL Supplement 763.

130 *Ibid.* 768.

131 Report of the International Law Commission (n. 113) 282.

132 Nordquist (n. 113) (2002) II 184 § 100.7(b).

relate exclusively to piracy) "apply to the exclusive economic zone in so far as they are not incompatible with" the regime of the EEZ.

The relationship between the meaning of "jurisdiction", on the one hand, and the meaning of "sovereignty" and "sovereign rights", on the other, is not the only one that is problematical in the LOSC. In fact, the way in which the relationship between the meaning of the word "jurisdiction" and that of the word "freedom" is portrayed in the Convention is even more problematical. This is illustrated by article 55, which describes the legal regime of the EEZ as one "under which the rights and jurisdiction of the coastal State and the rights and freedoms of other States are governed by the relevant provisions of th[e] Convention". By distinguishing between the coastal States, which have both rights and *jurisdiction*, and other States, which have both rights and *freedoms*, this provision could be interpreted as implying, on the one hand, that the coastal States do not have freedoms in their own EEZs and, on the other, that a State does not have any jurisdiction in an EEZ other than its own.

In order to confirm that this is not the case, one needs to turn to the legislative history of the provision. The part of the negotiating text devoted to the EEZ started initially with an earlier version of what was to become article 56, which deals with the rights, jurisdiction and duties of the coastal State in its EEZ.[133] Thereafter, the Castañeda Group proposed in 1977[134] the insertion of a new first provision, article 43*bis*, which focused on the legal position of the States other than the coastal States. That provision stated that the EEZ was "subject to the specific legal regime established in [the relevant] Chapter [of the Convention], under which the rights and freedoms of other States are governed by the relevant provisions of the" Convention.[135] This placed too great an emphasis on the "rights and freedoms" of the States other than the coastal States. For that reason, "a better basis for negotiation"[136] was found when the phrase "rights and jurisdictions of the coastal State" was added to make up article 55.[137] It was indeed felt that this formulation reflected better "the essential features of the specific legal regime of the exclusive economic zone without upsetting the balance [...] between the rights and duties of the coastal State and those of other States".[138] In that light, it is clear that the words "rights and freedoms" were chosen not so much to distinguish the concept of "freedom" from that of "jurisdiction", but to stress the continued application within the EEZ of many aspects of the high-seas regime referred to as the "freedoms of

133 Article 45 of Part II of the Informal Single Negotiating Text (ISNT; UN Doc. A/CONF.62/WP.8/PART II (1975)) and article 44 of Part II of the Revised Single Negotiating Text (RSNT; UN Doc. A/CONF.62/WP.8/REV.1/PART II (1976)).

134 Nordquist (n. 113) (2002) II 518 § 55.7 referring to R Platzoeder (ed) *Third United Nations Conference on the Law of the Sea: Documents* (1982) IV 419 and 426.

135 *Ibid.*

136 Memorandum by the President of the Conference on document A/CONF.62/WP.10 (A/CONF.62/WP.10/Add.1 (1977) in *Official Records* VII) 68.

137 Informal Composite Negotiating Text (ICNT; UN Doc. A/CONF.62/WP.10 (ICNT 1977)).

138 Memorandum (n. 136) 68.

the high seas".[139] As a result, the phrases "the rights and jurisdiction of the coastal State" and "the rights and freedoms of other States" do not compare accurately the legal positions of both categories of States. Indeed, although article 55 does not refer to the jurisdiction of States other than the coastal States, there is no doubt that those States have a measure of jurisdiction in the EEZ and that this jurisdiction is based on their "rights and freedoms".[140] Likewise, although article 55 does not refer to the freedoms of the coastal States, there is no doubt that those States enjoy those freedoms in their own EEZs in addition to their sovereign rights.[141]

Being different from "sovereignty", "sovereign rights" and "freedom", "State jurisdiction" is a complex concept in its application in the marine environment. This is illustrated by the use in the LOSC and other law-of-the-sea instruments of a number of terms such as "civil jurisdiction",[142] "criminal jurisdiction",[143] "exclusive jurisdiction"[144] and "penal jurisdiction".[145] Nevertheless, the common denominator appears to be that "State jurisdiction" refers to the international law authority of a State to be involved in a factual matter on the basis of a valid legal ground to perform authoritative acts impacting on that matter.[146] In other words, to discuss whether a State has jurisdiction in a factual matter relating to the oceans is to discuss whether the State has the legal authority to involve itself in that matter.[147] The development of a systematic and coherent theoretical framework to describe the attribution and exercise of State authority in ocean matters has received limited

139 See article 87(1) of the LOSC.

140 See further Chapter 4.

141 Article 58 of the LOSC deals with the rights and duties of States other than the coastal States, but paragraph 2 must also apply to coastal States because the latter neither gave any indication that they were prepared to give up their high-seas rights that were not converted into sovereign rights.

142 See e.g., article 28(1) of the LOSC and the 1952 Convention on Civil Jurisdiction in Matters of Collision. (439 UNTS 129; adopted: 10 May 1952; EIF: 14 September 1955).

143 See e.g., article 27(1) of the LOSC, article 6(5) of the 1988 Convention for the Suppression of Unlawful Acts against the Safety of Maritime Navigation (SUA; 1678 UNTS 201, (1988) 27 ILM 668, (1988) 11 LOSB 14; adopted: 10 March 1988; EIF: 1 March 1992) as amended by the 2005 Protocol to the Convention (IMO Doc. LEG/CONF.15/21 (2005); adopted: 14 October 2005; EIF: 28 July 2010) and article 3(5) of the 1988 Protocol for the Suppression of Unlawful Acts against the Safety of Fixed Platforms Located on the Continental Shelf to the SUA (SUA PROT; 1678 UNTS 304, (1988) 27 ILM 685, (1988) 11 LOSB 24; adopted: 10 March 1988; EIF: 1 March 1992).

144 See e.g., articles 60(2) and 92(1) of the LOSC.

145 See e.g., article 97(1) of the LOSC and the 1952 Convention on Penal Jurisdiction in Matters of Collision (CPJC; 439 UNTS 235; adopted: 10 May 1952; EIF: 20 November 1955).

146 Compare e.g., D Costelloe "Conceptions of State jurisdiction in the jurisprudence of the International Court of Justice and the Permanent Court of International Justice" in Allen *et al. Handbook* (n. 96) 455–480 at 460 ("'state jurisdiction' refers to the authority of a state to regulate conduct, persons or property within the limits of international law"). On normative pluralism with each State, see e.g., H Quane "Navigating diffuse jurisdictions" in Allen *et al. Handbook* (n. 96) 99–120.

147 See e.g., Papanicolopulu (n. 95) 389.

attention.[148] That is in contrast with the development and application of the legal regime governing the jurisdiction of dispute-settlement bodies, which is the focus of many contemporary law-of-the-sea writings.[149]

1.5 Analytical framework

It is against the above background that this work proposes a new analytical framework, which, it is hoped, will make a contribution to the accurate study and application of the international law regime governing State ocean jurisdiction.[150] The need for such a framework is well illustrated by the decision of the Permanent Court of International Justice (PCIJ) in the *Lotus Case*,[151] to which reference is still made almost a century later,[152] and the large amount of criticisms directed at that decision.[153]

The dispute flowed from a collision between the mail steamer *Lotus*, which was flying the French flag, and the collier *Boz-Kourt*, which was flying the Turkish flag.[154] The collision occurred between five and six nautical miles (NM) to the north of Cape Sigri, on the west coast of the Greek island of Lesbos.[155] At the time of the collision, in August 1926, there was no general rule of international law determining the breadth of the territorial sea[156] and Greece itself had not taken any decision in that regard.[157] Nevertheless, France and Turkey,[158] as well as the Court, proceeded on the basis that the collision had occurred on the high seas.[159]

148 M Chadwick *Piracy and the Origins of Universal Jurisdiction* (2019); M Gavouneli *Functional Jurisdiction in the Law of the Sea* (2007); LS Johnson *Coastal State Regulation of International Shipping* (2004); Marten (n. 97); R Rayfuse *Non-Flag State Enforcement in High Seas Fisheries* (2004).
149 See e.g., IV Karaman *Dispute Resolution in the Law of the Sea* (2012).
150 See e.g., IA Shearer "Problems of jurisdiction and enforcement against delinquent vessels" (1986) 35 ICLQ 320–343, who points out some of the consequences of "the doctrinal incoherence" (at 321).
151 *(France v. Turkey)*, judgment of 7 September 1927, 1927 PCIJ Reports, Series A No 10.
152 See e.g., *The M/V "Norstar" Case (Panama v. Italy)*, judgment of 10 April 2019, (2019) 58 ILM 673 § 216; Allen (n. 96) 6–7 ("[t]he orthodox starting point for international lawyers in assessing questions of jurisdictional limits remains the *Lotus* case [...]. The judgment remains decisive [...]"); Costelloe (n. 146) 468 (it "is perhaps the most famous of international decisions").
153 See e.g., A von Bogdandy & M Rau "Lotus, the" 2006 MPEPIL § 1 ("[f]ew decisions of the [PCIJ] have been so vividly and controversially discussed, to this day [...]"). See further e.g., S Beaulac "The *Lotus* case in context" in Allen *et al. Handbook* (n. 96) 40–58.
154 *Lotus Case* (n. 151) 10.
155 *Ibid.*
156 Gidel (n. 78) III 123. States were unable to agree on this issue at the 1930 Hague Conference. They were still unable to do so, thirty years later, at the First United Nations Conference on the Law of the Sea (UNCLOS I) and the Second United Nations Conference on the Law of the Sea, in 1958 and 1960 respectively. See R Churchill, V Lowe & A Sander *The Law of the Sea* (2022) 138.
157 Gidel (n. 78) III 105.
158 The two parties to the dispute.
159 *Lotus Case* (n. 151) 12.

As a result of the incident, the *Boz-Kourt* was cut in two and sank.[160] Eight Turkish sailors and passengers who were on board perished, but ten persons were saved and taken to Istanbul, where the *Lotus* arrived the day after the collision.[161] The Turkish police immediately initiated an enquiry into the event and, two days later, the Turkish authorities requested lieutenant Demons, the officer of the watch on board the *Lotus* at the time of the collision, to go ashore to give evidence.[162] After having done so, the officer was arrested and charged with involuntary manslaughter.[163] The case was heard by the Criminal Court of Istanbul, which sentenced lieutenant Demons to 80 days' imprisonment and a fine of 22 Turkish pounds.[164]

The special agreement in terms of which France and Turkey submitted their dispute regarding jurisdiction over lieutenant Demons to the PCIJ required the latter to decide whether Turkey had violated article 15 of the Convention Respecting Conditions of Residence and Business and Jurisdiction adopted in Lausanne in 1923[165] and, if so, what pecuniary reparation was due to the officer.[166] Article 15 provided that, "[s]ubject to the provisions of Article 16, all questions of jurisdiction shall, as between Turkey and the other contracting Powers [including France], be decided in accordance with the principles of international law".[167]

France argued that Turkey did not have jurisdiction because

> according to international law as established by the practice of civilized nations, in their relations with each other, a State is not entitled, apart from express or implicit special agreements, to extend the criminal jurisdiction of its courts to include a crime or offence committed by a foreigner abroad solely in consequence of the fact that one of its nationals has been a victim of the crime or offence.[168]

In reply, Turkey argued that it was not necessary for it to be able to rely on an express or implicit special agreement allowing it to extend the criminal jurisdiction of its courts to cases such as the one at hand. What mattered was that "no principle of international criminal law exist[ed] which would debar Turkey from exercising [its] jurisdiction".[169] The Court ruled, by its President's casting vote, that "the contention of the French Government to the effect that Turkey must in each case be able to cite a rule of international law authorizing her to exercise jurisdiction, is opposed to the generally accepted international law to which Article

160 *Ibid.* 10.
161 *Ibid.*
162 *Ibid.*
163 *Ibid.* 11 and 13.
164 *Ibid.* 11.
165 28 LNTS 153, 1924 ATS 12, 1923 UKTS 16; adopted: 24 July 1923.
166 *Lotus Case* (n. 151) 5.
167 *Ibid.* 16.
168 *Ibid.* 7.
169 *Ibid.* 9.

15 of the Convention of Lausanne refers".[170] For the Court, that law was based on the principle of freedom of States and there was no principle of international law within the meaning of article 15 which precluded the institution of the criminal proceedings under consideration.[171] The Court based its decision on its understanding that "[i]nternational law governs relations between independent States" and "[r]estrictions upon the independence of States cannot [...] be presumed".[172] The Court readily acknowledged that "the first and foremost restriction" is that jurisdiction "cannot be exercised by a State outside its territory except by virtue of a permissive rule derived from international custom or from a convention".[173] But the Court stressed that it does not follow from this restriction "that international law prohibits a State from exercising jurisdiction *in its own territory*, in respect of any case which relates to acts which have taken place abroad, and in which it cannot rely on some permissive rule of international law".[174] On the contrary, States have "a wide measure of discretion" to "extend the application of their laws and the jurisdiction of their courts to persons, property and acts outside their territory", "which is only limited in certain cases by prohibitive rules".[175]

At the same time that the Court found that Turkey had jurisdiction, it agreed with France when the latter contended that it did have jurisdiction because it was the flag State.[176] In addition, the Court agreed that the jurisdiction of the flag State with regard to acts performed on the high seas on board a merchant ship is, "in principle and from the point of view of criminal proceedings", exclusive.[177] However, the Court held that this rule does not prohibit "the State to which the ship on which the effects of the offence have taken place belongs, from regarding the offence as having been committed in its territory and prosecuting, accordingly, the delinquent".[178] The Court based its decision on the fact that there existed no evidence, in the case where an offence is committed on one vessel and the effects of that offence are felt on another vessel, that "States recognize themselves to be under an obligation towards each other only to have regard to the place where the author of the offence happens to be at the time of the offence".[179] In other words, there was "no rule of international law in regard to collision cases to the effect that criminal proceedings are exclusively within the jurisdiction of the State whose flag is flown".[180]

Some of the criticisms of the Court's decision flow from the fact that there was room for a more careful and systematic distinction between four fundamental

170 *Ibid.* 19.
171 *Ibid.* 31.
172 *Ibid.* 18.
173 *Ibid.* 18–19.
174 *Ibid.* 19 (emphasis added).
175 *Ibid.*
176 *Ibid.* 7.
177 *Ibid.* See also 25.
178 *Ibid.* 23.
179 *Ibid.*
180 *Ibid.* 30.

aspects of State ocean jurisdiction: its form, its ground, its scope and its purpose. A discussion of those aspects is the object of the chapters that follow.

Chapter 2 is devoted to the form of State ocean jurisdiction. It highlights the fact that the involvement of States in human activities takes a wide variety of forms. Identifying those forms and ascertaining the degree of their impact on the persons concerned is essential if one is to accurately map the gradated pattern along the lines of which international law attributes jurisdiction to States in ocean matters. That pattern takes into account that State organs exercise their authority on the basis of their respective domestic law and that, in most cases, the latter distinguishes between "legislative jurisdiction", "executive jurisdiction" and "adjudicative jurisdiction". The chapter also tries to unravel the complex relationship between the three jurisdictions, the three categories of organs called upon to exercise them and the three categories of acts performed to that end. In the process, it is stressed that the determinant factor is not the nature of the organ concerned, but the nature of the act performed.

Chapter 3 turns to the ground of State ocean jurisdiction. It identifies and discusses the connecting factors on the basis of which States have been attributed authority in ocean matters. This is done because a thorough examination of those factors provides the necessary foundation to establish whether a State has any authority at all in a specific matter. The answer to that question is important for two reasons. First, attempting to establish the extent of a State's jurisdiction is only necessary when the State does have a ground on which to exercise jurisdiction. Secondly, in the case where a ground exists, it is that very ground that will determine the precise extent of the jurisdiction. In this light, more types of jurisdiction are distinguished in this work than is usually the case. They are, in alphabetical order: the coastal zone jurisdictions, the collective jurisdictions, the delegated jurisdictions, flag State jurisdiction, personal jurisdiction, port State jurisdiction, the protective jurisdictions and the universal jurisdictions.

Chapter 4 focuses on the scope of State ocean jurisdiction. It examines the extent of each jurisdiction identified in Chapter 3 in the case of each category of acts identified in Chapter 2. On that basis, it then examines, in the case of each jurisdiction, the relationship between two different States exercising that jurisdiction and the relationships between one State exercising that jurisdiction and other States, each of which exercises one of the other jurisdictions. This makes it possible to describe the gaps and areas of overlap of jurisdictions *de lege lata*.

Finally, Chapter 5 zooms in on the purpose of State ocean jurisdiction. It dwells briefly on the premise on which the exercise of State ocean jurisdiction is based, i.e., the sovereign equality of States and the independence that it entails. The chapter then outlines the historical development of the principles of the international law of the sea. In the course of that process, a number of principles that point towards the lawful purpose of State ocean jurisdiction are identified. Light is also shed on parameters within which the purpose for which State ocean jurisdiction is exercised is to be lawfully achieved.

Together with the conclusions reached at the end of the work, the chapters lay the foundation for future research on: (a) the extent to which, and the reasons why,

States fail to make full use of their existing ocean jurisdictions; (b) whether, why and how the gaps and areas of overlap of jurisdictions should be addressed; and (c) whether it is necessary to create any additional ground(s) of jurisdiction, expand the scope of any existing jurisdiction(s) and/or take further steps to determine the purpose(s) for which State ocean jurisdiction is to be exercised. In contrast, this book is not meant to make any contribution, in ocean-related matters, to the development and application of the legal regime governing the jurisdiction of domestic and international dispute-settlement bodies,[181] the private international laws of States, the laws of war and the regime governing State responsibility.[182]

181 See Costelloe (n. 146) 458.
182 The book does not deal either with the jurisdiction of States regarding matters arising in the air space above the oceans.

2 The form of State ocean jurisdiction

2.1 Introduction

As indicated in Chapter 1, the first aspect of the international-law regime governing the attribution and exercise of State authority in ocean matters is the form of that authority. That form varies and, in order to recognise its different manifestations more easily, State authority is divided in the constitutional regimes of many States, on the basis of the principle of separation of powers,[1] into legislative authority, executive authority and adjudicative authority.[2] That division is mirrored in international law by the distinction between legislative jurisdiction, executive jurisdiction and adjudicative jurisdiction.[3] Each of these jurisdictions will be examined in

1 See e.g., T Campbell *Separation of Power in Practice* (2004) 19–25; F Solano Carrera "Constitutional justice and the separation of powers: The case of Costa Rica" (2009) 47 *Duquesne Law Review* 871–904; J Crawford "Sovereignty as a legal value" in J Crawford & M Koskenniemi (eds) *The Cambridge Companion to International Law* (2012) 117–133 at 118; PY Lo & AHY Chen "The judicial perspective of separation of powers in the Hong Kong Special Administrative Region of the People's Republic of China" (2018) 5 *Journal of International and Comparative Law* 337–362.

2 That is the case e.g., in Brazil (see the 1988 *Constituição da República Federativa do Brasil*, published in *Diário Official da União* of 5 October 1988 at 1), France (see the 1958 *Constitution*, published in *Journal Officiel* of 5 October 1958 at 9151), India (see the 1950 Constitution of India, published in *Gazette of India Extraordinary* of 26 November 1949) and South Africa (see the 1996 Constitution of the Republic of South Africa, published in *Government Gazette* 17678 of 18 December 1996). See further e.g., B Simma & AT Müller "Exercise and limits of jurisdiction" in Crawford & Koskenniemi (n. 1) 134–157 at 147.

3 A distinction is always made between legislative jurisdiction and other forms of jurisdiction. The latter are grouped together under the word "enforcement" in article 73 of the LOSC and under the term "enforcement jurisdiction" by many writers (see e.g., DW Bowett "Jurisdiction: Changing patterns of authority over activities and resources" (1982) 53 BYIL 1–26 at 1; LS Johnson *Coastal State Regulation of International Shipping* (2004) 46–50; R O'Keefe "Universal jurisdiction: Clarifying the basic concept" (2004) 2 JICJ 735–760 at 736–737; MT Ladan *Materials and Cases in International Law* (2008) 34; D Nelson "Maritime jurisdiction" 2010 MPEPIL § 1; R Beckman "Jurisdiction over pirates and maritime terrorists" in C Schofield, S Lee & M-S Kwon (eds) *The Limits of Maritime Jurisdiction* (2014) 349–371 at 350; ST Mouland "Rethinking adjudicative jurisdiction in international law" (2019) 29 *Washington International Law Journal* 173–202 at 181; D Costelloe "Conceptions of State jurisdiction in the jurisprudence of the International Court of Justice and the Permanent Court of International Justice" in S Allen *et al.* (eds) *The Oxford Handbook of Jurisdiction in International Law* (2019) 455–480 at 457–458). Other writers distinguish between executive jurisdiction and judicial jurisdiction (see e.g., D Ireland-Piper "Extraterritorial criminal jurisdiction: Does

DOI: 10.4324/9781003383871-2

turn in the following three sections, after which the relationship between them will be discussed. Before doing so, it must be stressed that it is the nature of the acts performed by States (i.e., whether the acts are of a legislative nature, an executive nature or an adjudicative nature) that will be the primary object of the discussion and not the nature of the organs performing those acts (i.e., whether the organs are categorised as legislative organs, executive organs or adjudicative organs). That is the case for two reasons.

The first reason is that there is no complete match between the nature of a State organ performing an act and the nature of that act. Admittedly, the great majority of legislative acts are performed by legislative organs, the great majority of executive acts are performed by executive organs and the great majority of adjudicative acts are performed by adjudicative organs. However, any theory of State ocean jurisdiction must take into account that, for instance, executive organs also perform legislative acts,[4] adjudicative organs also perform executive acts[5] and legislative organs also perform adjudicative acts.[6] This state of affairs can be built into the theory by referring to:

(a) a State organ performing a legislative act as either a "legislative organ" (when its primary function is to perform legislative acts) or a "legislating organ" (when it is not its primary function to perform legislative acts);
(b) a State organ performing an executive act as either an "executive organ" (when its primary function is to perform executive acts) or an "executing organ" (when it is not its primary function to perform executive acts); and
(c) a State organ performing an adjudicative act as either a "adjudicative organ" (when its primary function is to perform adjudicative acts) or an "adjudicating organ" (when it is not its primary function to perform adjudicative acts).

In other words, while the great majority of legislative acts are performed by legislative organs, some legislative acts are performed by other organs acting as legislating organs. Likewise, while the great majority of executive acts are performed by executive organs, some executive acts are performed by other organs acting as executing organs. In addition, while the great majority of adjudicative acts are

the long arm of the law undermine the rule of law" (2012) 13 *Melbourne Journal of International Law* 122–157 at 125; AN Honniball "The exclusive jurisdiction of flag States: A limitation on pro-active port States?" (2016) 31 IJMCL 499–530 at 501; M Akehurst "Jurisdiction in international law" (1972–1973) 46 BYIL 145–257 at 145–178; MN Shaw *International Law* (2017) 486; WS Dodge "Jurisdiction, State immunity, and judgments in the Restatement (Fourth) of US Foreign Relations Law" (2020) 19 *Chinese Journal of International Law* 101–135 at 107; C Ryngaert "The Restatement and the law of jurisdiction: A commentary" (2021) 32 *European Journal of International Law* 1455–1469 at 1463. See further e.g., *The "Enrica Lexie" Incident (Italy v. India)*, award of 21 May 2020 (2021) 60 ILM 180 § 526.

4 See e.g., § 401 comment (c) *Restatement of the Law (Fourth): The Foreign Relations Law of the United States* (2018). See further e.g., section 2.2.2.4.

5 See e.g., section 2.4.4.3.

6 See e.g., section 2.2.5.

performed by adjudicative organs, some adjudicative acts are performed by other organs acting as adjudicating organs.

The second reason why the primary object of the discussion that follows is the nature of the acts performed by States (rather than the nature of the organs performing those acts) is that international law does not involve itself in the attribution of authority among State organs within the domestic constitutional order of each State.[7] Instead, what matters to international law is the impact of the acts performed by a State on other States and, indirectly, on non-State actors (NSAs).[8] That impact depends on the nature of the acts performed, rather than the nature of the organs performing the acts. For instance, when international law confers legislative jurisdiction on a State, it is of no concern to international law whether the acts performed in the exercise of that jurisdiction are performed by legislative organs, executive organs or adjudicative organs.

2.2 Legislative jurisdiction

2.2.1 Introduction

Legislative jurisdiction[9] (also called, for instance, "prescriptive jurisdiction",[10] "prescriptive competence"[11] and "jurisdiction to prescribe"[12]) has been defined in

7 See article 2(7) of the Charter of the United Nations (1 UNTS xvi; adopted: 26 June 1945; EIF: 24 October 1945).

8 See e.g., P Vincent *Droit de la Mer* (2008) 13. While it ought to be acknowledged that "[t]he label 'non-state actor' can hardly be considered to constitute a term of art because it includes such [a] wide range of" entities (M Noortmann and C Ryngaert "Non-State actors: International law's problematic case" in M Noortmann and C Ryngaert (ed) *Non-State Actor Dynamics in International Law: From Law-Takers to Law-Makers* (2010) 1–6 at 1), for present purposes the term "non-State actor" refers to any natural person and to any juristic person who is not a State (see e.g., M Wagner "Non-State actors" 2013 MPEPIL § 1 ("[t]he term non-State actors is a superordinate concept that encompasses all those actors in international relations that are not States")). See further e.g., A Mills "Private interests and private law regulation in public international law jurisdiction" in Allen *et al.* (n. 3) 330–354.

9 That is the term used, for instance, in Akehurst (n. 3) 179–212; WLM Reese "Legislative jurisdiction" (1978) 78 *Columbia Law Review* 1587–1608; R Churchill "Under-utilized coastal state jurisdiction: Causes and consequences" in H Ringbom (ed) *Jurisdiction over Ships* (2015) 278–298 at 279.

10 See e.g., *The "Enrica Lexie" Incident* (n. 3) § 526; Bowett (n. 3) 1; Johnson (n. 3) 35–46; D Guilfoyle *Shipping Interdiction and the Law of the Sea* (2009) 8; AJ Colangelo "What is extraterritorial jurisdiction?" (2014) 99 *Cornell Law Review* 1303–1352 at 1304; B Marten *Port State Jurisdiction and the Regulation of International Shipping* (2014) 8; Beckman (n. 3) 350; AT Gallagher & F David *The International Law of Migrant Smuggling* (2014) 212; C Ryngaert *Jurisdiction in International Law* (2015) 9; Honniball (n. 3) 501.

11 See e.g., BH Oxman "Jurisdiction of States" 2007 MPEPIL § 3.

12 See e.g., § 407–413 *Restatement of the Law (Fourth)* (n. 4) and the 1997 revision of the 1968 Council of Europe Model Plan for the Classification of Documents concerning State Practice in the Field of Public International Law (Rec R (97) 11 of 12 June 1997); O'Keefe (n. 3) 736; A Cassese *International Law* (2005) 49; L Sohn *et al. Law of the Sea in a Nutshell* (2010) 71.

different ways.[13] All those definitions point to the fact that the exercise of legislative jurisdiction includes the performance of legislative acts. Whether an act is a legislative act does not depend on the form of the act (e.g., whether it consists in a vote in a legislature or a signature by a government minister) nor on the category within which the legislative instrument produced, amended or repealed by the act falls (e.g., whether the instrument constitutes primary legislation, such as an Act of Parliament, or secondary legislation, such as regulations). What matters is the content of the provisions contained in the instrument. Indeed, it is that content that makes it possible to distinguish between, on the one hand, legislative acts (which produce, amend or repeal legislative instruments containing legislative provisions) and, on the other, executive acts and adjudicative acts. At the same time, it has already been alluded to, and it will be shown below,[14] that, while the exercise of legislative jurisdiction involves primarily the performance of legislative acts, it also involves the performance of executive acts and adjudicative acts. For that reason, in order to accurately define the term "legislative jurisdiction",[15] one must first identify and describe the various categories of legislative provisions contained in the legislative instruments produced, amended or repealed by the legislative acts performed in the exercise of legislative jurisdiction.[16] It is only thereafter that one can discuss the impact of those provisions[17] and turn to the executive acts and adjudicative acts performed in the exercise of legislative jurisdiction.[18]

2.2.2 *Categories of legislative provisions*

2.2.2.1 Introduction

It has just been posited that whether an act performed by an organ of State is a legislative act depends on whether the provisions contained in the instrument

13 For instance, it has been defined as: "the authority of a state to make law applicable to persons, property, or conduct" (§ 401(a) *Restatement of the Law (Fourth)* (n. 4); the authority of a State to establish rules (Oxman (n. 11) § 3); "the power of a state to apply its law to create or affect legal interests" (Reese (n. 9) 1587); "the power to enact legal commands or authorizations binding upon the individuals and State instrumentalities in the territory belonging to the State, and also, under certain circumstances, upon individuals abroad" (Cassese (n. 12) 49); "the power to make decisions or rules" (Marten (n. 10) 8); "the power to make and apply law to persons or things" (Colangelo (n. 10) 1310); "the authority of a State to make laws in relation to persons, property, or conduct" (*The "Enrica Lexie" Incident* (n. 3) § 526); the "competence to make laws and regulations governing a matter" (Gallagher & David (n. 10) 212); "those acts by a State, usually in legislative form, whereby the State asserts the right to characterize conduct as delictual" (Bowett (n. 3) 1); O'Keefe (n. 3) 736 (legislative jurisdiction "refers, in the criminal context, to a state's authority under international law to assert the applicability of its criminal law to given conduct, whether by primary or subordinate legislation, executive decree or, in certain circumstances, judicial ruling").

14 See sections 2.2.4 and 2.2.5, respectively.

15 See section 2.2.6.

16 See section 2.2.2.

17 See section 2.2.3.

18 See sections 2.2.4 and 2.2.5, respectively.

produced, amended or repealed by the act are legislative provisions. For the purposes of a proper understanding of State ocean jurisdiction, it is helpful to divide those provisions into three categories: constitutive provisions, normative provisions and performative provisions.

2.2.2.2 Constitutive provisions

A legislative provision is a constitutive provision when it either creates a ground of jurisdiction for the State that adopts it or describes the features of that ground. For instance, the law of the sea attributes to each coastal State[19] the legislative jurisdiction to adopt a legislative instrument containing a provision in terms of which it establishes an EEZ[20] and, when it does so, to include a provision determining the breadth of that zone.[21] The first provision impacts on the authority of the coastal State by creating an additional ground of jurisdiction for that State.[22] The second provision defines the geographical extent of that jurisdiction by setting the spatial limit within which it may be exercised.[23] Because constitutive provisions relate to fundamental features of a State's legal system, the instruments in which they are contained are often adopted by the States' highest legislative organs. That is the case of Seychelles, for instance, where the National Assembly adopted the Maritime Zones Act, 1999,[24] which sets out the State's maritime-zones framework.[25]

2.2.2.3 Normative provisions

The great majority of legislative provisions can be referred to as "normative provisions", i.e., provisions containing statements laying down authoritatively what natural and juristic persons may do, ought to do or ought not to do. For instance, coastal States exercise their legislative jurisdiction by performing legislative acts producing legislative instruments containing normative provisions, when they exercise their authority to set legal norms relating to the actions of individuals inside their territorial seas in respect of marine scientific research and hydrographic surveys.[26]

19 On the concept of "coastal State", see Chapter 3 section 3.3.2.2.
20 The EEZ differs from the continental shelf in that the latter exists without the need for a legislative act to claim it. See article 77(3) of the LOSC and Chapter 3 section 3.3.3.3.
21 See article 57 of the LOSC, which does not prescribe how States must exercise their jurisdiction in that regard. It merely sets a limit to that jurisdiction by setting the maximum breadth that may be claimed.
22 Jurisdiction on that ground is a type of extraterritorial coastal zone jurisdiction. See Chapter 3 section 3.3.3.2.
23 See further Chapter 4 section 4.6.1.4.
24 Act 2 of 1999.
25 See e.g., sections 9–10.
26 The existence of the coastal States' jurisdiction to do so is confirmed by article 21(1)(g) and 245 of the LOSC.

2.2.2.4 *Performative provisions*

The term "performative provision" is used here to refer to a provision that either confers on an organ of the State the authority to perform an act or sets the parameters within which an act must be performed. Performative provisions are often necessary in a State governed by the rule of law because the only authority that organs of the State have is the authority that they derive from the law.[27]

An example of a performative provision relating to legislative jurisdiction is a provision in terms of which legislative authority is conferred on an executive organ. Such a provision is used because legislative organs often confine the exercise of their legislative authority to the adoption of legislative instruments containing normative provisions setting the principles and main norms of the relevant legal regimes. In those cases, the more detailed and technical norms that need to fill the gaps left by the provisions of the legislative instruments adopted by the legislative organs, are usually adopted by executive organs acting as legislating organs. In South Africa, for example, most of the normative provisions contained in the instruments adopted by the IMO are incorporated into domestic law by means of regulations made by the minister responsible for transport matters,[28] who acts in terms of section 356 of the Merchant Shipping Act, 1951.[29] As already pointed out,[30] the delegation by a legislative organ of its legislative authority to an executive organ – which then acts as a legislating organ – has no import as far as international law is concerned because it merely relates to the nature of the organ given authority to perform an act, the impact of which is not affected by the provision.

It must be stressed that performative provisions do not all relate to legislative jurisdiction. Indeed, although performative provisions are legislative provisions contained in legislative instruments produced by legislative acts, many of them empower State organs to perform legislative, executive or adjudicative acts in the exercise of a jurisdiction other than legislative jurisdiction. In those cases, the performative provisions relating to executive or adjudicative jurisdiction are contained in legislative instruments produced by means of legislative acts. The latter are, however, best understood not as being performed in the exercise of legislative jurisdiction, but rather as being performed in the exercise of executive jurisdiction or adjudicative jurisdiction.[31]

27 See e.g., KM Stack "An administrative jurisprudence: The rule of law in the administrative State" (2015) 115 *Columbia Law Review* 1985–2018 at 1992; P Lazaroiu & I Cochintu "The constitutionalisation of law through the principle of legality" (2018) 9 *Journal of Law and Administrative Sciences* 163–168 at 164. See further UNGA Declaration of the High Level Meeting of the General Assembly on the Rule of Law at the National and International Levels (Resolution 67/1 of 24 September 2012) 2.

28 See e.g., the Merchant Shipping (Dangerous Goods) Regulations, 1997, published by GN R574 of 1997 in GG 17921 of 18 April 1997.

29 Act 57 of 1951. See further J Hare *Shipping Law & Admiralty Jurisdiction in South Africa* (2009).

30 See section 2.1.

31 See further sections 2.3.2 and 2.4.2, respectively.

2.2.2.5 *Combination of provisions*

The analysis of the nature of a legislative provision is often complicated by the fact that a single legislative instrument might contain legislative provisions falling within more than one of the categories and might even contain provisions falling within all the categories at the same time. In addition, the legislative act producing the instrument might be performed at the same time in the exercise of the State's legislative jurisdiction, its executive jurisdiction and its adjudicative jurisdiction.[32] The Maritime Zones Act of Seychelles, already mentioned above,[33] is a good example. Sections 9 and 10 of the Act are constitutive provisions adopted in the exercise of legislative jurisdiction, in that they relate to the existence and extent of the Seychellois EEZ as well as the ambit of the State's jurisdiction in the zone. Section 18 is a normative provision adopted in the exercise of legislative jurisdiction because it regulates the exercise of the right of archipelagic sea lanes passage in the archipelagic waters of Seychelles. Section 33(1)(a) is a performative provision adopted in the exercise of legislative jurisdiction in that it authorises the President of Seychelles to make regulations governing the conduct of any person on the State's continental shelf. Section 33(1)(b)(v) is a performative provision adopted in the exercise of executive jurisdiction in that it authorises the President to make regulations governing the authorisation and control of marine scientific research in the EEZ. Finally, section 24(2) is a performative provision adopted in the exercise of adjudicative jurisdiction in that it limits the range of options available to the courts of Seychelles when imposing a sentence for a violation of the State's fisheries laws.

2.2.3 *Impact of legislative acts performed in the exercise of legislative jurisdiction*

2.2.3.1 *Introduction*

As explained earlier,[34] what matters in international law is not the nature of the organ performing an act, but the nature of that act. That is the case because it is the nature of an act that determines the impact of that act on other States and NSAs. While the impact of legislative acts differs from the impacts of executive acts and adjudicative acts,[35] legislative acts do not all have the same impact at the international level. This becomes apparent when one focuses on the performance of the legislative acts[36] and the contents of the legislative provisions.[37]

2.2.3.2 *Performance of legislative acts*

In practice, the performance of a legislative act, that is to say the taking of a decision to adopt, amend or repeal a legislative instrument, does not normally have an impact on

32 Each jurisdiction being exercised in respect of the relevant provision(s).
33 See section 2.2.2.2.
34 See section 2.1.
35 See sections 2.2.4 and 2.2.5.
36 See section 2.2.3.2.
37 See section 2.2.3.3.

foreign States. The reason is that State organs perform legislative acts in most, if not all, instances within their own territory. State organs do so because the performance of legislative acts within the territory of another State or on a vessel flying the flag of another State would require both the consent of that State as well as abiding by any stipulation that the State might decide to make.[38] Those two constraints do not exist when a legislative act is performed by a State organ within the State's territory. They also do not exist when the act is performed on board a vessel flying the flag of the State while it is not within the marine component of the territory of a foreign State.[39] In such a case, it would clearly be against international law for a State to perform a legislative act beyond its territorial sea as an element of a practice to support a claim that the area in which the vessel is located when the act is performed is part of its territory.[40] By contrast, there appears to be no legal obstacle standing in the way of a State organ performing a legislative act beyond its territorial sea without any intention to rely on that performance to support a territorial claim. That would be the case, for instance, were a legislative organ of a State to adopt, while convened on the high seas on a vessel flying the flag of the State, a statute incorporating into its domestic law a new international regime governing the living resources of the high seas in order to demonstrate to other States its commitment to the successful implementation of that regime.

2.2.3.3 Contents of legislative provisions

(A) INTRODUCTION

In addition to the actual performance of a legislative act, the contents of the legislative provisions contained in the legislative instrument produced by the act also have an effect on the impact of the act on foreign States and NSAs. Building on the earlier discussion,[41] it is best to approach this aspect of State ocean jurisdiction by examining the three categories of legislative provisions one after the other.

(B) CONSTITUTIVE PROVISIONS

Constitutive provisions have a direct impact on foreign States when both the creation of a ground of jurisdiction and the proclamation of the extent of that jurisdiction have the effect of limiting the scope of the jurisdictions of other States. For instance, the proclamation of an EEZ by a State has the effect of reducing the geographical extent of the jurisdictions of other States with regard to living resources and non-living resources at sea.[42] By contrast, the contents of constitutive provisions do not have a direct impact on NSAs. The reason is that constitutive

38 See e.g., *Island of Palmas Case (United States of America v. The Netherlands)*, award of 4 April 1928, II RIAA 829 at 838.

39 On the extent of the marine component of the territory of a coastal State, see Chapter 4 section 2.3.1.

40 See article 89 of the LOSC with regard to the high seas.

41 See section 2.2.2.

42 See article 56(1)(a) of the LOSC. See further Chapter 4 section 4.6.1.2.

provisions merely lay the foundation for the State to adopt the normative provisions and the performative provisions necessary to govern the activities of the NSAs. In other words, while the performance of a legislative act producing a legislative instrument containing a constitutive provision is a precondition for a State's organs to perform one or more acts having a direct impact on NSAs, the impact of that provision is only felt by NSAs when the State performs additional acts in the exercise of its legislative jurisdiction, its executive jurisdiction or its adjudicative jurisdiction on the ground created by that provision.

It is in light of the above that one would probably best interpret State protests against, for instance, the performance by a State of a legislative act producing a legislative instrument containing a provision in terms of which the outer limit of its EEZ is set further than 200 NM from its baselines and, therefore, in violation of article 57 of the LOSC. Such protests do not relate to the direct impact of the provision on ocean activities beyond 200 NM, because the provision does not have such an impact. Instead, the protests constitute objections by foreign States to the fact that the State extended, in its domestic legal order, the geographical scope of its EEZ-related legislative, executive and adjudicative jurisdictions beyond the limit within which international law allows States to exercise those jurisdictions. The protests also indicate that any later performance of a legislative, executive or adjudicative act based on the constitutive provision (for instance in the form of the adoption of a legislative instrument containing normative provisions relating to fisheries) will be objected to by the protesting States (in this example to the extent that the provisions govern fishing activities beyond 200 NM).[43]

The fact that a constitutive provision does not have a direct impact does not exclude the possibility that the State, an organ of which adopted the instrument containing that provision, breached one of its international obligations through the adoption of that instrument. The ILC confirmed that there is no general answer applicable in all cases to the question

> whether an obligation is breached by the enactment of legislation by a State, in cases where the content of the legislation *prima facie* conflicts with what is required by the international obligation, or whether the legislation has to be implemented in the given case before the breach can be said to have occurred.[44]

The ILC explained that

> [c]ertain obligations may be breached by the mere passage of incompatible legislation. Where this is so, the passage of the legislation without more

43 See further Chapter 4 section 4.6.1.4.

44 See the commentary to article 12 of the ILC Articles on State Responsibility (Report of the International Law Commission covering the work of its 53rd session, 23 April – 1 June and 2 July – 10 August 2001, to the General Assembly, UN Doc. A/56/10 (2001) reproduced in (2001) II YILC 57).

> entails the international responsibility of the enacting State, the legislature itself being an organ of the State for the purposes of the attribution of responsibility. In other circumstances, the enactment of legislation may not in and of itself amount to a breach, especially if it is open to the State concerned to give effect to the legislation in a way which would not violate the international obligation in question. In such cases, whether there is a breach will depend on whether and how the legislation is given effect.[45]

(C) PERFORMATIVE PROVISIONS

In contrast to constitutive provisions and normative provisions, performative provisions do not have a direct impact on foreign States or NSAs. This is because the effect of a provision in terms of which authority is conferred on an organ of State to perform an act is either: (a) to vest in the organ capacity to perform at a later stage an act that might impact foreign States and NSAs; or (b) to set the parameters within which the organ is expected to perform the act.

In the case of the EEZ, for instance, it has just been pointed out above that it is the proclamation of the zone that has the direct effect of reducing the spatial extent of the jurisdictions of other States with regard to living and non-living resources at sea.[46] The concurrent or subsequent adoption by the legislature of a coastal State of a legislative instrument containing a performative provision[47] does not reduce the spatial extent of the jurisdictions of other States any further.

At the same time, performative provisions relating to legislative jurisdiction do not have a direct impact on NSAs because they do not state the norms that govern activities at sea. Indeed, it is only when the organs that the provisions capacitate make use of their legislative authority by performing legislative acts producing legislative instruments containing normative provisions that the performative provisions have an indirect impact on NSAs. For instance, a fisheries statute containing a performative provision giving authority to the minister responsible for fisheries to adopt regulations complementing the normative provisions of the statute does not, on its own, have a direct impact on ocean activities in the EEZ of the State concerned. The provision only has an indirect impact when the minister exercises the authority conferred by the provision in the form of the adoption of a legislative instrument containing normative provisions relating, for instance, to technical control measures based on criteria, such as time, location, kind of gear, mesh size, type of fishing, species as well as number and size of the fish captured.

45 *Ibid.* See also *The M/V "Norstar" Case (Panama v. Italy)*, judgment of 10 April 2019 (2019) 58 ILM 673 § 225; *Alleged Violations of Sovereign Rights and Maritime Spaces in the Caribbean Sea (Nicaragua v. Colombia)*, judgment of 21 April 2022, ICJ Case No 155, § 194.

46 See section 2.2.3.3(b).

47 For instance, a provision giving authority to the State's minister responsible for fisheries to adopt normative provisions governing the exploitation of living resources in the EEZ. The position is the same with regard to the performative provisions setting the parameters within which the minister is to act as legislating organ.

In light of the above, a foreign State's protest against performative provisions relating to legislative jurisdiction is best understood as not to relate to the direct impact of the provisions on the State or NSAs, because the provisions do not have such an impact. Instead, the protest may be interpreted in one or both of the following ways. First, the protest may be understood as a renewed expression by the foreign State of the objection raised against the constitutive provision on the basis of which the State adopted the legislative instrument containing the performative provision.[48] Secondly, the protest may be seen as an indication that the later adoption of a legislative instrument containing normative provisions is likely to be objected to by the protesting State.[49]

(D) NORMATIVE PROVISIONS

(i) Introduction The actual impact of the normative provisions of a legislative instrument on human activities at sea is affected by the subject matter of those provisions as well as the criteria determining the scope of application of those provisions. Those criteria define the extent of that application on a spatial basis, a personal basis or a hybrid basis.

(ii) Spatial application In most cases, normative provisions apply within the whole geographical area for which the legislative or legislating organ that performed the act producing the legislative instrument containing the provisions, has the authority to legislate. Thus, provisions contained in an instrument adopted by a legislative or legislating organ of a municipality normally apply within the territory of that municipality, provisions contained in an instrument adopted by a legislative or legislating organ of a province or a constituent state normally apply within the territory of that province or state, while provisions contained in an instrument adopted by a legislative or legislating organ of a unitary or federal State normally apply within the territory of that State. In those cases, the precise extent of the territorial application of the rules is often not expressly stated.[50] The reason is that there is a presumption that legislation applies within the whole area for which the legislative or legislating organ that performed the act has the authority to legislate.[51]

Two difficulties can arise with regard to the application of that presumption in ocean matters. The first difficulty is in the case of legislative or legislating organs below the national level. It revolves around the geographical extent of the geographical areas for which those organs have legislative authority. It might indeed be unclear whether the territory of a coastal municipality, province or constituent

48 In a case where such a constitutive provision was needed. See section 2.2.2.2.

49 In a case where the normative provisions are not contained in the same legislative instrument. See section 2.2.2.5.

50 See e.g., M Hirst *Jurisdiction and the Ambit of the Criminal Law* (2003) 2.

51 In the case of South Africa, see e.g., GM Cockram *The Interpretation of Statutes* (1987) 134. In the case of the United States, see e.g., FA Gevurtz "Extraterritoriality and the Fourth Restatement of Foreign Relations Law: Opportunities lost" (2019) 55 *Willamette Law Review* 449–474; Dodge (n. 3) 111.

state includes the adjacent ocean waters and, if so, how far out at sea.[52] The second difficulty is, as far as a legislative or legislating organ at the national level is concerned, regarding whether the presumption applies at all in matters relating to ocean matters. It might indeed be that, although an organ has legislative authority over the whole national territory, the rules which it adopts must be presumed in domestic law to apply in an area that does not include all or part of the ocean spaces within what is considered to be the State's territory in international law. That is the case in England, for instance, where the territorial waters are outside the realm.[53]

The second difficulty flows from the fact that, in many cases, international law allows or compels States to provide for the application outside of their territory of the normative provisions contained in the legislative instruments that they adopt,[54] leading courts to "often pay lip-service to the territoriality presumption".[55] Examples are the provisions contained in an instrument adopted by a coastal State to govern the exploration and exploitation of the natural resources of its continental shelf[56] and the provisions contained in an instrument adopted by a flag State to govern administrative, technical and social matters relating to vessels flying its flag.[57] The authority to perform legislative acts producing legislative instruments containing normative provisions applying beyond the border of a State, is often vested in the relevant organs at the national level within the State.[58] At the same time, international law places limitations on the extent to which States may provide for the application outside of their territory of the normative provisions contained in the legislative instruments that they adopt. For instance, a State may not adopt legislative instruments containing normative provisions that are based on the premise that the State has sovereignty over a part of the high seas.[59] Likewise, a State may not unilaterally adopt rules meant to apply, for instance, to all fisheries matters arising

52 See e.g., *United States v. California* 332 US 19 (1947) at 38; *Reference re Offshore Mineral Rights of British Columbia* 1967 SCR 792 at 816 confirmed in *Reference re Property in and Legislative Jurisdiction over the Seabed and Subsoil of the Continental Shelf Offshore Newfoundland* 1984 SCR 86 (regarding the continental shelf); *New South Wales v. Commonwealth* 8 ALR 1 at 11); *Reference re Ownership of the Bed of the Strait of Georgia and Related Areas* 1984 SCR 388 at 427; P Vrancken *South Africa and the Law of the Sea* (2011) 38–39 and 42–43. In India, each coastal constituent state has its own legislation governing fisheries up to 12 NM (see e.g., the Tamil Nadu Marine Fishing Regulation Act, 1983 (Tamil Nadu Act 8 of 1983)). On the position in Brazil, see e.g., J Nakamura & F Hazin "Assessing the Brazilian federal fisheries law and policy in light of the Voluntary Guidelines for Securing Sustainable Small-scale Fisheries" (2020) 113 MP 103798 at 3–4.

53 See e.g., *R v. Keyn* 1876 2 Ex D 63; DP O'Connell *The International Law of the Sea* (1982) I 53–57 and 84–121; Hirst (n. 50) 2.

54 See further e.g., Chapter 4 sections 4.2.1 and 4.4.1 and Chapter 5 section 5.4.3.3.

55 Ryngaert (n. 10) 77.

56 See article 77(1) of the LOSC.

57 See article 94(1) of the LOSC.

58 See e.g., section 51(x) of the 1900 Australian Constitution.

59 See article 89 of the LOSC.

in the territorial sea or the EEZ of another State. This does not mean, however, that normative provisions adopted by a State may never apply to such matters.[60]

(iii) Personal application The basis for the application of a normative provision can also be of a personal nature. In that case, a provision applies only to matters involving natural and/or juristic persons who have the characteristic(s) specified in the provision itself or another provision determining its scope of application. For instance, sections 267–279 of Mauritania's 1995 Merchant Marine Code[61] apply to seafarers as defined in section 266. The fact that a provision applies on a personal basis does not mean that the provision applies irrespective of where the persons find themselves. Indeed, it has just been pointed out above that the organ that performs a legislative act producing a legislative instrument containing normative provisions has only the authority to do so within the confines of the geographical area over which that authority extends.[62]

In the domestic legal order of many States, the right to equality does constitute an obstacle to a departure from the principle of general application of a normative provision on a spatial basis by providing for the application of that provision on a personal basis.[63] By contrast, international law allows, and in specific cases even compels, States to provide for the application of the rules which they adopt to apply on a personal basis outside of their territory.[64] In order to do so, a legally valid connection is needed between the State which adopts the instrument containing the provisions and the persons to whom the provisions are made to apply. In most instances, the connection relied upon is nationality. This is the case, for instance, of article 117 of the LOSC, which provides that "[a]ll States have the duty to take, or to cooperate with other States in taking, such measures for their respective nationals as may be necessary for the conservation of the living resources of the high seas".

Whether the provisions apply everywhere beyond a State's territory depends on whether the limitation of the application of the provision on a personal basis is combined with a limitation of the application of the provision on a spatial basis. A State might provide for such a combination when, for instance, it wishes to avoid the situation where its own provision would apply to a person on a personal basis at the same time that a conflicting provision contained in an instrument adopted by another State applies to that same person on a spatial basis. That is the case, for instance, when a person having the nationality of one State is within the internal waters, archipelagic waters or territorial waters of another State.[65]

The fact that two normative provisions contained in instruments adopted by two different States apply at the same time is not inevitably a problem. Indeed, the provisions might be identical or so similar that they do not have different impacts on

60 See further e.g., Chapter 4 sections 4.3.3.2 and 4.6.3.2.
61 Act 95–009 of 31 January 1995.
62 See section 2.2.3.3(d)(ii).
63 See e.g., article 1 of the Dutch Constitution.
64 See further Chapter 4 section 4.4.1 and Chapter 5 section 5.4.3.3.
65 See further Chapter 4 section 4.4.4.

the persons to whom they apply. By contrast, a serious problem does arise when the provisions have very different or even opposite impacts. One way of avoiding that problem is to provide that the provisions apply only on a personal basis outside of the geographical areas where other States are entitled to make their own provisions applicable on a spatial basis, as in the example just mentioned.

Limiting the application of a provision in that way can however create more difficulties than the one the limitation attempts to avoid. An example is where a provision contained in an instrument adopted by State A applies to a person on a personal basis outside of the territory of another State, that person is within the territory of State B, but the latter has not exercised its legislative jurisdiction. In this case neither the provisions of State A nor any provisions of State B do apply to the person. In addition, a difficulty would still remain, for instance, were State B to exercise its legislative jurisdiction, but the impact of its provisions be more limited than the impact of the provisions adopted by State A. Indeed, in such a case, although provisions enacted by State B do apply to the person, they have a lesser impact on the issue that State A wishes to address, than the impact that State A considers they should have.

States are therefore faced with a choice. In many instances, States appear to consider that the subject matter of the provisions contained in the instruments that they adopt is of such a nature that it is more important to ensure that their nationals are not confronted with a situation where they are expected to abide by conflicting provisions at the same time (with the ensuing negative impact on the mobility of those persons, for instance),[66] than to ensure that their provisions apply to their nationals wherever they are. However, in specific instances, such as serious crimes,[67] many States clearly take the view that avoiding the simultaneous application of conflicting provisions to their nationals is less important than ensuring that those persons are never in a position not to have to abide by the States' provisions.[68]

(iv) Hybrid application The basis for the application of a normative provision may be of a hybrid nature, with both personal and spatial features.[69] In the law of the sea, a hybrid basis is used in cases when a provision is meant to apply only to matters arising on, or related to, vessels.[70] This is also the case with regard to artificial islands, installations and structures, which are referred to in this book as "artificial features". The hybrid basis has a spatial element in that the provision applies

66 See e.g., JL Brierly "The 'Lotus' case" (1928) 44 *Law Quarterly Review* 154–163 at 162.

67 See e.g., Ryngaert (n. 10) 104–110.

68 On the handling of the ensuing conflicts, see e.g., K Brookson-Morris "Conflicts of criminal jurisdiction" (2007) 56 ICLQ 659–666; P Caeiro "Jurisdiction in criminal matters in the EU: Negative and positive conflicts, and beyond" (2010) 93(4) *Kritische Vierteljahresschrift für Gesetzgebung und Rechtswissenschaft* 366–379.

69 See e.g., G Gidel *Le Droit international public de la mer* (1932) I 253.

70 See e.g., F Chevillard "Le statut du navire en fin de vie" in A de Marffy-Mantuano (ed) *Droit International de la Mer et Droit de l'Union Européenne* (2014) 275–289 at 275. "For purposes of the LOS Convention, other treaties, many national laws, and this text, the terms 'ship' and 'vessel' are synonymous" (Sohn *et al.* (n. 12) 62).

to matters arising on, or with regard to, specific (and very limited) spaces (i.e., vessels) irrespective of the nationality or State of residence of the persons in those spaces.[71] At the same time, the basis has a personal element in that the geographical area within which the vessel finds itself in does not have an impact on whether the normative provision applies. Instead, whether the provision applies depends on whether there is a legal link symbolised by the flag that the ship flies between the vessel and the State, an organ of which has performed the legislative act that has produced the legislative instrument containing the provision.[72]

As in the case of personal application, international law allows, and in specific cases even compels, States to provide for the application of the provisions contained in the instruments which they adopt to apply on a hybrid basis outside of their territory. This is the case, for instance, of article 99 of the LOSC, which provides that "[e]very State shall take effective measures to prevent and punish the transport of slaves in ships authorized to fly its flag and to prevent the unlawful use of its flag for that purpose".[73] Whether a provision applies everywhere beyond the State's territory depends on whether the hybrid basis is combined with a spatial one. That would be the case, for instance, were State A to wish to avoid the situation where its own normative provisions applying to the vessels flying its flag apply at the same time as the normative provisions contained in an instrument adopted by an organ of State B applying to all vessels within the marine component of the territory of State B.[74]

It has already been pointed out that the fact that normative provisions contained in legislative instruments adopted by organs of different States apply at the same time is only a problem when the provisions have different or even opposite impacts.[75] The likelihood of this occurring is obviously increased by the existence of provisions that apply on a hybrid basis. Indeed, in the most complex cases, the normative provisions of State A that apply to all persons on a vessel on a personal basis, conflict with the normative provisions of State B that apply on a spatial basis in the geographical area where the vessel finds itself, as well as with the normative provisions of State C that apply to the vessel on a hybrid basis. The ways to avoid such conflicts differ in the cases of conflicts between provisions applied on a hybrid basis and provisions applied on a spatial basis, on the one hand, and in the cases of conflicts between provisions applied on a hybrid basis and provisions applied on a personal basis, on the other.

In the cases of conflicts between normative provisions applied on a hybrid basis and provisions applied on a spatial basis, the approach is largely the same as in the cases of conflicts between normative provisions applied on a personal basis and provisions applied on a spatial basis.[76] It involves the normative provisions

71 See e.g., Gidel (n. 69) I 252.
72 See article 91(1) of the LOSC. See further Chapter 3 section 3.2.3.
73 See further Chapter 4 section 4.8.1.3.
74 See further Chapter 4 section 4.3.3.2.
75 See section 2.2.3.3(d)*(iii)*.
76 See section 2.2.3.3(d)*(iii)*.

that apply on a hybrid basis being made to apply only outside of the geographical areas where other States are entitled to make their own normative provisions applicable on a spatial basis. That would be the case, for instance, were a State to provide for the application of normative provisions applying to vessels flying its flag to all geographical areas outside the territories of other States. However, as in the case of personal application, that approach can create more difficulties than the one it attempts to avoid. For instance, the coastal State through the territorial sea of which a vessel is passing might not have exercised its legislative jurisdiction. In such a case, no normative provisions would apply to the vessel at all. Another possibility is that the coastal State has exercised its legislative jurisdiction, but the impact of its provisions is more limited than the impact of the provisions adopted by the flag State.

States must therefore, as in the case of personal application, decide which situations they want to avoid. However, the factors to be taken into account in the case of hybrid application do not correspond entirely to those to be taken into account in the case of personal application. The main reason is that vessels are meant to be moving and many of them do so by passing, at one stage or another, through waters where coastal States have legislative jurisdiction. As a result, were a State to provide that the normative provisions contained in the legislative instruments adopted by its organs apply on a hybrid basis only outside the territories of other States, those provisions would not apply permanently to the vessels flying its flag. In addition, those vessels would be subject to regulatory changes when they enter the waters where the normative provisions, the contents of which differ from the contents of the provisions adopted by the flag State, apply on a spatial basis. Such changes might be of such a nature that it might be impossible for a vessel to comply at all times with the applicable provisions and, as a result, to make full use of the navigational rights that it holds. That is the case, for instance, with regard to normative provisions setting technical standards relating to the physical features of ships.[77] In such a case, States might take the view that the subject matter of the norms is of such a nature that avoiding the concurrent application of conflicting provisions to the ships flying their flags is less important than ensuring that those ships are permanently subjected to the same regulatory regime. States might even go further by removing the source of the conflict. That is the case, for instance, of article 24(1)(a) of the LOSC, which forbids that a coastal State "impose requirements on foreign ships which have the practical effect of denying or impairing the right of innocent passage".[78]

77 See e.g., F Attard 'IMO's contribution to international law regulating maritime security' (2014) 45 JMLC 479–565.

78 Another example is article 21(2) of the LOSC, which is based on the premise that, in the interests of international navigation, the hybrid basis of certain normative provisions is not combined with a spatial one (see e.g., R Churchill, V Lowe & A Sander *The Law of the Sea* (2022) 157; MH Nordquist (ed) *United Nations Convention on the Law of the Sea 1982: A Commentary* (1993) II 201 § 21.11(f)). An example of a domestic provision in which the hybrid basis is not combined with a spatial one is article 546 of Guinea's 1995 Code de la Marine Marchande.

The position is somewhat different in the cases of conflicts between provisions applied on a hybrid basis and provisions applied on a personal basis. The reason is that the provisions applying on a hybrid basis apply to all persons on board a vessel, irrespective of the nationality or State of residence of those persons. The reason is that the space within which the individuals operate on board that vessel needs to be governed by a single legal regime, for similar reasons and to a similar extent that dry land forming part of the territory of a State needs to be governed by a single system. Indeed, each vessel is inherently a "collectivité organisée" in which "les individualités doivent s'absorber dans [...] l''agrégation' dont [elles] font partie d'une manière passagère ou permanente".[79] For that reason, like on dry land, it is not an option for the flag State to exclude from the sphere of application of its own normative provisions on a hybrid basis, individuals to whom the normative provisions of other States apply on a personal basis.

(v) Subject matter The impact of the normative provisions of a legislative instrument on human activities at sea is affected not only by the basis on which those provisions are applied, but also by the subject matter of the provisions. That impact is both direct and indirect.

The impact is indirect when the subject matter affects the decision made by the organ of a State that performs the legislative acts producing the legislative instrument containing normative provisions, regarding the basis on which those provisions are to apply. In other words, the impact is indirect when the subject matter of a normative provision affects the number of grounds of jurisdiction on the basis of which the State may or must decide that the provision applies. In this sense, the subject matter of the normative provisions of a legislative instrument impacts human activities at sea indirectly because the provisions only apply to those activities when the State has relied on the ground(s) of jurisdiction available to it. It will be explained in later chapters that there is often a link between the nature of the matters to be regulated, on the one hand, and whether, and to which extent, States have legislative jurisdiction over those matters, on the other.[80]

The impact of the subject matter of the normative provisions on human activities at sea is direct when the subject matter is defined in such a way that it goes a step further in limiting the impact of those provisions, after their sphere of application has already been limited by the use of the spatial, personal or hybrid applicability criterion. That is the case, for instance, when the application of a normative provision is limited on a spatial basis to the EEZ of the State, while the subject-matter of the provision is limited to fisheries. In such a case, the impact of the legislative act is limited to activities taking place within the EEZ of the State and, in addition, to activities relating to living resources in that zone. That means, for instance, that the legislative act has no impact on container vessels. This is the case not only while those vessels are outside the EEZ of the State (because they are outside the

79 Gidel (n. 69) I 253.
80 See further Chapters 3 and 4.

sphere of spatial application of the normative provision), but also while the vessels are inside the EEZ of the State (because they are outside the sphere of application *ratione materiae* of the provision).

2.2.4 Executive acts

2.2.4.1 Introduction

As alluded to earlier, it is sometimes necessary for legislative and legislating organs vested with legislative jurisdiction to perform executive acts in order for them to be able to perform the legislative acts that that jurisdiction primarily entails. For present purposes, it is arguably helpful to divide those executive acts (understood for present purposes as involving the application of legal rules outside adjudicative processes) into logistic acts, process acts and enforcement acts.

2.2.4.2 Logistic acts

The logistic acts performed in the exercise of legislative jurisdiction are the executive acts performed for the purpose of setting legislative organs up and putting in place the resources and mechanisms necessary for legislative organs and legislating organs to perform legislative acts, executive acts and adjudicative acts in the exercise of that jurisdiction. For instance, an organ of State performs logistic acts in the exercise of that State's legislative jurisdiction when it establishes the administrative structures necessary for a legislative organ to deliberate upon, and perform a legislative act producing, a legislative instrument containing normative provisions governing marine pollution.

The logistic acts performed in the exercise of legislative jurisdiction also include the executive acts performed for the purpose of putting in place the resources and mechanisms necessary for legislating organs to perform legislative acts in the exercise of legislative jurisdiction. For instance, a State would perform logistic acts in the exercise of its legislative jurisdiction were it to put in place the resources and mechanisms necessary for its ministry responsible for shipping to make the regulations that are necessary, in terms of its domestic law, to incorporate IMO instruments into that law.

Logistic acts have no direct impact on NSAs. Normally, as in the case of legislative acts,[81] the performance of logistic acts also has no impact outside the territory of the State concerned as a result of the fact that, in the light of a wide range of factors,[82] States do perform their logistic acts in most, if not all, instances within their own territory. The reasons are the same as those that explain the position as far as legislative acts are concerned.[83]

81 See section 2.2.3.2.
82 Such as the financial and logistical implications of the performance of the acts.
83 See section 2.2.3.2.

2.2.4.3 Process acts

The process acts performed in the exercise of legislative jurisdiction are the executive acts that are performed by State organs in the process of exercising the State's legislative jurisdiction and that do not involve the threat or actual use of force. For instance, the members of the administrative staff of a legislative organ perform process acts when they provide administrative support in the process followed by the members of that organ to deliberate upon, and perform the legislative act producing, a legislative instrument containing normative provisions relating to maritime security.

As in the case of logistic acts, the process acts performed in the exercise of legislative jurisdiction have no direct impact on NSAs. The position with regard to any possible impact of a process act outside the territory of the State, of which an organ has performed that act, is the same as in the case of logistic acts.[84]

2.2.4.4 Enforcement acts

Under certain circumstances, legislative organs are called upon to perform enforcement acts, that is to say executive acts involving the threat or the actual use of force. That would be the case, for instance, were steps to be taken to remove from a parliamentary chamber one or more individuals who unlawfully interfere with the process of deliberating upon, and later performing, a legislative act.

In contrast with logistic acts and process acts, enforcement acts can have a direct impact on NSAs as the abovementioned example illustrates. However, the position with regard to any possible impact of an enforcement act outside the territory of the State, an organ of which has performed that act, is the same as in the case of logistic acts.[85]

2.2.5 Adjudicative acts

In exceptional cases, legislative organs[86] are called upon, in relation to the exercise of the State's legislative jurisdiction, to perform adjudicative acts. Those acts may be defined as those performed by the said organs when they settle internal disputes that relate to the exercise of that jurisdiction. That is the case, for instance, when a committee of a legislative body reaches a decision at the end of disciplinary proceedings instituted against a member of that body. Those adjudicative acts do not have a direct impact on individuals outside the organs concerned. The position with regard to any possible impact of an adjudicative act outside the territory of the

84 See section 2.2.4.2.
85 *Ibid.*
86 And other organs to the extent that they act as legislating organs.

State, an organ of which has performed that act, is once again the same as in the case of logistic acts.[87]

2.2.6 Definition of "legislative jurisdiction"

On the basis of the above, it is possible to define the term "legislative jurisdiction" as the international-law authority of a State to be involved in a factual matter by performing,

(a) legislative acts producing, amending or repealing legislative instruments containing constitutive provisions;
(b) legislative acts producing, amending or repealing legislative instruments containing normative provisions; and, incidentally,
(c) legislative acts producing, amending or repealing legislative instruments containing performative provisions necessary for the performance of:
  (i) the legislative acts referred to in paragraphs (a)–(b);
  (ii) other legislative acts referred to in this paragraph;
  (iii) the executive acts referred to in paragraph (d); and
  (iv) the adjudicative acts referred to in paragraph (e);
(d) logistic acts, process acts and enforcement acts related to the performance of:
  (i) the legislative acts referred to in paragraphs (a)–(c);
  (ii) other executive acts referred to in this paragraph; and
  (iii) the adjudicative acts referred to in paragraph (e); and
(e) adjudicative acts related to the performance of:
  (i) the legislative acts referred to in paragraphs (a)–(c);
  (ii) the executive acts referred to in paragraph (d); and
  (iii) other adjudicative acts referred to in this paragraph.

2.3 Executive jurisdiction

2.3.1 Introduction

Executive jurisdiction[88] (also called, for instance, "enforcement jurisdiction",[89] "enforcement competence",[90] "jurisdiction to enforce",[91] "enforcement or prerogative jurisdiction"[92] and "arrest jurisdiction"[93]) has been defined in different

87 See section 2.2.4.2.
88 The term is also used by e.g., Akehurst (n. 3) 145.
89 See e.g., *The "Enrica Lexie" Incident* (n. 3) § 526; Johnson (n. 3) 46–50; Guilfoyle (n. 10) 8; Colangelo (n. 10) 1305; Beckman (n. 3) 350; Gallagher & David (n. 10) 212; Honniball (n. 3) 501.
90 See e.g., Oxman (n. 11) § 3.
91 See e.g., § 401(c) *Restatement of the Law (Fourth)* (n. 4); the Council of Europe's 1997 Amended Model Plan (n. 12); Cassese (n. 12) 49; Sohn *et al.* (n. 12) 71.
92 See e.g., Marten (n. 10) 8.
93 See e.g., Churchill (n. 9) 279.

ways.[94] In most instances, the exercise of executive jurisdiction involves the performance of executive acts.[95] In fewer cases, executive jurisdiction is exercised by performing a legislative act[96] or an adjudicative act.[97]

2.3.2 Legislative acts

It was pointed out earlier in this chapter that, in a State governed by the rule of law, the only authority that organs of the State have is the authority that they derive from the law.[98] For that reason, the exercise of executive jurisdiction must often start by performing legislative acts producing legislative instruments containing performative provisions that: (a) confer on one or more organs of the State the authority to perform acts in the exercise of the State's executive jurisdiction; and (b) set the parameters within which the acts must be performed.

Those provisions can have different purposes. A provision might be meant to confirm the existence of the State's executive jurisdiction. For instance, section 22 of the 2017 Territorial Sea and Maritime Zones Law of Myanmar[99] proclaims that "[t]he relevant government departments and government organizations may, in accordance with the existing laws, search, query [and] arrest [...] any ship for exploring, exploiting, conserving and managing the natural resources in the exclusive economic zone". Another provision might have the effect of establishing an organ of the State, while other provisions confer on that organ the authority to perform a range of acts in the exercise of the State's executive jurisdiction. For instance, section 5 of the Australian Maritime Safety Authority Act, 1990,[100] establishes the Authority and section 6(1) sets out the functions of the Authority. In addition, some performative provisions incorporate into domestic law provisions contained in international-law instruments. Section 7 of the Act is an example when it provides that "[t]he Authority must perform its functions in a manner

94 For instance: "the authority of a state to exercise its power to compel compliance with law" (§ 401(c) *Restatement of the Law (Fourth)* (n. 4)); the authority to "forcibly impos[e] consequences such as loss of liberty or property for breaches or, pending adjudication, alleged breaches of the rules" (Oxman (n. 11) § 3); "the power to ensure through coercive means that legal commands and entitlements are complied with" (Cassese (n. 12) 49); "the power to take executive action in pursuance of or consequent on the making of decisions or rules" (Marten (n. 10) 8); the right of a State to "regulate conduct by taking executive or administrative action which impinges more directly on the course of events [than legislative and judicial jurisdiction], as by enforcing its laws or the decisions of its courts" (R Jennings & A Watts (eds) *Oppenheim's International Law* (1992) 456); the "States' capacity to apply law to specific facts and to enforce that law's application through coercive power" (Gallagher & David (n. 10) 222); "the authority of a State to exercise its power to compel compliance with law" (*The "Enrica Lexie" Incident* (n. 3) § 526).

95 See section 2.3.3.

96 See section 2.3.2.

97 See section 2.3.4.

98 See section 2.2.2.4.

99 (2019) 99 LOSB 28.

100 Act 78 of 1990.

consistent with the obligations of Australia under any agreement between Australia and another country".

It is important to keep in mind that the performative provisions setting the parameters within which State organs perform acts in the exercise of executive jurisdiction in ocean matters are often not contained only in ocean-specific instruments. Indeed, the provisions may also be contained in generic instruments that apply by default to all State organs exercising executive jurisdiction in any matter. That is the case, in Germany for example, of the Administrative Procedure Act, 1976.[101] In fact, State organs might perform acts in the exercise of executive jurisdiction in ocean matters within parameters that are not set by ocean-specific performative provisions.[102]

The impact of performative provisions adopted in the exercise of executive jurisdiction is similar to the impact of performative provisions adopted in the exercise of legislative jurisdiction.[103] Indeed, performative provisions adopted in the exercise of executive jurisdiction do not have a direct impact on foreign States or NSAs. That is because performative provisions do not limit the scope of the jurisdictions of other States further than constitutive provisions do. To use the example of the EEZ again, it has been pointed out above that it is the proclamation of the zone that has the direct effect of reducing the spatial extent of the legislative, executive and adjudicative jurisdictions of other States with regard to living and non-living resources at sea.[104] The concurrent or subsequent performance of a legislative act producing a legislative instrument containing a performative provision establishing an organ, the function of which is to perform acts in the exercise of the State's executive jurisdiction, does not reduce the spatial extent of the jurisdictions of other States any further. The position is the same with regard to performative provisions setting the parameters within which acts are to be performed in the exercise of the State's executive jurisdiction.[105]

As far as they are concerned, NSAs are not directly impacted either by an act producing a legislative instrument containing performative provisions relating to executive jurisdiction. Indeed, the NSAs are only impacted by the legislative act when executive acts are performed in terms of, and in accordance with, those provisions. At the same time, it must be pointed out here that the absence of performative provisions relating to executive jurisdiction does have a direct impact on NSAs. The reason is that there is, in such a case, no legal basis for the performance of any executive act in the exercise of executive jurisdiction. In the case of the living resources of an EEZ, this could mean that, although an EEZ has been

101 See § 1(1)(1) of the Verwaltungsverfahrensgesetz (VwVfG).

102 See e.g., European Commission *Guidelines for Integrated Border Management in European Commission External Cooperation* (2010) 36–39.

103 See section 2.2.3.3(c).

104 See section 2.2.3.3(b).

105 See section 2.2.3.3(c).

established in terms of a constitutive provision[106] and a normative provision prohibits the exploitation of the resources without a licence, foreign fishing vessels are able to fish with impunity without such a licence because there is no legal basis for the performance of the executive acts required to prevent them from doing so.

In light of the above, a foreign State's protest against the performance of a legislative act producing a legislative instrument containing performative provisions relating to executive jurisdiction probably does not relate to the direct impact of the provisions on the State or NSAs, because the provisions do not have such an impact. Instead, the protest is best understood in one or two of the following ways. First, the protest might constitute a concurrent or renewed expression by the foreign State of an objection raised against the performance of the legislative act producing the legislative instrument containing the constitutive provision(s) on the basis of which the State created the ground upon which the State exercised its executive jurisdiction by performing the legislative act that produced the legislative instrument containing the performative provisions. Secondly, the protest might provide an indication that the performance by the State at a later stage of an executive act in terms of, and in accordance with, the performative provisions, is likely to be objected to by the protesting State.

2.3.3 Executive acts

2.3.3.1 Types of executive acts

(A) INTRODUCTION

It has been explained earlier that executive acts are understood, for present purposes, as involving the application of legal rules outside adjudicative processes.[107] In addition, it has already been pointed out that executive acts might involve the use of force, but they often do not.[108] This is the reason why the term "enforcement jurisdiction" is avoided here. Executive acts take a wide variety of forms, some of which are expressly referred to in the international instruments that apply in the ocean environment.[109] As in the case of executive acts performed in the exercise of legislative jurisdiction,[110] executive acts performed in the exercise of executive jurisdiction can usefully be divided into logistic acts, process acts and enforcement acts.

(B) LOGISTIC ACTS

The logistic acts performed in the exercise of executive jurisdiction are the executive acts performed for the purpose of: (a) setting executive organs up; and (b)

106 And, as a result, the State has sovereign rights over those resources. See article 56(1)(a) of the LOSC.

107 See section 2.2.4.1.

108 On the meaning of the concept "use of force" as a form of exercise of executive jurisdiction, see e.g., K Neri *L'Emploi de la Force en Mer* (2013) 34–37.

109 See e.g., article 22 of the Fish Stocks Agreement.

110 See section 2.2.4.

putting in place the resources and mechanisms necessary for executive organs and executing organs to perform executive acts, legislative acts and adjudicative acts in the exercise of that jurisdiction. For instance, an organ of State performs logistic acts in the exercise of its executive jurisdiction when it recruits staff or develops the internal mechanisms to manage the State's ocean fisheries, including those necessary to process applications for fishing licences.

(C) PROCESS ACTS

(i) Definition The process acts performed in the exercise of executive jurisdiction are the executive acts that are performed in the process of exercising the State's executive jurisdiction and that do not involve the threat or actual use of force. For instance, a State organ performs process acts in the exercise of the State's executive jurisdiction when it processes an application for a fishing licence.[111] It is important to point out here that, while each State is free to determine in its domestic law which bodies are the organs of the State and which acts performed by other bodies must be seen as having been performed on behalf of the State, international law distinguishes between process acts performed *iure imperii* and process acts performed *iure gestionis*.[112]

(ii) Acts performed iure imperii The primary task of State executive organs is to perform acts *iure imperii*, that is to say acts performed in the exercise of State jurisdiction because they fall within the States' core functions. An example of such an act is given in article 41(4) of the LOSC, which relates to the referral of proposals for strait sea lanes and traffic separation schemes "to the competent international organization with a view to their adoption", while paragraph (5) deals with cooperation in formulating proposals and paragraph (6) deals with indicating sea lanes and traffic separation schemes designated or prescribed by bordering States on charts as well as giving due publicity to those charts.

The abovementioned acts are examples of acts the very nature of which results in them being performed *iure imperii*. That is the case because such acts can only be performed for the purpose of fulfilling a State's core functions.[113] By contrast, there are acts that can be performed either for the purpose of fulfilling a State's core function or for another purpose. As far as those acts are concerned, one cannot rely on the nature of an act to determine whether it is performed *iure imperii*. It is

111 See further e.g., *The "Enrica Lexie" Incident* (n. 3) § 497.

112 In *Jurisdictional Immunities of the State (Germany v. Italy, Greece intervening)*, judgment of 3 February 2012, 2012 ICJ Reports 99, the ICJ stressed that "the terms 'jure imperii' and 'jure gestionis' do not imply that the acts in question are lawful [...]" (§ 60).

113 See e.g., *Jurisdictional Immunities of the State* (n. 112) § 60; B Hess *The Private–Public Divide in International Dispute Resolution* (2019) 275. One must point out that some functions are not regarded by all States as core functions. "For instance, in common law countries anyone may serve a writ on a defendant in civil proceedings; in civil law countries writs are served by officers of the court" (Akehurst (n. 3) 146).

necessary to ascertain instead the purpose for which the act has been performed. For instance, taking steps to obtain information regarding the movements of a vessel is not an act that is performed *iure imperii* when it is performed by a State official for the purpose of securing goods for carriage on a State-owned container vessel. The reason is that the carriage of goods by sea does not fall within a State's core functions. By contrast, when questions are asked for the purpose of ascertaining whether any member of the crew on a State-owned container vessel has contracted a communicable disease, the act is performed for the purpose of applying the State's quarantine rules, i.e., in order to fulfil a core function of the State. In this case, the act is performed *iure imperii*.[114]

(iii) Acts performed iure gestionis To varying extents, States do perform executive acts *iure gestionis*, that is to say acts that are not performed in the exercise of State jurisdiction because they do not fall within the States' core functions.[115] As it has just been alluded to above, most of those acts are performed as part of the commercial activities of States, in which the latter must be seen to be acting on the same basis as all other persons involved in those activities.[116] This state of affairs is reflected in the distinction made in the LOSC between articles 27 and 28, which apply to "merchant ships and government ships operated for commercial purposes", and articles 29 to 32, which apply to "warships and other government ships operated for non-commercial purposes".[117]

(D) ENFORCEMENT ACTS

In most instances, NSAs to whom normative provisions apply do act in conformity with those provisions. When they do not, State organs are either unwilling or unable to take action, or they do take action by performing enforcement acts, that is to say executive acts involving the threat or the actual use of force.[118] Examples of enforcement acts are given in article 110(2) of the LOSC, which provides that,

> [i]n the cases provided for in paragraph 1, the warship may proceed to verify the ship's right to fly its flag. To this end, it may send a boat under the command of an officer to the suspected ship. If suspicion remains after the

114 Sanitary laws are included among the laws and regulations with regard to which coastal States have executive jurisdiction in their respective contiguous zones, as confirmed by article 33 of the LOSC. See further Chapter 4 section 4.5.1.

115 See e.g., *Jurisdictional Immunities of the State* (n. 112) § 60.

116 See e.g., Cassese (n. 12) 100–101.

117 See e.g., Churchill, Lowe & Sander (n. 78) 164.

118 On the distinction between process acts and enforcement acts in the exercise of executive jurisdiction, see e.g., *Alleged Violations of Sovereign Rights and Maritime Spaces in the Caribbean Sea* (n. 45) § 100.

> documents have been checked, it may proceed to a further examination on board the ship, which must be carried out with all possible consideration.[119]

As far as it is concerned, article 221(1) provides that nothing in Part XII of the LOSC

> shall prejudice the right of States, pursuant to international law, both customary and conventional, to take and enforce measures beyond the territorial sea proportionate to the actual or threatened damage to protect their coastline or related interests, including fishing, from pollution or threat of pollution following upon a maritime casualty or acts relating to such a casualty, which may reasonably be expected to result in major harmful consequences.[120]

2.3.3.2 *Impact of executive acts*

(A) LOGISTIC ACTS

Logistic acts seldom give rise to protests by other States for two reasons. The first is that, as it was indicated above, logistic acts relate merely to setting organs of State up as well as putting in place the resources and mechanisms necessary for those organs to perform other acts in the exercise of executive jurisdiction.[121] The second reason is that, as in the case of logistic acts performed in the exercise of legislative jurisdiction,[122] logistic acts performed in the exercise of executive jurisdiction do not normally have a direct impact outside the territory of the State concerned. When a protest is made, it is therefore best interpreted in the same manner as in the case of a protest against a legislative act producing a legislative instrument containing constitutive provisions.[123] For instance, it is likely that a protest by a foreign State against the performance by a coastal State of logistic acts aimed at making it possible for State organs to perform enforcement acts in the case of infringement of its fisheries' normative provisions by foreign vessels further than 200 NM from its baselines, does not relate to the direct impact of those acts on the State or NSAs because logistic acts do not have such an impact. Rather, the protests must probably be understood to entail an objection to the fact that, as the performance of the logistic acts reveals, the coastal State has arrogated to itself an executive jurisdiction that international law does not attribute to the State. The protest would also indicate that the later performance of other executive acts made possible by the logistic acts is likely to be objected to.

119 See further e.g., D Guilfoyle "Article 110" in A Proelss (ed) *United Nations Convention on the Law of the Sea – A Commentary* (2017) 767–772 at 770.

120 See e.g., K Bartenstein "Article 221" in Proelss (n. 119) 1512–1521 at 1517–1521. See further e.g., *The "Enrica Lexie" Incident* (n. 3) § 491 quoting Guilfoyle (n. 10) 4–5.

121 See section 2.3.3.1(b)

122 See section 2.2.4.2.

123 See section 2.2.3.3(b).

(B) PROCESS ACTS

In contrast to logistic acts, process acts can have a direct impact on NSAs. That would be the case, for instance, when a State organ turns down an application for an oil-exploration permit submitted by a foreign juristic person. That is also the case, for instance, when customs officials engage in a patrol in the contiguous zone of a coastal State for the purpose of exercising the control necessary to prevent the infringement of the State's customs laws and regulations within the State's territory, including its territorial sea.[124] Although the act of patrolling does not constitute, on its own, a threat or actual use of force (and is therefore not an enforcement act), its performance is likely to influence the behaviour of vessels in the patrolled area. Its performance might also cause the customs officials or any other law enforcement officers to perform enforcement acts against one or more vessels.

Because process acts performed *iure gestionis* are not performed in the scope of a State's core functions, their performance by one State does not have a direct impact on the exercise by another State of its own core functions. This explains, for instance, why "the representative of one State who signs a commercial contract in another State is not acting contrary to international law".[125] In fact, the impact of those acts is not different from the impact of the same acts performed by private legal subjects. The position is different with regard to process acts performed *iure imperii*, for instance when a health official of State A takes steps on a vessel flying the flag of State A, while the vessel is in a port of State B, for the purpose of ascertaining the state of health of the crew before the vessel sails to a port of State A. The reason is that, although those acts do not entail the threat or actual use of force, they are performed in the scope of a State's core functions. As a result, their performance might have a negative impact on the exercise by another State of its own core functions, for instance when it results in a conflict between the different courses of action followed by the two States.[126]

(C) ENFORCEMENT ACTS

Because enforcement acts involve the threat or actual use of force over which the State normally has a monopoly, they are performed *iure imperii*.[127] Therefore, as in the case of process acts performed *iure imperii*, their performance can have an impact on the exercise by another State of its own core functions. In fact, that impact is greater than the impact of process acts performed *iure imperii*. The reason is that the performance of enforcement acts in the territory of a foreign State

124 See article 33(1)(a) of the LOSC.

125 Akehurst (n. 3) 145. That is the case, obviously, provided that the representative is lawfully in the territory of the foreign State.

126 In the example, the health official of State A might order that an individual disembark at the same time that a health official of State B determines that the individual is not allowed to disembark. See further Chapter 4.

127 See e.g., M Zwanenburg "Military vessel protection detachments: The experience of the Netherlands" (2012) 51 *Military Law and Law of War Review* 97–116 at 112.

would be contrary to international law on the ground that the State exercises, or threatens to exercise, its physical power in that territory.[128] That would be the case, for instance, were a fisheries officer of State A to arrest a fisher in a port of State B for an alleged violation of a fisheries normative provision of State A.[129]

While, as it will be explained in a later chapter, the position is similar with regard to the performance of enforcement acts against, or on, foreign vessels on the high seas,[130] it is more complex when the acts are performed in an EEZ or on a continental shelf. The reason is that, in those zones, the attribution of executive jurisdiction is the product of the extension and overlap of the regime applicable within the marine component of the territory of the coastal State and the regime applicable with regard to vessels on the high seas.[131]

2.3.4 Adjudicative acts

In exceptional cases, executive organs and executing organs might be called upon, in relation to the exercise of the State's executive jurisdiction, to perform adjudicative acts. Those acts are performed by the said organs when they settle internal disputes that relate to the exercise of that jurisdiction. That is the case, for instance, when a departmental committee reaches a decision at the end of internal disciplinary proceedings instituted against a member of the government department concerned. As in the case of legislative jurisdiction,[132] adjudicative acts performed in the exercise of executive jurisdiction do not have a direct impact on foreign States and NSAs.

As pointed out earlier,[133] in practice, the actual performance of an adjudicative act, i.e., the actual taking of a decision on an internal dispute, has normally no impact outside the territory of the State concerned. The reason is that, in the light of the same factors as for legislative acts,[134] States do perform their adjudicative acts in most, if not all, instances within their own territory. There does not appear to be any reason why a State organ would act unlawfully, as far as international law is concerned, were it to perform an adjudicative act in the exercise of the State's executive jurisdiction in the territory of another State. Indeed, adjudicative acts do not involve the threat or actual use of force. As a result, they cannot be contrary to

128 See e.g., J Boucht "Cross-border use of police power within the EU – A Finnish, Norwegian and Swedish perspective" (2012) 2 *European Criminal Law Review* 203–235 at 203; Colangelo (n. 10) 1311. On the reasons why it is important to distinguish between an act that constitutes force in the sense of article 2(4) of the UN Charter, on the one hand, and "a 'mere' violation of a state's territorial integrity or of the duty of non-intervention", on the other, see e.g., T Ruys "The meaning of 'force' and the boundaries of the *jus ad bellum*: Are 'minimal' uses of force excluded from UN Charter article 2(4)?" (2014) 108 AJIL 159–210 at 160–163.

129 See further Chapter 4 section 4.4.4.

130 See article 92(1) of the LOSC. See further Chapter 4 section 4.2.2.

131 See further Chapter 4 section 4.6.3.

132 See section 2.2.5.

133 See section 2.2.5.

134 See section 2.2.3.2.

international law on the ground that the State exercises, or threatens to exercise, its physical power in that territory. At the same time, an adjudicative act performed in the exercise of the State's executive jurisdiction in the territory of another State arguably does not interfere with the latter's own core functions. This is because those functions do not include the performance of adjudicative acts performed to settle internal disputes that relate to the exercise of executive by a foreign State. By contrast, as it has already been pointed out in the case of legislative acts,[135] it would clearly be against international law for a State to perform an adjudicative act beyond its territorial sea as an element of a practice to support a claim that the area is part of its territory. But there appears to be no legal obstacle standing in the way of a State performing the act without any intention to use it to support a territorial claim. That would be the case, for instance, were an executive organ of a State, while on a vessel flying the flag of the State on the high seas, to give a ruling on an internal disciplinary matter relating to an arrest made a few days earlier in the EEZ of another State.[136]

2.3.5 Definition of "executive jurisdiction"

On the basis of the above, it is possible to define the term "executive jurisdiction" as the international-law authority of a State to be involved in a factual matter by performing:

(a) process acts and enforcement acts related to the application of normative provisions; and, incidentally,
(b) legislative acts producing legislative instruments containing performative provisions necessary for the performance of:
  (i) the executive acts referred to in paragraphs (a) and (c);
  (ii) other legislative acts referred to in this paragraph; and
  (iii) the adjudicative acts referred to in paragraph (d);
(c) executive acts related to the performance of
  (i) the executive acts referred to in paragraph (a);
  (ii) the legislative acts referred to in paragraph (b);
  (iii) other executive acts referred to in this paragraph; and
  (iv) the adjudicative acts referred to in paragraph (d); and
(d) adjudicative acts related to the performance of:
  (i) the legislative acts referred to in paragraph (b);
  (ii) the executive acts referred to in paragraph (c); and
  (iii) other adjudicative acts referred to in this paragraph.

135 See section 2.2.3.2.
136 See further Chapter 4 section 4.6.3.

2.4 Adjudicative jurisdiction

2.4.1 Introduction

Adjudicative jurisdiction[137] (also called "adjudicative competence",[138] "jurisdiction to adjudicate"[139] "judicial jurisdiction"[140] and "curial jurisdiction"[141]) has been defined in different ways.[142] The exercise of adjudicative jurisdiction involves, primarily, the performance of adjudicative acts.[143] In addition, adjudicative jurisdiction can also be exercised by performing legislative acts[144] and executive acts.[145]

2.4.2 Legislative acts

It was pointed out earlier in this chapter that, in a State governed by the rule of law, the only authority that organs of the State have is the authority that they derive from the law.[146] For that reason, the exercise of adjudicative jurisdiction must often start by performing legislative acts producing legislative instruments containing performative provisions that: (a) confer on one or more organs of the State the authority to perform acts in the exercise of the State's adjudicative jurisdiction; and (b) set the parameters within which the acts must be performed.[147]

That is the case, for example, when an organ of a coastal State exercises the latter's "jurisdiction [...] with regard to [...] the establishment and use of artificial islands, installations and structures" in its EEZ,[148] by performing a legislative

137 See e.g., *The "Enrica Lexie" Incident* (n. 3) § 526; Colangelo (n. 10) 1304; Honniball (n. 3) 501.

138 See e.g., Oxman (n. 11) § 3.

139 See e.g., § 401(b) *Restatement of the Law (Fourth)* (n. 4); the Council of Europe's 1997 Amended Model Plan (n. 12); Cassese (n. 12) 49; C Staker "Jurisdiction" in MD Evans (ed) *International Law* (2018) 289–315 at 293.

140 See e.g., C Wassterstein Fassberg "Judicial and legislative jurisdiction in the Hague Conventions on Private International Law" (1993) 27 *Israel Law Review* 460–486 at 461–464; Churchill (n. 9) 279.

141 See e.g., Jennings & Watts (n. 94) 458; Staker (n. 137) 292.

142 For instance, adjudicative jurisdiction has been defined as: "the authority of a state to apply law to persons or things, in particular through the processes of its courts or administrative tribunals" (§ 401(b) *Restatement of the Law (Fourth)* (n. 4)); the authority to establish "procedures for identifying breaches of the rules and the precise consequences thereof" (Oxman (n. 11) § 3), "the power to settle legal disputes through binding decisions, or to interpret the law with binding force for all the persons and entities concerned" (Cassese (n. 12) 49) and "the authority of a State to apply law to persons or things" (*The "Enrica Lexie" Incident* (n. 3) § 526).

143 See section 2.4.3.

144 See section 2.4.2.

145 See section 2.4.4.

146 See section 2.2.2.4.

147 The performance of legislative acts producing legislative instruments containing performative provisions is by no means always necessary. In private international law matters, for instance, adjudicative bodies often rely on common-law rules rather than provisions contained in legislation. See e.g., § 407 comment (f) *Restatement of the Law (Fourth)* (n. 4); P Vrancken & F Marx "Birth, marriage and death at sea in South African law" (2015) 40 SAYIL 58–102.

148 Article 56(1)(b)(i) of the LOSC.

act producing a legislative instrument containing provisions giving authority to its courts to settle disputes arising from the use of those artificial features. Those provisions differ from the normative provisions governing the use of the features that might, for instance, set the fire-prevention requirements to be met on those islands, installations and structures. They also differ from the performative provisions relating to the exercise of legislative jurisdiction or executive jurisdiction with regard to the features, such as those governing the appointment and activities of fire-prevention officers, for instance.

The impact on foreign States and NSAs of a legislative act producing a legislative instrument containing performative provisions relating to adjudicative jurisdiction is not different from the impact of a legislative act producing a legislative instrument containing performative provisions relating to legislative jurisdiction or executive jurisdiction.[149]

2.4.3 Adjudicative acts

2.4.3.1 Introduction

It has already been pointed out that, although State organs vested with adjudicative jurisdiction may perform legislative acts and executive acts, their main function is to perform adjudicative acts.[150] For present purposes, it is helpful to divide those adjudicative acts, which involve the application of legal rules in the course of adjudicative processes, into: (i) acts performed to settle disputes between States and other legal persons;[151] (ii) acts performed to settle disputes between private legal persons;[152] and (iii) acts performed to settle internal disputes relating to the exercise of adjudicative jurisdiction.[153]

2.4.3.2 Acts performed to settle disputes between States and other legal persons

Adjudicative jurisdiction includes the authority to perform adjudicative acts to settle disputes between States and other legal persons, including foreign States and organs of State that either do not have sovereign immunity or waived their immunity.[154] Those disputes can be settled at the end of civil proceedings such as, for instance, the "civil proceedings in respect of any claim for loss or damage resulting from pollution of the marine environment" referred to in article 229 of the LOSC,

149 See sections 2.2.3.1 and 2.3.2.

150 See section 2.4.1.

151 See section 2.4.3.2.

152 See section 2.4.3.3.

153 See section 2.4.3.4.

154 See e.g., J Finke "Sovereign immunity: Rule, comity or something else?" (2011) 21 *European Journal of International Law* 853–881 at 864–866; P-T Stoll "State immunity" 2011 MPEPIL §§ 25–48; Mouland (n. 3). See also section 2.3.3.1(c).

or criminal or penal proceedings such as those to which articles 73 and 97 of the LOSC apply.[155]

Adjudicative acts between States and other legal persons often have a significant direct impact on the persons concerned, especially in the case of criminal proceedings. For that reason, when the accused is a foreign national, the performance of the act frequently gives rise to public debate in the foreign State which, as a result, finds itself compelled to protest against that performance.[156] That protest can relate to the scope of the jurisdiction. That would be the case, for instance, were a foreign national, in the absence of an agreement by the two States, to be sentenced to a period of imprisonment despite the fact that article 73(3) forbids such a penalty.[157] The protest can also relate to the ground of the jurisdiction. That would be the case, for instance, were a foreign national to be sentenced for an offence relating to a collision at sea although the sentencing State is neither the flag State nor the State of nationality. The State organ performing the adjudicative act would indeed be acting in violation of article 97(1), which provides that

> [i]n the event of a collision or any other incident of navigation concerning a ship on the high seas, involving the penal or disciplinary responsibility of the master or of any other person in the service of the ship, no penal or disciplinary proceedings may be instituted against such person except before the judicial or administrative authorities either of the flag State or of the State of which such person is a national.[158]

2.4.3.3 Acts performed to settle disputes between private legal persons

Adjudicative jurisdiction includes also the authority to perform adjudicative acts to settle disputes between private legal persons. Those disputes are settled during civil proceedings. Such a dispute would arise, for instance, were the existence of a bill of lading be challenged[159] or a marine-insurance claim be dishonoured.[160]

Like the adjudicative acts performed to settle disputes between a State and another legal person,[161] the adjudicative acts performed to settle disputes between

155 See further e.g., Churchill (n. 9) 278–298.

156 See e.g., WE Beckett "The exercise of criminal jurisdiction over foreigners" (1925) 6 BYIL 44–60 at 45.

157 See further Chapter 4 section 4.6.1.2 and Chapter 5 section 4.4.3.3.

158 See *The "Enrica Lexie" Incident* (n. 3) § 650. See also the CPJC and article 11 of the CHS. See further e.g., D Guilfoyle "Article 97" in Proelss (n. 119) 721–724 at 723; C Ha "Criminal jurisdiction for ship collision and marine pollution in high seas – Focused on the 2015 judgement on *M/V Ernest Hemingway* case" (2020) 4 *Journal of International Maritime Safety, Environmental Affairs, and Shipping* 8–15.

159 See e.g., *Delta Kikori Ltd v. ANDQ Trading Ltd* [2017] PGNC 89; N6707 (19 May 2017).

160 See e.g., *Kingdom of Tonga & Shipping Corporation of Polynesia Ltd v. Allianz Australia Insurance Ltd* [2005] TOSC 8, CV 723 2003 (25 February 2005).

161 See section 2.4.4.4.

private legal persons do have a direct impact on the persons concerned. However, because the acts do not have criminal implications, the performance of those acts seldom gives rise to public debate in foreign States when the disputes involve nationals of those States. That does not mean that a foreign State might not refuse to recognise a decision on the ground that the adjudicating State acted either without a ground of adjudicative jurisdiction or outside the scope of its adjudicative jurisdiction, as laid out in the applicable private-international-law regime.[162]

2.4.3.4 Acts performed to settle internal disputes

As explained above, adjudicative acts can be performed in the exercise of legislative jurisdiction or executive jurisdiction.[163] Likewise, some adjudicative acts are performed in the exercise of adjudicative jurisdiction to settle internal disputes related to issues that arise while State organs exercise that jurisdiction by performing legislative acts, executive acts or adjudicative acts. That is the case, for instance, when a committee reaches a decision at the end of internal disciplinary proceedings relating to actions of a judicial officer.

Adjudicative acts performed in the exercise of adjudicative jurisdiction to settle internal disputes do not have a direct impact on foreign States and NSAs. Furthermore, those acts do not normally have a direct impact outside of the State's territory for the same reasons, and to the same extent, as in the case of adjudicative acts performed in the exercise of legislative jurisdiction or executive jurisdiction.[164]

2.4.4 Executive acts

2.4.4.1 Introduction

Executive acts need to be performed to make it possible for the State organs expected to exercise the State's adjudicative jurisdiction to assume their functions. As in the case of executive acts performed in the exercise of legislative jurisdiction or executive jurisdiction,[165] it is helpful to divide the executive acts performed in the exercise of adjudicative jurisdiction into logistic acts,[166] process acts[167] and enforcement acts.[168]

162 See e.g., G Solomons "Enforcement of foreign judgments – Jurisdiction of foreign court" (1976) 25 ICLQ 665–674 at 665.
163 See sections 2.2.5 and 2.3.4, respectively.
164 *Ibid.*
165 See sections 2.2.4 and 2.3.3, respectively.
166 See section 2.4.4.2.
167 See section 2.4.4.3.
168 See section 2.4.4.4.

2.4.4.2 Logistic acts

The logistic acts performed in the exercise of adjudicative jurisdiction are the executive acts performed for the purpose of: (a) setting adjudicative organs up; and (b) putting in place the resources and mechanisms necessary for adjudicative organs and adjudicating organs to perform adjudicative acts, legislative acts and executive acts in the exercise of that jurisdiction. For instance, a flag State performs logistic acts in the exercise of its adjudicative jurisdiction when it puts in place the resources and mechanisms necessary for a court, to which it has given authority to settle disputes relating to the illicit traffic in narcotic drugs or psychotropic substances,[169] to perform that function. For that reason and because they are performed within the State's structures, with very little, if any, involvement of NSAs, logistic acts do not normally have a direct impact on those actors. That is one of the reasons why logistic acts performed in the exercise of adjudicative jurisdiction seldom give rise to protests by other States. When a foreign State protests, that step is probably best interpreted in the same manner as in the case of a protest against the adoption of a legislative instrument consisting of constitutive provisions.[170] For instance, a protest by a foreign State against the performance by a coastal State of logistic acts aimed at punishing the infringement of its fisheries laws and regulations by foreign vessels beyond 200 NM from its baselines probably does not relate to the impact of those acts on the foreign State or its nationals. The reason is that the provisions do not have, on their own, a direct impact on that State or those persons. Rather, the protest is likely meant to object to the fact that, as the performance of the logistic acts reveals, the coastal State arrogated to itself an adjudicative jurisdiction that international law does not attribute to that State. The protest indicates also that the later performance of adjudicative acts made possible by the logistic acts is likely to be objected to.

2.4.4.3 Process acts

The process acts performed in the exercise of adjudicative jurisdiction are the executive acts that do not involve the threat or actual use of force. In contrast to logistic acts, process acts performed in the exercise of adjudicative jurisdiction can have a direct impact on NSAs. That would be the case, for instance, when the prosecuting authority of a State decides to prosecute a person for an alleged violation of that State's environmental-protection legislation.[171]

169 See article 108(1) of the LOSC. See further Chapter 4 section 4.2.

170 See section 2.2.3.3(b).

171 France had no doubt in *Lotus* that a decision to prosecute is taken by "judicial authorities" (see 1927 PCIJ Reports, Series A No 10 at 6). On the relationship between prosecution services and the executive branch of government, see e.g., United Nations Office on Drugs and Crime *The Status and Role of Prosecutors* (2014) 10, where it is stressed that the overriding goal is to protect the independence of prosecutors.

2.4.4.4 Enforcement acts

The exercise of adjudicative jurisdiction may also require the performance of enforcement acts, that is to say executive acts involving the threat or the actual use of force. Most of those acts are performed by individuals employed in an executive organ, from the time a decision has been taken to start adjudicative proceedings until the conclusion of those proceedings. This means that enforcement acts taken to detain an individual who is suspected of having committed a criminal offence are best understood as no longer being performed in the exercise of executive jurisdiction once a decision has been taken to prosecute that individual. The acts are then performed in the exercise of adjudicative jurisdiction until the adjudicative proceedings are concluded. Thereafter, the enforcement acts taken to incarcerate the individual after he or she has been sentenced to a period of imprisonment, for instance, are again performed in the exercise of executive jurisdiction.

2.4.5 Definition of "adjudicative jurisdiction"

On the basis of the above, it is possible to define the term "adjudicative jurisdiction" as the international-law authority of a State to be involved in a factual matter by performing,

(a) acts performed to settle disputes between States and private legal subjects;
(b) acts performed to settle disputes between private legal subjects; and, incidentally,
(c) legislative acts producing legislative instruments containing performative provisions necessary for the performance of:
   (i) the adjudicative acts referred to in paragraphs (a) and (b);
   (ii) other legislative acts referred to in this paragraph;
   (iii) the executive acts referred to in paragraph (d); and
   (iv) the adjudicative acts referred to in paragraph (e);
(d) executive acts related to the performance of:
   (i) the legislative acts referred to in paragraphs (c)
   (ii) other executive acts referred to in this paragraph; and
   (iii) the adjudicative acts referred to in paragraph (e); and
(e) adjudicative acts related to the performance of:
   (i) the adjudicative acts referred to in paragraphs (a) and (b);
   (ii) the legislative acts referred to in paragraph (c);
   (iii) the executive acts referred to in paragraph (d); and
   (iv) other adjudicative acts referred to in this paragraph.

2.5 Relationship between the legislative, executive and adjudicative jurisdictions

State ocean jurisdiction is complex for three reasons. The first reason is that, as already pointed out, there is no complete match between the nature of State organs and the nature of the acts that they perform.[172] The second reason is that, as also already pointed out, there is no complete match between the three main categories of acts (i.e., legislative acts, executive acts and adjudicative acts) and the three forms of State jurisdiction.[173] The third reason is that, while those jurisdictions are "logically independent of each other",[174] they are intricately related. Indeed, the existence and exercise of adjudicative jurisdiction is affected by the existence and exercise of executive jurisdiction, which, in turn, is affected by the existence and exercise of legislative jurisdiction.[175] At the same time, the efficacy of legislative jurisdiction depends on the existence and exercise of executive jurisdiction, the efficacy of which is affected, in turn, by the existence and exercise of adjudicative jurisdiction.

More specifically, to the extent that executive jurisdiction entails the performance of both process acts and enforcement acts related to the application of normative provisions,[176] the attribution of executive jurisdiction among States presupposes the attribution of legislative jurisdiction conferring the authority to perform legislative acts producing legislative instruments containing the normative provisions to be applied.[177] Indeed, it would make little sense for international law to attribute to a State the authority to exercise executive jurisdiction were that State not given also the authority to adopt the legislative provisions that the relevant organs of the State are expected to apply. Moreover, when legislative and executive jurisdictions do co-exist, the performance of process acts and enforcement acts related to the application of normative provisions depends on the prior exercise by organs of State of the latter's legislative jurisdiction,[178] mainly by performing legislative acts producing legislative instruments containing the necessary constitutive, normative and performative provisions. In other words, it is necessary for a State, in order for its organs to have a legal basis for performing process acts and enforcement acts related to the application of normative provisions (i.e., to make

172 See section 2.1.
173 See section 2.1.
174 O'Keefe (n. 3) 741.
175 See e.g., MM Roggenkamp "Petroleum pipelines in the North Sea: Questions of jurisdiction and practical solutions" (1998) 16 *Journal of Energy & Natural Resources Law* 92–109 at 93 ("[a]fter all, there can be no enforcement jurisdiction without legislative jurisdiction"); I Papanicolopulu "A missing part of the Law of the Sea Convention: Addressing issues of State jurisdiction over persons at sea" in Schofield, Lee & Kwon (n. 3) 387–404 at 391 ("[a]djudication may be seen as *sub-generis* of prescriptive jurisdiction, if one considers that the competence of courts is stated in legal instruments adopted by States in their exercise of legislative jurisdiction [...]").
176 See section 2.3.5.
177 See e.g., A Murdoch "Ships without nationality: Interdiction on the high seas" in MD Evans & S Galani (eds) *Maritime Security and the Law of the Sea* (2020) 157–179 at 158 ("[i]f domestic criminal law has not been extended to apply to activities on board ships without nationality on the high seas, law enforcement agencies will not be able to undertake an interdiction, or elements of it, even if they believe that unlawful activity is occurring on board"). See further section 2.2.6.
178 Gallagher & David (n. 10) 222 confirm that "[t]he question of enforcement jurisdiction [...] only arises once prescriptive jurisdiction has been both established and exercised".

use of the State's executive jurisdiction), to actually make use of the State's legislative jurisdiction.

Likewise, to the extent that adjudicative jurisdiction entails the performance of acts performed to settle disputes between States and other legal persons, or between private legal persons, over the application of legislative provisions,[179] the attribution of adjudicative jurisdiction among States presupposes the attribution of legislative jurisdiction. Indeed, it would once again make little sense for international law to attribute to a State the authority to exercise adjudicative jurisdiction were that State not given also the authority to adopt its own legislative provisions. While that is the case in criminal matters, for instance, because the organs of a State do not apply the criminal law of another State,[180] that is not to say that the exercise by the organs of a State of the latter's adjudicative jurisdiction only involves the settlement of disputes over the application of the State's own legislative provisions. For instance, a State may make it possible for its adjudicative organs to settle a dispute over the application of a foreign normative provision in specific civil matters by performing a legislative act producing a legislative instrument containing performative provisions that are part of its private international law.[181]

As far as it is concerned, the efficacy of legislative jurisdiction depends on the existence and exercise of executive jurisdiction. The reason is that the impact of the performance of legislative acts producing legislative instruments containing normative provisions is limited when the State concerned has not been attributed the executive jurisdiction to perform acts, such as enforcement acts, relating to the application of those provisions. Moreover, when a State does have executive jurisdiction, the impact of the normative provisions remains limited as long as the organs of the State do not exercise that jurisdiction. That is the case when the relevant organs do not perform the necessary logistic acts or refrain from performing the process acts and/or enforcement acts that are required.

By contrast, while the efficacy of executive jurisdiction is affected by the existence and exercise of adjudicative jurisdiction, it does not always depend on it. It is clear that the efficacy of the arrest of an individual suspected of having committed an act that constitutes an offence for which the sentence is a period of imprisonment depends on the individual being found guilty by an organ exercising the State's adjudicative jurisdiction. However, the efficacy of a decision to turn down an application for a licence does not depend on the involvement of an organ exercising the State's adjudicative jurisdiction when the decision is not the object of a dispute. That would be the case, for instance, when there is little doubt that the applicant does not meet one of

179 See section 2.4.5.

180 See e.g., MJL Decroos "Criminal jurisdiction over transnational speech offenses – From unilateralism to the application of foreign public law by the national courts" (2005) 13 *European Journal of Crime, Criminal Law and Criminal Justice* 365–400 at 392 ("[t]he taboo surrounding the fact that a court can not apply foreign public law, or that there is a strict concurrence between prescriptive and adjudicative criminal jurisdiction, is an enduring one").

181 See e.g., Oxman (n. 11) § 6. The performance of a legislative act might not be necessary in the case where the performative provisions are part of the common law.

the requirements for the issuance of the licence. At the same time, the impact of a decision would be negated had the State been attributed adjudicative jurisdiction and, for instance, one of its organs were to exercise that jurisdiction by ruling that the decision is invalid for lack of compliance with the relevant performative provisions applicable to the State's fisheries administration.

2.6 Conclusion

At the end of this chapter, it is possible to illustrate the importance of distinguishing the different forms of State ocean jurisdiction and taking into account their complex relationship, by identifying, for instance, the range of acts that the organs of a State must perform in order to levy execution on an asset for a violation, in the EEZ of that State, of a provision in ministerial regulations regarding fisheries. A possible sequence can be described as follows:

(a) Legislative jurisdiction is exercised by performing a legislative act producing a legislative instrument containing a constitutive provision having the effect of proclaiming the EEZ.
(b) The legislative act producing the fisheries statute involves:
    (i) the exercise of legislative jurisdiction to the extent that the statute contains normative provisions;
    (ii) the exercise of legislative jurisdiction to the extent that the statute contains performative provisions for the purpose of the making of ministerial regulations complementing the statute;
    (iii) the exercise of executive jurisdiction to the extent that the statute contains performative provisions for the purpose of applying the statute and the regulations; and
    (iv) the exercise of adjudicative jurisdiction to the extent that the statute contains performative provisions for the purpose of the settlement of disputes relating to the application of the statute and the regulations.
(c) Legislative jurisdiction is exercised by performing the process acts required to draft the regulations.
(d) Legislative jurisdiction is exercised by adopting the regulations containing the normative provision that has been violated.
(e) Executive jurisdiction is exercised by performing the logistic acts required to set up an organ responsible for the application of the regulations and to put in place the resources and mechanisms necessary for that organ to perform its function.
(f) Executive jurisdiction is exercised by performing process acts and enforcement acts involved in the application of the regulations in the EEZ.
(g) Adjudicative jurisdiction is exercised by performing the logistic acts required to set up an organ responsible for the settlement of disputes relating to the application of the regulations and to put in place the resources and mechanisms necessary for that organ to perform its function.
(h) Adjudicative jurisdiction is exercised by taking the decision to prosecute the person who allegedly violated the provision.

(i) Adjudicative jurisdiction is exercised by performing process acts and enforcement acts during the process leading to the settlement of the dispute.
(j) Adjudicative jurisdiction is exercised by performing the adjudicative act settling the dispute.
(k) Executive jurisdiction is exercised by performing process acts and enforcement acts involved in levying execution on an asset.

Many among the wide variety of acts performed by organs of States in the exercise of the latter's legislative, executive and adjudicative jurisdictions have no direct impact on other States or NSAs and are performed within the territory of the States concerned. For those reasons, they are most often not the focus of law-of-the-sea scholarship. They must nevertheless not be ignored because their non-performance, or inadequate performance, can have a negative effect on the ability of a State to perform the acts that have a direct impact on other States or NSAs and, in many instances, are performed outside the territory of the States concerned. As a result, the attribution of State ocean jurisdiction in international law does not always achieve its purpose. As explained earlier, this problem will be dealt with at a later stage because, in order to tackle it, it is necessary to first establish the grounds of State ocean jurisdiction and, thereafter, to determine the scope of that jurisdiction in each specific case. Before doing so, however, one must revisit the PCIJ decision in the *Lotus* case through the lenses of the approach to the form of State ocean jurisdiction expounded in this chapter.

The judgment stressed that, in terms of the special agreement between France and Turkey, the main question that the Court had to decide arose as a result of Turkey "instituting […] criminal proceedings in pursuance of Turkish law against" lieutenant Demons.[182] In other words, the dispute did not arise from the exercise by Turkey of its legislative jurisdiction by making unlawful the act that lieutenant Demons was convicted of having committed.[183] Neither did the dispute arise from the exercise by Turkey of its executive jurisdiction from the moment the *Lotus* docked in Istanbul until the decision to institute proceedings was taken. This was confirmed by France when it confined its argument to the legal issues relating to "the Turkish judicial authorities […] prosecuting, imprisoning and convicting M. Demons".[184] It was also confirmed by the Court when it explained that "the arguments put forward by the Parties […] relate[d] exclusively to the question whether Turkey ha[d] or ha[d] not, according to the principles of international law, jurisdiction to prosecute in th[e] case".[185]

182 *Lotus Case* (n. 171) 5. The relevant facts are recorded at 10–11.
183 The Court touched upon the normative provisions applied at 14–15.
184 *Lotus Case* (n. 171) 6 and 8.
185 *Lotus Case* (n. 171) 12–13. At the end of the paragraph, the Court reiterated that "[t]he discussions have borne exclusively upon the question whether criminal jurisdiction does or does not exist in this case". As explained in this chapter, the term "criminal jurisdiction" is broad in that it encompasses the three forms of jurisdiction, i.e. legislative criminal jurisdiction, executive criminal jurisdiction and adjudicative criminal jurisdiction. The latter appears to be the form of jurisdiction that the Court had in mind, when the sentence is read in its context.

When reasoning on whether Turkey had jurisdiction in the case, the Court started by stating that

> the first and foremost restriction imposed by international law upon a State is that – failing the existence of a permissive rule to the contrary – it may not exercise its power in any form in the territory of another State. In this sense jurisdiction is certainly territorial; it cannot be exercised by a State outside its territory except by virtue of a permissive rule derived from international custom or from a convention.[186]

This chapter shows that this statement is problematical and it explains the three reasons why that is the case. The first reason is that the Court used the word "jurisdiction" without making it clear whether it was referring to legislative jurisdiction, executive jurisdiction or adjudicative jurisdiction, or all of them at the same time. This would not be an issue were the statement to be correct with regard to all the forms of jurisdiction, but it will be explained in a later chapter that this is not the case.[187] The second reason is that the Court used the words "exercise its power in any form", the meaning of which is so broad as to include the exercise of all forms of legislative authority, executive authority and adjudicative authority. This would once again not be an issue were the statement to be correct with regard to all the forms of exercise of authority but, in view of the wide range of acts distinguished in this chapter, it is to be expected that this is not the case. The third reason is that the Court uses the words "in the territory of another State" without explaining whether it is referring to: (a) the performance of an act in the territory of another State; (b) the impact of an act in the territory of another State; and/or (c) the link between the act and the territory of another State. This would not be an issue were the statement to be correct in all those cases, but it has been alluded to in this chapter, and it will be fully explained in a later chapter,[188] that this is not the case.

While the statement is correct with regard to the performance of enforcement acts, it is not correct with regard to acts that are performed within the territory of a State in the exercise of that State's adjudicative jurisdiction and that have a link with acts that occurred outside that territory.[189] The Court was quick to stress that fact when it stated that

> [i]t does not [...] follow that international law prohibits a State from exercising jurisdiction in its own territory, in respect of any case which relates to acts which have taken place abroad, and in which it cannot rely on some permissive rule of international law".[190]

186 *Lotus Case* (n. 171) 18–19.
187 See further Chapter 4.
188 *Ibid.*
189 See e.g., S Beaulac "The *Lotus* case in context" in Allen *et al.* (n. 3) 40–58 at 51.
190 *Lotus Case* (n. 171) 19.

Having made that clear, it then remained for the Court to establish "whether the foregoing considerations really apply as regards criminal jurisdiction, or whether this jurisdiction is governed by a different principle".[191] Once again, the term "criminal jurisdiction" must be read in its context. The latter makes it clear that the Court is referring here to adjudicative criminal jurisdiction and not legislative criminal jurisdiction or executive criminal jurisdiction. This was confirmed by the Court, later in its judgment, when it reiterated that it had to "ascertain whether or not there exists a rule of international law limiting the freedom of States to extend *the criminal jurisdiction of their courts* to a situation uniting the circumstances of the present case".[192] To do so, the first step is to determine whether Turkey had a ground on which to base its adjudicative jurisdiction in the matter, an issue to which we turn in the next chapter.

191 *Ibid.* 20.
192 *Ibid.* 21 (emphasis added).

3 The ground of State ocean jurisdiction

3.1 Introduction

For a State to have the legal authority to be involved in a matter, international law requires that the State has a valid ground for exercising that authority. That ground takes the form of a connecting factor, which links the State to the matter.[1] In other words, when international law is satisfied that there is a "sufficiently close connection"[2] between the matter and the State, the latter has a ground on which to exercise its authority.[3] It is not difficult to understand why such a requirement exists. Indeed, if it did not, all States would be entitled to exercise their legislative authority, executive authority and adjudicative authority at all times over all matters, including all ocean-related matters. That state of affairs would go some way towards ensuring that the authority of at least one State is exercised everywhere and at all times. At the same time, however, it has the potential to give rise to a multitude of overlapping and competing claims, some of which are likely to threaten international peace and security because they challenge the principle of sovereign equality of States[4] and the principle of non-intervention in the domestic affairs of States.[5]

The decision of the PCIJ in *Lotus* has been criticised for not requiring the existence of "a direct and substantial connection" on the basis of which a State may exercise its jurisdiction within its territory over acts occurring outside its territory.[6] The Court did indeed hold that States have "a wide measure of discretion" to "extend the application of their laws and the jurisdiction of their courts to persons, property and acts outside their territory", "which is only limited in certain cases

1 In French, a "titre juridique" defined as "tout fait, acte ou situation qui est la cause et le fondement d'un droit" (J Basdevant (ed) *Dictionnaire de la Terminologie du Droit International* (1969) 604).

2 R Jennings & A Watts (eds) *Oppenheim's International Law* (1992) 458. See also e.g., B Simma & AT Müller "Exercise and limits of jurisdiction" in J Crawford & M Koskenniemi (eds) *The Cambridge Companion to International Law* (2012) 134–157 at 137; § 407 *Restatement of the Law (Fourth): The Foreign Relations Law of the United States* (2018).

3 C Staker "Jurisdiction" in MD Evans (ed) *International Law* (2018) 289–315 at 295–296.

4 Article 2(1) of the UN Charter.

5 Article 2(7) of the UN Charter. See further Chapter 5 section 5.2.

6 See e.g., J Dugard, M du Plessis & E Cohen "Jurisdiction and international crimes" in J Dugard *et al.* (eds) *Dugard's International Law* (2018) 210–244 at 213.

DOI: 10.4324/9781003383871-3

by prohibitive rules".[7] In other words, States are entitled to extend the scope[8] of their legislative jurisdiction and their adjudicative jurisdiction beyond their territory as long as such an extension does not violate a rule prohibiting them from doing so. However, nowhere in its decision did the Court suggest that States do not need a ground on which to exercise those jurisdictions. It is true that the Court did not focus its attention on the ground(s) on which Turkey could base its adjudicative jurisdiction. However, that is not, it would appear, because the Court was of the opinion that a ground was not required. Rather, the Court's silence can be explained by the fact that the Court did not understand its task to be to state "principles which would permit Turkey to take criminal proceedings".[9] Nevertheless, the decision contains references to three grounds on which Turkey could base its jurisdiction: (i) the fact that the sunken vessel flew its flag; (ii) the fact that the victims were its nationals; and (iii) the fact that offences committed by the French officer of the watch and the Turkish officer of the watch were related.[10]

The decision of the PCIJ also contains repeated references to territoriality[11] because territoriality was a century ago, and it is still today, seen as "the primary basis for jurisdiction".[12] This view is understandable when one takes into account that most human activities take place on dry land.[13] The latter has been almost completely divided among States, and what matters first is to establish whether there exists a link between a specific territory and the matter at hand. When that link exists, the principle is that the territorial State, which has sovereignty over the territory, has exclusive and full jurisdiction over the matter.[14] For that reason, it is indeed correct to state that territoriality is the main ground of State jurisdiction when one refers to State jurisdiction as a whole.[15] However, it will be shown in this chapter that the statement is not accurate when one looks at the specific regime of State ocean jurisdiction. In other words, it is problematical to deduce from the fact that territory is the primary ground of State jurisdiction in general, that it is also the primary ground in the specific field of State ocean jurisdiction.

One reason why this deduction is nevertheless often made is that, when one asserts that sovereignty is the basis of jurisdiction, it is logical to reason that territoriality, when it is seen as the spatial equivalent of sovereignty, is the primary

7 1927 PCIJ Reports, Series A No 10 at 19.
8 The Court itself used the term (at 20).
9 *Lotus Case* (n. 7) 18.
10 *Lotus Case* (n. 7) 22–23 and 31.
11 See e.g., *Lotus Case* (n. 7) 18–19.
12 Jennings & Watts (n. 2) 458. See also e.g., E Scalieris *L'Exercice du Pouvoir Discrétionnaire de l'Etat Côtier en Droit de la Mer* (2011).
13 See e.g., M Vœlckel *Rien que la Mer* (1981) 18.
14 See e.g., Jennings & Watts (n. 2) 382; *The North Atlantic Coast Fisheries Case (Great Britain v. United States)*, award of 7 September 1910, XI RIAA 173 at 180.
15 See e.g., DW Bowett "Jurisdiction: Changing patterns of authority over activities and resources" (1982) 53 BYIL 1–26 at 4; Staker (n. 3) 303.

ground of jurisdiction.[16] However, as explained in Chapter 1,[17] sovereignty is not the source of State ocean jurisdiction. Rather, sovereignty is an evolving and still very important feature of the allocation to States of the legal authority to be involved in ocean matters.[18] From this perspective, territoriality is not the primary ground of State ocean jurisdiction.[19] Rather, territoriality is merely one of the main grounds on the basis of which legal authority to be involved in ocean matters is attributed to States.

Another reason why the deduction is made is that the international legal regime, including the part of that regime that governs the oceans, was built, at least during its initial stages, by borrowing domestic-law concepts and institutions developed within the territoriality paradigm.[20] This process is understandable because human beings are land creatures.[21] When we started interacting with the ocean environment, we had already at our disposal normative tools adapted to social life on land which, it was very tempting and to some extent sensible, to use also to govern human activities at sea.[22] That was especially so because, as explained in the previous chapter, many of the acts performed in the exercise of ocean jurisdiction are actually performed on land. What is overlooked, however, is that human beings are present in the oceans on a temporary basis and, in most cases, they are constantly moving aboard vessels within that environment.[23] In that light, there is little doubt that the personal paradigm is at least as important as the territoriality paradigm because it guarantees a certain level of continuity in the legal regime governing

16 See e.g., HL Buxbaum "Territory, territoriality, and the resolution of jurisdictional conflict" (2009) 57 *American Journal of Comparative Law* 631–676 at 632; S Beaulac "The *Lotus* case in context" in S Allen *et al.* (eds) *The Oxford Handbook of Jurisdiction in International Law* (2019) 40–58 at 45.

17 See section 3.4.

18 See e.g., the sovereign rights of a coastal State over the resources in its EEZ. See further Chapter 4 section 4.6.1.2.

19 This is in contrast to land jurisdiction, with regard to which "territoriality functions [...] as the conceptual foundation of regulatory authority over transactions or conduct" (Buxbaum (n. 16) 636). See further e.g., S Allen *et al.* "Defining State jurisdiction and jurisdiction in international law" in Allen *et al.* (n. 16) 3–22 at 7 and 9.

20 See e.g., H Lauterpacht *Private Law Sources and Analogies of International Law* (1927); R Lesaffer "Argument from Roman law in current international law: Occupation and acquisitive prescription" (2005) 16 EJIL 25–58. The process is still built into the sources of international law through the concept of the "general principles of law" mentioned in article 38(1)(c) of the Statute of the International Court of Justice (see e.g., Jennings & Watts (n. 2) 36–40; ILA *Report of the Study Group on the Use of Domestic Law Principles in the Development of International Law* (2018); ILC "Second report on general principles of law" (2020) (UN Doc. A/CN.4/741 (9 April 2021))).

21 See e.g., J-P Pancracio *Droit de la Mer* (2010) 15.

22 See e.g., Vœlckel (n. 13) 42.

23 See e.g., G Gidel *Le Droit International Public de la Mer* (1932) I 4; Voelckel (n. 13) 24; P Vincent *Droit de la Mer* (2008) 13. See also M Bedjaoui "Peuples en mer – Une ère nouvelle de colonisation des espaces maritimes" in V Coussirat-Coustère *et al.* (eds) *La Mer et son Droit* (2003) 67–77 at 67. On the deterritorialisation of human lives on land, see e.g., PS Berman "Jurisdictional pluralism" in S Allen *et al.* (n. 16) 121–160 at 122–128. On the effects of the means of transport used, see e.g., W Walters "migration, vehicles, and politics" (2015) 18 *European Journal of Social Theory* 469–488.

each vessel.[24] In fact, the legal relationship symbolised by the flag, which, as far as State ocean jurisdiction is concerned, combines the personality and territoriality paradigms,[25] is arguably the most important ground of State ocean jurisdiction.[26]

That is the reason why, in this chapter, flag State jurisdiction is dealt with first. Because the personality and territoriality paradigms have not been subsumed into flag State jurisdiction, the focus then turns to the coastal zone jurisdictions[27] and to personal jurisdiction.[28] The combination of those jurisdictions is not sufficient to maintain law and order at sea – if not in theory, certainly in practice – and, for that reason, additional grounds of State ocean jurisdiction exist or have been asserted. They may be referred to as collective jurisdictions,[29] delegated jurisdictions,[30] port State jurisdictions,[31] protective jurisdictions[32] and universal jurisdictions.[33]

3.2 Flag State jurisdiction

3.2.1 Introduction

The LOSC, the Part XI Agreement and the Fish Stocks Agreement do not use, let alone define, the term "flag State jurisdiction". However, the LOSC does deal with flag State jurisdiction ("F jurisdiction") in many of its provisions. For instance, article 211(2) refers to legislative flag State jurisdiction ("FL jurisdiction") when it provides that "States shall adopt laws and regulations for the prevention, reduction and control of pollution of the marine environment from vessels flying their flag or of their registry […]". Article 217(1) refers to executive flag State jurisdiction ("FE jurisdiction") when it states that

> States shall ensure compliance by vessels flying their flag or of their registry with applicable international rules and standards [...] and with their laws and regulations adopted in accordance with th[e] Convention [...] and [...] shall provide for the effective enforcement of such rules, standards, laws and regulations, irrespective of where a violation occurs.

24 See e.g., Gidel (n. 23) I 230.

25 See e.g., Simma & Müller (n. 2) 139; ST Helmersen "The *sui generis* nature of flag State jurisdiction" (2015) 58 *Japanese Yearbook of International Law* 319–335. See further Chapter 2 section 2.2.3.3(d)*(iv)*.

26 In other words, flag State jurisdiction is not merely a substitute for territorial jurisdiction, as suggested by Jennings & Watts (n. 2) 734. See also T Treves "Flags of convenience before the Law of the Sea Tribunal" (2004) 6 *San Diego International Law Journal* 179–189 at 189.

27 See section 3.3.

28 See section 3.4.

29 See section 3.8.

30 See section 3.7.

31 See section 3.6.

32 See section 3.9.

33 See section 3.5.

As far as it is concerned, article 109(3)(a) refers to adjudicative flag State jurisdiction ("FA jurisdiction") when it confirms that "[a]ny person engaged in unauthorized broadcasting may be prosecuted before the court of [...] the flag State of the ship". By contrast, the term "flag State jurisdiction" is widely used in other international instruments,[34] by adjudicative bodies[35] and in law-of-the-sea writings.[36]

For present purposes, it is important to distinguish, in the case of vessels, between: (a) the nature of the connecting factor that allows or compels a State to exercise flag State jurisdiction;[37] (b) the establishment of that connecting factor, i.e., the legal relationship of nationality;[38] (c) the evidence of the relationship;[39] (d) the nature of the relationship;[40] (e) the cessation and change of the relationship;[41] and (f) the multiplicity of relationships.[42] One must also focus on the position with regard to artificial objects other than vessels.[43]

3.2.2 Connecting factor

The connecting factor that allows or compels a State to exercise flag State jurisdiction over a matter is the fact that the matter or incident relates in one way or another to a vessel that has the necessary pre-existing legal relationship with the State. That legal relationship is sometimes called "registration".[44] However, the term is problematical because it leads to confusion between the legal relationship itself and the process followed to establish that relationship, including the document(s) issued to confirm the existence of that relationship.[45] The term "nationality", which is used

34 See e.g., article XIV(6) of the 1973 Convention on the International Trade in Endangered Species of Wild Fauna and Flora (993 UNTS 243, (1973) 12 ILM 1085; adopted: 3 March 1973; EIF: 1 July 1975); article II(1) of the 1979 International Convention on Maritime Search and Rescue (SAR 1979) (1405 UNTS 97; adopted: 27 April 1979; EIF: 22 June 1985); and article X(2) of the 1983 Agreement for Cooperation Relating to the Marine Environment between Canada and Denmark (1348 UNTS 122; adopted: 26 August 1983; EIF: 26 August 1983).

35 See e.g., *The "Enrica Lexie" Incident (Italy v. India)*, award of 21 May 2020, (2021) 60 ILM 180 § 368; and *The M/T "San Padre Pio" (No 1) Case (Switzerland v. Nigeria)*, order of 6 July 2019, 2018–2019 ITLOS Reports 375 § 106.

36 See e.g., JNK Mansell *Flag State Responsibility: Historical Development and Contemporary Issues* (2009) 5–10; Helmersen (n. 25); Y Yu, Y Zhao & Y-C Chang "Challenges to the primary jurisdiction of flag States over ships" (2018) 49 ODIL 85–102 at 89.

37 See section 3.2.2.

38 See section 3.2.3.

39 See section 3.2.4.

40 See section 3.2.5.

41 See section 3.2.6.

42 See section 3.2.7.

43 See section 3.2.8.

44 For R Churchill, V Lowe & A Sander *The Law of the Sea* (2022) 464, "expressions such as 'the State of registration' or the 'flag State' are synonyms for the State whose nationality the vessels bears".

45 See e.g., *The "Enrica Lexie" Incident* (n. 35) §§ 1029 and 1033. See further section 3.2.3.

more frequently,[46] including by the LOSC,[47] does not present that difficulty. It is nevertheless also misleading because, "in spite of their common names, the legal relationship ascribed to the nationality of ships does differ from that arising from the nationality of natural or juridical persons".[48] It was indeed pointed out during debates on that issue at the ILC that "[t]he concept of nationality implie[s] an idea of allegiance, which [i]s possible for a natural person, but not for an inanimate object" such as a vessel.[49] It must however be conceded that "[t]he term 'nationality of a ship' [is] a long-established and very convenient one".[50]

It can be argued that the use of the legal relationship of nationality as the connecting factor between a ship and the flag State reflects the fact that the authority of the flag State is more personal than territorial.[51] In addition, it has been pointed out earlier that, although it is undoubtedly incorrect to see a ship as being a floating part of the flag State's territory,[52] flag State jurisdiction is a spatial jurisdiction, like the coastal zone jurisdictions, in that it applies in a specific, although very limited, space – the vessel – irrespective of the nationality of the individuals who find themselves within that space.[53]

46 See e.g., article 1 of the 1961 Agreement on Cooperation in Matters Concerning the Merchant Marine between Burkina Faso and France (1990 UNTS 53; adopted: 24 April 1961; EIF: 30 August 1961). See also e.g. VP Cogliati-Bantz "Disentangling the 'genuine link': Enquiries in sea, air and space law" (2010) 79 NJIL 383–432 at 387.

47 See e.g., article 91(1).

48 L Sohn *et al. Law of the Sea in a Nutshell* (2010) 44. See also e.g., M Kamto "La nationalité des navires en droit international" in Coussirat-Coustère *et al.* (n. 23) 343–373 at 345. Because of the differences, some writers do not use the term "nationality" (see e.g., H Meyers *The Nationality of Ships* (1967), who uses the term "allocation").

49 ILC 121st meeting, 10 July 1951, discussion of UN Doc. A/CN.4/42, § 16 in (1951) 1 YILC 328. For MH Nordquist (ed) *United Nations Convention on the Law of the Sea 1982: A Commentary* (2002) III 106 § 91.9(a), "[t]here is no analogy between the nationality of ships and the concept of nationality as applied to individuals or corporations". This was also, for instance, the view of Guatemala during UNCLOS I (Summary Records of the Second Committee, UN Doc. A/CONF.13/40 (1958) in (1958) IV *UNCLOS I Official Records* 4 § 2). See also Case C–221/89, *R v. Secretary of State for Transport ex parte Factortame*, judgment of 25 July 1991, C–221/89, EU:C:1991:320 § 27.

50 ILC 121st meeting (n. 49) 329. See further e.g., Cogliati-Bantz (n. 46) 387–388.

51 See e.g., *Cunard SS Co v. Mellon* 262 US 100 (1923) 123; D Momtaz "La haute mer" in R-J Dupuy & D Vignes (eds) *Traité du Nouveau Droit de la Mer* (1985) 354; ED Brown *The International Law of the Sea* (1994) I 287; AT Gallagher & F David *The International Law of Migrant Smuggling* (2014) 215.

52 See e.g., DP O'Connell *The International Law of the Sea* (1982) I 735–737; Y Tanaka *International Law of the Sea* (2019) 190.

53 See e.g., *The M/V "Saiga" (No 2) Case (Saint Vincent and the Grenadines v. Guinea)*, judgment of 1 July 1999, 1999 ITLOS Reports 10 § 106; *The M/V "Virginia G" Case (Panama v. Guinea-Bissau)*, judgment of 14 April 2014, 2014 ITLOS Reports 4 § 126; *The "Arctic Sunrise" Arbitration (Netherlands v. Russia)*, award of 14 August 2015, XXXII RIAA 205 §§ 171 and 175; *The M/V "Norstar" Case (Panama v. Italy)*, judgment of 4 November 2016, 2016 ITLOS Reports 44 § 231; *The "Duzgit Integrity" Arbitration (Malta v. São Tomé and Príncipe)*, award of 5 September 2016, PCA Case No. 2014–07 § 150; *The M/T "San Padre Pio" (No 1)* (n. 35) § 128; Gidel (n. 23) I 254–255; Jennings & Watts (n. 2) 731.

It is not always easy to establish whether a matter or incident is sufficiently related to a vessel for the connecting factor to exist. There is no doubt in that regard when the matter or incident relates entirely and exclusively to a specific vessel, for instance when a theft takes place on the vessel. By contrast, the position is not as obvious when only some of the aspects of the matter or incident relate to a specific vessel. For instance, a vessel might be damaged or sink as a result of an act performed by the officer in charge of another vessel, which caused a collision between the two vessels. One will recall that this is part of the facts that gave rise to the dispute in *Lotus*.[54] One will also recall that the PCIJ ruled in that case that the State with which the damaged or sunk vessel had a legal relationship of nationality had jurisdiction.[55] Today, article 97(1) of the LOSC, read with article 58(2), makes it clear that the State only has very limited flag State jurisdiction "[i]n the event of a collision or any other incident of navigation concerning a ship" beyond the outer limits of the territorial seas "involving the penal or disciplinary responsibility of the master or of any other person in the service of the ship".[56] In other cases, however, the principle on which the PCIJ based its decision continues to apply.[57] This means, for instance, that, when an offence is started on one vessel and completed on another vessel, the latter's flag State has objective flag State jurisdiction ("Fo jurisdiction"), while the State with which the other vessel has a legal relationship of nationality has subjective flag State jurisdiction ("Fs jurisdiction").[58]

3.2.3 Establishment of the legal relationship

All coastal and landlocked States have FL jurisdiction to perform a legislative act producing a legislative instrument containing one or several constitutive provisions creating the legal relationship of nationality.[59] In that regard, article 91(1) of the LOSC states that "[e]very State shall fix the conditions for the grant of its nationality to ships [...]". In other words, the LOSC compels every State that wishes to make use of its right to sail ships flying its flag, to exercise its FL jurisdiction by performing a legislative act producing a legislative instrument containing the constitutive provisions describing the features of the legal relationship of nationality between the State and vessels.[60] The LOSC does not prescribe what the conditions for the

54 See Chapter 1 section 1.5.
55 See Chapter 1 section 1.5.
56 See article 94(6)–(7) of the LOSC.
57 See e.g., D Guilfoyle "Article 97" in A Proelss (ed) *United Nations Convention on the Law of the Sea – A Commentary* (2017) 721–724 at 723.
58 See e.g., *The "Enrica Lexie" Incident* (n. 35) § 366. The terms are derived from the terms "objective territorial jurisdiction" and "subjective territorial jurisdiction" often used with regard to incidents occurring across land borders (see e.g., Jennings & Watts (n. 2) 460; Staker (n. 3) 297). See further e.g., M Akehurst "Jurisdiction in international law" (1972–1973) 46 BYIL 145–257 at 152.
59 Evidence of the existence of this jurisdiction is found in article 90 of the LOSC. See e.g., Churchill, Lowe & Sander (n. 44) 831; Nordquist (n. 49) 101 § 90.8(a); D Guilfoyle "Article 90" in Proelss (n. 57) 690–692 at 690.
60 See *M/V "Saiga" (No 2)* (n. 53) separate opinion of Vice-President Wolfrum § 19.

grant must be.[61] The majority of States make registration a requirement for a vessel to have their respective nationalities.[62] That is the case of Belize,[63] Mauritius,[64] Saint Vincent and the Grenadines[65] and Tanzania,[66] for instance. However, registration is not a necessary requirement.[67] For instance, section 57 of New Zealand's Ship Registration Act, 1992,[68] provides that both "ships that are registered under th[e] Act" and "ships entitled under section 8 to be registered [...]" must "for all purposes be treated as being New Zealand ships and having New Zealand nationality". An advantage of establishing the link of nationality independently from, and before, registration resides in that persons are not able to avoid the duties placed upon them by the State of nationality by refraining from registering a vessel. Thus, South Africa's Ship Registration Act, 1998,[69] provides that, should a ship which is entitled to be registered in South Africa – and is therefore a South African ship – depart from a South African port to a place outside South Africa without having been registered, that ship is nevertheless to be

> dealt with in the same manner in all respects as if the ship were registered for the purposes of any law providing for –
>
> (a) the payment of levies, fees or other charges;
> (b) the liability for fines, detention and forfeiture; and
> (c) the punishment of offences committed on board a ship or by any person belonging to a ship.[70]

61 See e.g., *The M/V "Saiga" (No 2)* (n. 53) § 63; *The "Enrica Lexie" Incident* (n. 35) § 1022. NP Ready "Nationality, registration, and ownership of ships" in DJ Attard (ed) *The IMLI Manual of International Maritime Law* (2016) II 19–38.
62 See e.g., *The M/V "Saiga" (No 2)* (n. 53) § 64; *The "Enrica Lexie" Incident* (n. 35) § 1022.
63 See reg. 2(1) of the 1991 Registration of Merchant Ships (Registration and Miscellaneous Provisions) Regulations made in terms of section 24(1) of the Registration of Merchant Ships Act, 1989 (Act 32 of 1989). See also *The "Grand Prince" Case (Belize v. France)*, judgment of 20 April 2001, 2001 ITLOS Reports 17 § 83.
64 See section 14(1) of the Merchant Shipping Act, 2007 (Act 26 of 2007).
65 See section 5 of the Merchant Shipping Act, 2004 (Act 11 of 2004).
66 See section 12 of the Merchant Shipping Act, 2003 (Act 21 of 2003).
67 See e.g., P Birnie "Reflagging of fishing vessels on the high seas" (1993) 2(3) *Review of European, Comparative and International Environmental Law* 270–276 at 272; D Guilfoyle "Article 91" in Proelss (n. 57) 692–699 at 694 and 697; GM Gauci & K Aquilina "The legal fiction of a genuine link as a requirement for the grant of nationality to ships and humans – The triumph of formality over substance?" (2017) 17 *International and Comparative Law Review* 167–191 at 169; R Coles & E Watt *Ship Registration – Law and Practice* (2018) § 1.12.
68 Act 89 of 1992.
69 Act 58 of 1998 (SRA).
70 Section 46(2) read with section 44(2). See further J Hare *Shipping Law and Admiralty Jurisdiction in South Africa* (2009) 199–200.

3.2.4 Evidence of the legal relationship

3.2.4.1 The right to fly a flag

The most conspicuous evidence of the legal relationship of nationality between a State and a ship is the flag that the ship flies.[71] As in the case of the grant of nationality, article 91(1) of the LOSC states that "[e]very State shall fix the conditions [...] for the right to fly its flag [...]". In other words, the LOSC compels every State that wishes to make use of its right to sail ships flying its flag, to exercise its FL jurisdiction by performing a legislative act producing a legislative instrument containing the normative provisions governing the right to fly the flag of the State. Once again, the LOSC does not prescribe what the contents of those provisions should be. An example is the Ghana Shipping Act, 2003,[72] which provides that "[a] ship registered or licensed in accordance with th[e] Act as a Ghanaian ship shall fly the national flag of Ghana"[73] and prescribes when the flag must be hoisted.[74]

Article 91(1) of the LOSC states that "[s]hips have the nationality of the State whose flag they are entitled to fly". It is important to keep in mind, however, that, while the flag symbolises the legal relationship of nationality, "the actual flag itself is only *prima facie* evidence of nationality".[75] That is the reason why article 91(2) of the LOSC compels "[e]very State [to] issue to ships to which it has granted the right to fly its flag documents to that effect". That is also why warships[76] may, in specific cases,[77] proceed to verify a foreign vessel's right to fly its flag by sending a boat under the command of an officer to the vessel to check the latter's documents.[78]

The issuing of the documents "is regulated by domestic law".[79] When registration is not a requirement for the grant of the nationality of a State as well as the exercise of the right to fly the flag of the State, the registration documents are not available until registration has taken place, in the cases when it is required. The State must then provide for the issuance of one or more other documents.[80] Because registration is normally a requirement for the grant of the nationality of a State as well as the exercise of the right to fly the flag of the State, the documents that are expected to be produced to give evidence of the legal relationship of nationality are

71 See e.g., *The "Enrica Lexie" Incident* (n. 35) § 1029. See further e.g., Ready (n. 61) 25.

72 Act 645.

73 Section 94(1).

74 See section 95(1).

75 RG Rayfuse *Non-Flag State Enforcement in High Seas Fisheries* (2004) 22. See further e.g., *The "Enrica Lexie" Incident* (n. 35) § 1029; Gidel (n. 23) I 83; CJ Colombos *The International Law of the Sea* (1967) 291.

76 As well as military aircraft and "duly authorized ships or aircraft clearly marked and identifiable as being on government service" (article 110(4)–(5) of the LOSC).

77 See article 110(1) of the LOSC.

78 See article 110(2) of the LOSC.

79 *The M/V "Saiga" (No 2)* (n. 53) § 63.

80 See e.g., section 4(5) of the SRA, which provides for the issuance of a certificate stating that the vessel concerned is entitled to fly the national flag.

those issued upon registration by the organ of State in charge of the relevant ship register.[81]

3.2.4.2 Ship registries

Registration is "a constitutive act of the competent authorities of the flag State by which a ship enters a public register of that State".[82] The LOSC compels every State that wishes to make use of its right to sail ships flying its flag, to "maintain a register of ships containing the names and particulars of ships flying its flag, except those which are excluded from generally accepted international regulations on account of their small size".[83] The LOSC does not require that the particulars of the owners of the ships be included in the register.[84] This is in contrast to the 1986 United Nations Convention on the Registration of Ships ("the Registration Convention"),[85] which requires that the information included in the register includes also that concerning the ship's owner or owners, bareboat charterer and/or operator.[86] The Convention is not in effect,[87] but a similar requirement exists with regard to fishing vessels in terms of the 1993 Agreement to Promote Compliance with International Conservation and Management Measures by Fishing Vessels on the High Seas ("the Compliance Agreement"),[88] which came into force in 2003.[89] That information is necessary because it plays a crucial role in the fulfilment by the flag States of their various duties,[90] if necessary through the exercise of their ter-

81 See e.g., section 26(1) and section 28(2) of Fiji's Ship Registration Decree, 2013 (Decree 19 of 2013).

82 D König "Flags of ships" 2009 MPEPIL § 19. On the many functions of registration, see e.g., Ready (n. 61) 25–27. On flags of convenience, see e.g., SM Kim & J Kim "Flags of convenience in the context of the OECD BEPS Package" (2018) 49 JMLC 221–238.

83 Article 94(2)(a) of the LOSC. See *The "Enrica Lexie" Incident* (n. 35) § 1034; D Guilfoyle "Article 94" in Proelss (n. 57) 707–714 at 711. There are different types of registries available to States, which sometimes have more than one registry (see e.g., Pancracio (n. 21) 80–84; Ready (n. 61) 32–36; UNCTAD *Review of Maritime Transport* (2019) 36–41). See also e.g., S Sucharitkul "Liability and responsibility of the State of registration or the flag State in respect of sea-going vessels, aircraft and spacecraft registered by national registration authorities" (2006) 54 *American Journal of Comparative Law* (special issue) 409–442 at 421–429.

84 Sohn *et al.* (n. 48) 57.

85 (1987) 28 ILM 1229, (1986) 7 LOSB 87. Adopted: 7 February 1986; EIF: not yet. See e.g., D Momtaz "La Convention des Nations Unies sur l'immatriculation des navires" (1986) 32 AFDI 715–735; HW Wefers Bettink "Open registry, the genuine link and the 1986 Convention on Registration Conditions for Ships" (1987) 18 *Netherlands Yearbook of International Law* 69–119; ML McConnell "Business as usual: An evaluation of the 1986 United Nations Convention on Conditions for Registration of Ships" (1987) 18 JMLC 435–450.

86 See articles 6(1), 11(2)(f), 11(2)(h) and 11(3)(b). See further section 3.2.5.2(c).

87 See e.g., R Barnes "Flag States" in DR Rothwell *et al.* (eds) *The Oxford Handbook of the Law of the Sea* (2015) at 307.

88 2221 UNTS 91, (1994) 33 ILM 968. Adopted: 24 November 1993; EIF: 24 April 2003. See article IV read with article VI(1)(d).

89 See article IV read together with article VI.

90 See further section 3.2.5.2.

ritorial jurisdiction on land.[91] In other words, the information is important to hold the persons in charge of the management and operation of vessels accountable for their actions, including illegal activities at sea such as dumping, illegal, unreported and unregulated (IUU) fishing and terrorism.[92] For that reason, the Registration Convention contains also a requirement that measures be taken by the flag State to make the information easily accessible "by persons having a legitimate interest in obtaining such information".[93]

3.2.4.3 Nature of the evidence

It has just been indicated that, while registration is not always a requirement to establish the legal relationship of nationality between a State and a vessel, the registration documents constitute the pieces of evidence that are often used to confirm the existence of that relationship.[94] That evidence is particularly important for a State to ensure that the attribution of its nationality is respected by an organ of a foreign State when the exercise of the latter's executive jurisdiction is contemplated at sea.[95] The LOSC takes into account that reliance on such evidence might give rise to a dispute when it states that the members of the crew of a foreign warship who exercise the right of visit may, when suspicions remain regarding the right of the vessel to fly the flag it flies after having checked the documents, "proceed to a further examination on board the ship".[96] This second step in the verification process confirms that, "although it is necessary that [...] nationality be easily identifiable" because "the juridical order of the maritime spaces is based upon the institution of the nationality of ships",[97] the process may involve having regard to other evidence than the documents that are expected to be issued in terms of article 91(2) of the LOSC.

Disputes relating to nationality are "subject to the procedures under Part XV of the [LOSC], especially in cases where issues of interpretation or application of provisions of the Convention are involved".[98] In the course of those procedures, "the nationality of a ship is a question of fact to be determined, like other facts in dispute [...], on the basis of evidence adduced by the parties".[99] In that regard, it must be kept in mind that issues relating to the nature of the evidence confirming nationality do not only arise at sea, but also, for instance, when an adjudicative body is called upon to establish whether it has jurisdiction in a case or whether an

91 Cogliati-Bantz (n. 46) 402.
92 See e.g., Sohn *et al.* (n. 48) 58.
93 Article 6(2).
94 See Ready (n. 61) 23.
95 See e.g., *The M/V "Saiga" (No 2)* (n. 53) separate opinion of Vice-President Wolfrum § 22.
96 Article 110(2) of the LOSC. In terms of article 110(5), the right is held by any "duly authorized ships or aircraft clearly marked and identifiable as being on government service".
97 See e.g., *The M/V "Saiga" (No 2)* (n. 53) separate opinion of Vice-President Wolfrum § 17.
98 *The M/V "Saiga" (No 2)* (n. 53) § 65.
99 *Ibid.* § 66. See also e.g., *The "Enrica Lexie" Incident* (n. 35) § 1023.

applicant has legal standing to bring claims. Two examples are *M/V "Saiga" (No 2)*[100] and *Grand Prince*,[101] in which ITLOS was called upon to make rulings.

The *Saiga* was an oil tanker, which was provisionally registered in Saint Vincent and the Grenadines[102] at the time when, on 28 October 1997, it was boarded and arrested by members of the crew of two Guinean patrol boats, while it was drifting "south of the southern limit of the exclusive economic zone of Guinea".[103] Thereafter, the vessel and its crew were brought to Conakry.[104] Upon a request of Saint Vincent and the Grenadines under article 292 of the LOSC, the Tribunal decided to prescribe provisional measures in its order of 11 March 1998.[105] A year later, during the proceedings on the merits of the case, one of Guinea's objections to the admissibility of the claims made by Saint Vincent and the Grenadines was that the latter did "not have legal standing to bring claims in connection with the measures taken by Guinea against the *Saiga*" because "on the day of its arrest the ship was 'not validly registered under the flag of Saint Vincent and the Grenadines' [...]".[106]

As far as it is concerned, the *Grand Prince* was a fishing vessel flying the flag of Belize[107] when, on 26 December 2000, it "was boarded by the crew of the French surveillance frigate *Nivose* in the exclusive economic zone of the Kerguelen Islands in the French Southern and Antarctic Territories".[108] In the process of determining whether it had jurisdiction, the Tribunal had to "satisfy itself that the Application was 'made on behalf of the flag State of the vessel', as required by article 292, paragraph 2, of the" LOSC.[109] The matter was complicated by the fact that there was an issue relating to whether the legal relationship had ceased, an issue that will be dealt with later in this chapter.[110] What matters for present purposes is that the Tribunal stated that "[i]t is necessary that there is sufficient evidence to establish that a vessel is registered and, therefore, has the right to fly the flag of Belize [...]".[111] The only document that had been issued in respect of the vessel by Belize was a "provisional patent of navigation".[112] That document had expired by the time it could be relied upon and, therefore, the Tribunal did not have to pronounce on its validity. Nevertheless, the Tribunal gave no indication that the patent was not, while it was valid, a suitable document to confirm the right to fly the flag. What

100 See *The M/V "Saiga" (No 2)* (n. 53) § 65.
101 *The "Grand Prince" Case* (n. 63).
102 See *The M/V "Saiga" (No 2)* (n. 53) § 31. That this was indeed the case was disputed by Vice-President Wolfrum in his separate opinion (§ 26).
103 *The M/V "Saiga" (No 2)* (n. 53) § 33.
104 *Ibid.*
105 *Ibid.* § 86.
106 *Ibid.* § 55.
107 See *The "Grand Prince" Case* (n. 63) § 34.
108 *Ibid.* § 35.
109 *Ibid.* § 80.
110 See section 3.2.6.
111 *The "Grand Prince" Case* (n. 63) § 83.
112 *Ibid.* §§ 32 and 84.

the Tribunal did, however, was to rule that a certification from the International Merchant Marine Registry of Belize in which it asserted, three months after the expiry of the provisional patent, that the vessel was "still considered as registered in Belize" could not be treated as a "document" within the meaning of article 91(2) of the LOSC.[113] The Tribunal did so for three reasons.

The first reason is that Belize had not discharged the initial burden of establishing that the vessel had its nationality at the time when the flag State jurisdiction was challenged,[114] because the certification was "in the nature of [an] administrative [letter], unsupported by references to any entries in the merchant marine register of Belize or any other action required by law".[115] The second reason is that the certification had been issued after the application to the Tribunal had been made.[116] Finally, the certification contradicted an earlier official communication by Belize with France. That communication had taken the form of a note verbale that did set "out the legal position of the Government of Belize with respect to the registration of the vessel".[117] In that note, Belize confirmed that the vessel had been entered in its register, but added that it had been de-registered with effect on the date of the note.[118] That third reason is noteworthy in that it refers to a factor already identified by the Tribunal in *M/V "Saiga" (No 2)*.[119] That factor resides in that the conduct of a State that contends that it is the flag State is "an important consideration in determining the nationality or registration of a ship".[120] In *M/V "Saiga" (No 2)*, the Tribunal had decided that, although the registration was no longer valid, Saint Vincent and the Grenadines had "at all times material to the dispute operated on the basis that the *Saiga* was a ship of its nationality".[121] In addition, the State had "acted as the flag State of the ship during all phases of the proceedings".[122]

This approach highlights the fact that, although the requirement of article 91(2) of the LOSC that "[e]very State shall issue to ships to which it has granted the right to fly its flag documents to that effect" confirms a practice illustrated by "hundreds of treaties of friendship, commerce, and navigation",[123] that requirement does not mean that, in a case where no valid document exists or the validity of the document has expired, it is impossible for the vessel concerned to have a nationality and the related right to fly the flag of the relevant State. The effect of the lack of valid documentation is only to complicate situations at sea where a vessel's right to fly the flag it flies is being verified and to place a burden on the State that claims

113 *Ibid.* § 85.
114 See *The M/V "Saiga" (No 2)* (n. 53) §§ 67 and 72.
115 *The "Grand Prince" Case* (n. 63) § 86.
116 *Ibid.*
117 *Ibid.* § 32.
118 *Ibid.* § 87.
119 See *The M/V "Saiga" (No 2)* (n. 53) § 68.
120 *The "Grand Prince" Case* (n. 63) § 89.
121 *The M/V "Saiga" (No 2)* (n. 53) § 68.
122 *Ibid.*
123 *The M/V "Saiga" (No 2)* (n. 53) separate opinion of Vice-President Wolfrum § 22.

to be the flag State to demonstrate the existence of the link of nationality by other appropriate means.[124]

In cases where valid documents do exist and there is a discrepancy between the flag flown by a ship and the documents the latter carries, because the documents point to a different nationality than the one pointed to by the flag, the documents would normally prevail.[125] That means that third States are entitled to act on the basis that it is the State to which the documents point that has flag State jurisdiction, and not the State to which the flag points. In fact, States other than the flag State

> are under an obligation to respect these documents as being accurate and valid, in particular, they must not – except under special circumstances[126] – challenge the validity or accuracy of such documents on the ground that they do not correspond to the national law of the State having issued the documents.[127]

3.2.5 Nature of the legal relationship

3.2.5.1 Exclusive competence of every State

ITLOS confirmed, in *M/V "Saiga" (No 2)*, that it is "a well-established rule of general international law" that all States have exclusive legislative jurisdiction with regard to the requirements that need to be met for the grant of their nationalities.[128] Those are indeed matters that are regulated by each State in its domestic law.[129] Nevertheless, as already indicated above, disputes regarding the nature of the legal relationship of nationality between a State and a vessel "may be subject to the procedures under Part XV of the Convention, especially in cases where issues of interpretation or application of provisions of the Convention are involved".[130] Those disputes, which often involve States with "flags of convenience" or "open registries",[131] may relate to specific contractual requirements or exclusions accepted by the State concerned[132] or to the general requirement of genuineness.[133]

124 See *The M/V "Saiga" (No 2)* (n. 53) §§ 66–68.
125 *The Merritt* 84 US 582, 586 (1873).
126 "[S]uch as reasonable grounds for suspecting a falsification" (König (n. 82) § 20).
127 *The M/V "Saiga" (No 2)* (n. 53) separate opinion of Vice-President Wolfrum § 23.
128 *The M/V "Saiga" (No 2)* (n. 53) § 63. See also e.g., *Muscat Dhows (Great Britain v. France)*, award of 8 August 1905, XI RIAA 83. As far as vessels flying the flag of the United Nations, its specialised agencies and the International Atomic Energy Agency are concerned, see article 93 of the LOSC.
129 See *The M/V "Saiga" (No 2)* (n. 53) § 63. See also section 3.2.3.
130 *The M/V "Saiga" (No 2)* (n. 53) § 65.
131 See e.g., Churchill, Lowe & Sander (n. 44) 466. On flags of convenience and open registries, see e.g., Treves (n. 26) 179–189; D König "Flags of convenience" 2008 MPEPIL; CF Llinás Negret "Pretending to be Liberian and Panamanian; flags of convenience and the weakening of the nation State on the high seas" (2016) 47 JMLC 1–28; Kim & Kim (n. 82).
132 See section 3.2.5.3.
133 See section 3.2.5.2.

3.2.5.2 The requirement of genuineness

(A) INTRODUCTION

The LOSC, in article 91(1), appears to place only one limitation upon each State's right to determine the criteria for granting its nationality to ships: there must exist "a genuine link between the State and the ship".[134] However, there is a lack of consensus on whether a genuine link is actually a requirement for the grant of nationality.[135] In addition, the meaning of the concept is far from perfectly clear[136] and it is debated whether a State may refuse to recognise the nationality of a ship on the ground of a lack of a genuine link.[137]

(B) THE EXISTENCE OF THE REQUIREMENT THAT THE LINK BE GENUINE

It is not entirely clear whether it is a requirement that the link between a vessel and a State be genuine before the State is entitled to grant its nationality to the ship. The wording of the provision that was to become article 91(1) was already agreed upon at the beginning of UNCLOS III by the informal consultative group on the high seas.[138] It corresponds to the wording of article 5(1) of the CHS, except for the excision in the sentence that started with the words "[t]here must exist a genuine link between the State and the ship" of the words that followed, i.e., "in particular, the State must effectively exercise its jurisdiction and control in administrative, technical and social matters over ships flying its flag". That excision can be explained by the fact that the words were repeated in the provision that was to become article 94(1) of the LOSC.[139] However, that explanation does not address the issue

134 See also *Filleting within the Gulf of St. Lawrence (Canada v. France)*, award of 17 July 1986, XIX RIAA 225 § 27. Although the term "genuine link" was borrowed from the ICJ judgment in *Nottebohm* (*Nottebohm Case (Second Phase) (Liechtenstein v. Guatemala)*, judgment of 6 April 1955, 1955 ICJ Reports 4), there is little to gain in this discussion from the judgment in view of the important differences between the nationality of persons and the nationality of vessels as well as the "mixed precedential value" of the case (O Dörr "*Nottebohm Case*" 2007 MPEPIL § 16). See also MS Mc Dougal, WT Burke & IA Vlasic "The maintenance of public order at sea and the nationality of ships" (1960) 54 AJIL 25–116 at 36–40; Ready (n. 61) 30.

135 See section 3.2.5.2(b).

136 See section 3.2.5.2(c).

137 See section 3.2.5.2(d).

138 See Nordquist (n. 49) 105 § 91.5, referring to Doc. C.2/Blue Paper No 7 (1975) provision 140 (reproduced in R Platzöder *Third United Nations Conference on the Law of the Sea: Documents* (1983) IV 130) and Doc. C.2/Blue Paper No 9/Rev 1 (1975) provision 140 reproduced in Platzöder (*ibid.*) 139. Provision 140 became article 77 of Part II of the Informal Single Negotiating Text (UN Doc. A/CONF.62/WP.8/Part II (ISNT, 1975) ((2009) IV *UNCLOS III Official Records* 164)), article 79 of Part II of the Revised Single Negotiating Text (UN Doc. A/CONF.62/WP.8/Rev.1/Part II (RSNT, 1976) ((2009) V *UNCLOS III Official Records* 165–166)) and article 91 of the Informal Composite Negotiating Text (UN Doc. A/CONF.62/WP.10 (ICNT, 1977) ((2009) VIII *UNCLOS III Official Records* 18)). The word "each" was replaced by the word "every" in the Draft Convention (UN Doc. A/CONF.62/L.78 (Draft Convention, 1981) ((2009) XV *UNCLOS III Official Records* 189–190)).

139 See Nordquist (n. 49) 105 § 91.5.

whether the words "in particular" were meant to indicate that the words that followed them elaborated on the meaning of the words that preceded them, in which case the whole sentence belonged in article 94(1) and only there, or whether they were meant to stress the existence of a separate and consequential duty described by the words that follow them, in which case it made sense to separate the two parts of the sentence. To shed light on this matter, it is necessary to scrutinise the drafting history of article 5(1).

The provision finds its origin in article 29 of the Draft Articles on the Law of the Sea adopted by the ILC in 1956. The Commission's deliberations leading to the adoption of the provision were based on the preparatory work of its special rapporteur on matters regarding the high seas.[140] In 1951, the rapporteur noted in its second report that there were no uniform rules in the domestic laws of States regarding the grant of nationality to ships.[141] He also expressed the view that it would not be possible to propose uniform rules in the light of the differing economic and political factors influencing States in the management of their respective maritime sectors.[142] At the same time, the rapporteur wondered whether States were completely free when granting their nationalities to vessels.[143] This was because nationality is a corollary of the principle of the freedom of the high seas in the sense that, in order to avoid abuses of the principle, the only vessels that are entitled to make use of the freedom are vessels with a nationality and, therefore, with a State monitoring and controlling them.[144] The rapporteur was also concerned that complete freedom would encourage States "to look behind the flag".[145] For those reasons, the rapporteur expressed the view that the relationship between a State and a vessel must entail more than mere registration,[146] before he called for minimum requirements being set in the interest of all ocean users[147] and proposed what those requirements should entail.[148]

During the meeting in the course of which the members of the Commission discussed "the principles formulated on th[e] subject by the Rapporteur",[149] the latter acknowledged that the principle that

> there were certain general international directives regarding the nationality of ships, which States were required to observe [...] had only been formulated by a very few writers. It was rarely stated, because nearly all legal

140 Professor JPA François.
141 See UN Doc. A/CN.4/42 (n. 49) § 2.
142 *Ibid.* (quoting in French A Pearce Higgins & JC Colombos *The International Law of the Sea* (1943) 190).
143 See UN Doc. A/CN.4/42 (n. 49) § 3.
144 *Ibid.* referring to Gidel (n. 23) I 73. See also e.g., Cogliati-Bantz (n. 46) 387.
145 UN Doc. A/CN.4/42 (n. 49) § 4.
146 *Ibid.* § 3.
147 *Ibid.*
148 *Ibid.* § 18. See further section 3.2.5.2(c).
149 Summary record of the 121st meeting held on 10 July 1951 § 10 ((1951) I YILC 327).

> authorities [...] recognized States as having complete sovereignty in respect of the nationality of ships.[150]

Nevertheless, when the members were asked to decide whether States were "absolutely free to fix as they deemed fit the conditions for the granting of their nationality to ships" or "certain general rules of international law had to be observed in that connexion",[151] they "recognized, by 8 votes to 1 with 2 abstentions, that the grant of nationality to ships was limited by certain principles of international law".[152] Having overwhelmingly agreed that States were not absolutely free to fix the conditions for the granting of their nationality to vessels as they deemed fit, the Commission then focussed its attention on what the minimum requirements should be.[153] The rapporteur proceeded also on the basis of the outcome of the vote in his third report[154] and in his sixth report.[155]

The matter was raised again four years later when one of the members proposed a new provision that stated merely that "[e]ach State is entitled to fix the conditions to which registration and transfer of registration are subject".[156]The rapporteur expressed his opposition to the text[157] on the ground that the Commission had earlier agreed that "States were not entirely at liberty to lay down conditions governing the nationality of ships as they thought fit but [had to] observe certain general rules of international law governing the subject".[158] In his reply, the proposer explained that he did not mean to disagree with the principle, but that he rather felt that the minimum requirements formulated by the Commission should not be too detailed.[159] The provision proposed by the rapporteur was ultimately adopted with a few amendments by seven votes to four, with two abstentions,[160] and became article 5 of the ILC's Provisional Draft Articles on the High Seas.[161] In its regard, the Commission explained that

> [e]ach State lays down the conditions on which seagoing ships may fly its flag. Obviously the State enjoys complete liberty in the case of ships owned by it or ships which are the property of a nationalized company. With regard

150 *Ibid.* 328. See further e.g., Cogliati-Bantz (n. 46) 391.
151 Summary record of the 121st meeting (n. 149) 330.
152 *Ibid.*
153 *Ibid.* 330–334.
154 See UN Doc. A/CN.4/51 (1952) ((1952) II YILC 44–49 at 44). The Commission did not discuss the reports during its fourth session (summary record of the 178th meeting held on 1 August 1952 § 38 ((1952) I YILC 223)) and its fifth session (summary record of the 237th meeting held on 11 August 1953 § 51–59 ((1953) I YILC 367–368)).
155 See UN Doc. A/CN.4/79 (1954) § 4 ((1954) II YILC 8).
156 Summary record of the 294th meeting held on 18 May 1955 § 1 fn. 1 ((1955) I YILC 61).
157 *Ibid.* § 2.
158 *Ibid.* § 11.
159 *Ibid.* § 5.
160 *Ibid.* § 25.
161 See UN Doc. A/2934 (1955) § 18 ((1955) II YILC 22).

> to other ships, the State must accept certain restrictions. As in the case of the granting of nationality to persons, national legislation on the subject must not diverge too far from the principles adopted by the majority of States, which may be regarded as forming part of international law. Only on that condition will the freedom granted to States not give rise to abuse and to friction with other States.[162]

None of the States that commented on article 5 challenged the stance of the Commission[163] and the latter restated its view *verbatim* in its comment on article 29(1) of its Final Draft Articles Concerning the Law of the Sea ("the Final Draft Articles"),[164] which formed the basis of the debates at the 1958 First United Nations Conference on the Law of the Sea (UNCLOS I).[165] The Conference adopted article 5(1) of the CHS which, with regard to the issue of the existence of a genuine-link requirement, was substantially the same as article 29(1) of the ILC's Final Draft Articles.

The ICJ did not discuss the issue of whether there exists a genuine-link requirement for the grant of nationality in its advisory opinion given in *Inter-Governmental Maritime Consultative Organisation*, two years after the adoption of the Convention.[166] Likewise, there was no discussion of the issue at UNCLOS III.[167] In *M/V "Saiga" (No 2)*, ITLOS considered that it needed to address two questions in connection with article 91(1). "The first [was] whether the absence of a genuine link between a flag State and a ship entitles another State to refuse to recognize the nationality of the ship. The second question [was] whether or not a genuine link existed between the *Saiga* and [the flag State] at the time of the incident".[168] The content of the genuine-link requirement and the implications of the absence of a

162 *Ibid.*

163 See UN Doc. A/CN.4/97/Add.1 (1956) § 38–59 ((1956) II YILC 14–16). See further UN Doc. A/CN.4/99 and Add.1 to 9 (1956) ((1956) II YILC 37–103).

164 See UN Doc. A/3159 (1956) ((1956) II YILC 253–302 at 278) and UN Doc. A/CONF.13/40 (n. 49) 113).

165 The rapporteur explained in the Conference's Second Committee that, in the Commission's view, there was a link between the position that it held regarding the establishment of the legal relationship of nationality between a State and a vessel, and the fact that "every freedom must be regulated if it is desired that it be exercised in the interest of those entitled to benefit by it. The essential corollary to the freedom of the seas must be that states exercise the same jurisdiction over ships sailing the high seas under their flag as they exercise in their own territory" (UN Doc A/CONF.13/C.2/L.14 § 26, reproduced in UN Doc. A/CONF.13/40 (n. 49) 34).

166 *Constitution of the Maritime Safety Committee of the Inter-Governmental Maritime Consultative Organisation*, advisory opinion of 8 June 1960, 1960 ICJ Reports 150. See further e.g., Churchill, Lowe & Sander (n. 44) 468; TA Mensah "International Maritime Organization (IMO)" 2011 MPEPIL § 11.

167 RR Churchill (with the assistance of C Hedley) *The Meaning of the "Genuine Link" Requirement in Relation to the Nationality of Ships* (2000) 46, available at http://seafarersrights.org/wp/wp-content/uploads/2014/11/INTERNATIONAL_ARTICLE_GENUINE-LINK-REQUIREMENT-IN-NATIONALITY-OF-SHIPS_2000_ENG.pdf.

168 See *The M/V "Saiga" (No 2)* (n. 53) § 79.

genuine link will be discussed later.[169] One may note however that, in the process of dealing with those issues, the Tribunal recalled that the ILC had, in article 29(1) of its Final Draft Articles, "proposed the concept of a 'genuine link' as a criterion [...] for the attribution of nationality to a ship".[170] The Tribunal then noted that "the obligation regarding a genuine link was maintained in the 1958 Convention"[171] and that the latter's approach was followed in article 91(1) of the LOSC, which "retains the part of the third sentence of article 5, paragraph 1, of the 1958 Convention which provides that there must be a genuine link between the State and the ship".[172] The Tribunal might appear to have contradicted itself when it stated that "the purpose of the provisions of the Convention on the need for a genuine link between a ship and its flag State is [...] not to establish criteria by reference to which the validity of the registration of ships in a flag State may be challenged by other States".[173] However, this statement was made while the Tribunal was discussing the implications of the absence of a genuine link, not the issue whether the existence of a genuine link is a requirement for the grant of nationality. That is the way Judge Anderson understood the statement[174] and President Mensah had no doubt that article 91(1) "does not [...] support the proposition that a ship can acquire nationality merely because an official of the State declares that it has such nationality".[175]

The Tribunal confirmed in 2007, in *Tomimaru*, that article 91(1) deals with the conditions for the granting of nationality to ships, while article 94 deals with the "network of mutual rights and obligations" produced by the grant.[176] Unfortunately, the Tribunal appears to have overlooked this fundamental distinction seven years later, in *Virginia G*, when it stated that, in its view,

> once a ship is registered, the flag State is required, under article 94 of the Convention, to exercise effective jurisdiction and control over that ship in order to ensure that it operates in accordance with generally accepted international regulations, procedures and practices. This is the meaning of "genuine link".[177]

This *obiter* statement seems to imply, against all the evidence discussed above, that, although the term "genuine link" appears in article 91 and does not appear in article 94, it has no import regarding the issue of the nationality of ships in article 91 because it relates instead to the duties of the flag State spelled out in article

169 See sections 3.2.5.2(c) and 3.2.5.2(d), respectively.
170 See *The M/V "Saiga" (No 2)* (n. 53) § 80.
171 *Ibid.*
172 *Ibid.* § 81.
173 *Ibid.* § 83. See e.g., Churchill (n. 167) 50–51.
174 See the separate opinion of Judge Anderson at 1.
175 Separate opinion of President Mensah § 13.
176 *The "Tomimaru" Case (Japan v. Russian Federation)*, judgment of 6 August 2007, 2005–2007 ITLOS Reports 74 § 70. See further section 3.2.6.
177 *The M/V "Virginia G" Case* (n. 53) § 113.

94. That interpretation is supported by Judge Jesus who read the judgment of the Tribunal in *M/V "Saiga" (No 2)* to mean that

> [t]he genuine link that should exist between a ship and its flag State is not a prerequisite or condition for the granting of nationality to the ship and therefore it does not condition the validity of the nationality or registration of such ship.[178]

On that basis, Judge Jesus expressed the view that

> at the time a State grants its nationality to a ship, it is totally free to do so and is not bound by any prerequisite and condition, including that of a genuine link, other than those it may freely impose on itself.[179]

This view is clearly at odds with the view of all the authorities mentioned earlier and there is little doubt that, while all States, whether coastal or land-locked, have exclusive legislative jurisdiction to perform legislative acts producing legislative instruments containing normative provisions setting the requirements that need to be met for the grant of their nationalities, that jurisdiction is limited by the requirement that the link between a State and a vessel must be genuine for the legal relationship of nationality to be validly established between the State and the vessel. It is now necessary to ascertain what the genuineness of the link entails.

(C) THE MEANING OF "GENUINENESS"

(i) Introduction It is difficult to understand the purpose of the third sentence of article 91(1) if the genuine link entails nothing more than registration.[180] Indeed, the need for registration is already implied in the first sentence. The third sentence would therefore add nothing to the provision. For that reason, the only conclusion appears to be that, while registration plays a central role in the process of establishing a legal relationship of nationality between a State and a vessel,[181] the link between the State and the vessel must entail more than mere registration if it is to be genuine.[182] While the legislative history of article 91(1) appears to support this conclusion, it has already been alluded to above that identifying the element(s) of genuineness has proven to be an inordinately challenging task.[183] It would appear that the main reason is that arguments are often made, or suspected to be made, with a view to their impact on the position of each State or group of States in

178 Dissenting opinion of Judge Jesus § 42.
179 *Ibid.* § 45.
180 "There must exist a genuine link between the State and the ship".
181 See section 3.2.3.
182 See e.g., Kamto (n. 48) 347.
183 See section 3.2.5.2(b).

the highly competitive shipping and fishing industries. From that perspective, it is unlikely that any binding agreement will ever be reached.[184]

What the legislative history of article 91(1) makes quite clear, however, is that, irrespective of those commercial considerations, there is a relation between the requirement that there be a genuine link when establishing the legal relationship of nationality, on the one hand, and the need to ensure law and order at sea, especially on the high seas, on the other.[185] That relation consists in the genuine link being seen not as a requirement for the establishment of the legal relationship of nationality *per se*, but as a requirement flowing from the fact that a flag State is unlikely to be able to contribute to ensuring law and order at sea *after* it has granted its nationality to a vessel, when it has not ensured, *before* it granted that nationality, that there is a sufficiently close link between it and the vessel. In other words, the requirement of genuineness must be defined purposively in the light of the duties of the flag States, including those mentioned in article 94 of the LOSC.[186]

As far as legislative jurisdiction is concerned, there is no apparent need for anything more than registration. In fact, the easier it is to establish the legal relationship of nationality, the easier it is for States to extend the application of their normative provisions at sea on the ground of flag State jurisdiction.[187] The same reasoning applies to adjudicative jurisdiction and, at first sight, to executive jurisdiction. Indeed, the easier it is to establish the legal relationship between a State and a vessel, the easier it is for the flag State to justify the exercise of its executive powers at sea. However, the problem is that the exercise of its executive jurisdiction by a flag State requires much greater means than the exercise of its legislative and adjudicative jurisdictions, which, in most if not all cases, takes place on land.[188] In fact, the means that are required for a State to exercise its executive jurisdiction everywhere at sea are so great that it has never been convincingly argued that any flag State has ever had such means. It might be that technological developments have already reached a point where, on paper, the systematic and consistent exercise of their executive jurisdictions by the flag States is possible.[189] However, until a consensus arises as to the use of the technology and until the necessary financial and human resources are available,[190] the requirement of genuineness cannot be aimed at ensuring a systematic and consistent exercise of executive jurisdiction because the latter will remain inevitably sporadic and erratic.[191]

184 See further below.
185 See e.g., Churchill (n. 167) 38.
186 See e.g., F-M Fay "La nationalité des navires en temps de paix" (1973) 77 RGDIP 1000–1080 at 1022–1023; Cogliati-Bantz (n. 46) 403.
187 The downside, however, is an increase in the number of conflicts of laws. See further below.
188 See Chapter 2.
189 See e.g., BS Kothari *The Role of Technology in Maritime Security: A Survey of its Development, Application and Adequacy* (2008) 48–81.
190 See e.g., JP Craven "The technology and the law of the sea: The effect of prediction and misprediction" (1985) 45 *Louisiana Law Review* 1143–1160 at 1151.
191 See e.g., Gidel (n. 23) I 74. See further Chapter 5 section 5.5.5.

Instead, a more realistic understanding of the genuineness requirement is that it aims to address the inability of flag States to exercise their executive jurisdiction systematically and consistently *at sea*, by requiring that the link between the State and the vessel is such that the flag State is able to exercise its executive jurisdiction *on land* whenever necessary.[192] This was made abundantly clear during the 1950–1956 ILC deliberations on matters regarding the high seas.[193] The inability of the flag State to exercise its executive jurisdiction systematically and consistently at sea can be addressed to some extent when the vessel is within a port of the flag State but, as the rapporteur pointed out, the vessel might never call at such a port. The solution alluded to by the rapporteur is to require that the link between the State and the vessel include at least one element on the basis of which the flag State may exercise its personal jurisdiction over one or more of the natural and/or juristic persons who control the vessel. As indicated above, the ILC devoted a lot of efforts during its deliberations to the pursuit of identifying the said elements.[194]

(ii) Discussions at the International Law Commission The Commission based its first discussion of the matter on the rapporteur's second report. In the latter, the rapporteur conceded that it was not possible to propose a set of uniformly applicable rules.[195] At the same time, he argued, on the basis of a comparison with the nationality of persons, that "a certain minimum" was required and that it could be determined by letting oneself be guided by the principles adopted by the great majority of States.[196] The rapporteur then referred to the work undertaken 50 years earlier by the Institute of International Law (IDI).[197] It is important to point out that the IDI was not attempting to determine the minimum content of the genuine link, but was trying to ensure that each merchant vessel only had one nationality[198] in order to avoid disputes between States in the application of the laws of war at sea and tax legislation as well as private and commercial law whenever the relevant rules of private international law require the application of the law of the flag State.[199] To the latter end, the IDI proposal did set the bar very high when it required that at least two-thirds of the shares in the ship be owned either: (i) by natural persons who are nationals of the State or have been domiciled in the State for an uninterrupted period of at least five years; or (ii) by juristic persons controlled by natural persons at least two-thirds of whom are nationals of the State or have been domiciled in the State for an uninterrupted period of at least five years.[200] In addition, the seat of the

192 See e.g., Cogliati-Bantz (n. 46) 414.
193 See UN Doc. A/CN.4/42 (n. 49) § 3).
194 See section 3.2.5.2(b).
195 See UN Doc. A/CN.4/42 (n. 49) § 2, quoting Higgins & Colombos (n. 142) 19.
196 *Ibid.* § 3.
197 (1896) 15 AIDI 51.
198 *Ibid.* 53.
199 *Ibid.* 51–53.
200 *Ibid.* 72.

business had to be located in the territory of the State.[201] In contrast, the proposal stated that it was not necessary for the captain or the members of the crew to have the nationality of the State.[202]

After referring to the IDI proposal, the ILC rapporteur summarised the findings of his own comparative survey of national legislation[203] before proposing to set the bar somewhat lower than the IDI had done by requiring that at least half of the shares in the ship be owned either: (i) by natural persons who are nationals of the State or who are established in the State; (ii) by a partnership or commandite company of which more than half of the personally liable associates are nationals of the State or who are established in the State; or (iii) a joint stock company having its seat in the territory of the State.[204] In addition, the proposal required that the captain have the nationality of the flag State.[205]

As indicated above, the members of the Commission turned their attention to the requirements for the establishment of the legal relationship of nationality after they had resolved that the discretion of States was indeed limited by certain principles of international law.[206] Unfortunately, the Commission's deliberations were from the very beginning affected by the separate issue of whether "a State might refuse to recognize the right of a ship to fly a particular flag when its nationality had been acquired in violation of the rules".[207] In other words, the Commission did not focus on ascertaining the minimum conditions that had to be met for a genuine link to exist. Rather, the Commission assumed, despite the fact that the rapporteur's second report had not touched on the matter, that States had the right not to recognise the nationality granted by another State to a vessel, and focussed its attention on ascertaining the minimum conditions that had to be met for the grant to be recognised.[208] Nevertheless, the deliberations shed useful light on the meaning of "genuineness".

At the outset, the members of the ILC agreed to adopt, with regard to the issue of recognition of a grant of nationality to a vessel, the ownership requirement proposed by the rapporteur.[209] However, they rejected the nationality requirement regarding the captain.[210] The rapporteur proceeded on that basis in his third report[211] and in his sixth report.[212] At the start of the discussions on the draft article 10 proposed in the latter report, one of the members expressed his concern that "the

201 *Ibid.*
202 *Ibid.*
203 UN Doc. A/CN.4/42 (n. 49) § 6–17.
204 *Ibid.* § 18.
205 *Ibid.*
206 See section 3.2.5.2(b).
207 (1951) I YILC 330 § 49.
208 *Ibid.* § 59.
209 *Ibid.* § 60–127.
210 *Ibid.*
211 See UN Doc. A/CN.4/51 (n. 154) 44–45. The Commission did not discuss the report during its fourth session ((1952) I YILC 223 § 38) and its fifth session ((1953) I YILC 367–368 § 51–59).
212 See UN Doc. A/CN.4/79 (n. 155) § 4. See also the draft article 10 and its commentary (at 10–11).

time was not yet ripe for achieving the ideal in the shape of a generally accepted law for universal application, and little purpose would be served by striving to draw up a set of perfect rules which would have no chance whatsoever of adoption".[213] Nevertheless, the Commission continued to discuss the draft provisions,[214] which were amended, mainly by removing the condition regarding the nationality of the captain, to become article 5 of the ILC's Provisional Draft Articles on the High Seas.[215]

That provision received a relatively high number of replies from governments.[216] While the majority of them suggested only minor amendments, some proposed more substantial changes aimed at shortening the provision. The Netherlands proposed to shorten the provision in such a way that it would merely state that "there must exist a genuine connexion between the State and the ship".[217] However, they did not do so having the issue of recognition in mind, but because "[t]hey doubt[ed] whether it [was] possible to lay down detailed regulations which the State granting the right to fly its flag [was] bound to observe".[218] There is no doubt that the Netherlands were aware that the issue of recognition was distinct from that of the conditions of grant. Indeed, they indicated that, apart from the issue of recognition, which they saw as being

> aim[ed] only at the prevention of abuse in a negative way, the Netherlands Government deem[ed] it desirable to prescribe that States by taking the necessary legal measures create safeguards lest ships flying their flag disregard their legislation as to the safety at sea etc.[219]

As far as it is concerned, the United Kingdom did agree that "it would be preferable for the articles to be confined to broad principles which are established in international law".[220] At the same time, the United Kingdom expressed the concern that, the way article 5 was drafted, it did not "provide for the control and jurisdiction which, according to the Commission's comment to article 5, should be effectively exercised by the flag State".[221] For that reason, the United Kingdom proposed that it be a condition for the grant of nationality that "the flag State [be] in a position to exercise, and does exercise, effective jurisdiction and control over ships flying its flag, and the right to fly its flag is limited and regulated accordingly by its domestic

213 (1955) I YILC 13 § 70.
214 *Ibid.* § 7–25.
215 See UN Doc. A/2934 (n. 161) 20–34.
216 See UN Doc. A/CN.4/97/Add.1 (n. 163) § 38–59. See further UN Doc. A/CN.4/99 and Add.1 to 9 (n. 163).
217 UN Doc. A/CN.4/97/Add.1 (n. 163) § 50.
218 *Ibid.* § 17.
219 UN Doc. A/CN.4/99/Add.1 (n. 163) § 17.
220 *Ibid.* § 23.
221 *Ibid.*

law".[222] In addition, a State would be allowed to "permit a ship that would be entitled to fly its own national flag under domestic law, to fly the flag of another State, provided the requirement of the exercise of effective jurisdiction and control on the part of that other State [was] fulfilled".[223]

During the ensuing deliberations, there was clear support for the British and Dutch amendments.[224] However, that support was not always wholehearted. Indeed, one of the members expressed the concern that "[b]ehind the stress on the necessity for 'genuine connexion between the State and the ship' was probably the fear of competition from States with very liberal registration laws".[225] He nevertheless believed that the formulation was better than "detailed conditions [which] might have some effect on the freedom of the high seas".[226] Article 5, redrafted by a sub-committee[227] to provide that "there must exist a genuine link between the State and the ship",[228] was then adopted without objection.[229] That formulation thus appeared in article 29(1) of the Final Draft Articles,[230] in his commentary of which the rapporteur explained that the Commission "thought it best to confine itself to enunciating the guiding principle" because it did "not consider it possible to state in any greater detail what form th[e] link should take".[231] He stressed that, although this was admittedly "a vague criterion", it was better than "no criterion at all".[232] That was because the Commission wished not only to leave States "a wide latitude" in determining the conditions for the grant of their nationality to ships, but also

> to make it clear that the grant of its flag to a ship cannot be a mere administrative formality, with no accompanying guarantee that the ship possess a real link with its new State. The jurisdiction of the State over ships, and the control it should exercise [...], can only be effective where there exists in fact a relationship between the State and the ship other than mere registration or the mere grant of a certificate of registry.[233]

(iii) Developments at and after UNCLOS I As indicated above, article 29(1) formed the basis of the debates at the 1958 UN Conference on the Law of the Sea (UNCLOS I). At the outset of the proceedings in the Conference's Second Committee, the Netherlands proposed that the provision be amended to state that there must exist "a genuine link between the ship and the state, enabling the latter

222 *Ibid.*
223 *Ibid.*
224 See e.g., (1956) I YILC 37 §§ 22 and 26.
225 *Ibid.* § 25.
226 *Ibid.*
227 *Ibid.* 38 § 41 and 67 § 37.
228 *Ibid.* 66 § 34.
229 *Ibid.* 72 § 32.
230 See UN Doc. A/3159 (n. 164) 278 and UN Doc. A/CONF.13/40 (n. 49) 113.
231 UN Doc. A/3159 (n. 164) § 3.
232 *Ibid.*
233 *Ibid.*

to exercise the control necessary to ensure observance of the rule and regulations concerning navigation on the high seas".[234] That formulation had the advantage of distinguishing the issue of the recognition of the grant of nationality from the issue of the conditions for that grant. It also had the advantage of striking a better balance between, on the one hand, the vague concept of the "genuine link" and, on the other, detailed prescriptions regarding ownership, by stressing what the purpose of the genuine-link requirement is. Together with many other States,[235] the United Kingdom agreed,[236] while it believed, once again together with other States,[237] that, "[i]n view of the complexity of the issue, [...] the effective translation of the principle of the genuine link into practical rules required further thought and discussion".[238] For that reason, India was of the opinion, while it supported the principle of the "genuine link", that it was too early for it to be included in an instrument.[239]

While there was thus consensus on the fact that more than a formal link was required and that the additional elements of the link would have to be thrashed out at a later stage, Liberia expressed its concern, like one of the ILC members had done earlier that year,[240] that the deliberations around those issues were affected by "fear of competition from states with very liberal registration laws".[241] In other words, the debate around the meaning of genuineness was not only influenced by the need to ensure that the flag State is able to comply with its duties regarding the vessels flying its flag, but by entirely different considerations. In fact, Liberia went as far as to contend that the purpose of the conditions for the grant of nationality laid down in domestic laws and regulations "was not to secure compliance with the rules governing the high seas; they were based merely on those states' domestic, economic or social policies".[242] In that regard, Panama stated that "[f]or a long time certain maritime states, but by no means all of them, had been much concerned at the fact that for reasons of economy, and to some extent of security too, several shipping companies preferred their vessels to be registered in countries like Panama".[243] As far as it is concerned, Israel had no difficulty in acknowledging that

> [i]t would be difficult and hazardous for the Conference to reach a practical solution of the problem raised by the concept of the "genuine link" without studying the economic and social factors involved, which were

234 UN Doc. A/CONF.13/40 (n. 49) § 20.
235 For instance, China (§ 23), Panama (§ 35) and Liberia (§ 32). See also UN Doc A/CONF.13/C.2/L.12/Rev.l ((1958) IV *UNCLOS I Official Records* 119)).
236 UN Doc. A/CONF.13/40 (n. 49) § 27.
237 For instance, Australia (§ 26); Israel (§ 12) and the United States (§ 15).
238 UN Doc. A/CONF.13/40 (n. 49) § 28. See also UN Doc A/CONF.13/C.2/L.86 ((1958) IV *UNCLOS I Official Records* 138).
239 UN Doc. A/CONF.13/40 (n. 49) § 10.
240 See above.
241 UN Doc. A/CONF.13/40 (n. 49) § 33.
242 *Ibid.* § 35.
243 *Ibid.* § 23.

not sufficiently documented. Maritime states that subjected their merchant marines to normal taxes and obligations and to strict shipping laws would no doubt be interested in the universal application of such a regulation.[244]

Ultimately, the Committee adopted an Italian proposal,[245] as amended by France[246] and the Committee's drafting group, to add at the end of the paragraph the sentence: "In particular, the State must effectively exercise its jurisdiction and control in administrative, technical and social matters over ships flying its flag".[247] As a result, the Committee inserted into the provision a further factor contributing to confusion: the separate issue of the duty of the flag State *after* nationality is granted. When article 29(1) was put to the vote in the plenary, El Salvador readily agreed that "the Conference was entitled to lay down certain general conditions governing the grant of nationality to ships", but it proposed that the words "Nevertheless, for purposes of recognition of the national character of the ship by other States" be deleted because they "seemed to offend against the principle of sovereignty".[248] The provision so amended was adopted unanimously, thereby removing the separate issue of the recognition of the grant of nationality from the provision on the conditions for such a grant.

Article 5(1) was included *verbatim* as provision 140 of the Main Trends Working Paper which served as the basis for deliberations at UNCLOS III.[249] During the latter third session in 1975, as already indicated earlier, the informal consultative group on the high seas decided to remove the words which had been added as a result of the adoption of the Italian proposal at UNCLOS I because those words now also appeared in provision 142 (which ultimately became article 94(1) of LOSC).[250] The new wording appeared in Article 77 of Part II of the ISNT,[251] Article 79 of Part II of the RSNT[252] and Article 91 of the ICNT.[253]

As indicated earlier, the need for a dedicated process aimed at identifying the elements required for there to be a genuine link between a State and a vessel to which it grants its nationality had repeatedly been acknowledged during UNCLOS I. States did turn their attention to that matter as soon as UNCLOS III was coming to an end. However, the forum where they did so was not a law-of-the-sea forum, but the United Nations Conference on Trade and Development (UNCTAD). The latter's Committee on Shipping, during its third special session in 1981, did adopt

244 *Ibid.* § 12.
245 See UN Doc A/CONF.13/C.2/L.28 in UN Doc. A/CONF.13/40 (n. 49) 123.
246 See UN Doc A/CONF.13/C.2/L.93 in UN Doc. A/CONF.13/40 (n. 49) 141.
247 UN Doc. A/CONF.13/38 (1958) § 13–14 ((1958) II *UNCLOS I Official Records* 95).
248 *Ibid.* § 3.
249 See UN Doc. A/CONF.62/L.8/Rev.1 (1974), Annex II, Appendix I ((2009) III *UNCLOS III Official Records* 130).
250 Nordquist (n. 49) 105 § 91.5, referring to C.2/Blue Paper No 7 (n. 138) provision 142 and C.2/Blue Paper No 9/Rev 1 (n. 138) provision 142.
251 See UN Doc. A/CONF.62/WP.8/Part II (1975) (n. 138) 164.
252 See UN Doc. A/CONF.62/WP.8/Rev.1/Part II (1976) (n. 138) 165.
253 See UN Doc. A/CONF.62/WP.10 (1977) (n. 138) 18.

a resolution calling for "the conditions under which open-registry countries retain or accept vessels on their registers" to be tightened.[254] Although several States objected to the resolution on the ground that it violated the right of States to determine their own registration requirements,[255] the UN General Assembly decided, in 1982, that a conference should be convened to consider the adoption of an international agreement.[256] That conference, which met in 1984, 1985 and 1986,[257] produced the Registration Convention.

The preamble to the Convention makes no mention of the issue of recognition of the grant of nationality which, as was pointed out earlier, was separated from that of the conditions of grant during UNCLOS I. Instead, it starts by stressing "the need to promote the orderly expansion of world shipping as a whole".[258] It then stresses[259] that the expansion was expected to be a part of the International Development Strategy for the Third United Nations Development Decade[260] that aimed at the establishment of a new international economic order through *inter alia* "an increase in the participation by developing countries in world transport of international trade".[261] At the same time, the preamble acknowledges that, while it is for each State to "fix the conditions for the grant of its nationality to ships",[262] "there must exist a genuine link between a ship and a flag State".[263] The preamble then explains that the States parties' duties to exercise effectively their jurisdiction and control over vessels flying their flags requires that "those who are responsible for the management and operation of a ship [...] are readily identifiable and accountable".[264]

To that end, the Convention compels each State party to set conditions concerning the participation of its nationals in the manning and/or the ownership of a vessel, for the grant of its nationality to that vessel.[265] As far as ownership is concerned, the Convention requires that the flag State includes in its laws and regulations "appropriate provisions for participation by that State or its nationals as owners of ships flying its flag or in the ownership of such ships and for the level of such participation".[266] The Convention refrains from setting minimum requirements and merely requires that the laws and regulations must "be sufficient to permit the flag State to exercise effectively its jurisdiction and control over ships flying

254 Sohn *et al.* (n. 48) 51.
255 *Ibid.* 52.
256 Resolution 37/209 (20 December 1982).
257 See § 2 of the Final Act of the UN Conference on Conditions for Registration of Ships ((1987) 26 ILM 1229).
258 First paragraph of the preamble.
259 Second paragraph of the preamble.
260 Annexed to UN General Assembly Resolution 35/56 (5 December 1980).
261 Paragraph 128 of the Strategy.
262 Seventh paragraph of the preamble.
263 Third paragraph of the preamble.
264 Fifth paragraph of the preamble.
265 See article 7.
266 Article 8(2).

its flag".[267] As far as manning is concerned, the Convention requires that each State Party observes "the principle that a satisfactory part of the complement consisting of officers and crew of ships flying its flag be nationals or persons domiciled or lawfully in permanent residence in that State".[268] That principle must be applied "on a ship, company or fleet basis",[269] having regard to:

> (a) the availability of qualified seafarers within the State of registration, (b) multilateral or bilateral agreements or other types of arrangements valid and enforceable pursuant to the legislation of the State of registration, [and] (c) the sound and economically viable operation of its ships.[270]

The Convention is not in force and it is unlikely that it will ever be.[271] The main reason is probably that the issue of the conditions for the grant of nationality to ships is obscured by the problem of flags of convenience, which "seems, broadly, to derive from international competition in the shipping and fishing industry [...]".[272] Although the provisions of the Convention are relatively flexible, they are nevertheless seen by many States as an unacceptable interference in that competition, even when attenuated by provisions on joint ventures, measures to protect the interests of labour-supplying countries and measures to minimise adverse economic effects.[273] However, the Convention confirms the crucial point made earlier that the genuine-link requirement aims to address the inability of flag States to exercise their executive jurisdiction systematically and consistently *at sea*, by requiring that the link between the State and the ship is such that the flag State is able to exercise its executive jurisdiction *on land* whenever necessary. Indeed, the Convention requires that the flag State has "a competent and adequate national maritime administration",[274] one of the main duties of which is to ensure that the State has adequate information about the owners or operators of the ships flying its flag in order to be able to identify them "for the purpose of ensuring their full accountability".[275] That accountability is possible because, as indicated above, either the State's nationals are "owners of ships flying its flag or in the ownership of such ships" at an adequate level of participation[276] or "a satisfactory part of the complement consisting of officers and crew of ships flying its flag [are] nationals or persons domiciled or lawfully in permanent residence in" the State.[277]

267 *Ibid.*
268 Article 9(1).
269 Article 9(3).
270 Article 9(2).
271 See Churchill, Lowe & Sander (n. 44) 467.
272 Tanaka (n. 52) 196. See also e.g., McConnell (n. 85) 449); L Lucchini & M Voelckel *Droit de la Mer* (1990) I 283; Rayfuse (n. 75) 27.
273 See articles 13–15.
274 Article 5(1).
275 Article 6(6).
276 Article 8(2).
277 Article 9(1).

Another attempt at reaching a binding agreement was made a few years later by the Food and Agriculture Organisation (FAO) during the process leading to the adoption of the Compliance Agreement. The first draft of the Agreement contained a provision that listed factors to be taken into account when a State determines whether there exists a genuine link.[278] The provision was however removed when it became clear that no agreement would be reached.[279] Such a provision is also absent in the Fish Stocks Agreement adopted in 1995. A decade later, an ad hoc consultative meeting of senior representatives of DOALOS, the FAO, the International Labour Organisation (ILO), the IMO and UNCTAD, convened by the IMO on the subject of the genuine link, reached the conclusion that "the questions relating to the precise criteria or conditions adopted by a State with respect to the grant of its nationality to a ship were a matter beyond the purview of the organizations participating in the Meeting".[280]

(D) THE RECOGNITION OF GENUINENESS[281]

As indicated above, the ILC deliberations regarding the requirements that need to be met for the grant of nationality to be valid were from the very beginning affected by the separate issue of whether "a State might refuse to recognize the right of a ship to fly a particular flag when its nationality had been acquired in violation of the rules".[282]

It will be recalled that article 5 of the ILC's Provisional Draft Articles on the High Seas[283] received a relatively high number of replies from governments[284] and that, while the majority of them suggested only minor amendments, some proposed more substantial changes aimed at shortening the provision.[285] As far as they were concerned, the Netherlands expressed their uneasiness with the last sentence

278 See article IV(2)(a) of the draft Agreement on the Flagging of Vessels Fishing on the High Seas to Promote Compliance with Internationally Agreed Conservation and Management Measures ((1993) 9 *International Organisations and the Law of the Sea. Documentary Yearbook* 639).

279 See G Moore "The Food and Agriculture Organisation of the United Nations Compliance Agreement" (1995) 10 IJMCL 412–425 at 413.

280 IMO "Report of the Ad Hoc Consultative Meeting of senior representatives of international organisations on the 'genuine link'" § 28 (UN Doc. A/61/160 of 17 July 2006 at 9). The meeting was held on 7–8 July 2005. See also the 2009 FAO Draft Criteria for Flag State Performance (FAO "Report of the Expert Consultation on Flag State Performance" FAO Doc. FIEL/R918 Appendix F.1), which do not specify what a genuine link entails.

281 This issue relates to the scope of F jurisdiction, which is discussed in section 4.2.1 of Chapter 4. It is nevertheless discussed here for greater ease of understanding in its historical and contextual aspects.

282 (1951) I YILC 330 § 49.

283 See section 3.2.5.2(b) .

284 See UN Doc. A/CN.4/97/Add.1 (n. 163) § 38–59. See further UN Doc. A/CN.4/99 and Add.1 to 9 (n. 163).

285 See e.g., Brazil (UN Doc. A/CN.4/97/Add.1 (n. 163) § 45). See further UN Doc. A/CN.4/99 (n. 163) 40.

of article 29(1) of the Final Draft Articles[286] because it linked the genuine-link requirement to the issue of the "recognition of the national character of the ship by other States".[287] For that reason, the Netherlands proposed that the provision be amended to state that there must exist "a genuine link between the ship and the state, enabling the latter to exercise the control necessary to ensure observance of the rule and regulations concerning navigation on the high seas".[288] That formulation had the advantage of distinguishing the issue of the recognition of the grant of nationality from the issue of the conditions for that grant. The need for that distinction was also stressed by other States, including Mexico, which voiced what was undoubtedly the main concern, i.e., the fact that, "by conceding to other states the right to decide for themselves whether there was a genuine link between the ship and the flag state, the Commission had opened the door to the creation of insoluble problems".[289]

Ultimately, the last sentence of article 29(1) did not find its way into article 5(1) of the CHS, nor article 91(1) of the LOSC. On that basis, ITLOS confirmed, in *M/V "Saiga" (No 2)*, that

> the need for a genuine link between a ship and its flag State is to secure more effective implementation of the duties of the flag State, and not to establish criteria by reference to which the validity of the registration of ships in a flag State may be challenged by other States.[290]

As a result, the fact that a State "discovers evidence indicating the absence of proper jurisdiction and control by a flag State over a ship" does not entitle that State "to refuse to recognize the right of the ship to fly the flag of the flag State".[291]

At first sight, such a state of affairs might appear disturbing. Indeed, one might ask what one hopes to achieve by requiring that there be a genuine link between a State and a vessel when there appears to be no sanction in cases where that link does not exist.[292] There is no escaping the fact, however, that a right not to recognise the nationality of a vessel on the basis of the fact that the link of nationality

286 See UN Doc. A/3159 (n. 164) 259–260 and UN Doc. A/CONF.13/40 (n. 49) 113.
287 UN Doc. A/CONF.13/40 (n. 49) § 20.
288 *Ibid.* See also UN Doc A/CONF.13/C.2/L.22 ((1958) IV *UNCLOS I Official Records* 122).
289 UN Doc. A/CONF.13/40 (n. 49) § 17. See further the *Virginius* incident, the settlement of the dispute arising from which included the admission by Spain that it was not entitled to refuse to take into account that the vessel was flying the flag of the United States although the latter itself had good reason to believe that the vessel had no right to do so (see the Protocol of the conference held at the Department of State, at Washington, on the 29th of November, 1873, between Hamilton Fish, Secretary of State, and Rear-Admiral Don José Polo de Bernabé, envoy extraordinary and minister plenipotentiary of Spain dated 29 November 1873 (available at <https://history.state.gov/historicaldocuments/frus1873p1v1/d1>). See also Mc Dougal, Burke & Vlasic (n. 134) 41–42.
290 *The M/V "Saiga" (No 2)* (n. 53) § 83. See also *Commission v. Ireland*, judgment of 2 December 1992, C–280/89, EU:C:1992:481 § 23–24.
291 *The M/V "Saiga" (No 2)* (n. 53) § 82. See also *The M/V "Virginia G" Case* (n. 53) § 111.
292 See e.g., Wefers Bettink (n. 85) 86.

that it has with a State is not genuine "[i]s not justified by international practice".[293] As explained above, one of the reasons is that States are all in agreement that it is impossible to give a very precise meaning to the concept of "genuineness".[294] Therefore, States are likely to disagree with each other in that regard.[295] At the same time, many States are highly suspicious of other States' motives for advocating the adoption of specific requirements as well as what they perceive as attempts to interfere with their sovereignty.[296] In these conditions, it is difficult not to conclude that it would be against the principle of peaceful international co-operation to allow a State to challenge the ground of jurisdiction of another State on the basis that there is no genuine link between the latter State and a vessel[297] without the endorsement of a competent body.[298]

What the above means is that, while the existence of a genuine link is a requirement for the establishment of the legal relationship of nationality, it is not a requirement for all purposes. Indeed, the absence of a genuine link does not have an impact on the *scope* of the jurisdiction of the flag State. In other words, whether a genuine link exists does not matter when it comes to determining the extent of the jurisdictions of the States involved in any given situation.[299] By contrast, the absence of a genuine link has an impact on the *purpose* of the jurisdiction of the flag State. In other words, whether a genuine link exists does matter when it comes to the reasons for which flag State jurisdiction is attributed to States.[300] That is the case regarding the fulfilment of the duties spelled out in article 94 of the LOSC.[301] That is also the case, for instance, regarding high-seas fishing because, without a genuine link, a State party to the Compliance Agreement will find it very difficult to be "satisfied that it is able, taking into account the links that exist between it and the fishing vessel concerned, to exercise effectively its responsibilities under th[e] Agreement in respect of" the vessel when it decides whether to grant an authorisation to fish on

293 (1956) I YILC 70 § 3. See also e.g., the *Magda Maria Case* ((1989) 20 *Netherlands Yearbook of International Law* 349 at 351); Mc Dougal, Burke & Vlasic (n. 134) 54. See however e.g., JHW Verzijl *International Law in Historical Perspective* (1972) V 149; Churchill (n. 167) 39.

294 The concept has been criticised for that reason (see e.g., McDougal, Burke & Vlasic (n. 134) 28–43). However, as was pointed during UNCLOS I, "[d]ifficulty of definition in no way invalidate[s] the force of a principle and, after all, even fundamental constitutional principles of different countries sometimes required interpretation by the courts" (UN Doc. A/CONF.13/40 (n. 49) § 53).

295 See e.g., Cogliati-Bantz (n. 46) 410.

296 See UN Doc. A/CONF.13/40 (n. 49) § 21.

297 *Ibid.* § 2.

298 See e.g., UNSC Resolution 787 (1992) (16 November 1992).

299 See further Chapter 4.

300 See e.g., UNGA Resolution 58/240 (23 December 2003) § 28; IMO "Report of the Ad Hoc Consultative Meeting of senior representatives of international organisations on the 'genuine link'" § 28 (UN Doc. A/61/160 (17 July 2006) 9); Cogliati-Bantz (n. 46) 403.

301 See *Strengthening of Flag State Implementation. Submitted by the Secretariat of the IMO* (UN Doc. A/AC.259/11 (11 May 2004) § 14.

the high seas.[302] The same applies regarding the duties of the flag States in terms of article 18 of the Fish Stocks Agreement.

2.2.5.3 Additional requirements and restrictions

States are free to accept binding requirements and restrictions regarding the vessels that they are prepared to register. Although States have generally been reluctant to do so,[303] one can find examples of additional requirements in treaty provisions in terms of which a State Party may "not reduce the ownership requisite for registration below 50%".[304] In *Muscat Dhows*, the arbitrators confirmed that "a Sovereign may be limited by treaties in the exercise of" its right "to decide to whom [it] will accord the right to fly [its] flag and to prescribe the rules governing such grants".[305] The instrument in question was the General Act of the Brussels Conference Relative to the African Slave Trade of 2 July 1890, article 32 of which limited the competence of the States parties to grant their flags to vessels "for the purpose of suppressing slave trading and in the general interests of humanity, irrespective of whether the applicant for the flag may belong to a state signatory of th[e] Act or not [...]".[306]

Other examples of additional restrictions to the discretion of a State to set the requirements for the grant of its nationality to vessels are found in European Union (EU) law. In that regard, the European Court of Justice (ECJ) stated in *Poulsen* that "[i]t was for the State that conferred its nationality in the first place to determine at its absolute discretion the conditions on which it would grant its nationality".[307] Two days later, in *Commission v. Ireland*, the ECJ repeated, without using the term "absolute discretion", that "under international law a vessel has the nationality of the State in which it is registered and that it is for that State to determine in the exercise of its sovereign powers the conditions for the grant of such nationality".[308] It must be stressed, however, that the cases did not relate to the maintenance of law and order at sea, which, as was explained above, appears to be the purpose of the requirement of genuineness. Instead, the disputes revolved around the application of the EU-law rules on non-discrimination and freedom of establishment.

In the *Factortame* cases, the United Kingdom had amended its legislation regarding the conditions for the grant of the British nationality to ships "in order

302 Article 3(3) of the Agreement. See further e.g., Moore (n. 279) 413; A D'Andrea *The "Genuine Link" Concept in Responsible Fisheries: Legal Aspects and Recent Developments* (2006) 9; R Rayfuse "Article 117" in Proelss (n. 57) 803–817 at 811. See further Chapter 5 section 5.4.3.

303 LB Sohn *et al. Cases and Materials on the Law of the Sea* (2014) 117.

304 König (n. 82) § 21.

305 GG Wilson (ed) *The Hague Arbitration Cases* (1915) 72–73.

306 *Ibid.* 73.

307 *Anklagemyndigheden v. Poulsen and Diva Navigation*, judgment of 24 November 1992, C–286/90, EU:C:1992:453 § 15.

308 *Commission v. Ireland* (n. 290) § 24. The Advocate General did not deal with Ireland's genuine-link argument which, in his opinion, had to be rejected on a procedural basis (see § 11).

to put a stop to the practice known as 'quota hopping' whereby, according to the United Kingdom, its fishing quotas [were] 'plundered' by vessels flying the British flag but lacking any genuine link with the United Kingdom".[309] Factortame and the European Commission argued that the amended rules constituted discrimination on ground of nationality.[310] The Court confirmed that "competence to determine the conditions for the registration of vessels [was] vested in the Member States".[311] As a result, it is

> for the Member States to determine, in accordance with the general rules of international law, the conditions which must be fulfilled in order for a vessel to be registered in their registers and granted the right to fly their flag, but, in exercising that power, the Member States must comply with the rules of Community law.[312]

The United Kingdom argued, referring to article 5(1) of the CHS, that the position was different "when it comes to the competence of each State under public international law to define as it thinks fit the conditions upon which it grants to a vessel the right to fly its flag".[313] To this, the Court replied curtly that

> [t]hat argument might have some merit only if the requirements laid down by Community law with regard to the exercise by the Member States of the powers which they retain with regard to the registration of vessels conflicted with the rules of international law.[314]

This statement can only mean that, as far as the Court is concerned, member States do not have to choose between complying with their global-international-law obligations and complying with their regional-law obligations when setting the conditions for the registration of vessels because those two sets of obligations do not conflict. The Court refrained however from explaining what it understood the States' global-international-law obligations to entail. As the AG explained, the Court did not have to do so because, insofar as compliance with EU rules "in relations between the Member States does not jeopardise non-member countries' rights under the 1958 Geneva Convention", as was the case in the dispute, the United Kingdom could not "rely on that Convention in order to justify infringements of those rules". Those infringements consisted in a violation of article 7 (prohibition

309 *Factortame* (n. 49) § 4. See further §§ 5–7.

310 *Commission v. United Kingdom, Factortame II*, judgment of 4 October 1991, C–246/89, EU:C:1991:375 § 9.

311 *Factortame* (n. 49) § 13. See also *Factortame II* (n. 310) § 11.

312 *Factortame* (n. 49) § 14. See also *Factortame II* (n. 310) § 12.

313 *Factortame II* (n. 310) § 13.

314 *Ibid.* § 14.

of discrimination),[315] article 52 (freedom of establishment)[316] and article 221 ("obligation to accord nationals of the other Member States the same treatment as their own nationals as regards participation in the capital of companies or firms within the meaning of Article 58")[317] of the EU Treaty as a result of the setting by the United Kingdom of the requirement that

> a fishing vessel is to be eligible to be registered in the register only if:
> "(a) the vessel is British-owned;
> (b) the vessel is managed, and its operations are directed and controlled, from within the United Kingdom; and
> (c) any charterer, manager or operator of the vessel is a qualified person or company".[318]

It must be stressed that the ruling of the ECJ only applied to the relationships between the United Kingdom and the other EU member States while the United Kingdom was a member of the EU. The Court did not pronounce on whether the requirement was valid with regard to States which are not members of the EU.[319]

3.2.6 Cessation and change of the legal relationship

The legal relationship of nationality between a State and a vessel can come to an end for several reasons. As was mentioned earlier with regard to *Grand Prince*, one possible reason is the expiration of the period of validity of a provisional registration.[320] Another possible reason is the fact that the vessel is actually or constructively lost, burnt or broken up.[321]

315 *Ibid.* § 18.
316 *Ibid.* § 31.
317 *Ibid.* § 33.
318 *Ibid.* § 4.
319 See also e.g., *Commission v. France*, judgment of 7 March 1996, C–334/94, EU:C:1996:90; *Commission v. Greece*, judgment of 27 November 1997, C–62/96, EU:C:1997:565; *Commission v. Ireland*, judgment of 12 June 1997, C–151/96, EU:C:1997:294; *Commission v. Netherlands*, judgment of 14 October 2004, C–299/02, EU:C:2004:620; *International Transport Workers' Federation and Finnish Seamen's Union v. Viking Line ABP and OÜ Viking Line Eesti*, judgment of 11 December 2007, C–438/05, EU:C:2007:772; *Deutscher Naturschutzring — Dachverband der deutschen Natur- und Umweltschutzverbände eV v. Germany*, judgment of 13 June 2018, C–683/16, EU:C:2018:433; *The North of England P & I Association Ltd v. Bundeszentralamt für Steuern*, judgment of 15 April 2021, C–786/19, EU:C:2021:276; *Anklagemyndigheden v. VAS Shipping ApS (formerly Sirius Shipping ApS)*, opinion delivered on 10 June 2021, C–71/20, EU:C:2021:474.
320 See section 3.2.4.3.
321 See e.g., section 62 of the Merchant Shipping Act, 1958 (Act 44 of 1998), of India; F Chevillard "Le statut du navire en fin de vie" in A de Marffy-Mantuano (ed) *Droit International de la Mer et Droit de l'Union Européenne* (2014) 275–289.

Further possible reasons are the need to receive effective protection[322] and a change of ownership in the ship. Such a change occurred in *Tomimaru*,[323] where ITLOS agreed that "[c]onfiscation changes the ownership of a vessel", but it also stressed that "ownership of a vessel and the nationality of a vessel are different issues".[324] For that reason, the Tribunal ruled that "the confiscation of a vessel does not result *per se* in an automatic change of the flag or in its loss".[325]

Changes of ownership also take place as part of voluntary business transactions, sometimes for the specific purpose of breaking the legal relationship of nationality between a vessel and the flag State so as to remove the ground on which the latter may exercise jurisdiction over the vessel. Such a step is often taken as part of a practice, referred to as "flag hopping", that involves "repeated and rapid changes of a vessel's flag for the purposes of circumventing international legal requirements regarding ship safety, labo[u]r conditions, protection of the marine environment, and fishery management and conservation".[326] The ILC was aware of this practice[327] when it included in article 30 of its Final Draft Articles, the sentence that stated that "[a] ship may not change its flag during a voyage or while in a port of call, save in the case of a real transfer of ownership or change of registry".[328] As a middle path, the sentence was "intended to condemn any change of flag which cannot be regarded as a *bona fide* transaction".[329] During UNCLOS I, a proposal by the Netherlands that the sentence be removed was overwhelmingly rejected.[330] A proposal by the United States that the wording of the sentence be amended suffered the same fate.[331] The reason appears to be that replacing the words "change of registry" with "change of documentation", as the United States proposed, "implied that a ship changed its nationality and flag whenever it changed its papers".[332] However, as was already explained above,[333] "[t]he change of a ship's papers [is] a consequence of the change of registry. Therefore the International Law Commission's text seemed preferable from the juridical point of view".[334] Ultimately, the sentence found its way *verbatim* in article 6(1) of the CHS and article 92(1) of the LOSC.

The sentence has been criticised for appearing "to authorise a change of flag upon the high seas without change of registry, thus destroying the security of

322 See e.g., the statement by Under Secretary for Political Affairs, MH Armacost, before the US Senate Foreign Relations Committee on 16 June 1987 ((1987) 26 ILM 1429–1431). See further e.g., Sucharitkul (n. 83) 421.
323 *The "Tomimaru" Case* (n. 176).
324 *Ibid.* § 70.
325 *Ibid.*
326 Sohn *et al.* (n. 48) 62. See also Birnie (n. 67) 271; Moore (n. 279) 412 fn. 3.
327 See UN Doc. A/3159 (n. 164) § 3.
328 *Ibid.* 260.
329 *Ibid.* 279.
330 See UN Doc. A/CONF.13/40 (n. 49) § 47.
331 *Ibid.* § 50.
332 UN Doc. A/CONF.13/40 (n. 49) § 33.
333 See section 3.2.4.3.
334 UN Doc. A/CONF.13/40 (n. 49) § 33.

the registry and encouraging artistry in quick and fraudulent change of flags".[335] However, there appears to be no basis for interpreting the sentence that way. This would have been made clear by the second amendment proposed by the United States at UNCLOS I, an amendment that entailed replacing the words "may not change its flag" with the words "may not change its nationality, and hence its flag".[336] Indeed, no State appears to have had any doubt that the sentence refers to changes of nationality and not changes of flags *per se*.[337] In other words, the sentence refers to changes of flags that may not lawfully occur without a change of nationality, because they flow from the latter.[338] From that perspective, the sentence may not be interpreted as allowing changes of flag without changes of registry when registration is required for the establishment of the legal relationship of nationality in terms of the domestic law of the States concerned because, as was confirmed earlier, the setting of the requirements for the establishment of that relationship is within the exclusive competence of the States.[339] Any doubt in that regard would have been removed had the States acted on the suggestion that the words "in the case of a real transfer of ownership or change of registry" be replaced by the words "in accordance with the laws of the States concerned".[340] The latter are indeed where the answer to flag hopping lies.

That answer appears to consist in States ensuring that their legislation empower them to vet the loss of their nationality, for instance by blocking the deregistration of vessels on their registries. The States' exclusive competence to determine the conditions for the grant of their nationalities to ships must surely also include the determination of the conditions for the loss of the nationalities,[341] so as to protect the important principle that "a State could not afford any ship a means of escaping the jurisdiction of the State under which it had previously been registered".[342] That principle might give rise to the fear that the State of registration would have "the power of absolute veto on any change of registration",[343] something that would be undesirable.[344] In practice, however, the competition between flag States makes it unlikely that the exercise of that power by the flag States would be so wide as to render their nationalities unattractive due to the fear that a ship would be "locked" inside a nationality at the full discretion of the flag State.[345] The vetting power should however be wide enough to enable flag States to prevent the loss of their nationalities whenever such a step is needed to combat an unacceptable practice

335 M McDougal & W Burke *The Public Order of the Oceans* (1962) 1086.
336 UN Doc. A/CONF.13/C.2/L.41 (1958) § 2 ((1958) IV *UNCLOS I Official Records* Annexes 127).
337 See e.g., UN Doc. A/CONF.13/40 (n. 49) § 19.
338 See section 3.2.4.1.
339 See section 3.2.5.1.
340 UN Doc. A/CONF.13/40 (n. 49) §§ 15 and 17.
341 See e.g., Kamto (n. 48) 356.
342 (1956) I YILC 67 § 37.
343 *Ibid.* § 56.
344 *Ibid.* § 44.
345 It has already been pointed out above that the registration of vessels is a competitive process.

such as flag hopping.[346] At the same time, States other than the flag State should ensure that they do not allow the establishment of a legal relationship of nationality between themselves and vessels of which the loss of a foreign nationality is blocked. Were they not to do so, issues related to a multiplicity of co-existing legal relationships of nationality would arise.

3.2.7 Multiplicity of legal relationships

Article 92(1) of the LOSC states that "[s]hips shall sail under the flag of one State only". Read with article 91(1),[347] this provision is understood to mean that vessels may not have multiple nationalities.[348] The Registration Convention confirms "the principle generally prohibiting a state from granting its nationality to a ship already authorised to fly the flag of another state [...]"[349] by providing that a ship must not "be entered in the registers of ships of two or more States at a time [...]".[350] To that end, "[b]efore entering a ship in its register of ships a State should assure itself that the previous registration, if any, is deleted".[351] When the legal relationship of nationality flows from registration, the deletion results in the termination of the relationship. There are however cases, such as when a ship is chartered on a bareboat basis,[352] where it is convenient for the first registration not to be deleted.[353] In those cases, the Convention does not require that the first registration be deleted, but merely that the registration and the related right to fly the flag of the relevant State be suspended.[354] In other words, while two legal relationships of nationality are in existence during the period of the charter, the registration that is in effect is that of the second State and the vessel only has the right to fly the flag of that State.[355]

346 It must be stressed that the power of the flag State to block, or at least delay, the break of the link of nationality is not unknown in legislation presently in force. For instance, in South African law, a court may, in the case where the vessel concerned is subject to an unsatisfied mortgage, make "an order that the registration may not be regarded as closed for the period that the court may determine" (s. 42(6)(c) of the SRA).

347 See section 3.2.4.1.

348 See e.g., D Guilfoyle "Article 92" in Proelss (n. 57) 700–704 at 702.

349 Sohn *et al.* (n. 48) 48.

350 Article 4(4).

351 Article 11(4).

352 See e.g., section 18(1) of the 1989 Registration of Merchant Ships Act of Belize; *The North of England* (n. 319). See further Ademuni-Odeke "An examination of bareboat charter registries and flag of convenience registries in international law" (2005) 36 ODIL 339–362 at 344–346; Ready (n. 61) 36–38.

353 See Pancracio (n. 21) 78. On other cases, see e.g., Kamto (n. 48) 354–355, who mentions the loan of a flag, the use of a vessel for a non-commercial purpose of a foreign State and the judicial sale.

354 See article 11(5).

355 See article 12(1). See further e.g., section 24(1) of the Merchant Shipping Act, 2014 (Act 75 of 2014), of Denmark. On the dual nationality of vessels, see e.g., LFE Goldie "Recognition and dual nationality – A problem of flags of convenience" (1963) 39 BYIL 220–283.

3.2.8 Artificial objects other than ships

There is an increasing variety of artificial objects at sea. Many objects that one would not immediately consider as ships can be assimilated to ships by adopting a broad definition of the term. For instance, for purposes of the Ship Registration Act, 1981,[356] of Australia, the meaning of the word "ship" includes "a structure that is able to float or be floated and is able to move or be moved as an entity from one place to another".[357] This would include an offshore oil rig which, in international law, appears "to be regarded as having the nationality of the State of registry while [it is] in transit [...]".[358] It would also include an installation for "the transmission of sound radio or television broadcasts".[359] The LOSC assumes that scientific research installations and equipment must be registered in a State when they do not belong to an international organisation.[360] In this regard, the Convention appears to be at odds with State practice, which is not uniform,[361] and it seems that, "[i]f no registration occurred, the emplacing state or the state of the owner of the objects may exercise jurisdiction".[362] Nevertheless, the position in terms of the LOSC is shared by the 1993 Draft Convention on Ocean Data Acquisition Systems, Aids and Devices (Second Revision), which provides for ocean data acquisition systems (ODASs)[363] to be registered in "a special register",[364] an ODAS having "the nationality of the State in which it is registered".[365] However, no final text has been adopted yet.[366] In the absence of flags, the LOSC requires that scientific research

356 Act 8 of 1981.

357 Section 3(1).

358 Staker (n. 3) 300. See also Barnes (n. 87) 311.

359 Article 109(2) read with article 109(3)(b) of the LOSC. See e.g., D Guilfoyle "Article 109" in Proelss (n. 57) 763–767 at 766. By contrast, it would appear that "a glider cannot be considered as a ship under the international law of the sea [...]" (T Hofmann & A Proelss "The operation of gliders under the international law of the sea" (2015) 46(3) ODIL 167–187 at 176).

360 See article 262 read with article 258. See also e.g., I Papanicolopulu "Article 262" in Proelss (n. 57) 1746–1749 at 1748; K Bork *et al.* "The legal regulation of floats and gliders In quest of a new regime?" (2008) 39 ODIL 298–328 at 309.

361 See Papanicolopulu (n. 360) 1748.

362 Bork (n. 360) 313. See also e.g., L Caflisch & J Piccard "The legal regime of marine scientific research and the Third United Nations Conference on the Law of the Sea" (1978) 38 *Zeitschrift für ausländisches öffentliches Recht und Völkerrecht* 848–901 at 889.

363 An ODAS is defined as "a structure, platform, installation, buoy or other device, not being a ship, together with its appurtenant equipment deployed at sea for non-military purposes essentially for the purpose of collecting, storing or transmitting samples and data relating to the marine environment or the atmosphere or the uses thereof" (article 1(2)).

364 Article 10(1), which adds that "[n]o ODAS may be registered by more than one Registry State". See also article 10(4).

365 Article 11(2).

366 See e.g., A Proelss "International legal challenges concerning marine scientific research in the era of climate change" in HN Scheiber, J Kraska & M-S Kwon (eds) *Science, Technology and New Challenges to Ocean Law* (2015) 280–295 at 291.

installations and equipment "bear identification markings indicating the State of registry".[367]

3.3 Coastal zone jurisdictions

3.3.1 Introduction

The relative importance of flag State jurisdiction is linked to the geographical extent of the high seas. Indeed, flag State jurisdiction was by far the main ground of State ocean jurisdiction while only some confined bodies of water, as well as a very narrow strip of water adjacent to the coast, had a different status.[368] The broadening of that strip and the creation of additional maritime zones since the Second World War has been an arduous process that culminated in diplomatic compromises taking the form of complex legal regimes.[369] As a result, flag State jurisdiction has not given significant way to a single "coastal (State) jurisdiction", as it is often referred to,[370] but rather to several "coastal zone jurisdictions". Indeed, the latter do not all play the same role within the State ocean jurisdiction regime. That explains why the connecting factors and the scopes of the jurisdictions are not the same. That also explains why it is necessary, for present purposes, to distinguish between, on the one hand, territorial jurisdiction[371] and, on the other, the extraterritorial coastal zone jurisdictions, i.e., contiguous zone jurisdiction,[372] exclusive economic zone jurisdiction[373] and continental shelf jurisdiction.[374]

3.3.2 Territorial jurisdiction

3.3.2.1 Introduction

The LOSC refers to the three forms of territorial jurisdiction ("T jurisdiction"), i.e., legislative territorial jurisdiction ("TL jurisdiction"), executive territorial

367 Article 262.

368 See further section 3.3.2.3.

369 See e.g., R-J Dupuy *L'Océan partagé* (1979) 19–27; JA Knauss "Creeping jurisdiction and customary international law" (1985) 15 ODIL 209–216; B Kwiatkowska "Creeping Jurisdiction beyond 200 miles in the light of the 1982 Law of the Sea Convention and State practice" (1991) 22 ODIL 153–188 at 159–160; S Kaye "Maritime security in the post 9/11 world: A new creeping jurisdiction in the law of the sea?" in C Schofield, S Lee & M-S Kwon (eds) *The Limits of Maritime Jurisdiction* (2014) 327–348 at 328; EJ Molenaar "New maritime zones and the law of the sea" in H Ringbom (ed) *Jurisdiction over Ships* (2015) 249–277.

370 See e.g., GG Schram "The case for coastal State jurisdiction" (1974–1975) 44 *Nordisk Tidsskrift for International Ret* 17–26; A Bardin "Coastal State's jurisdiction over foreign vessels" (2002) 14 *Pace International Law Review* 27–76; DR Rothwell & T Stephens *The International Law of the Sea* (2016) 17; Tanaka (n. 52) 9–10; EJ Molenaar "Multilateral creeping coastal State jurisdiction and the BBNJ negotiations" (2021) 36 IJMCL 5–58.

371 See section 3.3.2.

372 See section 3.3.3.

373 See section 3.3.4.

374 See section 3.3.5.

jurisdiction ("TE jurisdiction") and adjudicative territorial jurisdiction ("TA jurisdiction"), in a number of its provisions. For instance, article 21(1) provides that "[t]he coastal State may adopt laws and regulations, in conformity with the provisions of th[e] Convention and other rules of international law, relating to innocent passage through the territorial sea [...]". Article 28(1) states that "[t]he coastal State should not stop or divert a foreign ship passing through the territorial sea [...]". As far as it is concerned, article 32 provides that, "[w]ith such exceptions as are contained in [articles 17 to 26] and in articles 30 and 31, nothing in th[e] Convention affects the immunities of warships and other government ships operated for non-commercial purposes".

The connecting factor that is the basis of T jurisdiction is the fact that the matter in one way or another relates to the marine component of the territory of the State.[375] Whether the connecting factor exists in a specific set of facts depends on whether the State claiming that it has T jurisdiction is the coastal State.[376] If that is the case, the State has a maritime territory[377] and one needs to establish whether a link exists between the matter and the territory.[378]

3.3.2.2 The concept of "coastal State"

The LOSC does not provide a definition of the term "coastal State" despite the fact that it occurs in a large number of its provisions.[379] However, several of those provisions[380] make it clear that, if a State is not a coastal State, it is a "land-locked State", a term which the LOSC defines as "a State which has no sea-coast". Thus, the LOSC defines the term "coastal State" indirectly as "a State having a sea coast".[381] What the LOSC does not do, even indirectly, is to

> provide guidance on the identification of the "coastal State" in cases where sovereignty over the land territory fronting a coast is disputed. Nor is

375 Compare e.g., § 408 comment (a) *Restatement of the Law (Fourth)* (n. 2). One was reminded a century ago that to "call part of the sea 'territory' [...] is etymologically incorrect. Nevertheless 'territory' is now a term of international law with well-defined connotations. It has long been used adjectively of the marginal sea" (PC Jessup *The Law of Territorial Waters and Maritime Jurisdiction* (1927) 453).

376 See section 3.3.2.2.

377 See section 3.3.2.3.

378 See section 3.3.2.4.

379 See e.g., articles 2(1), 33(1), 56(1) and 76(1).

380 Articles 17, 58(1), 87(1), 90, 140(1) and 141 of the LOSC.

381 *Chagos Marine Protected Area Arbitration (Mauritius v. United Kingdom)*, award of 18 March 2015, XXXI RIAA 359 § 203. Compare e.g., R Churchill "Under-utilised coastal State jurisdiction: Causes and consequences" in Ringbom (n. 369) 278–298 at 278. Low-tide elevations (i.e. the "naturally formed area[s] of land which [are] surrounded by and above water at low tide but submerged at high tide" (article 13(1) of the LOSC)) "do not form part of the land territory of a State in the legal sense" (*In the Matter of the South China Sea Arbitration (Philippines v. China)*, award of 12 July 2016, XXXIII RIAA 153 § 309).

> provision made for circumstances of war or secession in which a coast might effectively be occupied by authorities exercising de facto governmental powers, or other complex permutations of territorial sovereignty, such as condominium governments. In each of these cases, the identity of the coastal State for the purposes of the Convention would be a matter to be determined through the application of rules of international law lying outside the international law of the sea.[382]

The application of those rules is expressly allowed by article 293(1) of the LOSC, provided that they are not incompatible with the Convention. That does not mean that the rules will actually be applied in any given case.

This is illustrated by *Chagos*. The 2015 arbitral award in that case was the outcome of arbitration proceedings initiated by Mauritius against the United Kingdom pursuant to article 287 of the LOSC and in accordance with article 1 of Annex VII to the Convention,[383] after the United Kingdom had established a marine protected area (MPA) around the Chagos Archipelago. One of the elements of the claim of Mauritius was that "the United Kingdom [was] not 'the coastal State' (within the meaning of the 1982 Convention) and so [was] not entitled to declare an 'MPA' (or indeed any other maritime zone) around the Chagos Archipelago".[384] However, three of the five arbitrators declined to deal with the issue.[385] They did so after having characterised the claim as relating to land sovereignty, a matter that did not relate to the interpretation or application of the LOSC within the ambit of article 288(1) of the LOSC, on which the arbitral tribunal's jurisdiction was based.[386]

As far as it is concerned, the ICJ had an opportunity to express its advisory opinion on the sovereignty dispute in 2019 when it stated that "the United Kingdom ha[d] an obligation to bring to an end its administration of the Chagos Archipelago as rapidly as possible, and that all Member States must co-operate with the United Nations to complete the decolonization of Mauritius".[387] In its Resolution 73/295, the UN General Assembly welcomed the opinion of the ICJ and "[d]emand[ed] that the United Kingdom of Great Britain and Northern Ireland withdraw its colonial administration from the Chagos Archipelago unconditionally".[388] However, the United Kingdom has made it clear that it still considers itself bound by the arbitral award.[389] As a result, whether the United Kingdom is the coastal State in

382 *Chagos Marine Protected Area Arbitration* (n. 381) § 203.

383 In terms of article 287(5) of the LOSC, the dispute could only be submitted to arbitration in accordance with Annex VII because the parties had not accepted the same procedure for the settlement of the dispute.

384 Final Transcript 16:6–9.

385 *Chagos Marine Protected Area Arbitration* (n. 381) § 221.

386 *Ibid.* § 220.

387 *Legal Consequences of the Separation of the Chagos Archipelago from Mauritius in 1965*, advisory opinion of 25 February 2019, ICJ General list No 169 § 182.

388 Paragraph 3. The Resolution was adopted on 22 May 2019 by 116 votes to 6 and 56 abstentions (UN Doc. A/73/PV.83 (22 May 2019) § 25).

389 Paragraph 9.14 of the Written Statement of the United Kingdom to the ICJ.

the case of the Archipelago remains a disputed matter.[390] In this regard, ITLOS explained in *Maritime Boundary between Mauritius and Maldives* that, while

> [a]n advisory opinion is not binding because even the requesting entity is not obligated to comply with it in the same way as parties to contentious proceedings are obligated to comply with a judgment [...], judicial determinations made in advisory opinions carry no less weight and authority than those in judgments because they are made with the same rigour and scrutiny by the "principal judicial organ" of the United Nations with competence in matters of international law.[391]

In addition, the Tribunal considered that, "[i]n light of the general functions of the General Assembly on decolonization and the specific task of the decolonization of Mauritius with which it was entrusted, [...] resolution 73/295 is relevant to assessing the legal status of the Chagos Archipelago".[392] On that basis, ITLOS concluded that Mauritius could "be regarded as the coastal State in respect of the Chagos Archipelago for the purpose of the delimitation of a maritime boundary even before the process of the decolonization of Mauritius is completed".[393]

While the abovementioned pronouncements illustrate the fact that the *Chagos* dispute is very much alive,[394] the disputes regarding the claims to sectors of Antarctica[395] are dormant since the coming into effect of the 1959 Antarctic Treaty,[396] article IV of which has the effect of freezing those claims and the related counterclaims.[397]

390 See further e.g., LN Nguyen "The Chagos Marine Protected Area Arbitration: Has the scope of LOSC compulsory jurisdiction been clarified?" (2016) 31 IJMCL 120–143; W Qu "The issue of jurisdiction over mixed disputes in the Chagos Marine Protected Area Arbitration and beyond" (2016) 47 ODIL 40–51; S Talmon "The Chagos Marine Protected Area Arbitration: Expansion of the jurisdiction of UNCLOS Part XV courts and tribunals" (2016) 65 ICLQ 927–951; PHG Vrancken & SY Ntola "Land sovereignty and LOSC: The Chagos Marine Protected Area Arbitration (*Republic of Mauritius v. United Kingdom*)" (2014) 39 SAYIL 105–134; J-L Iten "L'avis consultatif de la Cour internationale de Justice du 25 février 2019 sur les *Effets juridiques de la séparation de l'archipel des Chagos de Maurice en 1965*" (2019) 123 RGDIP 391–408; P Vrancken "The identity of the coastal State – Reflections following two judicial pronouncements in the Chagos Archipelago dispute" (2019) 1 (2) *Seychelles Research Journal* 15–24.

391 *Dispute Concerning Delimitation of the Maritime Boundary between Mauritius and Maldives in the Indian Ocean (Mauritius v. Maldives)*, judgment of 28 January 2021, ITLOS Case No. 28 § 203.

392 *Ibid.* § 227.

393 *Ibid.* § 250.

394 See also e.g., *Dispute Concerning Coastal State Rights in the Black Sea, Sea of Azov, and Kerch Strait (Ukraine v. Russia)*, award of 21 February 2020, PCA Case No 2017-06 § 154.

395 By Argentina, Australia, Chile, France, New Zealand, Norway and the United Kingdom.

396 402 UNTS 71. Adopted: 1 December 1959; EIF: 23 June 1961.

397 See further e.g., B Conforti "Territorial claims in Antarctica: A modern way to deal with an old problem" (1986) 19 *Cornell International Law Journal* 249–258; P Vrancken "Southern limit of the international seabed area" (1995) 20 SAYIL 144–181; KN Scott "Managing sovereignty and jurisdictional disputes in the Antarctic: The next fifty years" (2010) 20 *Yearbook of International*

3.3.2.3 The existence of the marine territory

Pakistan is one of the States the legislation of which states that the State's sovereignty "has always extended" to its territorial sea.[398] However, such a statement is "historically incorrect: the true picture of the development of the concept is rather more complex".[399] It is correct that it was very early accepted that clearly defined small bodies of ocean waters immediately adjacent to the shore, such as ports and small coastal indentations, are part of the territory of the coastal States.[400] By contrast, only a century has passed since all States have come to regard narrow strips of waters along their whole coasts, together with the seabed and subsoil beneath those waters as well as the airspace above those waters, as part of their territory.[401] Today, the LOSC confirms that the territory of a coastal State includes, beyond its land territory, the waters up to the outer limit of its territorial sea as well as the airspace above those waters and the seabed and subsoil beneath those waters.[402]

It is not only clear that the territories of the coastal States extend offshore along their whole coasts, but it is also clear that this is the case as a matter of course. This was confirmed in 1909 by the arbitral tribunal called upon to rule in *Grisbadarna*.[403] In other words, all coastal States automatically have a territorial sea.[404] This means that the existence of the T jurisdiction of a coastal State does not depend on the performance by an organ of that State of a legislative act producing a legislative instrument containing a constitutive provision establishing the territorial sea.[405]

Environmental Law 3–40; SV Scott "Ingenious and innocuous? Article IV of the Antarctic Treaty as imperialism" (2011) 1 *The Polar Journal* 51–62.

398 See section 2(1) of the Territorial Waters and Maritime Zones Act, 1976.

399 Churchill, Lowe & Sander (n. 44) 130.

400 See e.g., Gidel (n. 23) II 35–37.

401 See articles 1(1) and 2(1) of the text adopted by the 1930 Hague Conference for the Codification of International Law on the legal status of the territorial sea (League of Nations Doc. C. 351. M. 145. 1930. V. at 165). See also e.g. P Vrancken "The marine component of the South African territory" (2010) 127 *South African Law Journal* 207–223; § 408 comment (a) *Restatement of the Law (Fourth)* (n. 2). On the complexities that may arise as a result of land being divided into several States, see e.g., *Land, Island and Maritime Frontier Dispute (El Salvador v. Honduras, Nicaragua intervening)*, judgment of 11 September 1992, 1992 ICJ Reports 351 § 385 and 401; *Bay of Piran (Croatia v. Slovenia)*, award of 29 June 2017, PCA Case No 2012–04 § 882–883; D Arnaut "Adriatic blues: The former Yugoslavia's final frontier" in Schofield, Lee & Kwon (n. 369) 145–173.

402 See article 2(1)–(2). Those waters include not only the waters of the territorial sea, but also the internal waters and, in the case of an archipelagic State, its archipelagic waters (see articles 8(1) and 49(1)). See further Chapter 4 section 4.3.1.

403 *Grisbadarna Case (Norway v. Sweden)*, award of 23 October 1909, XI RIAA 147 at 159.

404 See the *obiter* statement of Judge McNair in his dissenting opinion in the *Norwegian Fisheries Case (United Kingdom v. Norway)*, judgment of 18 December 1951, 1951 ICJ Reports 116 at 160. See also e.g., O'Connell (n. 52) I 52.

405 By contrast, constitutive provisions are required to determine the extent of the marine component of the territory of the coastal State and, therefore, the scope of its territorial jurisdiction (see further Chapter 4 section 4.3.1). Normative provisions also have to be made to apply to the marine component of the State's territory (see e.g., O'Connell (n. 52) I 52.

3.3.2.4 The link between the matter and the territory

As indicated earlier, for a coastal State to have T jurisdiction in an ocean-related matter, the latter must in one way or another be linked to the marine component of the territory of the State. The link is clear when all the aspects of the matter relate to that component. The existence of T jurisdiction is also clear when some of the aspects of the matter relate to the marine component of the territory of the coastal State and the other aspects of the matter or incident relate to the land component.[406] This is because, as far as international law is concerned, a State exercises its jurisdiction on the same spatial ground in the entirety of its territory. In other words, although there are limitations to the *scope* of territorial jurisdiction in the marine component of the territory of the coastal State that do not exist in the land component, the *ground* of jurisdiction is the same in that it is exercised within the territory of the State, over which the latter has sovereignty.[407]

As in the case of F jurisdiction,[408] the position is not as obvious when some of the aspects of the matter relate to the marine component of the territory of the coastal State and the other aspects of the matter relate to waters beyond the outer limit of the territorial sea or within the territorial sea of an adjacent State. For instance, the perpetrator of a crime might be outside the territorial sea and the victim of the crime inside the territorial sea and vice versa. In such a case,

> [i]nternational law seems [...] to have satisfied itself with requiring that either the criminal act or its effects have taken place within a State's territory for the State to legitimately exercise territorial jurisdiction, irrespective of the municipal characterization of the act or the effects (in practice, usually the effects) as a constituent element of the offense.[409]

This means that a coastal State also has a ground to exercise T jurisdiction when a matter was initiated on the landward side of the outer limit of the territorial sea, but was completed beyond that limit. This form of T jurisdiction is based on subjective territoriality and may be referred to as subjective territorial jurisdiction ("Ts jurisdiction").[410] It also means that a coastal State has a ground to exercise T jurisdiction when the matter was initiated beyond the outer limit of the territorial sea, but was completed on the landward side of that limit. This form of T jurisdiction

406 In civil matters, a very tenuous link is sometimes sufficient to establish the connecting factor giving rise to T jurisdiction in the sense that, when the defendant is not physically present in the territory of the State, his, her or its "constructive presence" suffices. That would be the case "where circumstances establish a basic level of contact by the defendant with the forum state sufficient to justify the exercise of jurisdiction over him", her or it (Jennings & Watts (n. 2) 458).

407 See article 2(1)–(2). See further e.g., RA Barnes "Article 2" in Proelss (n. 57) 27–34 at 32.

408 See section 3.2.2.

409 C Ryngaert *Jurisdiction in International Law* (2015) 78.

410 See § 408 comment (c) *Restatement of the Law (Fourth)* (n. 2).

is based on objective territoriality and may be referred to as objective territorial jurisdiction ("To jurisdiction").[411]

In most instances, the answer to the question whether a State has To jurisdiction depends to a large extent on how the matter concerned is defined.[412] For instance, States have full authority over radio and television communications within their territory and that authority includes the control of both elements of those communications, i.e., their broadcasting and their reception, as well as taking the necessary steps to eliminate interferences with the communications.[413] This means that, in an instance where communications are broadcast beyond the outer limit of a coastal State's territorial sea but received within the State's territory, at least one element of the communications – their reception – is sufficiently related to the coastal State for the latter to have To jurisdiction. ToA jurisdiction in that case is confirmed by article 109(3)(d) of the LOSC when "the transmission of sound radio or television broadcasts" is "intended for reception by the general public contrary to international regulations".[414] It is important to note that the provisions of the LOSC directly relating to radio and television communications do not give jurisdiction to a State in cases of mere threats of broadcasting.[415]

The existence of To jurisdiction has given risen to debate when the link between a matter and the territory of the State claiming to have To jurisdiction has been perceived as being too tenuous because the matter arose entirely outside the territory of the State and only the effects or impact of the matter are felt in that territory. The danger posed by extending the connecting factor of T jurisdiction to include such a case (the so-called "effects doctrine") is that the concepts of "effect" and "impact" are difficult to define and their meaning can be stretched to such an extent that T jurisdiction would allow a State to exercise its authority in a matter that does not have a sufficiently close connection with that State. While jurisdiction based on the effects doctrine has been interpreted as a form of To jurisdiction,[416] it is arguably best to see it as a form of protective jurisdiction in order not to taint the otherwise uncontroversial character of To jurisdiction.[417]

411 See e.g., *The "Enrica Lexie" Incident* (n. 35) § 366; § 408 comment (c) *Restatement of the Law (Fourth)* (n. 2).

412 See e.g., Gallagher & David (n. 51) 219.

413 See e.g., Churchill, Lowe & Sander (n. 44) 397.

414 Article 109(2) of the LOSC, which expressly excludes "the transmission of distress calls". See also article 109(3)(e) in the case "where authorized radio communication is suffering interference".

415 See article 109(3) confers ToA jurisdiction over "[a]ny person *engaged* in unauthorized broadcasting" (emphasis added). On whether a State has protective jurisdiction in such a case, see section 3.9, and Chapter 4 section 4.12.

416 See e.g., A Abass *Complete International Law* (2014) 532; Buxbaum (n. 16) 635.

417 See e.g., Akehurst (n. 58) 154. See further Chapter 4 section 4.12.

3.3.3 Extraterritorial coastal zone jurisdictions

3.3.3.1 Contiguous zone jurisdiction

A second ground of coastal zone jurisdiction is contiguous zone jurisdiction ("Cz jurisdiction"), in the case of which the connecting factor that is the fact that the matter in one way or another relates to the contiguous zone of the State. Whether the connecting factor exists in a specific set of facts depends on whether the State claiming that it has Cz jurisdiction is a coastal State, whether the State has a contiguous zone and whether a link exists between the matter and the zone of the State. What has been discussed for the purposes of T jurisdiction regarding the first aspect applies *mutatis mutandis* for the purposes of Cz jurisdiction. That is not the case regarding the third aspect, because of the limited scope of Cz jurisdiction,[418] and the second aspect.

In contrast to the territorial sea, coastal States do not automatically have a contiguous zone[419] and only 60% of them have claimed one.[420] The development of the concept was complex[421] and, to a large extent, linked to the issue of the width of the territorial sea.[422] Nevertheless, although agreement was not reached on the issue during UNCLOS I, an agreement was reached on the existence of the contiguous zone and a dedicated provision included in the 1958 Convention on the Territorial Sea and the Contiguous Zone.[423] The first two paragraphs of that provision are reproduced without relevant changes for present purposes in article 33 of the LOSC. This provision is arguably best understood as only conferring an inchoate Cz jurisdiction on coastal States.[424] In other words, the only form of Cz jurisdiction that coastal States always have is the legislative jurisdiction ("CzL jurisdiction") to perform a legislative act producing a legislative instrument containing a constitutive provision having the effect of proclaiming a contiguous zone. It is only if and when that proclamation is made that the coastal State has full Cz jurisdiction, including, for instance, the CzL jurisdiction to perform a legislative act producing

418 See further Chapter 4 section 4.5.1.

419 See e.g., Churchill, Lowe & Sander (n. 44) 206.

420 See e.g., *Alleged Violations of Sovereign Rights and Maritime Spaces in the Caribbean Sea (Nicaragua v. Colombia)*, judgment of 21 April 2022, ICJ Case No 155 § 149; D-E Kahn "Article 33" in Proelss (n. 57) 254–271 at 270. See also e.g., Churchill (n. 381) 284–286; W Gullett "Can the contiguous zone be used for environmental protection purposes?" in K Zou (ed) *Sustainable Development and the Law of the Sea* (2017) 39–57 at 55–56.

421 See e.g., Gidel (n. 23) III 361–488; AV Lowe "The development of the concept of the contiguous zone" (1981) 52 BYIL 109–169; *Church v. Hubbart* 6 US (2 Cranch) 187 (1804).

422 See e.g., FV Garcia Amador *The Exploitation and Conservation of the Resources of the Sea* (1963) 59; R-J Dupuy "La mer sous compétence nationale" in Dupuy & Vignes (n. 51) 219–273 at 236; Pancracio (n. 21) 218.

423 516 UNTS 206. Adopted: 29 April 1958; EIF: 10 September 1964. See article 24.

424 See e.g., K Aquilina "Territorial sea and the contiguous zone" in DJ Attard (ed) *The IMLI Manual of International Maritime Law* (2014) I 26–70 at 60. This is also the case with regard to the archaeological aspects of the jurisdiction of the coastal State in the space concerned (see e.g., MJ Aznar "The contiguous zone as an archaeological maritime zone" (2014) 29 IJMCL 1–51 at 49–50).

a legislative instrument containing a constitutive provision setting the width of the zone, and the executive jurisdiction ("CzE jurisdiction") to perform a legislative act producing a legislative instrument containing a performative provision giving power to one or more organs of the State to perform executive acts in the exercise of the State's CzE jurisdiction.[425]

3.3.3.2 Exclusive economic zone jurisdiction

When they have both been proclaimed, the contiguous zone overlaps with the (much larger) EEZ,[426] the conceptual development of which was very quick in that it took only the three decades leading to the adoption of the LOSC for the existence of the zone to be recognised in article 55 of the Convention,[427] immediately after which its customary international status was confirmed by the ICJ in *Libya/Malta Continental Shelf*.[428] The connecting factor that is the basis of exclusive economic zone jurisdiction ("Eez jurisdiction") is the fact that the matter in one way or another relates to the EEZ of the State. As in the case of Cz jurisdiction, whether the connecting factor exists in a specific set of facts depends on whether the State claiming that it has Eez jurisdiction is a coastal State, whether the State has an EEZ and whether a link exists between the matter and the EEZ of the State. Except in the case of islands that "cannot sustain human habitation or economic life of their own",[429] the position is the same as for Cz jurisdiction to the extent that what has been discussed for the purposes of T jurisdiction regarding the first and third aspects applies *mutatis mutandis* for the purposes of Eez jurisdiction. That is not the case regarding the second aspect.

As in the case of the contiguous zone, coastal States do not automatically have an EEZ.[430] For that reason, as in the case of Cz jurisdiction, Eez jurisdiction is argu-

425 See further Chapter 4 section 4.5.1.

426 Compare articles 33(2), 55 and 57 of the LOSC.

427 See e.g., NS Rembe *Africa and the International Law of the Sea* (1980) 116–123; FV García-Amador "The origins of the concept of an exclusive economic zone: Latin American practice and legislation" in F Orrego Vicuña (ed) *The Exclusive Economic Zone – A Latin American Perspective* (1984) 7–26; Pancracio (n. 21) 170–175; A Proelss "Article 55" in Proelss (n. 57) 408–418 at 411–415.

428 *Case Concerning the Continental Shelf (Libya v. Malta)*, judgment of 3 June 1985, 1985 ICJ Reports 13 § 34. A decade earlier, the ICJ had confirmed that "[t]wo concepts have crystallized as customary law in recent years arising out of the general consensus revealed at [UNCLOS II]. The first is the concept of the fishery zone, the area in which a State may claim exclusive fishery jurisdiction independently of its territorial sea; the extension of that fishery zone up to a 12-mile limit from the baselines appears now to be generally accepted. The second is the concept of preferential rights of fishing in adjacent waters in favour of the coastal State in a situation of special dependence on its coastal fisheries [...]" (*Fisheries Jurisdiction Case (Germany v. Iceland)*, judgment of 25 July 1974, 1974 ICJ Reports 175 § 44; *Fisheries Jurisdiction Case (Great Britain v. Iceland)*, judgment of 25 July 1974, 1974 ICJ Reports 3 § 52). See also *Alleged Violations* (n. 420) § 56.

429 Article 121(3) of the LOSC. See further e.g., *In the Matter of the South China Sea Arbitration* (n. 381) § 478–553.

430 See e.g., Churchill, Lowe & Sander (n. 44) 227 and 253–254; *Alleged Violations* (n. 420) § 56.

ably best understood as being only inchoate at first. In other words, the only form of Eez jurisdiction that coastal States always have is the legislative jurisdiction ("EezL jurisdiction") to perform a legislative act producing a legislative instrument containing a constitutive provision having the effect of proclaiming an EEZ. It is only if and when that proclamation is made that the coastal State has full Eez jurisdiction, including, for instance, the EezL jurisdiction to perform a legislative act producing a legislative instrument containing a constitutive provision setting the width of the zone, and the adjudicative jurisdiction ("EezA jurisdiction") to perform a legislative act producing a legislative instrument containing a performative provision giving power to one or more organs of the State to perform adjudicative acts in the exercise of the State's EezA jurisdiction.[431]

3.3.3.3 Continental shelf jurisdiction

When an EEZ has been proclaimed, it overlaps with the legal continental shelf,[432] the extent of which is different from that of the geological continental shelf.[433] The connecting factor that is the basis of continental shelf jurisdiction ("Cs jurisdiction") is the fact that the matter in one way or another relates to the continental shelf of the State. As in the case of T jurisdiction, whether the connecting factor exists in a specific set of facts depends on whether the State claiming that it has Cs jurisdiction is a coastal State and whether a link exists between the matter and the shelf of the State. The issue of whether the coastal State has a continental shelf does not arise. Indeed, article 77(3) of the LOSC confirms that "[t]he rights of the coastal State over the continental shelf do not depend on occupation, effective or notional, or on any express proclamation". In other words, "a continental shelf exists *ipso facto* and *ab initio* and therefore need not be claimed".[434] This means that the Cs jurisdiction of a coastal State is not initially inchoate, as in the case of Cz jurisdiction and Eez jurisdiction, but, on the contrary, automatically and immediately of a full nature, as in the case of the T jurisdiction.

431 See e.g., *Bay of Piran* (n. 401) § 1065. On the States that have not proclaimed EEZs and their reasons for doing so, see e.g., Churchill, Lowe & Sander (n. 44) 295–297; S Kvinikhidze "Contemporary exclusive fishery zone or why some States still claim an EFZ" (2008) 23 IJMCL 271–295; M Grbec *Extension of Coastal State Jurisdiction in Enclosed and Semi-enclosed Seas* (2014) 76–124.

432 Compare articles 55, 57 and 76(1) of the LOSC. See also *Case Concerning the Continental Shelf* (n. 428) § 34.

433 See e.g. Churchill, Lowe & Sander (n. 44) 230. On the geological continental shelf, see e.g., CA Burk & CL Drake (eds) *The Geology of Continental Margins* (1974); J-F Pulvenis "Le plateau continental – Définition et régime des ressources" in Dupuy & Vignes (n. 51) 275–336 at 275–280.

434 Churchill, Lowe & Sander (n. 44) 227. See also *North Sea Continental Shelf (Germany v. Denmark, Germany v. Netherlands)*, judgment of 20 February 1969, 1969 ICJ Reports 3 § 19; *Dispute Concerning Delimitation of the Maritime Boundary between Ghana and Côte d'Ivoire in the Atlantic Ocean (Ghana v. Côte d'Ivoire)*, judgment of 23 September 2017, 2017 ITLOS Reports 4 § 590.

3.4 Personal jurisdiction

3.4.1 Introduction

Personal jurisdiction ("P jurisdiction") plays a less prominent place in ocean-related instruments and adjudicative processes than F jurisdiction and the coastal zone jurisdictions. It is however much older than F jurisdiction[435] and it has, in the past, played a much greater role than it does today.[436] The LOSC does deal with personal jurisdiction in a number of its provisions. An example is article 97(1) which provides that,

> [i]n the event of a collision or any other incident of navigation concerning a ship on the high seas, involving the penal or disciplinary responsibility of the master or of any other person in the service of the ship, no penal or disciplinary proceedings may be instituted against such person except before the judicial or administrative authorities [...] of the State of which such person is a national.

However, the LOSC does not use, let alone define, the term "personal jurisdiction".

The LOSC does refer to legislative personal jurisdiction ("PL jurisdiction"). For instance, article 113 provides that

> [e]very State shall adopt the laws and regulations necessary to provide that the breaking or injury [...] by a person subject to its jurisdiction of a submarine cable beneath the high seas done wilfully or through culpable negligence [...] shall be a punishable offence [...].

The LOSC also refers to executive personal jurisdiction ("PE jurisdiction"). For instance, article 110(1)(c), read with article 109(3)(c), confirms that a warship of the personal State that encounters a foreign ship on the high seas is justified in boarding the ship when "there is reasonable ground for suspecting that ... the ship is engaged in unauthorized broadcasting". Moreover, the LOSC refers to adjudicative personal jurisdiction ("PA jurisdiction") in article 109(3)(c), for instance, when it provides that "[a]ny person engaged in unauthorized broadcasting may be prosecuted before the court of [...] the State of which the person is a national".

3.4.2 Connecting factor

The connecting factor that is the ground of P jurisdiction is the fact that the matter relates to a person who has the required link with the State wishing to exercise

435 See e.g., Cogliati-Bantz (n. 46) 387.

436 See e.g., Staker (n. 3) 299; K Tuori "The beginnings of State jurisdiction in international law until 1648" in Allen *et al.* (n. 16) 25–39 at 26–27. For "arguments in favour of a move to nationality-based jurisdiction", see e.g., P Arnell "The case for nationality-based jurisdiction" (2001) 50 ICLQ 955–962 at 958–961.

that jurisdiction. That link can take two forms. In most instances, the link is of a legal nature and is referred to as "nationality" or "citizenship".[437] In addition, in an increasing number of instances, the link is, in the absence of a link of nationality, of a factual nature and consists in one form or another of residence in the State concerned.[438]

3.4.3 Legal relationship between the State and the person

"The terms 'nationality' and 'citizenship' are used interchangeably and loosely by both politicians and lawyers to indicate a connection between individual and state".[439] Article 1 of the 1930 Hague Convention on Certain Questions Relating to the Conflict of Nationality Laws (CCNL)[440] confirms that "[i]t is for each State to determine under its own law who are its nationals".[441] A State usually grant its nationality to natural persons who are born in its territory (*ius soli*), who are the children of its nationals (*ius sanguinis*) and/or who have applied for its nationality (naturalisation).[442] The link of nationality may be severed by the State concerned (deprivation) or by the individual concerned (renunciation).[443] It is possible for individuals to have more than one nationality.[444] In that case, the connecting factor might be present in relation to more than one State, which then have concurrent P jurisdictions.[445]

In contrast to the link of nationality between a State and a ship, foreign States only have to recognise the link of nationality between a natural person and a State, when the latter's nationality law "is consistent with international conventions, international custom, and the principles of law generally recognised with regard to

437 See further section 3.4.3.

438 See e.g., Staker (n. 3) 301. See further section 3.4.4.

439 J Dugard "State responsibility, diplomatic protection and the treatment of aliens" in Dugard *et al.* (n. 6) 389–441 at 407–408). Compare *Nottebohm Case* (n. 134) 23.

440 179 LNTS 89. Adopted: 12 April 1930; EIF: 1 July 1937.

441 See also e.g., *Nationality Decrees issued in Tunis and Morocco (French Zone)*, advisory opinion of 7 February 1923, 1923 PCIJ Reports, Series B, No. 4 at 24; article 3(1) of the 1997 European Convention on Nationality (ECN; 2135 UNTS 213; adopted: 6 November 1997; EIF: 1 March 2000); the commentary on article 4 of the 2006 ILC Draft Articles on Diplomatic Protection (UN Doc. A/61/10 (2006) ((2006) II YILC 29)).

442 See e.g., AH Philipse "La nationalité à la Première Conférence de Codification" (1931) 2 *Nordisk Tidsskrift for International Ret* 85–94; C Amunátegui Perelló "Race and nation: On *ius sanguinis* and the origins of a racist national perspective" (2018) 24(2) *Fundamina* 1–20; § 410 comment (b) *Restatement of the Law (Fourth)* (n. 2).

443 See e.g., G-R de Groot "The European Convention on Nationality: A step towards a *ius commune* in the field of nationality law" (2000) 7(2) *Maastricht Journal of European and Comparative Law* 117–157 at 139–148; R Bauböck & V Paskalev "Cutting genuine links: A normative analysis of citizenship deprivation" (2015) 30 *Georgetown Immigration Law Journal* 47–104.

444 See e.g., PJ Spiro *At Home in Two Countries – The Past and Future of Dual Citizenship* (2015).

445 See e.g., article 6(1) of the 2006 ILC Draft Articles on Diplomatic Protection (UN Doc. A/61/10 (n. 441) 33). See further Chapter 4 section 4.4.2.

nationality".[446] However, that issue does not have an impact on the existence of the *ground* of personal jurisdiction,[447] but on the *scope* of that jurisdiction.[448]

The establishment of a legal link between a State and a corporation "is also a matter for each State to determine under its own laws; but here the practice is more complex".[449] As the ICJ indicated in *Barcelona Traction*, no single test exists. The traditional rule establishes the link between the corporation and "the State under the laws of which it is incorporated and in whose territory it has its registered office".[450] However, some States do establish a legal link with

> a company incorporated under their law [...] solely when it has its seat (*siège social*) or management or centre of control in their territory, or when a majority or a substantial proportion of the shares has been owned by nationals of the State concerned.[451]

Like natural persons, corporations can change their nationality. However, a change of nationality "is only a real alternative if the corporation can be registered in another country and acquire a new nationality without having to be dissolved in the state of departure and reincorporated in the state of arrival (identity-preserving nationality change)".[452]

3.4.4 Factual link between the State and the person

A State might have a ground to exercise P jurisdiction over a matter relating to an individual even though there is no legal link between that State and the individual. In such a case, a factual link is necessary and that link must meet certain requirements. For instance, article 6(2)(a) of the 1988 Convention for the Suppression of Unlawful Acts against the Safety of Maritime Navigation (SUA)[453] allows a State party to establish its jurisdiction over one of the offences

446 Article 1 of the CCNL. See also e.g., article 3(2) of the 1997 European Convention on Nationality (n. 441).

447 See e.g., G-R de Groot "Sports and unfair competition via nationality law" (2006) 13(2) *Maastricht Journal of European and Comparative Law* 161–172 at 163 ("a conferral of nationality without genuine link as such is valid").

448 See further Chapter 4 section 4.4.

449 Staker (n. 3) 299.

450 *Case Concerning the Barcelona Traction, Light and Power Company, Limited, Second Phase (Belgium v. Spain)*, judgment of 5 February 1970, 1970 ICJ Reports 3 § 70. See also commentary on article 9 of the 2006 ILC Draft Articles on Diplomatic Protection (UN Doc. A/61/10 (n. 441) 37).

451 *Case Concerning the Barcelona Traction* (n. 450) § 70.

452 KE Sørensen & M Neville "Corporate migration in the European Union" (2000) 6(2) *Columbia Journal of European Law* 181–208 at 191.

453 The Convention is the 1988 Convention for the Suppression of Unlawful Acts against the Safety of Maritime Navigation (1678 UNTS 222, (1988) 27 ILM 672, (1988) 11 LOSB 14; adopted: 10 March 1988; EIF: 1 March 1992) as amended by the 2005 Protocol to the Convention (IMO Doc. LEG/CONF.15/21 (1 November 2015); adopted: 14 October 2005; EIF: 28 July 2010).

set forth in articles 3, 3*bis*, 3*ter* and 3*quater* of the Convention when "it is committed by a stateless person whose habitual residence is in that State".[454]

3.4.5 Link between the matter and the person

The link between a matter and a person is clear when the matter relates to actions or inactions of the person. For instance, the link between the breaking of a submarine cable and a person is clear when the latter directly caused the break by allowing an anchor to be dragged across the path of the cable.[455]

The question arises whether a sufficient link exists between an incident and a person in order to exercise P jurisdiction, when the person is merely a victim of the action or inaction of another person. Jurisdiction in such a case is referred to as "passive personal jurisdiction" ("Pp jurisdiction") and, "[i]n the past[,] Anglo-American countries objected strongly to this basis of jurisdiction" in criminal matters.[456] Pp jurisdiction in criminal matters relating to collisions at sea is explicitly excluded by article 1 of the 1952 Convention on Penal Jurisdiction in Matters of Collision (CPJC),[457] an exclusion reiterated in article 11(1) of the CHS as well as article 97(1) of the LOSC, the text of which has already been reproduced above.[458] In contrast, Pp jurisdiction is confirmed in instruments such as the 2000 UN Convention against Transnational Organised Crime,[459] article 15(2)(a) of which allows a State party to exercise its jurisdiction over any offence established in accordance with articles 5, 6, 8 and 23 of the Convention when "[t]he offence is committed against a national of that State Party". In civil matters, article 1(1)(b) of the 1952 Convention on Civil Jurisdiction in Matters of Collision[460] only makes room for indirect Pp jurisdiction when the personal State is also the State the TE jurisdiction of which has been exercised to arrest "the defendant ship or [...] any other ship belonging to the defendant which can be lawfully arrested, or where arrest could have been effected and bail or other security has been furnished".

3.5 Universal jurisdictions

3.5.1 Introduction

In order to maintain law and order at sea, the oldest grounds added to flag State jurisdiction, the coastal zone jurisdictions and personal jurisdiction, are those of

454 See further e.g., § 410 comment (c) *Restatement of the Law (Fourth)* (n. 2).
455 See articles 113–114 of the LOSC.
456 Dugard, du Plessis & Cohen (n. 6) 221. See also *Case Concerning the Arrest Warrant of 11 April 2000 (DRC v. Belgium)*, judgment of 14 February 2002, 2002 ICJ Reports 3, joint separate opinion of Judges Higgins, Kooijmans and Bürgenthal § 47; § 411 *Restatement of the Law (Fourth)* (n. 2); Bowett (n. 15) 10; Simma & Müller (n. 2) 142–143; Staker (n. 3) 306–307.
457 439 UNTS 235. Adopted: 10 May 1952; EIF: 20 November 1955.
458 See section 3.4.1.
459 2225 UNTS 209, (2001) 40 ILM 353. Adopted: 15 November 2000; EIF: 29 September 2003.
460 439 UNTS 219. Adopted: 10 May 1952; EIF: 14 September 1955.

universal jurisdiction.[461] The epithet "universal" does not refer to some kind of overarching jurisdiction over all matters arising anywhere. Rather, it refers to the fact that all States, irrespective of whether they are coastal States or land-locked States, hold that jurisdiction concurrently.[462]

It is more accurate not to refer to a single universal jurisdiction, but rather to several universal jurisdictions because the scopes of the universal jurisdictions vary considerably[463] and, in addition, there have different connecting factors.[464] What those factors have in common, however, is that each of them creates a link between all States and a specific kind of matters over which the community of States wants every State to have jurisdiction.[465] The three grounds of universal jurisdiction confirmed by the LOSC relate to piracy,[466] the slave trade[467] as well as the suspicion that a vessel is without nationality and the assimilation of a vessel to a vessel without nationality.[468]

3.5.2 Piracy jurisdiction

Article 105 of the LOSC confirms that piracy is a ground of universal jurisdiction (which can be referred to as "piracy jurisdiction" ("Pi jurisdiction")), when it allows "every State [to] seize a pirate ship or aircraft, or a ship or aircraft taken by piracy and under the control of pirates, and arrest the persons and seize the property on board".[469] This means that a connecting factor exists between all States and a specific act when the latter constitutes a piratical act as defined in the LOSC.[470] An inordinate amount of efforts has been devoted to discussing that definition and it falls beyond the scope of this book to review the relevant literature

461 See e.g., S McVeigh "Critical approaches to jurisdiction and international law" in Allen *et al.* (n. 16) 182–205 at 192.

462 See e.g., *The "Enrica Lexie" Incident* (n. 35) § 1074. See further e.g., R O'Keefe "Universal jurisdiction: Clarifying the basic concept" (2004) 2 JICJ 735–760; C Ryngaert "Cosmopolitan jurisdiction and the national interest" in Allen *et al.* (n. 16) 209–227 at 212; M Chadwick *Piracy and the Origins of Universal Jurisdiction* (2019) 193.

463 See further Chapter 4 section 4.8.1.

464 See below in this section.

465 See e.g., § 407 *Restatement of the Law (Fourth)* (n. 2).

466 See section 3.5.2.

467 See section 3.5.3.

468 See section 3.5.4. There are arguably other (non-ocean-specific) grounds of universal jurisdiction (see e.g., § 413 *Restatement of the Law (Fourth)* (n. 2). See however e.g., Bowett (n. 15) 11–14.

469 States do so in fulfilment of their duty, codified in article 100 of the LOSC, to "cooperate to the fullest possible extent in the repression of piracy [...]". See e.g., P-M Dupuy & C Hoss "La chasse aux pirates par la communauté internationale. Le case de la Somalie" in SE Bedjaoui *et al* (eds) *L'Afrique et le Droit International: Variations sur l'Organisation Internationale* (2013) 135–146 at 136.

470 See article 101. See e.g., Brown (n. 51) I 300. For arguments to the effect that Pi jurisdiction should be eliminated, see J Goodwin "Universal jurisdiction and the pirate: Time for an old couple to part" (2006) 39 *Vanderbilt Journal of Transnational Law* 973–1011 at 1002–1007.

comprehensively.[471] Suffice it to say that the act must fall within any one of three categories.

The first category includes "illegal acts of violence or detention, or any act of depredation, committed for private ends by the crew or the passengers of a private ship or a private aircraft, and directed"[472] either: (i) beyond the outer limits of the territorial seas "against another ship or aircraft, or against persons or property on board such ship or aircraft";[473] or (ii) "against a ship, aircraft, persons or property in a place outside the jurisdiction of any State".[474] The second category includes acts "of voluntary participation in the operation of a ship or of an aircraft with knowledge of facts making it a pirate ship or aircraft".[475] The third category includes acts "of inciting or of intentionally facilitating an act" falling within one of the other categories.[476]

It is important to note that piracy might "involve relatively minor uses of force; and not every act of piracy can properly be described as heinous.[477] Yet for centuries, piracy was covered by universal jurisdiction, but murder, armed robbery, rape and arson on land, which could surely be equally heinous, were (and are) not".[478]

3.5.3 Slave trade jurisdiction

The LOSC confirms that engaging in the slave trade at sea is a ground of universal jurisdiction, which can be referred to as "slave trade jurisdiction" ("Sl jurisdiction"). More concretely, a connecting factor exists between all States and a vessel when

471 See e.g., AP Rubin *The Law of Piracy* (1998); P Koutrakos & A Skordas (eds) *The Law and Practice of Piracy at Sea* (2014). For a critical discussion of the reasons for Pi jurisdiction as a universal jurisdiction, see Goodwin (n. 470) 987–1002.

472 Tanaka (n. 52) 453. See further e.g., ALI Moffa "Two competing models of activism, one goal: A case study of anti-whaling campaigns in the South Ocean" (2012) 37 *Yale Journal of International Law* 201–214; F Villamizar Lamus "Piracy and whaling in Antractica" (2018) 51 *Revue Belge de Droit International* 483–503; A Petrig "The commission of maritime crimes with unmanned systems: An interpretive challenge for the United Nations Convention on the Law of the Sea" in MD Evans & S Galani (eds) *Maritime Security and the Law of the Sea* (2020) 104–131 at 128.

473 Article 101(a) read with article 58(2) of the LOSC. See e.g., *The "Arctic Sunrise" Arbitration* (n. 53) § 171. There is general agreement that hijacking does not constitute piracy (see e.g., Churchill, Lowe & Sander (n. 44) 386; Tanaka (n. 52) 455). See however GP McGinley "The Achille Lauro Affair – Implications for international law" (1985) 52 *Tennessee Law Review* 691–738 at 696. See further e.g., J-P Pancracio "L'affaire de l'*Achille Lauro* et le droit international" (1985) 31 AFDI 221–236; LC Green "The *Santa Maria*: Rebels or pirates" (1961) 37 BYIL 496–505.

474 Article 101(a) of the LOSC. "The provision appears [...] intended to cover acts by the crew of one vessel descending from the sea to a *terra nullius* island to attach those ashore" (D Guilfoyle "Article 101" in Proelss (n. 57) 737–744 at 742).

475 Article 101(b) of the LOSC. In terms of article 103, "[a] ship or aircraft is considered a pirate ship or aircraft if it is intended by the persons in dominant control to be used for the purpose of committing one of the acts referred to in article 101. The same applies if the ship or aircraft has been used to commit any such act, so long as it remains under the control of the persons guilty of that act".

476 Article 101(c) of the LOSC.

477 See e.g., Chadwick (n. 462) 147–170.

478 Staker (n. 3) 302.

the latter engages in the slave trade.[479] The Convention does not define that term, nor does it define the word "slave".[480] Slavery is defined in the 1926 Convention to Suppress the Slave Trade and Slavery[481] as "the status or condition of a person over whom any or all of the powers attaching to the right of ownership are exercised".[482] This is also the definition in the 1956 Supplementary Convention on the Abolition of Slavery, the Slave Trade, and Institutions and Practices Similar to Slavery (SCAS),[483] which adds that the word "slave" means "a person in such condition or status".[484] As far as the term "slave trade" is concerned, it is defined in the Supplementary Convention as meaning and including

> all acts involved in the capture, acquisition or disposal of a person with intent to reduce him to slavery; all acts involved in the acquisition of a slave with a view to selling or exchanging him; all acts of disposal by sale of exchange of a person acquired with a view to being sold or exchanged; and, in general, every act of trade or transport in slaves by whatever means of conveyance.[485]

It can be argued that "the concept of 'slaves' should be interpreted in a contemporary evolutionary perspective [...]".[486] Indeed, the 1948 Universal Declaration of Human Rights (UDHR)[487] does proclaim that "[n]o one shall be held in slavery or servitude; slavery and the slave trade shall be prohibited in all their forms".[488] The latter were identified by the Supplementary Convention, which acknowledged that there exist institutions and practices similar to slavery. It did so by extending the regime of the 1926 Convention to:

> (a) Debt bondage [...];
> (b) Serfdom [...];
> (c) Any institution or practice whereby:
>   (i) A woman, without the right to refuse, is promised or given in marriage on payment of a consideration in money or in kind to her parents, guardian, family or any other person or group; or
>   (ii) The husband of a woman, his family, or his clan, has the right to transfer her to another person for value received or otherwise; or
>   (iii) A woman on the death of her husband is liable to be inherited by another person;

479 See article 110(1)(b) of the LOSC.
480 The word is also used in article 99.
481 60 LNTS 253. Adopted: 25 September 1926; EIF: 9 March 1927.
482 Article 1(1).
483 266 UNTS 40. Adopted: 7 September 1956; EIF: 30 April 1957.
484 Article 7(a).
485 Article 7(c).
486 Tanaka (n. 52) 200.
487 UNGA Resolution 217A (III) (10 December 1948).
488 Article 4.

(d) Any institution or practice whereby a child or young person under the age of 18 years, is delivered by either or both of his natural parents or by his guardian to another person, whether for reward or not, with a view to the exploitation of the child or young person or of his labour.[489]

On that basis, it might be argued that there exists a ground of universal jurisdiction when a vessel is used to engage in the trade not only of slaves, but also persons subjected to the institutions and practices similar to slavery which are identified by the Supplementary Convention. There are also practices, such as migrant smuggling and human trafficking, which may result at a later stage in the individuals who are subjected to them finding themselves victims of slavery or a similar institution or practice.[490] However, it does appear that, although those practices "present criminal justice challenges that support a multi-jurisdictional approach, they are far from attracting the levels of State practice or *opinio juris* needed to become crimes of universal jurisdiction".[491] Indeed, "modern crimes of international importance are [...] generally tackled not through a customary rule of universal jurisdiction, but through consent-based treaty frameworks designed to comprehensively provide the bases of jurisdiction required for effective action".[492] That is the case, for instance, of the 2000 Protocol to Prevent, Suppress and Punish Trafficking in Persons, Especially Women and Children[493] and the 2000 Protocol against the Smuggling of Migrants by Land, Sea and Air, Supplementing the 2000 United Nations Convention against Transnational Organised Crime (PSM).[494]

3.5.4 Statelessness jurisdiction

3.5.4.1 Introduction

A further ground of universal jurisdiction, which can be referred to as "statelessness jurisdiction" ("St jurisdiction"),[495] resides in either the suspicion that a vessel

489 Article 1.

490 This is recognised in the preamble to the 2005 Convention on Acting against Trafficking in Human Beings of the Council of Europe (2569 UNTS 33; adopted: 16 May 2005; EIF: 1 February 2008). See also e.g., E Papastavridis "Interception of human beings on the high seas: A contemporary analysis under international law" (2008) 36(2) *Syracuse Journal of International Law and Commerce* 145–228 at 164–178; Tanaka (n. 52) 200.

491 Gallagher & David (n. 51) 221. See also e.g., D Guilfoyle *Shipping Interdiction and the Law of the Sea* (2009) 228–231.

492 Gallagher & David (n. 51) 221–222.

493 2237 UNTS 319, (2001) 40 ILM 377. Adopted: 15 November 2000; EIF: 25 December 2003.

494 2241 UNTS 480, (2001) 40 ILM 384. Adopted: 15 November 2000; EIF: 28 January 2004. See articles 3 and 8. See further e.g., Guilfoyle (n. 491) 184–187.

495 On whether the terms "unflagged vessel", "vessel without nationality" and "stateless vessel" are interchangeable, see Rob McLaughlin "Article 110 of the Law of the Sea Convention 1982 and jurisdiction over vessels without nationality" (2019) 51 *George Washington International Law Review* 373–406 at 376–388.

lacks a nationality[496] or in a vessel being assimilated to a vessel without nationality.[497] In other words, a connecting factor exists between all States and a vessel when the latter is suspected not to have a legal relationship of nationality with any State[498] or when it may be assimilated to a vessel not having such a relationship.[499]

3.5.4.2 Vessels without nationality

The LOSC confirms the existence of St jurisdiction with regard to vessels without nationality when it provides, in article 110(1)(d), that "a warship which encounters on the high seas a foreign ship [...] is not justified in boarding it unless there is reasonable ground for suspecting that [...] the ship is without nationality". The suspicion will normally arise when a vessel does not fly a flag or does not bear "equivalent markings identifying its nationality".[500] The suspicion could also arise when, although the vessel does fly a flag or bear the relevant markings, there is good reason to believe that the vessel does not actually have a nationality, either because it was never granted a nationality or because, after losing its nationality (either because the nationality was revoked by the State concerned[501] or because "the ship revoke[d] its registration of its own accord for some reasons [...]"),[502] it was not granted another one.

The ground also exists where a vessel does have a nationality, but the State wanting to exercise St jurisdiction does not recognise the government of another State that has granted the latter's nationality to the vessel.[503] In such a case, the State is entitled to suspect that the vessel is without nationality in light of the fact that vessels normally have only one nationality.[504] This case must be distinguished from the case where a vessel does have a nationality, the State that argues that it has St jurisdiction has recognised the flag State, but it does not recognise the genuineness of the link between the flag State and the vessel. As explained above, there appears to be no basis in law for a State to challenge the ground of jurisdiction of another State on the basis that there is no genuine link between the latter State and a vessel.[505] This is confirmed by the fact that "courts and other public bodies have

496 See e.g., Tanaka (n. 52) 201, who confirms that "stateless vessels exist in reality".
497 See TL McDorman "Stateless fishing vessels, international law and the UN High Seas Fisheries Conference' (1994) 25 JMLC 531–555 at 537.
498 See section 3.5.4.2.
499 See section 3.5.4.3.
500 Nordquist (n. 49) 245 § 110.11(b).
501 See Tanaka (n. 52) 201.
502 *Ibid.* 202.
503 See e.g., H Myers *The Nationality of Ships* (1967) 311–312; S Bouwhuis "South Africa: The *Samudera Pasific* and the exercise of jurisdiction over stateless vessels on the high seas" (2014) 29 IJMCL 363–372 at 365; McDorman (n. 497) 534; S Talmon *Recognition of Governments in International Law* (1998) 213–214.
504 See Tanaka (n. 52) 202.
505 See section 3.2.5.2(d) .

traditionally refrained from" doing "the equivalent of lifting the corporate veil"[506] and, in the few cases when they have done so, it was not for the purpose of denying any nationality to a vessel, but rather with the aim of dealing with the vessel on the basis that it had another nationality than the one symbolised by the flag flown by the vessel.[507]

3.5.4.3 Vessels with more than one nationality

The existence of St jurisdiction in the case where a vessel has legal relationships of nationality with two or more States is confirmed by article 92(2) of the LOSC, which allows States to assimilate a vessel that "sails under the flags of two or more States, using them according to convenience" to a vessel without nationality. This provision corresponds *verbatim* to article 6(1) of the CHS, which was adopted, once again *verbatim*, from article 31 of the Final Draft Articles. In its commentary, the ILC remarked that there was already at the middle of the last century "a definite school of thought which recognizes the right of other States to regard a ship sailing under two flags as having no proper nationality".[508]

3.6 Port State jurisdiction

A ground of jurisdiction that started complementing F jurisdiction, the coastal zone jurisdictions and P jurisdiction much more recently than the universal jurisdictions is port State jurisdiction ("Pt jurisdiction").[509] The connecting factor of Pt jurisdiction has two elements: a spatial element and a circumstantial element.

The LOSC does not use or define the term "port State jurisdiction", which has been defined as "the term given to the jurisdiction a state may exercise over vessels visiting its ports".[510] This definition points to the fact that the connecting factor of Pt jurisdiction only exists when a vessel is within a port of the port State. The terms "port" and "off-shore installation" are difficult to define. It comes therefore as no surprise that, although the LOSC uses the terms frequently,[511] it does not define them. It appears that the term "port", which may be defined as "'a facility on the sea coast [or] river shore [...] where ships can load and unload goods or livestock or embark or disembark passengers', forming part of the land territory and the internal

506 RR Churchill & AV Lowe *The Law of the Sea* (1999) 261.

507 See UNSC Resolution 787 (1992) (16 November 1992) § 10.

508 UN Doc. A/3159 (n. 164) 280.

509 See e.g., Churchill & Lowe (n. 506) 350; Yu, Zhao & Chang (n. 36) 87; Tanaka (n. 52) 355. Po jurisdiction as a separate ground of jurisdiction must not be confused with the term "port State jurisdiction" used to refer to mandatory T jurisdiction as compared to discretionary T jurisdiction (see R Rayfuse "The role of port States" in R Warner & S Kaye (eds) *Routledge Handbook of Maritime Regulation and Enforcement* (2016) 71–85 at 71).

510 B Marten *Port State Jurisdiction and the Regulation of International Shipping* (2014) 1.

511 See e.g., articles 25(2), 62(4)(h), 92(1), 111(7), 131 and 211(3) (as far as "port" is concerned) and articles 211(3), 216(1)(c), 218(3), 219 and 220(1) (as far as "off-shore terminal" is concerned).

waters of a State",[512] must be interpreted more broadly, for present purposes, as including an off-shore terminal of the port State[513] and, it would seem, a roadstead of that State.[514]

In addition to its spatial element, the connecting factor of Po jurisdiction has also a circumstantial element in that Po jurisdiction may only be exercised over vessels and persons voluntarily within a port.[515] Thus, in contrast to T jurisdiction where voluntariness has an impact on the *scope* of the jurisdiction,[516] voluntariness is an essential component of the connecting factor on the basis of which Pt jurisdiction is established.[517] There is no explanation of the word "voluntarily" on the record but, *a contrario*, the connecting factor does not exist when a vessel finds itself within a port, only because it was in distress or because it was compelled to enter the port by *force majeure*[518] or any other reason.[519]

3.7 Delegated jurisdictions

Delegated jurisdiction ("D jurisdiction") differs from the other grounds of jurisdiction in that, in each case, the connecting factor is the existence of a delegation of a jurisdiction by a State to another State that would not otherwise have the jurisdiction. Comparable to delegations by States to international institutions,[520] State-to-State delegations make it possible, for instance, for States with a limited capacity to act *in fact*, to confer upon States with a greater capacity to act the authority *in law* to do so. While they also relate to legislative jurisdiction and adjudicative jurisdiction, those arrangements are particularly important with regard to executive jurisdiction because "the physical nature of the seas and the significant maritime resources required to effectively patrol its vast spaces limits the capacity of any one

512 D König "Article 218" in Proelss (n. 57) 1487–1496 at 1492, quoting R Lagoni "Ports" MPEPIL 1). See also e.g., GK Walker (ed) *Definitions for the Law of the Sea* (2012) 276 ("[u]nder UNCLOS, 'port' means a place provided with various installations, terminals and facilities for loading and discharging cargo or passengers").

513 See e.g., article 218(1) of the LOSC. Off-shore terminals may be defined as "artificial islands or installations outside the internal waters, which serve as port facilities for loading or offloading mainly oil and gas [...]" (Lagoni (n. 512) § 2).

514 In terms of article 12 of the LOSC, "[r]oadsteads which are normally used for the loading, unloading and anchoring of ships, and which would otherwise be situated wholly or partly outside the outer limit of the territorial sea, are included in the territorial sea".

515 See e.g., article 218(1) of the LOSC.

516 See further Chapter 4 section 4.3.1.

517 MH Nordquist (ed) *United Nations Convention on the Law of the Sea 1982: A Commentary* (2002) IV 272 § 218.9(f).

518 See e.g., Nordquist (n. 517) 272 § 218.9(f); H-S Bang "Port State jurisdiction and article 218 of the UN Convention on the Law of Sea" (2009) 40 JMLC 291–314 at 300.

519 See e.g., L Schiano di Pepe "Port State control as an instrument to ensure compliance with international marine environmental obligations" in A Kirchner (ed) *International Marine Environmental Law* (2003) 137–157 at 142.

520 See e.g., CA Bradley & JG Kelley "The concept of international delegation" (2008) 71(1) LCP 1–36; OA Hathaway "International delegation and State sovereignty" (2008) 71(1) LCP 115–149.

State, particularly those without significant maritime power, to control the activities of its [...] ships at sea",[521] for instance high seas fishing activities.[522]

Ad hoc delegations may take various forms.[523] A delegation may take the form of a request by the delegating State to another State. An example is the request that a "State which has reasonable grounds for believing that a ship flying its flag is engaged in illicit traffic in narcotic drugs or psychotropic substances" may make to another State to assist it in suppressing that traffic.[524] In this case, the flag State delegates its FE jurisdiction to the other State, which would otherwise not have that jurisdiction because the ship concerned is not flying its flag.[525] Another example is article 218(2) of the LOSC, which makes the institution of proceedings by a State "in respect of a discharge violation in the internal waters, territorial sea or exclusive economic zone of another State" dependent on a request "by that State, the flag State, or a State damaged or threatened by the discharge violation", when "the violation has [not] caused or is [not] likely to cause pollution in the internal waters, territorial sea or exclusive economic zone of the" State wanting to exercise its adjudicative jurisdiction.[526]

A delegation may also take the form of an authorisation by the delegating State. An example is the PSM, in terms of which a flag State which is a party to the Protocol may authorise another State party *inter alia*:

> (a) [t]o board the vessel;
> (b) [t]o search the vessel; and
> (c) [i]f evidence is found that the vessel is engaged in the smuggling of migrants by sea, to take appropriate measures with respect to the vessel and persons and cargo on board [...].[527]

A similar regime applies between parties to the 2008 CARICOM Maritime and Airspace Security Co-operation Agreement.[528]

521 Gallagher & David (n. 51) 225. See also e.g., S Kaye "Maritime jurisdiction and the right to board" (2020) 26 *James Cook University Law Review* 17–30 at 18.
522 See e.g., Rayfuse (n. 302) 814.
523 Rayfuse (n. 302) 814.
524 Article 108(2) of the LOSC.
525 See e.g., Tanaka (n. 52) 208.
526 Nordquist (n. 517) 271 § 218.9(b). When "the violation has caused or is likely to cause pollution in the internal waters, territorial sea or exclusive economic zone of the" State wanting to exercise its adjudicative jurisdiction, the latter is exercising its relevant objective coastal zone jurisdiction (see section 3.3).
527 Article 8(2). Article 8(5) stresses that the flag State may "subject its authorisation to conditions to be agreed by it and the [other] State, including conditions relating to responsibility and the extent of effective measures to be taken". The other State party may not take "additional measures without the express authorisation of the flag State, except those necessary to relieve imminent danger to the lives of persons or those which derive from relevant bilateral or multilateral agreements".
528 (2008) 68 LOSB 20. Adopted: 4 July 2008; EIF: article 27. See e.g., article 9(2)(b). See further Y Gottlieb *International Cooperation in Combating Modern Forms of Maritime Piracy: Legal and Policy Dimensions* (2017) 206–208.

A delegation may also take the form of a duty created in a multilateral agreement. The SUA is an example. Article 6(4) states that "[e]ach State Party shall take such measures as may be necessary to establish its jurisdiction over the offences set forth in article 3 in cases where the alleged offender is present in its territory [...]", but the State may only "establish its jurisdiction" on that basis when the State "does not extradite [the alleged offender] to any of the States Parties which have established their jurisdiction in accordance with" article 6(1)–(2).[529] This wording makes it clear that this is a case of delegation. Indeed, in order for the "territorial" State party to have jurisdiction, at least one other State party must have beforehand relied on one of the grounds listed in article 6(1)–(2) to "take such measures as may be necessary to establish its [own] jurisdiction", measures that would have made it possible for the State to exercise its authority over the offender had he or she been extradited to it. After that is done, article 6(4) aims to ensure that the principle *aut dedere aut judicare* is applied by delegating the State's jurisdiction and requiring that it be exercised when the "territorial" State does not see its way open to extraditing the offender.[530]

The authorisation of a delegating State to exercise delegated jurisdiction must not be confused with the removal by a State of an obstacle to the exercise by another State of its own jurisdiction.[531] That is the case, for instance, when a State having TE jurisdiction authorises another State to exercise its FE jurisdiction in the marine component of the former's territory. In such a case, the State having TE jurisdiction is not delegating its jurisdiction to the other State but, by means of its authorisation, is removing the obstacle (i.e., the exclusive feature of its TE jurisdiction) that limited the scope of the FE jurisdiction of the other State.[532]

3.8 Collective jurisdictions

The connecting factor of a collective jurisdiction consists in the decision taken by a legal body with the capacity to confer to States the authority to be involved in a specific matter, in terms of which that body does confer that authority. An example of such a body is the UN Security Council (UNSC), which is from time to time called upon to "determine the existence of any threat to the peace, breach of the peace, or act of aggression".[533] In such a case, the Council is expected to make

529 See further article 6(3).

530 See also article 10(1). See further e.g., ILC "The obligation to extradite or prosecute (*aut dedere aut judicare*)" § 18 (UN Doc. A/69/10 (2014) ((2014) II YILC 97)); A Caligiuri "Governing international cooperation in criminal matters: The role of the *aut dedere aut judicare* principle" (2018) 18 *International Criminal Law Review* 244–274.

531 That confusion appears to have existed in *United States v. Suerte* (see S Murphy "Extraterritorial application of US laws to crimes on foreign vessels" (2003) 97 AJIL 183–185 at 183–184).

532 See further Chapter 4 section 4.3.3.

533 Article 39 of the UN Charter.

non-binding recommendations or take binding decisions "to maintain or restore international peace and security".[534]

The existence of collective jurisdiction depends not only on the existence of an act conferring that jurisdiction, but also on the fact that the conferring body has the authority to confer the jurisdiction to States. That authority was doubtful in the case of the Cuban "quarantine" imposed in 1962, the main ground of which was a decision of the Organisation of American States allegedly acting under Chapter VIII of the Charter of the United Nations (UNC).[535] By contrast, the authority of the UNSC has not been contested in the various cases where, in terms of article 42 of the Charter, it conferred jurisdiction on States to stop and search foreign vessels with the aim of preventing the circumvention of sanctions imposed by the Council.[536]

A decision to confer a collective jurisdiction must be distinguished from a decision to extend the scope of another jurisdiction. An example of the latter is the decision taken in 2008 by the UNSC in its Resolution 1816 that,

> for a period of six months from the date of this resolution, States cooperating with the [Transitional Federal Government of Somalia ("TFG")] in the fight against piracy and armed robbery at sea off the coast of Somalia, for which advance notification has been provided by the TFG to the Secretary-General, may:
>
> (a) Enter the territorial waters of Somalia for the purpose of repressing acts of piracy and armed robbery at sea, in a manner consistent with such action permitted on the high seas with respect to piracy under relevant international law; and
> (b) Use, within the territorial waters of Somalia, in a manner consistent with action permitted on the high seas with respect to piracy under relevant international law, all necessary means to repress acts of piracy and armed robbery[.][537]

534 Article 39 of the UN Charter. Article 25 of the Charter indicates that the members of the UN have agreed "to accept and carry out the decisions of the Security Council in accordance with the" Charter. See further e.g., M Selkirk "Judge, jury and executioner – Analysing the nature of the Security Council's authority under article 39 of the UN Charter" (2003) 9 *Auckland University Law Review* 1101–1139; ML Serna Galván "Interpretation of article 39 of the UN Charter (threat to the peace) by the Security Council – Is the Security Council a legislator for the entire international community?" (2011) 11 *Anuario Mexicano de Derecho Internacional* 147–185.

535 Churchill, Lowe & Sander (n. 44) 410.

536 See e.g., § 4 of Resolution 221 (1966) (9 April 1966); § 13 of Resolution 1973 (2011) (17 March 2011) replacing § 11 of Resolution 1970 (2011) (26 February 2011). See further e.g., K Neri *L'Emploi de la Force en Mer* (2013) 350, who cautions that "[l]e Chapitre VII est l'instrument de la sécurité collective, il s'agit donc par nature de protéger la paix et la sécurité internationales, et non l'ordre des mers. Il n'a donc pas vocation à être l'instrument de protection de la liberté de navigation".

537 Paragraph 7. The decision was taken again, for periods of 12 months, every year since then.

In this case, the decision did not confer a separate ground of jurisdiction, but rather entailed an extension of the scope of Pi jurisdiction *ratione loci* to the territorial waters of a specific State.[538]

3.9 Protective jurisdictions

Protective jurisdiction is a problematic form of State ocean jurisdiction,[539] which it is necessary to approach by distinguishing between two forms of protective jurisdiction: protective jurisdiction exercised for State security purposes ("Ps jurisdiction") and protective jurisdiction exercised for economic purposes or "effect jurisdiction" (Pe jurisdiction"). The connecting factor in the case of Ps jurisdiction may be defined as the fact that the matter with regard to which the State wants to exercise its jurisdiction constitutes a threat to the security of the State.[540] As far as it is concerned, the connecting factor in the case of Pe jurisdiction is arguably best defined as the fact that an activity taking place outside the territory of a State has an actual or intended economic effect or impact in the territory of the State.[541] Protective jurisdictions are probably best seen as subsidiary jurisdictions in that States normally rely on them either when they perceive that another ground on which they believe they can rely on is shaky,[542] or when they are unable to rely on any other ground of jurisdiction at all. These considerations affect the scope of the jurisdictions.[543]

3.10 Conclusion

The careful identification and description of the various grounds of State ocean jurisdiction shows both their multiplicity and the relatively limited role of T jurisdiction in ocean-related matters compared to its role in land-related matters. That is especially the case when one is careful to distinguish territorial jurisdiction *stricto sensu*, i.e., jurisdiction based on the fact that a matter in one way or another relates to the marine component of the territory of a State,[544] from other grounds of "territorial", spatial or zonal jurisdiction.[545] That is also the case when one frees oneself from the temptation of basing as many exercises of State authority in ocean-related matters as possible on the ground of T jurisdiction.

The PCIJ apparently struggled with this when it stated, in *Lotus*, that "[t]he collision which occurred on August 2nd, 1926, between the S.S. *Lotus*, flying the French

538 See further Chapter 4 section 4.8.1.2.
539 See e.g., Akehurst (n. 58) 158.
540 Compare e.g., § 412 *Restatement of the Law (Fourth)* (n. 2).
541 Compare e.g., § 409 comment (a) *Restatement of the Law (Fourth)* (n. 2). See further e.g., Bowett (n. 15) 7.
542 See Ryngaert (n. 409) 114.
543 See e.g., Bowett (n. 15) 10. See further Chapter 4 section 4.12.
544 See section 3.3.2.1.
545 See section 3.3.3.

flag, and the S.S. *Boz-Kourt*, flying the Turkish flag, took place on the high seas: the territorial jurisdiction of any State *other than France and Turkey* therefore does not enter into account".[546] Indeed, once it is agreed that a matter arose on the high seas, there is, in principle, no room for the exercise of T jurisdiction by any State, including the flag State(s) concerned.[547] To state, as the Court did, that "[a] corollary of the principle of the freedom of the seas is that a ship on the high seas is assimilated to the territory of the State the flag of which it flies [...]" does not speak to the ground of jurisdiction, i.e., F jurisdiction,[548] but to the scope of F jurisdiction, which is indeed akin to the scope of T jurisdiction when a vessel is on the high seas.[549]

A century later, in *Enrica Lexie*,[550] one of the two legal bases on which India relied was the "territoriality principle".[551] This is surprising because it was undisputed that the matter arose beyond the outer limit of the Indian territorial sea.[552] For that reason, one would have expected that any argument based on territoriality would be approached very cautiously in view of the fact that India and Italy agreed that "the 'Enrica Lexie' incident occurred in India's exclusive economic zone".[553] Nevertheless, the arbitral tribunal stated in its award that, "[a]ccording to the territoriality principle, both Italy and India [were] entitled to exercise jurisdiction over the incident".[554] To try and understand this statement, one needs to note that it was made by the tribunal when it dealt with India's argument that "[t]he territoriality principle [...] may be extended to a vessel, so that a State may exercise jurisdiction over any offence committed on board its vessel wherever it may be, as if the offence were committed in its territory".[555] In this regard, the tribunal indicated that, in its view, "such an extended territoriality principle is well established, and the domestic criminal legislation of a large number of States confers jurisdiction over offences committed on board national ships or aircraft".[556] At the same time, the tribunal cautioned, somewhat confusingly, that the principle does not amount "to assimilating a vessel with national territory 'for all purposes' as if 'a ship is a floating part of state territory' [...]".[557]

546 *Lotus Case* (n. 7) 12 (own emphasis).
547 See article 89 of the LOSC. See further Chapter 4 section 4.3.1.
548 *Lotus Case* (n. 7) 25.
549 See further Chapter 4 sections 4.2.1 and 4.3.1.
550 *The "Enrica Lexie" Incident* (n. 35). See e.g., M Gandhi "The *Enrica Lexie* incident: Seeing beyond the grey areas of international law" (2013) 53 *Indian Journal of International Law* 1–26; GM Farnelli "Back to *Lotus*? A recent decision by the Supreme Court of India on an incident of navigation in the contiguous zone" (2014) *International Community Law Review* 106–122.
551 *The "Enrica Lexie" Incident* (n. 35) § 362.
552 *Ibid.* § 180.
553 *Ibid.* § 373.
554 *Ibid.* § 367.
555 *Ibid.* § 364.
556 *Ibid.* § 365.
557 *Ibid.* Later in the award, the tribunal confirmed that "the legal fiction that ships may be assimilated for jurisdictional purposes with land territory of the flag State has [...] been universally rejected" (§ 869).

The key to unlock the riddle appears to be in the statement that,

> [i]n the view of the Arbitral Tribunal, it is [...] well established that, where the commission of an offence involves the territories of more than one State (for example, an offence was commenced in the territory of one State and completed in the territory of another State), both the State in whose territory an offence was commenced (subjective territoriality principle) and the State in whose territory it was completed (objective territoriality principle) may exercise jurisdiction over the offence. Likewise, where an offence was commenced on board one vessel and completed on board another vessel, the flag States of both vessels may have concurrent jurisdiction over the offence.[558]

The first sentence does not apply directly *in casu* because, as already pointed out above, it was undisputed that the matter arose beyond the outer limit of the Indian territorial sea. This could therefore not be a case "where the commission of an offence involves the territories of more than one State". Instead, the first sentence applies indirectly *in casu* by laying the ground for the second sentence. It does so by confirming the existence of two aspects of the "territoriality principle": the "subjective territoriality principle" and the "objective territoriality principle".[559] On that basis, an analogy is made in the second sentence between "territory" and "vessel", with the implication that the "subjective territoriality principle" and the "objective territoriality principle", as discreet aspects of the "territoriality principle", apply also in the case of vessels, even when none of them is within the territory of any State.

This approach to State ocean jurisdiction is problematic for at least three reasons. One of them is that, in order to apply the "territoriality principle" in cases where there is clearly no T jurisdiction (because the matter does not, in one way or another, relate to the marine component of the territory of the State),[560] it is necessary to resort to techniques such as "extension"[561] and "assimilation",[562] techniques that have the effect of making intricate jurisdictional situations even more complex. A second reason is that it opens the door for a conflation of F jurisdiction and T jurisdiction in situations where only the former's connecting factor exists. A third reason is that it perpetuates a practice, already alluded to above, of failing to distinguish between the ground of a jurisdiction and the scope of that jurisdiction. Having focused on the former in this chapter, it is now time to focus on the latter in the next chapter.

558 *The "Enrica Lexie" Incident* (n. 35) § 366.
559 See section 3.3.2.4.
560 See section 3.3.2.1.
561 Used by India (see above).
562 Used by the PCIJ and the tribunal (see above). The technique was also used by India in its counter-memorial (see § 339 of the award).

4 The scope of State ocean jurisdiction

4.1 Introduction

The fact that a State has a ground for exercising its authority in ocean matters does not automatically mean that it is entitled to exercise that authority everywhere, over all matters and irrespective of the persons or vessels involved. Indeed, the scope of State ocean jurisdiction varies depending on its form and its ground as well as: (i) its extent *ratione materiae* (i.e., with regard to the matter concerned); (ii) its extent *ratione navis* (i.e., with regard to the vessel involved); (iii) its extent *ratione personae* (i.e., with regard to the person involved); (iv) its extent *ratione loci* (i.e., with regard to the place where the matter arose, as far as legislative jurisdiction and adjudicative jurisdiction are concerned, or the authority is exercised, as far as executive jurisdiction is concerned); (v) the existence of one or more overlapping jurisdictions; and (vi) the opposability of the jurisdiction against another State, in that the latter is obliged to recognise that jurisdiction. The combination of all those factors produces an extremely complex picture that one can approach from different angles.

The approach adopted here starts by taking into account the range of matters over which States are entitled to act in the exercise of a specific ground of jurisdiction. It does so by distinguishing between primary jurisdictions and secondary jurisdictions. A ground of State ocean jurisdiction is referred to as "secondary" when its scope *ratione materiae* is limited to a specific category or categories of matters. By contrast, a ground of State ocean jurisdiction is referred to as "primary" when its scope is all-encompassing *ratione materiae*, but for specific exceptions in terms of international customary law or treaties. In other words, a ground of State ocean jurisdiction is primary when it is presumed to give authority to a State to be involved in all matters.

F jurisdiction is a primary ground of jurisdiction. This is because a flag State has, in principle, authority to perform legislative, executive and adjudicative acts with regard to a vessel flying its flag in respect of all matters relating to the vessel.[1] T jurisdiction is also a primary ground of jurisdiction. This is because a coastal State has, in principle, authority to perform legislative, executive and adjudicative acts in respect of all matters

1 See further section 4.2.1.

DOI: 10.4324/9781003383871-4

within its territory.[2] F jurisdiction and T jurisdiction have in common that they are not only all-encompassing *ratione materiae*, but also with regard to the persons involved (i.e., *ratione personae*). The latter is not the case for P jurisdiction because, as far as it is concerned, whether a State has P jurisdiction with regard to a person is a question relating to the ground of jurisdiction of the State, not the scope of that jurisdiction. Put differently, once it has been established that the ground of P jurisdiction exists in a matter, the answer to the question whether the matter falls within the scope of the State's P jurisdiction *ratione personae* is automatically answered affirmatively.[3] Subject to the above, P jurisdiction is a primary ground of jurisdiction in that the personal State has, in principle, authority to perform legislative, executive and adjudicative acts with regard to its nationals in respect of all matters.[4]

The above does not mean that primary jurisdictions are absolute with regard to the content and impact of the acts performed in their exercise. They are indeed limited, *inter alia*, by the jurisdictional immunities of States, their officials and their property,[5] the adjudicative-jurisdiction rules and principles,[6] the principles of non-discrimination and[7] peaceful use of the seas[8] as well as the acts of non-State subjects of international law, such as, for instance, the ISA.[9]

Before focusing on each jurisdiction in turn, it is important to explain the terminology used in the process of doing so. The term "potential overlap" is used to refer to an overlap that is possible when one does not take exclusions into account,[10] while the word "overlap" is used on its own when there is indeed no exclusion. In both cases, the term or word is usually complemented by a mention of the relevant aspect. The word "concurrence" is used only when there is overlap in all respects (i.e., *ratione materiae*, *ratione navis*, *ratione personae* and *ratione loci*),[11]

2 See further section 4.3.1.
3 See Chapter 3 section 3.4.2.
4 See section 4.4.1.
5 See e.g., article 16 of the 2004 International Convention on Jurisdictional Immunities of States and their Property ((2005) 44 ILM 803; adopted: 2 December 2004; EIF: article 30); *The "Enrica Lexie" Incident (Italy v. India)*, award of 21 May 2020, (2021) 60 ILM 180 § 841–874 (with regard to a vessel protection detachment); TL McDorman "Sovereign immune vessels: Immunities, responsibilities and exemptions" in H Ringbom (ed) *Jurisdiction over Ships* (2015) 82–102; P Gragl "Jurisdictional immunities of the State in international law" in S Allen *et al.* (eds) *The Oxford Handbook of Jurisdiction in International Law* (2019) 228–250.
6 For instance, the *ne bis in idem* principle. In that regard, C Ryngaert *Jurisdiction in International Law* (2015) 156 warns that "the absence of an unambiguous transnational *ne bis in idem* principle opens the door to multiple prosecutions of [an] offender in multiple jurisdictions".
7 See e.g., articles 26(2), 42(2), 52(2), 119(3) and 227 of the LOSC.
8 See e.g., article 301 of the LOSC.
9 See e.g., article 160(2)(f)(ii) of the LOSC. See further e.g., *Responsibilities and Obligations of States Sponsoring Persons and Entities with Respect to Activities in the Area*, advisory opinion of 1 February 2011, 2011 ITLOS Reports 10.
10 See e.g., section 4.5.3.
11 In specific instances, such as when jurisdiction derives from a treaty and the matter arose about the time when one of the States concerned became, or ceased to be, bound by the treaty, the temporal element also needs to be taken into account.

a situation sometimes referred to also as "complete overlap".[12] In this regard, it would clearly go far beyond the scope of this work to examine, in every single case, whether there is "actual" concurrence (i.e., whether the States concerned have exercised their respective jurisdictions). "Concurrence" thus refers only to a situation where the States *may* exercise their respective jurisdictions concurrently, irrespective of whether they have actually exercised them. Finally, the word "co-existence" is used to refer to an exceptional situation where there is no complete overlap (and therefore no concurrence), but two or more States may nevertheless exercise their respective jurisdictions in the same matter.[13]

4.2 Flag State jurisdiction

4.2.1 Extent of flag State jurisdiction

It has just been alluded to that F jurisdiction confers, upon a flag State, FL jurisdiction, FE jurisdiction and FA jurisdiction, which are, in principle, all-encompassing *ratione personae* and *ratione materiae*.[14] In addition, that authority is also all-encompassing *ratione loci*, subject to limitations resulting from potential overlaps with jurisdictions of other States,[15] the most important of which are pointed out below.[16]

When there is no legal relationship of nationality between a vessel and a State, the connecting factor establishing F jurisdiction does not exist and the State has therefore no F jurisdiction.[17] As a result, the scope of F jurisdiction is always limited *ratione navis*.[18] At the same time, it has been shown in the previous chapter that it does not matter whether a genuine link exists when it comes to the opposability of a State's F jurisdiction in any given situation.[19] In other words, when a legal relationship of nationality exists between a vessel and a State, another State may not refuse to recognise the F jurisdiction of the flag State on the ground that there is no genuine link between the latter and the vessel. It may be, however, that, instead of refusing to recognise the F jurisdiction of a flag State, a State refuses to recognise the fact that the flag State is indeed a State.[20]

12 See e.g., § 407 comment (d) *Restatement of the Law (Fourth): The Foreign Relations Law of the United States* (2018).
13 See e.g., section 4.2.2.
14 See e.g., B Simma & AT Müller "Exercise and limits of jurisdiction" in J Crawford & M Koskenniemi (eds) *The Cambridge Companion to International Law* (2012) 134–157 at 138.
15 On the relationship between F jurisdiction and the powers of the ISA over the Area, see e.g., E Røsæg "Framework legislation for commercial activities in the Area" in C Banet (ed) *The Law of the Seabed: Access, Uses, and Protection of Seabed Resources* (2020) 163–184 at 167.
16 See sections 4.3.3, 4.5.3, 4.6.3 and 4.7.3.
17 See Chapter 3 section 3.2.2.
18 See further e.g., N Oral "Jurisdiction and control over activities by non-State entities on the high seas" in RC Beckman *et al.* (eds) *High Seas Governance – Gaps and Challenges* (2019) 9–33.
19 See Chapter 3 section 3.2.5.2(d).
20 See Chapter 1 section 1.4.

To sum up, the flag State has, in principle, authority to perform acts in the exercise of its FL jurisdiction, FE jurisdiction and FA jurisdiction with regard to all matters relating to vessels with which it has a legal relationship of nationality, wherever those vessels are and irrespective of the nationality of the persons involved.

4.2.2 Relationship between flag State jurisdictions

Because F jurisdiction is limited *ratione navis*, there is, in all but very exceptional cases, no concurrence of F jurisdictions with regard to the same vessel. Indeed, it has already been pointed out that article 92(1) of the LOSC is understood to mean that vessels may not have multiple nationalities.[21] It does not mean, however, that F jurisdiction may never be held concurrently by two States, at least for limited purposes. Indeed, it was pointed out in the previous chapter that "[m]any countries have adopted dual registration procedures for the bareboat charterers, whereby the owner's original registration is suspended during the temporary registration by the bareboat charterer, but remains effective for certain purposes, such as the recording of mortgages against the ship".[22] The difficulty in reconciling these exceptional cases with article 92(1) – when it states that vessels are subject to the exclusive jurisdiction of the flag State on the high seas[23] – only relates to FE jurisdiction.[24] Indeed, article 92(1) does not refer to FL jurisdiction[25] nor, it would seem, to FA jurisdiction. In other words, article 92(1) does not stand in the way of two flag States exercising concurrently their FL jurisdictions[26] or their FA jurisdictions. The position is more complicated with regard to FE jurisdiction and three situations must be distinguished.

The first situation is where a vessel has legal relationships of nationality with two States, but is only entitled to fly the flag of one of those two States.[27] In such a case, there is no difficulty in applying article 92(1): the vessel is indeed under the exclusive FE jurisdiction of the only State the flag of which it is entitled to fly. The

21 See Chapter 3 section 3.2.7.

22 L Sohn *et al. Law of the Sea in a Nutshell* (2010) 61. See further Chapter 3 section 3.2.7.

23 See e.g., *The "Enrica Lexie" Incident* (n. 5) § 524; J-P Pancracio *Droit de la Mer* (2010) 329; J Kraska "Excessive coastal State jurisdiction: Shipboard armed security personnel" in Ringbom (n. 5) 167–193 at 170; D Guilfoyle "Transnational crime" in R Warner & S Kaye (eds) *Routledge Handbook of Maritime Regulation and Enforcement* (2016) 262–276 at 263.

24 See e.g., AN Honniball "The exclusive jurisdiction of flag States: A limitation on pro-active port States?" (2016) 31 IJMCL 499–530 at 508 and 520–521. *Contra* see e.g., D Fabris "Crime committed at sea and criminal jurisdiction: Current issues of international law of the sea awaiting the '*Enrica Lexie*' decision" (2017) 9(2) *Amsterdam Law Forum* 5–25 at 18.

25 See e.g., D Guilfoyle "Article 92" in A Proelss (ed) *United Nations Convention on the Law of the Sea – A Commentary* (2017) 700–704 at 702.

26 If it were the case, it would not be possible for the domestic law of one flag State to remain "effective for certain purposes", while the domestic law of another flag State governs all the other aspects. See e.g., Guilfoyle (n. 25) 700–701.

27 On the distinction between the legal relationship of nationality and the right to fly a flag, see Chapter 3 section 3.2.4.1.

position is arguably not different in the case where: (a) a vessel has legal relationships of nationality with two States; (b) the vessel is entitled to fly the flag of those two States; but (c) in practice, the vessel only flies the flag of one of those States. In that case, the vessel is under the exclusive FE jurisdiction of the State the flag of which it actually flies.

The problem only arises, as is confirmed by article 92(2) of the LOSC, in the third situation where a vessel actually "sails under the flags of two or more States, using them according to convenience", including, in many instances, for the purpose of evading the exercise of FE jurisdiction. In that case, it was already explained in the previous chapter that a form of universal jurisdiction exists: St jurisdiction.[28] It is clear that article 92(2) does not apply to any of the flag States, the flags of which a vessel is not flying at a specific time. Indeed, it cannot be that a ship sailing under two or more flags is able to rely on the exclusive FE jurisdiction of one of the flag States to oppose the exercise of FE jurisdiction by another flag State. Such a situation would defeat the very purpose for which third States have St jurisdiction (i.e., ensuring that the community of States has sufficient jurisdictional grounds to ensure law and order beyond the outer limits of the territorial seas).[29] Rather, any ship sailing under two or more flags must surely be in the same position as a person with two or more nationalities, that is to say unable to rely on one of its nationalities to oppose the exercise of jurisdiction by another State of which it also has the nationality.[30] The latter State is at least in the same position as a non-flag State that relies on article 110(1)(e) of the LOSC, when it provides that a warship that encounters a foreign ship on the high seas is justified in boarding the ship when there is reasonable ground for suspecting that, "though flying a foreign flag [...] the ship is [...] of the same nationality as the warship". In addition, the acts performed by the warship are performed not in the exercise of St jurisdiction, but in the exercise of the State's FE jurisdiction.[31]

In the normal situation where a vessel only has one legal relationship of nationality with a State, an overlap of F jurisdictions is nevertheless possible when a matter involves at least two vessels, each with the nationality of a different State, for example when an individual shoots a gun on a ship flying the flag of one State and injures or kills another individual on a ship flying the flag of another State. In such a case, it has been explained in the previous chapter that the former State has Fs jurisdiction and the latter State has Fo jurisdiction.[32] The two jurisdictions are not concurrent because, while they overlap *ratione materiae* and *ratione personae*, they do not overlap *ratione navis*, each State's T jurisdiction being limited to the vessel with which it has

28 See Chapter 3 section 3.5.4.
29 See Chapter 3 section 3.5.1.
30 See e.g., article 3 of the CCNL.
31 See e.g., D Guilfoyle "Article 110" in Proelss (n. 25) 767–772 at 772.
32 See Chapter 3 section 3.2.2.

a legal relationship of nationality.[33] Nevertheless, FsL jurisdiction and FoL jurisdiction, on the one hand, and FsA jurisdiction and FoA jurisdiction, on the other, coexist because the matter involves two or more vessels with different legal relationships of nationality. As a result, a person may violate, at the same time: (a) a normative provision contained in a legislative instrument produced by a legislative act performed by an organ of one of the flag States exercising that State's FoL jurisdiction; and (b) a normative provision contained in a legislative instrument produced by a legislative act performed by an organ of the other flag State exercising the latter's FsL jurisdiction. Likewise, a person may fall under the FoA jurisdiction of one of the two States and under the FsA jurisdiction of the other State, unless FoA jurisdiction is excluded, as is the effect of article 97 of the LOSC, for instance. By contrast, it has just been pointed out that, outside the territories of the coastal States, FE jurisdiction is, in principle, exclusive of any other executive jurisdiction.[34] Because neither Fs jurisdiction nor Fo jurisdiction appear to be exceptions to the principle, while a State with Fs jurisdiction has FsL jurisdiction and FsA jurisdiction, it does not have FsE jurisdiction beyond its territory over the vessel flying the flag of the State having Fo jurisdiction, and vice versa.

The above is subject to the fact that nothing prevents a flag State from waiving the exclusivity of its FE jurisdiction by means of a treaty[35] or ad hoc special arrangements.[36]

4.2.3 Summary

Flag States have, in principle, authority to perform acts in the exercise of their FL jurisdiction, FE jurisdiction and FA jurisdiction with regard to all matters relating to vessels with which they have a legal relationship of nationality, irrespective of the nationality of the persons involved and wherever those vessels are, subject to limitations flowing from precedence being given to another jurisdiction in specific cases of overlap. Because, in most cases, a vessel has only one legal relationship of nationality with a State, there is no overlap of F jurisdictions, unless the matter involves two or more vessels, each with the nationality of a different State.

33 See section 4.2.1.

34 This principle is confirmed, as far as the high seas are concerned, in article 92(1) of the LOSC.

35 See e.g., article X(1)(a) of the 1952 International Convention between the United States of America, Canada and Japan for the High Seas Fisheries of the North Pacific Ocean (205 UNTS 65; adopted: 9 May 1952; EIF: 12 June 1953). The waiver of the exclusivity of FE jurisdiction does not automatically have an impact on adjudicative jurisdiction (see e.g., article X(1)(c) of the 1952 Convention).

36 See e.g., CH Allen "Doctrine of hot pursuit: A functional interpretation adaptable to emerging maritime law enforcement technologies and practices" (1989) 20 ODIL 309–341 at 329 fn. 49 regarding arrangements made by the United States of America; Pancracio (n. 23) 332; T Herran "Le trafic maritime des stupéfiants" in L Grard (ed) *La Mer – Droit de l'Union Européenne – Droit International* (2018) 235–244 at 238 referring to art. 108(2) of the LOSC.

4.3 Territorial jurisdiction

4.3.1 Extent of territorial jurisdiction

As indicated above,[37] T jurisdiction confers upon the coastal State the authority to perform legislative, executive and adjudicative acts, which is, in principle,[38] all-encompassing *ratione materiae* and *ratione personae*.[39] That authority differs from that of the flag State in that it is limited *ratione loci*. Indeed, the connecting factor establishing T jurisdiction points to the fact that the latter is limited, in principle, to the land component and the marine component of the territory of the coastal State.[40]

While each coastal State automatically has a territorial sea, as explained in the previous chapter,[41] the LOSC does not prescribe the extent of the zone. Indeed, it merely sets at 12 NM, in most cases,[42] the maximum breadth that may be claimed by the coastal State in the exercise of its TL jurisdiction by means of a legislative act producing a legislative instrument containing the constitutive provision setting the breadth of the territorial sea.[43] That breadth is "measured from baselines determined in accordance with" the LOSC[44] and, therefore, the drawing of those baselines also has an impact on the extent of T jurisdiction *ratione loci*.

A coastal State does not have to perform any act in the exercise of its TL jurisdiction to establish the baseline. Indeed, the LOSC provides that the normal (or default) baseline is "the low-water line along the coast".[45] At the same time, that line is "a constructed line"[46] and the LOSC requires that the coastal State take the necessary steps to mark the line "on large-scale charts officially recognized by the coastal State".[47] In many instances, coastal States have, provided that the

37 See section 4.1.

38 See e.g., G Gidel *Le Droit international public de la mer* (1932) II 203.

39 See e.g., G Gidel *Le Droit international public de la mer* (1934) III 191; Simma & Müller (n. 14) 137–138. As in the case of F jurisdiction, T jurisdiction is not absolute because the contents of the measures taken in the exercise of that jurisdiction are subject to the States' "duties under human rights laws and similar constraints" (C Staker "Jurisdiction" in MD Evans (ed) *International Law* (2018) 289–315 at 296).

40 See Chapter 3 section 3.3.2.1.

41 See Chapter 3 section 3.3.2.3.

42 See article 12 of the LOSC.

43 See article 3. See also article 4.

44 Article 3.

45 Article 5. See also article 6.

46 K Trümpler "Article 5" in Proelss (n. 25) 45–60 at 52.

47 Article 5. See also Trümpler (n. 46) 52. Increasingly fast sea-level changes have brought to the fore the issue of the legal impact of changes in the position of the low-water line (see e.g., L Bernard *et al.* "Securing the limits of large ocean States in the Pacific: Defining baselines limits and boundaries amidst changing coastlines and sea level rise" (2021) 11 *Geosciences* 394). It seems clear, *de lege lata*, that the normal baseline is ambulatory (see e.g., ILA *Baselines under the International Law of the Sea* (2012) 32–33) and that a coastal State is expected to update its chart(s) on a reasonably regular basis when the position of the baseline does change (see e.g., Y Tanaka *The International Law of the Sea* (2019) 55; Trümpler (n. 46) 60). In practice, however, some States have started fixing their baselines (see e.g., Action 1B of the Framework for a Pacific Oceanscape, endorsed by Pacific Island leaders and ministers at the Pacific Islands Forum in 2010; the 2021 Declaration on

relevant requirements are met, TL jurisdiction to perform legislative acts producing legislative instruments containing constitutive provisions setting baselines that depart from the normal baselines[48] or are drawn using low-tide elevations sufficiently close to the shore.[49] In addition, coastal States that are archipelagic States[50] may draw straight archipelagic baselines.[51] An additional factor that affects the extent of the marine component of the territory of the coastal State is the delimitation of the maritime boundary between the territorial sea of the State and the territorial sea of a neighbouring State with an adjacent or opposite coast.[52]

An exception to the limitation of T jurisdiction *ratione loci* to the marine component of the territory of the coastal State is the case of hot pursuit, where TE jurisdiction may be exercised beyond the territorial sea,[53] provided that a number of requirements are met.[54] First, "the competent authorities of the coastal State [must] have good reason to believe that the ship has violated the laws and regulations of" the coastal State,[55] that is to say the laws and regulations adopted by the State in the exercise of its TL jurisdiction and that apply within the marine component of the territory of the State. Secondly, the pursuing ship must be a warship or another ship "clearly marked and identifiable as being on government service and authorized to that effect".[56] Thirdly, the pursuing ship must have "satisfied itself by such practicable means as may be available that the ship pursued or one of its boats or other craft working as a team and using the ship pursued as a mother ship is" landward

---

Preserving Maritime Zones in the Face of Climate Change-Related Sea-Level Rise adopted by the Pacific Island Forum Leaders; the 2021 Leaders' Declaration adopted by the Heads of State and Government of the Alliance of Small Island States; D Freestone & C Schofield "Pacific islands countries declare permanent maritime baselines, limits and boundaries" (2021) 36 IJMCL 685–695; C Schofield "A new frontier in the law of the sea? Responding to the implications of sea level rise for baselines, limits and boundaries" in R Barnes & R Long (eds) *Frontiers in International Environmental Law: Oceans and Climate Challenges* (2021) 171–193 at 182–185) and there is strong support, *de lege ferenda*, for the view that, "on the grounds of legal certainty and stability, provided that the baselines and the outer limits of maritime zones of a coastal or an archipelagic State have been properly determined in accordance with the 1982 Law of the Sea Convention, these baselines and limits should not be required to be recalculated should sea level change affect the geographical reality of the coastline" (ILA Res. 5/2018 ("Committee on International Law and Sea Level Rise")).

48 See articles 7 and 9–11 of the LOSC. See also articles 14 and 16.

49 See article 13 of the LOSC. See further e.g., C Schofield "Departures from the coast: Trends in the application of territorial sea baselines under the Law of the Sea Convention" (2012) 27 IJMCL 723–732.

50 The term "archipelagic State" is defined in article 46(a) of the LOSC and the term "archipelago" is defined in article 46(b).

51 See article 47 of the LOSC.

52 See further section 4.3.2.

53 On the impact of the pursued vessel entering a territorial sea, see section 3.2.

54 See e.g., Allen (n. 36) 312; *The "Arctic Sunrise" Arbitration (Netherlands v. Russia)*, award of 14 August 2015, XXXII RIAA 205 § 245 and 246 quoting *The M/V "Saiga" (No 2) Case (Saint Vincent and the Grenadines v. Guinea)*, judgment of 1 July 1999, 1999 ITLOS Reports 10 § 146.

55 Article 111(1) of the LOSC.

56 Article 111(5) of the LOSC. The pursuit may also be undertaken by an aircraft, in which case the rules apply *mutatis mutandis* (see article 111(6)(a)).

of the outer limit of the territorial sea.[57] And fourthly, "a visual or auditory signal to stop [must have] been given at a distance which enables it to be seen or heard by the foreign ship".[58] Once the pursuit has started, it may only be continued outside the territorial sea as long as it is not interrupted.[59]

A second exception to the principle that T jurisdiction is limited to the area landward of the outer limit of the territorial sea is confirmed by article 111(7) of LOSC.[60] A third exception is To jurisdiction.[61]

4.3.2 Relationship between territorial jurisdictions

There is a potential for spatial overlap of T jurisdictions within overlapping territorial seas, but there is no actual overlap when the coastal States concerned have agreed on the boundary that separates their respective territories. In the absence of agreement, the position might be very complex. Indeed, while a coastal State has no ground on which to deny an adjacent or opposite State a territorial sea, it might challenge, for instance, the breadth claimed by the other State.[62] The LOSC provides that, until the States have agreed, or an adjudicative body has decided otherwise, neither State "is entitled [...] to extend its territorial sea beyond the median line every point of which is equidistant from the nearest points on the baselines from which the breadth of the territorial seas of each of the [...] States is measured".[63] However, the LOSC itself acknowledges that the median line rule does not apply "where it is necessary by reason of historic title or other special circumstances to delimit the territorial seas of the two States in a way which is at variance therewith",[64] an exception that raises additional issues for disputes.[65]

There is a potential for spatial overlap of the TE jurisdiction of one State and the TE jurisdiction of another State when the latter exercises its right of hot pursuit and the pursuing vessel enters the territorial sea of the former. That overlap is however excluded in principle by the fact that the exercise of TE jurisdiction by a coastal State while exercising the right of hot pursuit is limited to areas outside the territorial seas of other coastal States. That limitation of the right, confirmed in article 111(3) of the LOSC, is based on the fact that, "[a]s a consequence of a State's territorial sovereignty extending into its territorial sea, a government vessel

57 Article 111(4) of the LOSC.

58 *Ibid.*

59 See article 111(1) of the LOSC. See further Allen (n. 36) 321–325 for an examination of the legitimacy of using various enforcement technologies and procedures.

60 See further ILC "Commentaries to the articles concerning the law of the sea" UN Doc. A/3159 (1956), reproduced in (1956) II YILC 253–302 at 285).

61 See sections 4.3.2 and 4.3.3.5 and Chapter 3 section 3.3.2.4.

62 See e.g., E Korkut *Turkey and the International Law of the Sea* (2017) 37 fn. 53.

63 Article 15.

64 *Ibid.*

65 See e.g., *Bay of Piran (Croatia v. Slovenia)*, award of 29 June 2017, PCA Case No 2012–04 §§ 955–961.

may not exercise law-enforcement jurisdiction within the […] territorial waters of another State without that State's consent".[66] When giving its consent, the State may determine whether the modalities of the continued exercise of the right of hot pursuit within its maritime territory are either the same as, or narrower or broader than, those set in article 111. Consent may be given on an ad hoc basis. It may also be given in advance by means of the conclusion of a treaty.[67] Examples are the many bilateral treaties concluded by the United States with other States in the Caribbean region[68] and the 2012 Agreement on Strengthening Implementation of the Niue Treaty on Cooperation in Fisheries Surveillance and Law Enforcement in the South Pacific.[69]

As in the case of F jurisdiction,[70] T jurisdictions can overlap when a matter involves the maritime territories of at least two States such as, for example, when a person located within the territorial sea of one State spills pollutants, which are then carried by a current into the territorial sea of another State. In such a case, the former State has Ts jurisdiction while the latter State has To jurisdiction.[71] The two jurisdictions are not concurrent because, while they overlap *ratione materiae* and *ratione personae*, they do not overlap *ratione loci*, each State's T jurisdiction being spatially limited to its own maritime territory.[72] TsL jurisdiction and ToL jurisdiction, on the one hand, and TsA jurisdiction and ToA jurisdiction, on the other, coexist nevertheless because the matter involves two or more maritime territories. As a result, a person may violate at the same time a normative provision contained in a legislative instrument produced by a legislative act performed by an organ of one of the coastal States exercising the latter's ToL jurisdiction, and a normative provision contained in a legislative instrument produced by a legislative act performed by an organ of the other coastal State exercising the latter's TsL jurisdiction. Likewise, the person may fall under the ToA jurisdiction of one of the two States and under the TsA jurisdiction of the other State. As far as ToE jurisdiction and TsE jurisdiction are concerned, it was explained above that their exercise within the maritime territory of another State is only allowed with the consent of, and within the parameters set by, that State.

66 D Guilfoyle "Article 111" in Proelss (n. 25) 772–779 at 776. See also e.g., Allen (n. 36) 320; K Neri *L'Emploi de la Force en Mer* (2013) 65 and 79–80.

67 See also Chapter 3 section 3.7.

68 See e.g., article 8(b) of the US' model bilateral Agreement Concerning Cooperation to Suppress Illicit Traffic by Sea (JE Kramek "Bilateral maritime counter-drug and immigrant interdiction agreements: Is this the world of the future" (2000) 31 *University of Miami Inter-American Law Review* 121–162 at 152–160). See further e.g., D Guilfoyle *Shipping Interdiction and the Law of the Sea* (2009) 92–94.

69 Adopted: 2 November 2012; EIF: 30 July 2014. See article 13(2)–(3).

70 See section 4.2.2.

71 See Chapter 3 section 3.3.2.4.

72 See section 4.3.1.

4.3.3 Relationship between territorial jurisdiction and flag State jurisdiction

4.3.3.1 Introduction

Because the connecting factor establishing F jurisdiction does not contain any geographical element[73] and both T jurisdiction and F jurisdiction are primary jurisdictions, there is an overlap of those jurisdictions *ratione loci* and *ratione materiae* when a vessel is within the marine component of the territory of a coastal State. That overlap presents no difficulty in international law when a vessel flies the flag of the State in the territory of which it finds itself. Indeed, in that case, no issue of attribution of competence arises because the same State exercises F jurisdiction and T jurisdiction. Issues only arise while a vessel flying the flag of one State finds itself within the maritime territory of another State. In such a case, the positions are different with regard to legislative jurisdiction,[74] executive jurisdiction[75] and adjudicative jurisdiction.[76] The position is also different in the cases where T jurisdiction is exercised outside of the territory of the coastal State.[77]

4.3.3.2 Legislative jurisdiction

The relationship between TL jurisdiction and FL jurisdiction is somewhat complex. Because TL jurisdiction is exercised in regard of the marine component of the territory of a coastal State, over which the latter has sovereignty,[78] the principle of non-intervention by a State in the internal affairs of another State would appear to exclude the concurrence of FL jurisdiction and TL jurisdiction.[79] However, the principle is "an extremely vague principle".[80] What appears to be clear, at least, is that "a particular jurisdictional assertion does not of itself violate the principle of non-intervention".[81] Irrespective of what the principle of non-intervention entails as far as legislative jurisdiction is concerned, there is undoubtedly room for FL jurisdiction in the maritime territories of the coastal States for at least four reasons.

The first reason is that the practice of coastal States consisting in leaving matters regarding only the "internal economy" of a foreign ship to the authorities of the flag State[82] is based on the expectation that the flag State does have, at least to

73 See Chapter 3 section 3.2.2.
74 See section 4.3.3.2.
75 See section 4.3.3.3.
76 See section 4.3.3.4.
77 See section 4.3.3.5.
78 See e.g., P Vincent *Droit de la Mer* (2008) 55. See further section 4.3.2.
79 See e.g., A Cassese *International Law* (2005) 53.
80 C Ryngaert (n. 6) 156.
81 *Ibid.* 155. See further Chapter 5 section 5.5.4.
82 See R Churchill, V Lowe & A Sander *The Law of the Sea* (2022) 124; R-J Dupuy "La mer sous compétence nationale" in R-J Dupuy & D Vignes (eds) *Traité du Nouveau Droit de la Mer* (1985) 219–273 at 222; L Lucchini & M Vœlckel *Droit de la Mer* (1990) I 148 and 156. See also *The "Sally" and "Newton"*, avis of 28 November 1806, *Bulletin des Lois* 2nd semester 1806 No 125 at 602 discussed in P Bonassies "Faut-il abroger l'avis du Conseil d'Etat du 28 octobre 1806?" in V

some extent, FL jurisdiction within the maritime territories of other States.[83] It is also based on the expectation that an organ of the flag State has actually exercised the latter's FL jurisdiction in such a way that its laws and regulations also apply to the vessels flying its flag while they are within the territories of other States. In this regard, the relevant organ(s) of a coastal State can adopt either one of two approaches. One approach is to exercise the State's TL jurisdiction by performing legislative acts producing legislative instruments containing normative provisions governing internal matters regarding foreign vessels within the State's territory, but to leave it to the organ(s) exercising the State's TE jurisdiction and TA jurisdiction to decide whether they ought to rely on those normative provisions to be involved in such matters.[84] The other approach is to refrain from exercising the State's TL jurisdiction, in which case other organs do not have to decide whether to exercise the State's TE jurisdiction and TA jurisdiction to the extent that they do not have a basis to do so in domestic law.[85]

The second reason is that the LOSC itself implies, when it limits the TL jurisdiction of the coastal States, that a flag State retains its FL jurisdiction to some extent when the vessels flying its flag are within the territories of other States and exercise the right of innocent passage, the right of transit passage or the right of archipelagic sea lanes passage.[86] The main limitation is that the coastal States do not have TL jurisdiction to deny the existence of the rights.[87] An example of a more specific limitation, in the case of the right of innocent passage, is article 21(2) of the LOSC, in terms of which coastal States are forbidden to adopt laws and regulations applying "to the design, construction, manning or equipment of foreign ships unless they are giving effect to generally accepted international rules or standards".[88] In the case of the right of transit passage, an example is article 42(2) of the LOSC, in terms of which coastal States are forbidden to adopt laws and regulations which "discriminate in form or in fact among foreign ships or in their application have the practical effect of denying, hampering or impairing the right of transit passage". This prohibition applies also in the case of the right of archipelagic sea lanes passage in terms of article 54 of the LOSC. In addition, article 24(1) confirms that FL jurisdiction excludes TL jurisdiction with regard to any matter that "might hamper the innocent passage of foreign ships through the territorial sea" otherwise than in accordance with the Convention.[89] There is no doubt that coastal States do not have

Coussirat-Coustère *et al* (eds) *La Mer et son Droit* (2003) 101–109; *"Wildenhus" Case* 120 US 1 (1887) at 12; *Spector v. Norwegian Cruise Lines Ltd* 545 US 119 (2005) 121.

83 See e.g., R Jennings & A Watts (eds) *Oppenheim's International Law* (1992) I 622.

84 See e.g., Gidel (n. 39) 148.

85 See e.g., *Spector v. Norwegian Cruise Lines Ltd* (n. 82).

86 Compare article 21(2) and article 94(1). See further e.g., Neri (n. 66) 101.

87 See articles 17, 38(1), 52(1) and 53(2) of the LOSC.

88 See e.g., Gidel (n. 39) 235. See further e.g., LS Johnson *Coastal State Regulation of International Shipping* (2004) 73.

89 See RA Barnes "Article 24" in Proelss (n. 25) 217–222 at 220. In particular, the coastal States may not "impose requirements which have the practical effect of denying or impairing the right of innocent passage" (article 24(1)(a)). See further e.g., Vincent (n. 78) 40.

TL jurisdiction to deny innocent passage when the requirements set by the LOSC for the exercise of the right are met.[90] It is also clear that coastal States do not have TL jurisdiction to impose "requirements so stringent either that access becomes impossible or that passage becomes too burdensome to be practical".[91] Even when that is not the case, however, coastal States arguably do not have TL jurisdiction when FL jurisdiction must prevail to best accommodate "the competing interests of the coastal State and [the world] community".[92]

The third reason is that the coastal State may impose limits to its own TL jurisdiction, thereby giving room to FL jurisdiction, for the purpose of complying with a bilateral or multilateral agreement entered into with one or more foreign States, for example with regard to access to ports[93] or air pollution.[94]

The fourth reason is that nothing appears to stand in the way of an organ of a flag State deciding to exercise the latter's FL jurisdiction by performing a legislative act producing a legislative instrument containing one or more normative provisions applicable in the territory of a coastal State, compelling the vessels flying the State's flag to comply with the duties and prohibitions imposed by the coastal State in the exercise of the latter's TL jurisdiction. Although the flag State would not, in principle, be able to exercise its FE jurisdiction while the vessels with which it has a legal relationship of nationality are in the maritime territory of a foreign coastal State,[95] it would be able to do so as soon as the vessels are not in such a territory[96] and, obviously, when they are within the maritime territory of the flag State itself.

4.3.3.3 Executive jurisdiction

(A) PRINCIPLE

The position is different regarding the relationship between FE jurisdiction and TE jurisdiction. The same principle that explains why the TE jurisdiction of one State excludes the TE jurisdiction of another State (i.e., the principle of exclusive

90 See articles 18–19 of the LOSC.
91 MS McDougal & WT Burke *The Public Order of the Oceans* (1962) 255.
92 Barnes (n. 89) 219–220. A decision in this regard can be made by applying the doctrine of abuse of rights (see DW Bowett *The Law of the Sea* (1967) 44) or the concepts of proportionality or reasonableness (see e.g., B Smith "Innocent passage as a rule of decision: Navigation v. environmental protection" (1982) 21 *Columbia Journal of Transnational Law* 49–102 at 91). See further Chapter 5 section 5.5.4.
93 See e.g., article 2 of the 1923 Convention and Statute on the International Regime of Maritime Ports (58 LNTS 285; adopted: 9 December 1923; EIF: 26 July 1926). See further e.g., Lucchini & Vœlckel (n. 82) 155.
94 See e.g., reg. 15(1) of Annex VI of MARPOL added to MARPOL in terms of its 1997 Protocol. See further e.g., B Lin & C-Y Lin "Compliance with international emission regulations: Reducing the air pollution from merchant vessels" (2006) 30 MP 220–225; C Pisani "Fair at sea: The design of a future legal instrument on marine bunker fuel emissions within the climate change regime" (2002) 33 ODIL 57–76.
95 See section 4.3.3.3.
96 See section 4.2.1.

executive jurisdiction of a State within its territory)[97] explains why the TE jurisdiction of a coastal State excludes, in principle, the FE jurisdiction of another State.[98] In other words, while the flag State has, in principle, exclusive FE jurisdiction over the vessels flying its flag on the high seas,[99] it has, in principle, no FE jurisdiction over the same vessels while they are within the maritime territories of other States, unless it has received the latter's consent to exercise that jurisdiction.[100]

One example of coastal-State consent is FE jurisdiction relating to the "internal economy" of vessels while they are within the maritime territories of foreign States. The practice of coastal States consisting in leaving matters relating to the "internal economy" of a foreign vessel to the authorities of the flag State[101] presupposes that the organ(s) having FE jurisdiction on a vessel may also exercise that jurisdiction on the vessel when the latter is within the territory of a coastal State. In that case, whether there is actual concurrence of FE jurisdiction and TE jurisdiction depends on the approach adopted by the relevant organ(s) of the coastal State in the exercise of the latter's TL jurisdiction[102] and the approach adopted by the relevant organ(s) of the flag State in the exercise of the latter's FL jurisdiction.[103] When there is concurrence and an organ of the coastal State decides to exercise the latter's TE jurisdiction, the sovereignty of the coastal State demands that its TE jurisdiction prevail over the FE jurisdiction of the relevant organ(s) on the foreign vessel. In other words, within the maritime territories of coastal States, TE jurisdiction excludes FE jurisdiction in most cases and, when it does not, it nevertheless prevails over FE jurisdiction whenever it is exercised.

The scope of the principle of exclusive executive jurisdiction of a State within its maritime territory is restricted in that, at the same time that the FE jurisdiction of a flag State may not be exercised by a vessel flying the flag of the State towards another vessel flying that flag without the consent of the coastal State,[104] the TE jurisdiction of the coastal State is subject to three sets of limitations: (i) those relating to either innocent passage, transit passage or archipelagic sea lanes passage;[105] (ii) those relating to warships and other government vessels operated for non-commercial purposes;[106] and (iii) those relating to cases of distress.[107]

97 See section 4.3.2.
98 See e.g., *The M/V 'Louisa' Case (Saint Vincent and the Grenadines v. Spain)*, judgment of 28 May 2013, 2013 ITLOS Reports 4 § 125.
99 See section 4.2.2.
100 See e.g., ED Brown *The International Law of the Sea* (1994) I 39–40; R O'Keefe "Universal jurisdiction: Clarifying the basic concept" (2004) 2 JICJ 735–760 at 739; S Bateman "The role of flag States" in Warner & Kaye (n. 23) 43–58 at 47.
101 See section 4.3.3.2.
102 See section 4.3.3.2.
103 The relevant organ(s) of the flag State might, deliberately or inadvertently, not have provided for the application of the relevant normative provisions within the maritime territory of foreign States.
104 See e.g., Neri (n. 66) 103.
105 See section 4.3.3.3(b).
106 See section 4.3.3.3(c).
107 See section 4.3.3.3(d).

(B) INNOCENT PASSAGE, TRANSIT PASSAGE AND ARCHIPELAGIC SEA LANES PASSAGE

(i) Introduction In specific parts of the maritime territory of a coastal State, foreign vessels have either the right of innocent passage, the right of transit passage or the right of archipelagic sea lanes passage.[108]

(ii) Innocent passage Wherever there is no right of transit passage or archipelagic sea lanes passage in the territorial sea and/or archipelagic waters, as well as, exceptionally, within internal waters, foreign vessels have the right of innocent passage.[109] Over and above the indirect limitations flowing from the limitations to TL jurisdiction,[110] the right limits the TE jurisdiction of the coastal State in that: (a) charges may only be levied on foreign vessels engaged in innocent passage "as payment [...] for specific services rendered to the ship";[111] (b) except in "straits used for international navigation", where innocent passage may not be suspended when it applies,[112] TE jurisdiction may only be exercised to suspend the innocent passage of foreign vessels "if such suspension is essential for the protection of [the coastal State's] security, including weapons exercises", in which case the suspension may only be temporary and "in specified areas";[113] and (c) TE jurisdiction may not, in principle, be exercised in such a way as to "hamper the innocent passage of foreign ships".[114] At the same time, there is no doubt that a coastal State has TE jurisdiction to "take the necessary steps in its territorial sea to prevent passage which is not innocent".[115] It has also TE jurisdiction "to take the necessary steps to prevent any breach of the conditions to which admission of" vessels to its internal waters or a call at a port facility outside those internal waters.[116]

In criminal matters, two categories of matters need to be distinguished regarding the exercise of TE jurisdiction on board foreign vessels. The first category consists of matters that arose before the vessel entered the maritime territory of the coastal State. When the matter does not in one way or another relate to the marine component of the territory of the State, the connecting factor does not exist and

108 The only parts of the maritime territories of coastal States where none of these rights exist are the internal waters that have not been enclosed by straight baselines established on the basis of article 7 of the LOSC (see article 8(2) of the LOSC). See further e.g., CR Symmons "Article 8" in Proelss (n. 25) 84–96 at 96.

109 See articles 17 and 8(2) of the LOSC. On the meaning of innocent passage, see articles 18–19 of the LOSC. See further e.g., *The "Duzgit Integrity" Arbitration (Malta v. São Tomé and Príncipe)*, award of 5 September 2016, PCA Case No. 2014–07 § 310.

110 See section 4.3.3.2.

111 Article 26(2) of the LOSC. See further e.g., RA Barnes "Article 26" in Proelss (n. 25) 226–229.

112 Article 45 of the LOSC. See further e.g., BB Jia "Article 45" in Proelss (n. 25) 327–333 at 332–333.

113 Article 25(3) of the LOSC, which also requires that the suspension only take effect "after having been duly published" and be applied on a non-discriminatory basis. See also article 52(2) of the LOSC. See further e.g., S Kaye "Maritime security in the post-9/11 world: A new creeping jurisdiction in the law of the sea?" in C Schofield, S Lee & M-S Kwon (eds) (2014) 327–348 at 330; RA Barnes "Article 25" in Proelss (n. 25) 222–226 at 225–226.

114 Article 24(1) of the LOSC. See further e.g., Barnes (n. 89) 219–221.

115 Article 25(1) of the LOSC. See further e.g., Barnes (n. 113) 224–225; Neri (n. 66) 89–90.

116 Article 25(2) of the LOSC. See further e.g., Barnes (n. 113) 225.

the coastal State cannot have T jurisdiction.[117] This is confirmed in article 27(5) of the LOSC with regard to cases of lateral innocent passage (i.e., passage without entering or exiting the internal waters of the coastal State) when it states that "the coastal State may not take any steps on board a foreign ship passing through the territorial sea to arrest any person or to conduct any investigation in connection with any crime committed before the ship entered the territorial sea [...]".[118] The position is different when the offence was initiated on a foreign vessel before it entered the territorial sea of the coastal State and was completed on the landward side of the outer limit of the territorial sea. Indeed, in such a case, the coastal State has To jurisdiction and the matter must arguably be dealt with as falling within the second category of matters (i.e., matters that arose on board a foreign vessel during its passage).

In the case of this second category of matters, there is no doubt that the connecting factor is established and the coastal State has T jurisdiction. This is confirmed by article 27 of the LOSC when: (a) "the consequences of the crime extend to the coastal State";[119] (b) "the crime is of a kind to disturb the peace of the country or the good order of the territorial sea";[120] (c) "the assistance of the local authorities has been requested by the master of the ship or by a diplomatic agent or consular officer of the flag State";[121] (d) the arrest of a person or the conduct of an investigation is "necessary for the suppression of illicit traffic in narcotic drugs or psychotropic substances";[122] and (e) when the foreign vessel is "passing through the territorial sea after leaving internal waters".[123] In other cases, article 27(1) provides that TE jurisdiction "should not be exercised [...] to arrest any person or to conduct any investigation [...]". It would appear that the phrase "should not" must be understood as giving a hortatory character to the statement,[124] leaving the determination of "whether or not to exercise criminal jurisdiction [to] be decided on a case-by-case basis according to the discretion of the coastal State",[125] unless the State is compelled to act in the case at hand.[126]

117 The decision of the French Cour de cassation of 3 May 1995 in *M/V "Ruby"* (Cour de Cassation Bulletin criminel 1995 No 161 at 446) is not a departure from this rule because the Court established the connecting factor on the basis of the indivisibility of the various factual elements of the case, which started outside the French territory but continued after the vessel entered the French territorial sea.

118 See RA Barnes "Article 27" in Proelss (n. 25) 229–237 at 237.

119 Article 27(1)(a). See e.g., Barnes (n. 118) 235.

120 Article 27(1)(b). See e.g., Barnes (n. 118) 235.

121 Article 27(1)(c).

122 Article 27(1)(d).

123 Article 27(2).

124 See e.g., Guilfoyle (n. 68) 12; Tanaka (n. 47) 115.

125 Barnes (n. 118) 233–234. See further e.g., Brown (n. 100) 64; H Yang *Jurisdiction of the Coastal State over Foreign Merchant Ships in Internal Waters and the Territorial Sea* (2005) 253–256.

126 See e.g., UNSC Resolution 1540 (2004) (28 April 2004) regarding the shipment of weapons of mass destruction. See further e.g., Guilfoyle (n. 68) 242.

In civil matters, the distinction that needs to be made is between matters relating to persons, on the one hand, and matters relating to vessels, on the other. With regard to the former, article 28(1) of the LOSC states that "[t]he coastal State should not stop or divert a foreign ship passing through the territorial sea for the purpose of exercising civil jurisdiction in relation to a person on board the ship". As in the case of article 27(1), the phrase "should not" must be understood as giving a hortatory character to the statement.[127] With regard to matters relating to a foreign vessel, the coastal State may only "levy execution against or arrest the ship for the purpose of any civil proceedings"[128] when the vessel is "lying in the territorial sea, or passing through the territorial sea after leaving internal waters"[129] or "in respect of obligations or liabilities assumed or incurred by the ship itself in the course or for the purpose of its voyage through the waters of the coastal State".[130] It is not entirely clear whether the phrase "the waters of the coastal State" refers only to the waters landward of the outer limit of the territorial sea,[131] but there is no doubt that it refers at least to the marine component of the territory of the coastal State and that, therefore, the latter has TE jurisdiction.

(iii) Transit passage In most "straits which are used for international navigation between one part of the high seas or an [EEZ] and another part of the high seas or an" EEZ[132] where there does not exist "through the strait a route through the high seas or through an [EEZ] of similar convenience with respect to navigational and hydrographical characteristics",[133] the right of transit passage enjoyed by foreign ships limits the TE jurisdiction of the States bordering the straits in that they may not hamper or suspend transit passage,[134] except in case of major damage, or a threat thereof, to the marine environment of the strait.[135] This is over and above the indirect limitations flowing from the limitations to TL jurisdiction.[136]

127 See RA Barnes "Article 28" in Proelss (n. 25) 237–241 at 240.

128 *Ibid.* referring to *The "Trade Resolve"* ([1999] 4 SLR 424 § 40 (Singapore)] and s. 22(1)(a) of the Admiralty Act, 1988, of Australia.

129 Article 28(3).

130 Article 28(2).

131 See e.g., DR Rothwell & T Stephens *The International Law of the Sea* (2016) 459; Barnes (n. 127) 241.

132 The exceptions are "straits in which passage is regulated in whole or in part by long-standing international conventions in force specifically relating to such straits" (article 35(c) of the LOSC) and where "the strait is formed by an island of a State bordering the strait and its mainland" and "there exists seaward of the island a route through the high seas or through an [EEZ] of similar convenience with respect to navigational and hydrographical characteristics" (article 38(1) of the LOSC). "Transit passage" is defined in article 38(2).

133 Article 36 of the LOSC.

134 See article 44 of the LOSC. See further e.g., BB Jia "Article 44" in Proelss (n. 25) 324–327; Neri (n. 66) 93.

135 See article 233 of the LOSC. See further e.g., V Becker-Weinberg "Article 233" in Proelss (n. 25) 1563–1566.

136 See section 4.3.3.2. See further e.g., H Caminos & VP Cogliati-Bantz *The Legal Regime of Straits* (2014); DD Caron & N Oral (eds) *Navigating Straits* (2014).

(iv) Archipelagic sea lanes passage Within the sea lanes and air routes designated by the archipelagic States[137] or, failing such designation, "through the routes normally used for international navigation",[138] the right of archipelagic sea lanes passage enjoyed by foreign ships[139] limits the TE jurisdiction of the archipelagic States in that the latter may not hamper or suspend archipelagic sea lanes passage.[140] This is over and above the indirect limitations of TE jurisdiction flowing from the limitations to TL jurisdiction.[141]

(C) WARSHIPS AND OTHER GOVERNMENT VESSELS OPERATED FOR NON-COMMERCIAL PURPOSES

The second set of limitations to the TE jurisdiction of the coastal States relates to warships and other government vessels operated for non-commercial purposes.[142] This limitation must be approached within the context of the other set of limitations in that these vessels may only enter the marine component of the territory of a foreign State with the consent of the State or in compliance with the requirements for the exercise of the right of innocent passage,[143] the right of transit passage or the right of archipelagic sea lanes passage. The fact that the coastal State has TL jurisdiction is confirmed, by implication, by articles 30, 42(5) and 54 of the LOSC. However, in order to take into account that warships and other government vessels operated for non-commercial purposes have immunities,[144] article 30 limits the measures that may be taken by the coastal State in the exercise of its TE jurisdiction with regard to vessels in innocent passage to: (a) requesting, in cases of lack of compliance "with the laws and regulations of the coastal State concerning passage through the territorial sea", that the vessel comply with those laws and regulations; and (b) in the case where the vessel disregards the request, requiring that the vessel "leave the territorial sea immediately".[145] Article 30 implies that the coastal State has no TE jurisdiction at all while warships and other government vessels operated

137 In terms of article 53(1) of the LOSC.
138 Article 53(12) of the LOSC.
139 See article 53(2) of the LOSC. The right is defined in article 53(3).
140 See article 54 of the LOSC read with article 44. On enforcement jurisdiction in respect of marine pollution, see e.g., Churchill, Lowe & Sander (n. 82) 197; RA Barnes & C Massarella "Article 44" in Proelss (n. 25) 404–407 at 407; Neri (n. 66) 93; L Bautista "The role of coastal States" in Warner & Kaye (n. 23) 59–70 at 63. On the possible exception in the case of major damage, or threat thereof, to the marine environment of the archipelago, see e.g., MH Nordquist (ed) *United Nations Convention on the Law of the Sea 1982: A Commentary* (2002) II 487 § 54.7(a); Vincent (n. 78) 84.
141 See section 4.3.3.2.
142 See e.g., articles 29–32 and 95–96 of the LOSC; *The Schooner Exchange v. McFaddon* 11 US (7 Cranch) 116 (1812); *The "Ara Libertad" Case (Argentina v. Ghana)*, order of 15 December 2012, 2012 ITLOS Reports 332 § 95; *Republic v. High Court (Comm. Div.) Accra* Ghana Supreme Court judgment of 20 June 2013 at 24–26 (available at https://pcacases.com/web/sendAttach/431).
143 See e.g., RA Barnes "Article 30" in Proelss (n. 25) 244–247 at 246.
144 See article 32 of the LOSC. See further Chapter 3 section 3.3.2.1.
145 Nordquist (n. 140) 255 § 30.6. See further e.g., BH Oxman "The regime of warships under the United Nations Convention on the Law of the Sea" (1984) 24 *Virginia Journal of International*

for non-commercial purposes are in innocent passage, with regard to its laws and regulations other than those concerning passage through the territorial sea.[146] That limitation no longer exists when passage is no longer innocent.[147] In that regard, it would appear that a coastal State may decide that a failure to comply with a request to leave, referred to in article 30, amounts to passage no longer being innocent, after "some investigation of the situation by the coastal State" and giving the vessel "an opportunity to correct its conduct".[148] Once that decision has been made, "the coastal State may use any force necessary to compel" the vessel to leave its territory.[149] The same steps may be taken in the cases of "violations of coastal States laws that are also conditions of innocent passage",[150] such as those listed in article 19(2) of the LOSC. Those steps "must necessarily comply with the requirements of necessity and proportionality" and the international order would be less at risk to be disrupted were the coastal State to "first consider other appropriate measures, such as diplomatic protest before resorting to force".[151]

The extent of TE jurisdiction in the case where a warship or other government vessel operated for non-commercial purposes is given permission to enter the maritime territory of a coastal State gave rise to a dispute between Argentina and Ghana in *ARA Libertad*.[152] The frigate *ARA Libertad* was an Argentinian frigate to which had been granted the request to call at the Ghanaian port of Tema[153] and which was forcefully detained once it had done so.[154] In its order, ITLOS confirmed that "a warship is an expression of the sovereignty of the State whose flag it flies".[155] It also confirmed that, "in accordance with general international law, a warship enjoys immunity, including in internal waters".[156] In other words, a coastal State that consents to a warship or other

---

Law 809–864 at 817; IA Shearer "Problems of jurisdiction and enforcement against delinquent vessels" (1986) 35 ICLQ 320–343 at 325.

146 This is confirmed by the fact that articles 27–28 of the LOSC are in a different subsection of Part II of the LOSC. See further Chapter 2 section 2.3.3.1(c)(*iii*).

147 The position of many States is that "the traditional view of the maritime states that warships, like other ships, are entitled to a right of innocent passage in the territorial is still the law of the sea" (TA Clingan Jr "Freedom of navigation in a post-UNCLOS III environment" (1983) 46(2) LCP 107–124 at 112). At the same time, many States are of the view that warships do not have an automatic right of innocent passage (see e.g., section 6(2) of China's 1992 Law on the Territorial Sea and the Contiguous Zone ((1992) 21 LOSB 24) and section 16(2) of the Maritime Zones Act, 1999 (Act 2 of 1999), of Seychelles ((2002) 48 LOSB 18)).

148 Barnes (n. 143) 247.

149 Churchill, Lowe & Sander (n. 82) 164.

150 See Barnes (n. 143) 246.

151 *Ibid.* 247.

152 See n. 142.

153 *Ibid.* § 38.

154 *Ibid.* § 40.

155 *Ibid.* § 94, recalled in *Case Concerning the Detention of Three Ukrainian Naval Vessels (Ukraine v. Russia)*, order of 25 May 2019, 2018–2019 ITLOS Reports 283, (2019) 58 ILM 1147 § 110.

156 *The "Ara Libertad" Case* (n. 142) § 95. See also e.g., *The Schooner Exchange v. McFaddon* (n. 142); CJ Colombos *The International Law of the Sea* (1967) 264–265; Jennings & Watts (n. 83) 460–461.

government vessel operated for non-commercial purposes calling at one of its ports thereby limits the scope of its TE jurisdiction over the vessel to the extent required for the State not to violate the immunity of the vessel.[157]

(D) CASES OF DISTRESS

The third set of limitations to the TE jurisdiction of the coastal States relates to cases of distress. Indeed, in those cases, the vessel flying the flag of a foreign State has a qualified right to enter a port[158] and the right to stop and anchor in the marine territory of a coastal State.[159] When it does so, the vessel is immune, to a not-uniformly-interpreted extent, from the TE jurisdiction of the coastal State.[160]

4.3.3.4 Adjudicative jurisdiction

Being dependent on the existence and exercise of legislative and executive jurisdiction,[161] the relationship between TA jurisdiction and FA jurisdiction is particularly complex. Irrespective of what the principle of non-intervention entails as far as legislative jurisdiction is concerned, it has been shown above that there is undoubtedly room for FL jurisdiction in the maritime territories of the coastal States.[162] This creates a basis for the concurrence of FA jurisdiction and TA jurisdiction.

Indeed, the practice of coastal States consisting in leaving matters regarding only the "internal economy" of a foreign ship to the authorities of the flag State[163] is based on the recognition that the flag State retains its FA jurisdiction while vessels flying its flag are within the marine components of the territories of other States. It also anticipates that the flag State will actually exercise its FA jurisdiction to deal with a dispute that: (a) arose within the maritime territory of a foreign State; and (b) relates to legislative provisions of the flag State applying in that territory.

Whether an organ of a flag State is in a position to exercise the latter's FA jurisdiction is affected by whether it was possible for FE jurisdiction to be exercised beforehand. For instance, in a case where an individual violates both a normative provision of the flag State and an identical normative provision of the coastal State in the territory of which the vessel is at the time of the violation, an organ of the coastal State might decide to exercise the TE jurisdiction of that State. Such a step would prevent an organ of the flag State on board the vessel from exercising the

157 See e.g., Vincent (n. 78) 42; Pancracio (n. 23) 148.

158 See e.g., Churchill, Lowe & Sander (n. 82) 115; A Chircop "Assistance at sea and places of refuge for ships: Reconciling competing norms" in Ringbom (n. 5) 140–163 at 163.

159 See articles 18(2) and 39(1)(c) of the LOSC.

160 See e.g., Colombos (n. 156) 329–330; Sohn *et al.* (n. 22) 197–198; A Choquet & A Sam Lefebvre "Détresse en mer en période de pandémie: Des navires de croisière à la recherche d'un port d'accueil" (2020) 124 RGDIP 261–288; JE Noyes "Ships in distress" 2021 MPEPIL; *The Eleanor* ((1809) 165 ER 1058), *The Brig Concord* (13 U.S. 387 (1815)).

161 See Chapter 2 section 2.5.

162 See section 4.3.3.2.

163 See section 4.3.3.2.

State's FE jurisdiction. In turn, the absence of control of the authorities of the flag State over the individual might then raise issues relating to whether the court has jurisdiction to hear the matter and/or order the relief sought. The same issues would arise in the exercise of TA jurisdiction should the relevant organ(s) of the coastal State have decided to refrain from exercising the latter's TE jurisdiction, thereby making it possible for FE jurisdiction to be exercised instead.[164]

4.3.3.5 Relationship outside of the territory of the coastal State

The relationship between T jurisdiction and F jurisdiction is different in the exercise of the right of hot pursuit. Indeed, once a pursuing vessel is no longer within the territory of the coastal State, it is no longer possible to rely on territorial sovereignty to exclude the exercise of FE jurisdiction. At the same time, there is no doubt that the principle of exclusive FE jurisdiction of the flag States over the vessels flying their flags outside the territories of coastal States does not apply in the case of hot pursuit.[165] However, nothing in international law appears to stand in the way of an organ of the flag State of a pursued vessel, acting not in the exercise of the right of hot pursuit (which is an attribute of TE jurisdiction) but in the exercise of the State's FE jurisdiction, assisting in the process of pursuing the vessel, taking control of it and, possibly, handing that control over to an organ of the coastal State.[166]

The relationship between To jurisdiction and F jurisdiction is also different outside of the territory of the coastal State. The rationale for the existence of To jurisdiction arguably requires that a coastal State may exercise its ToL jurisdiction and ToA jurisdiction not only with regard to the element(s) of the matter within its territory, but also the element(s) outside its territory.[167] By contrast, there does not appear to exist any basis for the FE jurisdiction of the flag States over the vessels flying their flags outside the territories of coastal States not to exclude ToE jurisdiction, except in cases of unauthorised broadcasting from a ship or installation located beyond the outer limits of the territorial seas, when the transmissions can be received in the territory of the coastal State or when authorised radio communication in that State is "suffering interference".[168] In those cases, the coastal State has ToE jurisdiction beyond the outer limits of its territorial sea, which may only be exercised by warships or "any other duly authorized ships or aircraft clearly marked and identifiable

164 See further e.g., Lucchini & Vœlckel (n. 82) 157–162.

165 Article 111(1) of the LOSC makes it clear that the provision relates to the pursuit of foreign ships. See further e.g., Allen (n. 36) 312. There is obviously no overlap of TE jurisdiction and FE jurisdiction when the vessel pursued is without nationality. In that case, the pursuit may also take place in the exercise of StE jurisdiction (see section 4.8.1.4).

166 See e.g., Allen (n. 36) 315.

167 *The M/V "Norstar" Case (Panama v. Italy)*, judgment of 10 April 2019, (2019) 58 ILM 673, joint dissenting opinion of judges Cot, Pawlak, Yanai, Hoffmann, Kolodkin and Lijnzaad and judge *ad hoc* Treves § 36.

168 Article 109(3)(d)–(e) of the LOSC.

as being on government service".[169] That jurisdiction may not be exercised against warships[170] or ships "owned or operated by a State and used only on government non-commercial service".[171] In addition, there needs to exist a "reasonable ground for suspecting" that the ship against which ToE jurisdiction is exercised, is engaged in unauthorised broadcasting.[172] When those requirements are met,

> the warship may proceed to verify the ship's right to fly its flag. To this end, it may send a boat under the command of an officer to the suspected ship. If suspicion remains after the documents have been checked, it may proceed to a further examination on board the ship, which must be carried out with all possible consideration.[173]

The State may then arrest the ship or any person on board and seize the broadcasting apparatus.[174]

4.3.4 Summary

Coastal States have, in principle, authority to perform acts within their respective territories in the exercise of their TL jurisdiction, TE jurisdiction and TA jurisdiction, with regard to all matters relating to the marine components of those territories, irrespective of the nationality of the persons involved and the legal relationship of nationality of the vessels involved. Within the maritime territory of a coastal State, T jurisdiction is limited primarily in matters involving the right of innocent passage, the right of transit passage, the right of archipelagic sea lanes passage, warships and other government vessels operated for non-commercial purposes and/or cases of distress. TE jurisdiction may be exercised outside the maritime territory of the State concerned, provided that the requirements for the exercise of the right of hot pursuit are met and as long as that exercise does not take place within the maritime territory of another State without the latter's consent.

4.4 Personal jurisdiction

4.4.1 Extent of personal jurisdiction

As indicated above, P jurisdiction is a primary form of jurisdiction in that it confers upon the personal State jurisdiction that is all-encompassing *ratione materiae*.[175] In

169 Article 110(1) and (5) of the LOSC.
170 See article 110(1) read with article 95 of the LOSC.
171 Article 110(1) read with article 96 of the LOSC. See e.g., *The "Enrica Lexie" Incident* (n. 5) § 799.
172 Article 110(1)(c) read with article 109(3)(d)–(e) of the LOSC.
173 Article 110(2) of the LOSC.
174 See article 109(4) of the LOSC.
175 See section 4.1.

addition, P jurisdiction is all-encompassing *ratione navis* and *ratione loci*.[176] This means that P jurisdiction includes, for instance, authority in fisheries-related matters arising on the high seas,[177] taking into account however that, as also pointed out above, the nature of the connecting factor establishing P jurisdiction means that the latter is limited *ratione personae*.[178] In light of the above, it is clear that the limited, albeit important,[179] role played in practice by P jurisdiction does not result from any limitation inherent to this ground of jurisdiction, but rather from the impact of the potential overlaps of P jurisdiction and other jurisdictions, an examination of which is necessary at this point.

4.4.2 Relationship between personal jurisdictions

There is usually no concurrence of P jurisdictions with regard to the same person because a person normally has only one nationality. However, international law does not forbid a person to have two or more nationalities.[180] Moreover, the fact that residence is also sufficient in limited cases for the connecting factor to exist increases the chance of overlap of P jurisdictions because international law does not forbid a person with the nationality of one State to reside within the territory of another State. In addition, in cases where, for instance, a national of one State kills at sea a national of another State, the objective P jurisdiction ("Po jurisdiction") of the latter State overlaps with the Ps jurisdiction of the former State.

In cases where there is more than one P jurisdiction, there is no obstacle in principle to the concurrence of the PL jurisdictions and the concurrence of the PA jurisdictions. In other words, the PL or PA jurisdiction of one State may not be relied upon to exclude the PL or PA jurisdiction of another State. Although the position is the same, in theory, with regard to PE jurisdiction, it is different in practice because executive jurisdiction is, in most cases, exercised either on dry land or on a vessel over which a form of executive jurisdiction other than PE jurisdiction is exercised. It will be explained shortly that, in most of these cases of potential overlap, PE jurisdiction is excluded by executive jurisdiction exercised on another ground. The main situation where that is not the case is that

176 See e.g., M Akehurst "Jurisdiction in international law" (1972–1973) 46 BYIL 145–257 at 156; Churchill, Lowe & Sander (n. 82) 382; O'Keefe (n. 100) 739; JM Goodwin "Universal jurisdiction and the pirate: Time for an old couple to part" (2006) 39 *Vanderbilt Journal of Transnational Law* 973–1012 at 985. See further e.g., § 410 comment (d) *Restatement of the Law (Fourth)* (n. 12).

177 This is confirmed by article 117 of the LOSC when it provides that "[a]ll States have the duty to take, or to cooperate with other States in taking, such measures for their respective nationals as may be necessary for the conservation of the living resources of the high seas". This duty is linked to the right of all States "for their nationals to engage in fishing on the high seas", confirmed in article 116 of the LOSC. See further e.g., R Rayfuse "Article 116" in Proelss (n. 25) 791–803 at 798.

178 See section 4.1.

179 See e.g., P Arnell "The case for nationality based jurisdiction" (2001) 50 ICLQ 955–962 at 955.

180 This was the basis on which the ICJ reasoned in *Nottebohm Case (Second Phase) (Liechtenstein v. Guatemala)*, judgment of 6 April 1955, 1955 ICJ Reports 4 at 21. See further e.g., PJ Spiro "Multiple nationality" 2008 MPEPIL; Simma & Müller (n. 14) 142.

of the exercise of PE jurisdictions over an individual with more than one nationality on a stateless vessel (or a vessel that "may be assimilated to a ship without nationality")[181] on the high seas. In such an instance, there is no connecting factor establishing F jurisdiction (because the vessel does not fly the flag of any State) and no connecting factor establishing T jurisdiction, Cz jurisdiction, Eez jurisdiction or Cs jurisdiction (because the vessel is not within any of the coastal zones). The two PE jurisdictions do not exclude each other and there is thus concurrence. In the light of the fact that there does not appear to be any basis for the PE jurisdiction of one State to prevail over the PE jurisdiction of another State, either State may exercise its PE jurisdiction over the individual. In the process of doing so, the personal State must however be careful not to arrogate FE jurisdiction to itself. In other words, the executive steps taken by the personal State must be limited to those necessary for it to exercise its authority over the person(s) over which it may exercise PE jurisdiction.

No issue of opposability arises in the case of concurrence of P jurisdictions because each personal State is entitled to treat, and, in practice, does treat, a person with multiple nationalities as having only the nationality of that State.[182]

4.4.3 Relationship between personal jurisdiction and flag State jurisdiction

There is concurrence of F jurisdiction and P jurisdiction as soon as, for instance, a natural person gets on board a vessel, provided that neither is without nationality.[183] When the vessel and the person have the nationality of the same State, the latter has both jurisdictions and no issue of attribution of competence arises as far as international law is concerned.[184] The position is more complex in cases where the flag State is not the same as the personal State.

As far as they are concerned, PL jurisdiction and FL jurisdiction are concurrent because the law of the sea does not contain any general exclusion of either jurisdiction by the other.[185] It must be stressed that article 92(1) of the LOSC does not create an exception when it provides that, "save in exceptional cases expressly provided for in international treaties or in" the LOSC, vessels are subject to the

181 See article 92(2) of the LOSC and section 4.2.2.

182 See article 3 of the CCNL. With regard to the exercise of PE jurisdiction in the form of diplomatic protection in such a case, compare article 4 of the Convention and article 7 of the 2006 ILC Draft Articles on Diplomatic Protection (ILC "Report of the International Law Commission on the work of its fifty-eighth session" (2006) 2(2) YILC 24).

183 A more complex example is, for instance, the case where a national of State A is shot and killed on a vessel flying the flag of State B by a national of State C shooting on a vessel flying the flag of State D. In such a case, State A has Po jurisdiction, State B as Fo jurisdiction, State C has Ps jurisdiction and State D has Fs jurisdiction.

184 In many cases, a substantial proportion, if not all the individuals, on board a ship do have the nationality of the flag State where national officers and a national crew are requirements for being entitled to fly the flag of the State concerned. See e.g., articles 7–9 of the Registration Convention; Sohn *et al.* (n. 22) 49.

185 Staker (n. 39) 323.

exclusive jurisdiction of the flag State while on the high seas. As it has already been explained above, the provision must indeed be understood to refer only to FE jurisdiction.[186] Article 97(1) of the LOSC confirms that the personal State has legislative jurisdiction together with the flag State. Indeed, a State would not have a basis for instituting proceedings against one of its nationals if it did not have the necessary legislative jurisdiction to enact the law, the violation of which is the ground for such proceedings. It is in the exercise of PL jurisdiction that, for instance, an increasing number of States are criminalising fisheries-related activities by their nationals.[187]

The position is different with regard to FE jurisdiction and PE jurisdiction because, unless the flag State decides otherwise, FE jurisdiction always excludes PE jurisdiction in cases where FE jurisdiction is not itself excluded by another executive jurisdiction.[188] This rule is confirmed by articles 92(1) and 97(3) of the LOSC. It would seem that it is in this context that the European Community must be understood when it made the (admittedly awkwardly-worded) interpretative declaration regarding the Fish Stocks Agreement that it

> and its Member States understand that the term "States whose nationals fish on the high seas" shall not provide any new grounds for jurisdiction based on the nationality of persons involved in fishing on the high seas rather than on the principle of flag State jurisdiction.[189]

It must be emphasised that, although the lack of PE jurisdiction substantially limits the ability of a personal State to exercise its PA jurisdiction in practice, the law of the sea does not contain any general exception to the exercise of FA jurisdiction or PA jurisdiction when they overlap. Disciplinary matters are exceptions, however, because the personal State does not have PA jurisdiction, when it is not the State which has issued the Master's certificate or the certificate of competence or licence involved, to pronounce the withdrawal of such certificates.[190]

It would appear that a State has very little room to challenge the existence of P jurisdiction of another State with regard to a specific person on the ground that the legal relationship of nationality between the person and that State has an inexistent or insufficient factual basis. Indeed, the ICJ decision in *Nottebohm*[191] related only to the exercise of PE jurisdiction in the form of diplomatic protection and only in the case of a State other than the State exercising PE jurisdiction with which the person concerned had stronger factual links than with the personal State. The Court stressed that it did "not propose to go beyond the limited scope of the question

186 See section 4.2.2.
187 See e.g., Rayfuse (n. 177) 798. See e.g., section 72 of the Fisheries Act, 2014 (Act 10 of 2014) of Vanuatu.
188 See section 4.3.3.
189 Sohn *et al.* (n. 22) 45.
190 Article 97(2) of the LOSC.
191 *Nottebohm Case (Second Phase)* (n. 180).

which it ha[d] to decide, namely whether the nationality conferred on Nottebohm [could] be relied upon as against Guatemala in justification of the proceedings instituted before the Court".[192] It is in answering this specific question that the Court stated that

> a State cannot claim that the rules [relating to nationality] it has [...] laid down are entitled to recognition by another State unless it has acted in conformity with th[e] general aim of making the legal bond of nationality accord with the individual's genuine connection with the State which assumes the defence of its citizens by means of protection as against other States.[193]

At the same time, the Court confirmed that it was "for Liechtenstein, as it is for every sovereign State, to settle by its own legislation the rules relating to the acquisition of its nationality, and to confer that nationality [...] in accordance with that legislation".[194] The Court did not suggest that this freedom was unlimited[195] and there is little doubt that the freedom would be exercised impermissibly were it to be exercised inconsistently with "applicable international conventions, customary international law and the principles of law generally recognised with regard to nationality".[196]

4.4.4 Relationship between personal jurisdiction and territorial jurisdiction

It has already been indicated earlier, with regard to the overlap of TL jurisdiction and FL jurisdiction, that it remains to some extent unclear to which extent the principle of non-intervention by a State in the internal affairs of another State stands in the way of the concurrence of TL jurisdiction and another legislative jurisdiction.[197] There is no doubt, however, that TL jurisdiction does not exclude PL legislation altogether.[198]

In contrast, the principle of exclusive executive jurisdiction of a State within its territory results in PE jurisdiction being excluded, bar exceptional cases such as

192 At 17.

193 At 23. Compare article 4 of the 2006 ILC Draft Articles on Diplomatic Protection, which "does not require a State to prove an effective or genuine link between itself and its national" (ILC "Report of the International Law Commission on the work of its fifty-eighth session" (2006) 2(2) YILC 29).

194 At 20. See also e.g., article 1 of the CCNL and article 3(1) of the ECN.

195 At 20.

196 Article 3(2) of the ECN, which repeats almost *verbatim* the latter part of article 1 of the CCNL. That would be the case, for instance, where the principle of non-discrimination is violated (see article 5 of the ECN; O Dörr "Nottebohm Case" (2007) MPEPIL 10), when nationality is imposed collectively upon unwilling people and where nationality is obtained by fraud or corruption (Staker (n. 39) 300).

197 See section 4.3.3.2.

198 Staker (n. 39) 299.

cases involving consular matters[199] as well as cases where the coastal State waives the exclusivity of its TE jurisdiction and authorises the personal State to exercise its PE jurisdiction within the coastal State's territory.[200]

Like the relationship between TA jurisdiction and FA jurisdiction, the relationship between TA jurisdiction and PA jurisdiction is complex because, as it was already explained earlier, it depends on the existence and exercise of the States' legislative and executive jurisdiction.[201] Irrespective of what the principle of non-intervention entails as far as legislative jurisdiction is concerned, it has been pointed out above that TL jurisdiction does not exclude PL jurisdiction, thereby creating a basis for the concurrence of PA jurisdiction and TA jurisdiction. Clearly, to the extent that the exercise of judicial jurisdiction involves the prior exercise of executive jurisdiction, the personal State is, in practice and in principle, unable to exercise its PA jurisdiction as long as the person concerned is within the territory of another State.

4.4.5 Summary

Personal States have, in principle, authority to perform acts in the exercise of their PL jurisdiction, PE jurisdiction and PA jurisdiction with regard to all matters relating to persons with whom they have the necessary link, irrespective of the location or the vessel(s) involved, subject to substantial limitations flowing from precedence being given to other (mainly executive) jurisdictions in most cases of potential overlap.

4.5 Contiguous zone jurisdiction

4.5.1 Extent of contiguous zone jurisdiction

The scope of Cz jurisdiction is, in principle, all-encompassing *ratione personae* and *ratione navis*. At the same time, Cz jurisdiction is a secondary form of State ocean jurisdiction in that it only confers authority on States with regard to a limited range of matters.[202] The latter are listed in article 33(1) of the LOSC as the matters relating to preventing "infringement of its customs, fiscal, immigration or sanitary laws and regulations within its territory or territorial sea" and to punishing "infringement of the above laws and regulations committed within its territory or

199 See the 1963 Vienna Convention on Consular Relations (596 UNTS 261; adopted: 24 April 1963; EIF: 19 March 1967).

200 See e.g., Akehurst (n. 176) 150.

201 See Chapter 2 section 2.5.

202 See e.g., Brown (n. 100) 134; Kaye (n. 113) 338; D-E Khan "Article 33" in Proelss (n. 25) 254–271 at 264.

territorial sea".[203] Whether the list is exhaustive[204] is affected by the relationship between article 33(1) and article 303(2) of the LOSC, which provides that, in order to control traffic in "objects of an archaeological and historical nature found at sea",

> the coastal State may, in applying article 33, presume that their removal from the seabed in the zone referred to in that article without its approval would result in an infringement within its territory or territorial sea of the laws and regulations referred to in that article.[205]

This provision, which arguably entails "legalistic lucubrations",[206] is the object of much debate.[207] However, that debate does not appear to revolve around the inclusion of matters relating to archaeological and historical objects within the scope *ratione materiae* of Cz jurisdiction in that portion of ocean space, whether or not labelled as a distinct overlapping zone,[208] but around the nature of the coastal State's authority in that regard.[209]

Cz jurisdiction is not only limited *ratione materiae*, it is also limited *ratione loci*. Indeed, provided that a coastal State has claimed a contiguous zone,[210] its Cz jurisdiction is, in principle, limited to the extent of that zone. The latter is located beyond the territorial sea and "may not extend beyond 24 nautical miles from the baselines from which the breadth of the territorial sea is measured".[211] As pointed out in the previous chapter, the breadth of each contiguous zone is determined by the coastal State, in the exercise of its inchoate CzL jurisdiction, by means of a legislative act producing a legislative instrument containing a constitutive provision to that effect.[212] The exception when a coastal State may exercise its CzE jurisdiction outside its contiguous zone is when it exercises that jurisdiction in the exercise of

203 The word "sanitary" may not be interpreted in such a way as to include the protection of the marine environment (see e.g., *Alleged Violations of Sovereign Rights and Maritime Spaces in the Caribbean Sea (Nicaragua v. Colombia)*, judgment of 21 April 2022, ICJ Case No 155 § 180). It would appear that the meaning of the word "sanitary" may not be broadened so as to include pollution as an indirect threat to public health (see e.g., EJ Molenaar *Coastal State Jurisdiction over Vessel-Source Pollution* (1998) 281; J Carlson "Presidential Proclamation 7219: Extending the United States' contiguous zone – Didn't someone say this had something to do with pollution?" (2001) 55 *University of Miami Law Review* 487–526 at 525.

204 See e.g., *Alleged Violations* (n. 203) §§ 134 and 177.

205 *Ibid.* § 188.

206 T Scovazzi "Article 303" in Proelss (n. 25) 1950–1961 at 1954.

207 See e.g., MJ Aznar "The contiguous zone as an archaeological maritime zone" (2014) 29 IJMCL 1–51.

208 For instance, the "archaeological maritime zone" (see e.g., Aznar (n. 207) 3 fn 5). As far as the Nigerian Maritime Zones (Enactment) Bill, 2020, and the Maritime Zones Act, 1994 (Act 15 of 1994), of South Africa are concerned, they use the term "maritime cultural zone" (see sections 4.7(1) and 4.6(1) respectively).

209 See further.

210 See Chapter 3 section 3.3.3.

211 Article 33(2) of the LOSC.

212 See Chapter 3 section 3.3.3.

its right of hot pursuit, in which case the same requirements have to be met, *mutatis mutandis*, as in the case of TE jurisdiction.[213] As a result, whether hot pursuit may be started in the contiguous zone depends *inter alia* on the nature of the coastal State's authority conferred in its contiguous zone by Cz jurisdiction.[214]

State practice and the doctrine reflect disagreement on the nature of that authority. There would appear, however, to be little room for any ambiguity in this regard. Indeed, "[a] literal reading [of article 33(1)] in accordance with generally recognized rules of interpretation [...] leaves no doubt": the LOSC does not give CzL jurisdiction and CzA jurisdiction to coastal States, but merely CzE jurisdiction.[215] As explained in Chapter 2, that does not mean that the coastal States have no authority to perform legislative acts with regard to their contiguous zone. That authority may however only be used in the exercise of their CzE jurisdiction.[216] In line with the protective nature of the contiguous zone, some States have nevertheless performed legislative acts producing legislative instruments containing normative provisions applying in their contiguous zones.[217] In other words, those States have exercised a CzL jurisdiction which they probably do not have. While the performance of those acts does "not appear to have evoked significant international opposition in practice", the instances where it has[218] arguably point out to the fact that the exercise of legislative jurisdiction in relation to the contiguous zone is best seen as a form of protective jurisdiction and ought to be assessed on that basis.[219]

The only matters with regard to which there is a growing consensus that the coastal States have CzL jurisdiction are those relating to archaeological and historical objects. Indeed, article 8 of the 2001 Convention on the Protection of the Underwater Cultural Heritage (CPUCH),[220] unambiguously gives legislative jurisdiction to coastal States to "regulate and authorize activities directed at underwater cultural heritage within their contiguous zone".[221]

The extent of the CzE jurisdiction of a coastal State to prevent or punish infringements of its laws and regulations is dependent on the extent of the prior exercise of its TL jurisdiction. In other words, the opportunity for an organ of a

213 See section 4.3.1.
214 See Khan (n. 202) 269.
215 See e.g., Lucchini & Vœlckel (n. 82) 199; Brown (n. 100) 133; Rothwell & Stephens (n. 131) 83; Khan (n. 202) 264; Fabris (n. 24) 16; Churchill, Lowe & Sander (n. 82) 214. As far as he is concerned, Tanaka stresses, after pointing out that article 33(1) does not refer to the internal waters, that "it would be inconceivable that the drafters of this provision intended to exclude the internal waters from the scope of this provision since these waters are under the territorial sovereignty of the coastal State" (Tanaka (n. 47) 147). The same reasoning applies in the case of the archipelagic waters. With regard to CzA jurisdiction, see e.g., Vincent (n. 78) 88.
216 See further Chapter 2 section 2.3.2.
217 See e.g., section 7(2)(b) of the Maritime Zones (Establishment) Decree, 1996 (Decree 11 of 1996), of Sierra Leone.
218 Churchill, Lowe & Sander (n. 82) 215.
219 See Chapter 3 section 3.9 as well as section 4.12.
220 2562 UNTS 3, (2002) 41 ILM 40, (2002) 48 LOSB 29. Adopted: 02.11.2001; EIF: 02.01.2009.
221 See further e.g., Aznar (n. 207) 3; Scovazzi (n. 206) 1955.

coastal State to exercise the State's CzE jurisdiction in a specific matter depends on an organ of the State having beforehand exercised the TL jurisdiction of the State by performing one or more legislative acts producing legislative instruments containing normative provisions with regard to that matter.[222] In the case of objects of an archaeological and historical nature, the relevant organ must give effect into its domestic law to the fact that article 303(2) entails

> a dual legal fiction. First, the removal of [those] objects is to be regarded as infringement of customs, fiscal, immigration or sanitary laws and regulations of the coastal State. Second, the removal of [those] objects within the contiguous zone is to be considered as an act within the territory or the territorial sea.[223]

As in the case of other executive jurisdictions, the performance of executive steps is also dependent on the prior performance of the legislative acts producing legislative instruments containing the necessary performative provisions.[224]

The CzE jurisdiction to prevent infringements, in terms of article 33(1)(a), appears to be exercisable only in respect of inbound vessels when the latter are suspected of being intended to be used for infringements, at one stage or another, once the vessel will enter the territorial sea of the coastal State. In the exercise of that jurisdiction, the only steps that may be taken appear to be "visit, search and eventually a refusal to let" the vessel enter the territorial sea.[225] As far as it is concerned, the CzE jurisdiction to punish infringements, in terms of article 33(1)(b), appears to be exercisable only in respect of vessels that have been within the territory of the coastal State. Although this is contested in the doctrine,[226] it is arguably the necessary implication of the absence of CzL jurisdiction and the limitation of the scope *ratione loci* of TL jurisdiction to the territory of the coastal State. As a result, a vessel can only infringe a law or regulation of a coastal State within the territory of that State and the vessel must have been there before any step to punish it from the infringement may be taken. There would appear, however, to be no temporal limitation as to when the steps must be taken. In other words, while one aspect of the rationale of the contiguous zone is to extend the area within which coastal States may take steps to punish infringements immediately or soon after they have taken place, there appears to be nothing in article 33(1)(b) that stands in the way of the coastal State taking steps at a later stage when the vessel is, in the course of a later voyage, either preparing to enter the State's territorial sea or merely passing laterally through the contiguous zone.[227]

222 See Chapter 2 section 2.2.2.3.
223 Tanaka (n. 47) 148.
224 See Chapter 2 section 2.3.2.
225 See Khan (n. 202) 265. See also article 19(2)(g) of the LOSC.
226 See e.g., S Oda "The concept of the contiguous zone" (1962) 11 ICLQ 131–153 at 153.
227 This is, obviously, within the limitations *ratione temporis* of domestic law and international law.

It is unlikely that the jurisdictional aspects of the legal regime governing archaeological and historical objects in a contiguous zone have matured into customary international law. As a result, a State's jurisdictional assertion in that regard might not be opposable to another State, especially if the latter is not a party to the LOSC and/or the CPUCH. This is in contrast to CzE jurisdiction in respect of customs, fiscal, immigration and sanitary matters, the main features of which have, although less than 100 States claim a contiguous zone,[228] probably matured into customary international law and, therefore, are opposable to all States.[229]

4.5.2 Relationship between contiguous zone jurisdictions

In view of the fact that CzE jurisdiction is exercised in relation to either TL jurisdiction or CzL jurisdiction,[230] the overlap of Cz jurisdictions is best understood, in cases other than the case of hot pursuit, by approaching it from two different angles *ratione materiae*.

Because CzE jurisdiction is dependent on the exercise of TL jurisdiction in cases where the coastal States do not have CzL jurisdiction,[231] the existence and extent of material overlaps between CzE jurisdictions is affected by the existence and extent of the material overlaps of TL jurisdictions.[232] In that regard, it has already been shown that T jurisdiction is all-encompassing *ratione materiae*.[233] As a result, the only factor affecting the material overlaps between CzE jurisdictions in any specific instance is the extent to which the States concerned have actually made use of their respective TL jurisdictions.

The position is more complex as far as spatial overlaps are concerned. Indeed, TL jurisdiction and CzE jurisdiction are exercised in different areas: the maritime territory and the contiguous zone, respectively. In the exceptional cases where there is a spatial overlap of TL jurisdictions[234] and contiguous zones have been claimed by all the States concerned, the latter all have CzE jurisdiction within their respective contiguous zones. In such cases, it is likely that there is a spatial overlap of CzE jurisdictions because the contiguous zones are geographical extensions of the territorial seas. However, cases of spatial overlap of CzE jurisdictions are not limited to cases of spatial overlap of TL jurisdictions. Indeed, contiguous zones can

228 103 States by 2019 (JA Roach *Excessive Maritime Claims* (2021) 145). See e.g., S Kaye "A zonal approach to maritime regulation and enforcement" in Warner & Kaye (n. 23) 3–15 at 8; Rothwell & Stephens (n. 131) 82; Khan (n. 202) 262.

229 The contiguous zone was already provided for in article 24 of the CTSCZ, which was ratified, or acceded to, by 52 States.

230 See section 4.5.1.

231 See section 4.5.1.

232 See section 4.3.2.

233 See section 4.3.1.

234 See section 4.3.2.

also potentially overlap in areas where the territorial seas have been delimited[235] or do not require delimitation.[236]

In contrast to the territorial sea,[237] the EEZ[238] and the continental shelf,[239] the LOSC does not contain any provision on the delimitation of the contiguous zone. It is unclear why that is the case[240] and State practice is of little assistance because it is "virtually negligible".[241] A possible explanation for this distinction between the contiguous zone, on the one hand, and the other three zones, on the other, is that Cz jurisdiction is much more limited than T jurisdiction, Eez jurisdiction and Cs jurisdiction.[242] Indeed, as pointed out above, Cz jurisdiction normally entails only CzE jurisdiction[243] and any spatial overlap of the zones does, therefore, not involve any overlap of legislative jurisdiction or adjudicative jurisdiction.

The above means that overlapping contiguous zones have limited impact on the EezL jurisdictions and CsL jurisdictions of States with EEZs and continental shelves overlapping those contiguous zones, because CzL jurisdiction only exists in those zones on an exceptional basis. By contrast, the CzE jurisdictions would overlap the EezE jurisdictions and the CsE jurisdictions *ratione loci*, although the latter would not overlap the former *ratione materiae* because the scope of CzE jurisdiction *ratione materiae* is completely different from the scopes of EezE jurisdiction and CsE jurisdiction.[244] In other words, there is no concurrence of CzE jurisdiction, on the one hand, and EezE jurisdiction or CsE jurisdiction, on the other. In this context, it is not entirely clear for what legal reason a State would object to overlapping contiguous zones.[245] This is especially so when one takes into account that, while the contiguous zone of a State might overlap the EEZ and continental shelf of a neighbouring State, this would also be the case of the latter's contiguous zone with regard to the former's EEZ and continental shelf. In this context, insisting on a delimitation of the contiguous zone appears to be only to the benefit of persons who either have already infringed or are planning to infringe a customs, fiscal, immigration or sanitary law or regulation of a coastal State because it would result in the limitation of the scope of the State's CzE jurisdiction *ratione loci*. In fact, the enforcement of such laws and regulations would probably be best served by the States cooperating with each other on a bilateral or regional basis, not

235 In the case of States with adjacent coasts.
236 In the case of States with opposite coasts more than 24 NM apart.
237 See article 15 of the LOSC. See further section 4.3.2.
238 See article 74 of the LOSC. See further section 4.6.2.
239 See article 83 of the LOSC. See further section 4.7.2.
240 See Khan (n. 202) 262.
241 NSM Antunes *Towards the Conceptualisation of Maritime Delimitation: Legal and Technical Aspects of a Political Process* (2003) 101.
242 Commonwealth Secretariat *Ocean Management – A Regional Perspective: The Prospects for Commonwealth Maritime Co-operation in Asia and the Pacific* (1984) 39, referred to in Khan (n. 202) 262.
243 See section 4.5.1.
244 See sections 4.6.6 and 4.7.6.
245 See however Khan (n. 202) 263.

only by avoiding to start from the premise that spatial overlaps must be avoided,[246] but also by conferring additional delegated jurisdiction to each other.[247]

The position is different with regard to the matters over which the coastal States have CzL jurisdiction. Indeed, the latter's existence means that, in the case of overlapping contiguous zones, more than one State is entitled to presume that the removal without its approval of objects of an archaeological and historical nature from the seabed in the area where contiguous zones overlap, results in an infringement of its own laws and regulations. Such a situation would certainly contribute to the protection of archaeological and historical objects at sea by increasing the number of States having jurisdiction over those objects. However, Cz jurisdiction over the objects includes not only regulation, but also authorisation.[248] In cases of spatial overlap, little benefit would be derived from requiring more than one authorisation, over and above the fact that States are unlikely to have agreed, when becoming parties to the LOSC or any other relevant instrument, to sharing their power in this regard.

The above points to the fact that, while the overlap of contiguous zone jurisdictions is not only acceptable but actually in the interest of the coastal States concerned with regard to customs, fiscal, immigration and sanitary matters, the overlap is probably best avoided with regard to archaeological and historical objects. A way to achieve these contradictory goals is to proclaim two different zones. The first zone is the contiguous zone *stricto sensu*, in which CzE jurisdiction is exercised with regard to customs, fiscal, immigration and sanitary matters. That zone may overlap with the same zones claimed by adjacent or opposite States where the geographical features of the area concerned have that effect. The second zone is a zone (however named by the coastal State) in which CzL jurisdiction, CzE jurisdiction and CzA jurisdiction are exercised with regard to archaeological and historical objects, and which should not overlap any other zone of the same kind.[249]

246 This would appear to be the position adopted by Japan in its Territorial Sea and the Contiguous Zone Act, 1977 (Act 30 of 1977) as amended by Territorial Sea Act Amendment Act, 1996 (Act 73 of 1996) ((1997) 35 LOSB 76). Indeed, in terms of the Act, now renamed "the Territorial Sea and Contiguous Zone Act", where the 24 NM line "extends beyond the median line from the baseline, the zone shall comprise the area up to the median line, or another line where such line has been agreed upon between Japan and another state" (article 4(2)), but also that the contiguous zone could extend beyond that line "where Japan and a neighbouring state consider it appropriate" (article 4(3)) (M Hayashi "Japan – New Law of the Sea Legislation" (1997) 12 IJMCL 572).

247 See further Chapter 5.

248 See article 303(2) of the LOSC ("without its approval") and article 8 of the CPUCH, quoted in section 4.5.1.

249 Delimitation should arguably take place on the same basis as the EEZ and the continental shelf in order to simplify the delimitation process and to avoid overlaps between different types of zones in any given geographical area. See e.g., Khan (n. 202) 263.

4.5.3 Relationship between contiguous zone jurisdiction and flag State jurisdiction

There is a potential for overlap of F jurisdiction and Cz jurisdiction within the contiguous zone. When the vessel has a legal relationship of nationality with the State in the contiguous zone of which it finds itself, that State has both F jurisdiction and Cz jurisdiction. As a result, no issue of attribution of competence arises as far as international law is concerned. The position is more complex in cases where the flag State is not the same as the coastal State.

There is a spatial overlap in that, although CzE jurisdiction is limited *ratione loci*,[250] FE jurisdiction is, in principle, all-encompassing *ratione loci*.[251] In addition, in contrast to the position in the territorial sea,[252] FE jurisdiction is not excluded by the principle of exclusive executive jurisdiction of a State within its territory because the contiguous zone is not part of the territory of the coastal State. There is also a personal overlap in that both CzE jurisdiction and FE jurisdiction are, in principle, all-encompassing *ratione personae*.[253] There is further a vessel overlap in that, although F jurisdiction is limited *ratione navis*,[254] Cz jurisdiction is, in principle, all-encompassing *ratione navis*.[255] There is a material overlap in that, although Cz jurisdiction is limited *ratione materiae*,[256] F jurisdiction is a form of primary jurisdiction and, in principle, all-encompassing *ratione materiae*.[257] In order to ascertain the extent of concurrence, it is once again necessary to distinguish between the two categories of matters over which a coastal State has CzE jurisdiction.

Where CzE jurisdiction is exercised in relation to matters over which the coastal State has exercised its TL jurisdiction (i.e., customs, fiscal, immigration and sanitary matters), there appears to be little doubt that the principle of non-intervention by a State in the internal affairs of another State[258] stands in the way of concurrence. Indeed, it is difficult to find any valid basis for the exercise by a State of its FL jurisdiction in respect of customs, fiscal, immigration and sanitary matters relating to another State's territory outside of a bilateral or regional arrangement, most probably on a reciprocal basis. By contrast, nothing appears to stand in the way of FE jurisdiction being exercised by an organ of a flag State in the contiguous zone of another State in respect of customs, fiscal, immigration and sanitary matters relating to the flag State's territory.[259] In that case, there is actually no material overlap

250 See section 4.5.1.
251 See section 4.2.1.
252 See section 4.3.3.3.
253 See sections 4.2.1 and 4.5.1.
254 See section 4.2.1.
255 See section 4.5.1.
256 See section 4.5.1.
257 See section 4.2.1.
258 See section 4.3.3.2.
259 See e.g., K Aquilina "Territorial sea and the contiguous zone" in DJ Attard (ed) *The IMLI Manual of International Maritime Law* (2014) I 26–70 at 60.

of CzE jurisdiction and FE jurisdiction because a coastal State does not have TL jurisdiction in respect of customs, fiscal, immigration and sanitary matters relating to another State's territory.

The position is more complex with regard to the matters over which the coastal States have CzL jurisdiction. Indeed, the flag States have F jurisdiction with regard to both the archaeological and historical objects with which a legal relationship of nationality exists and the vessels, with which such a relationship also exists, that engage in activities relating to those objects. As far as the objects are concerned, article 303(3) of the LOSC leaves the door open to a flag State exercising jurisdiction with regard to "the rights of identifiable owners, the law of salvage or other rules of admiralty, or laws and practices with respect to cultural exchanges".[260] In addition, article 10(7) of the CPUCH provides that "no activity directed at State vessels and aircraft shall be conducted without the agreement of the flag State".[261] As far as vessel activities are concerned, the relevant provisions of the CPUCH are premised on the existence of F jurisdiction.[262]

4.5.4 Relationship between contiguous zone jurisdiction and territorial jurisdiction

There is concurrence of T jurisdiction and Cz jurisdiction within the contiguous zone only in exceptional situations. When the same State has both T jurisdiction and Cz jurisdiction, there is obviously no issue of attribution of competence arising as far as international law is concerned.

There is a personal overlap in that both Cz jurisdiction and T jurisdiction are, in principle, all-encompassing *ratione personae*.[263] There is also a vessel overlap in that both Cz jurisdiction and T jurisdiction are, in principle, all-encompassing *ratione navis*.[264] There is a material overlap in that, although Cz jurisdiction is limited *ratione materiae*,[265] T jurisdiction is a form of primary jurisdiction and, in principle, all-encompassing *ratione materiae*.[266] However, there is, in principle, no spatial overlap in that both T jurisdiction and Cz jurisdiction are limited *ratione loci* and the respective geographical areas are separate.[267] The exception is the case of hot pursuit because, in that case, there is a spatial overlap of TE jurisdiction and CzE jurisdiction in that TE jurisdiction may be exercised in another State's con-

260 See further e.g., Scovazzi (n. 206) 1956–1957.

261 This is subject to the right of the "State Party in whose exclusive economic zone or on whose continental shelf underwater cultural heritage is located [...] to prohibit or authorize any activity directed at such heritage to prevent interference with its sovereign rights or jurisdiction as provided for by international law including the" LOSC (article 10(2)) and the taking of the necessary steps "to prevent any immediate danger to the underwater cultural heritage" (article 10(4)).

262 See articles 8–10.

263 See sections 4.3.1 and 4.5.1.

264 See sections 4.3.1 and 4.5.1.

265 See section 4.5.1.

266 See section 4.3.1.

267 See sections 4.3.1 and 4.5.1.

tiguous zone[268] and both TE jurisdiction and CzE jurisdiction may be exercised in the same area beyond the contiguous zones. In both situations, there is nevertheless no concurrence because, as already explained above, when jurisdiction is exercised in relation to matters over which the coastal State has TL jurisdiction, the principle of non-intervention by a State in the internal affairs of another State[269] stands in the way of concurrence. In other words, there is, in principle, no material overlap of the TL jurisdiction of the State exercising TE jurisdiction in the contiguous zone of another State with the TL jurisdiction of the latter State.

4.5.5 Relationship between contiguous zone jurisdiction and personal jurisdiction

There is a potential for overlap of P jurisdiction and Cz jurisdiction when a person is within a contiguous zone. In such a case, when the person has the nationality of the coastal State, the latter has both P jurisdiction and Cz jurisdiction and no issue of attribution of competence arises as far as international law is concerned. The position is more complex in cases where the personal State is not the same as the coastal State.

There is a spatial overlap in that, although Cz jurisdiction is limited *ratione loci*,[270] P jurisdiction is, in principle, all-encompassing *ratione loci*.[271] There is also a personal overlap in that, although P jurisdiction is limited *ratione personae*,[272] Cz jurisdiction is, in principle, all-encompassing *ratione personae*.[273] In addition, there is a vessel overlap in that both Cz jurisdiction and P jurisdiction are, in principle, all-encompassing *ratione navis*.[274] There is also a material overlap in that, although Cz jurisdiction is limited *ratione materiae*,[275] P jurisdiction is a form of primary jurisdiction and, in principle, all-encompassing *ratione materiae*.[276] The position in this regard is the same *mutatis mutandis* as in the case of overlap of Cz jurisdiction and F jurisdiction.[277]

4.5.6 Summary

Coastal States have, in principle, authority to perform acts in the exercise of their CzE jurisdiction only within their respective contiguous zones and with regard to customs, fiscal, immigration or sanitary matters, but irrespective of the person(s)

268 See section 4.5.2. CzE jurisdiction may not be exercised in hot pursuit within the marine component of another State, because it is excluded by the principle of exclusive executive jurisdiction of a State within its territory (see article 111(3) of the LOSC and section 3.2).
269 See section 4.3.3.2.
270 See section 4.5.1.
271 See section 4.4.1.
272 See section 4.4.1.
273 See section 4.5.1.
274 See sections 4.4.1 and 4.5.1.
275 See section 4.5.1.
276 See section 4.4.1.
277 See section 4.5.3.

and vessel(s) involved. In addition, coastal States have, within the same spatial limits, CzL jurisdiction, CzE jurisdiction and CzA jurisdiction with regard to archaeological and historical objects, irrespective of the person(s) and vessel(s) involved. CzE jurisdiction may be exercised beyond the contiguous zone in case of hot pursuit, except within the marine component of the territory of another State.

4.6 Exclusive economic zone jurisdiction

4.6.1 Extent of exclusive economic zone jurisdiction

4.6.1.1 Introduction

The scope of Eez jurisdiction is, in principle, all-encompassing *ratione personae* and *ratione navis*. By contrast, like Cz jurisdiction, Eez jurisdiction is a secondary form of State ocean jurisdiction in that it only confers authority on States with regard to a limited range of matters.[278] Most of those matters are mentioned in article 56 of the LOSC. At the same time, many other matters, which do not fall within the ambit of Eez jurisdiction, are mentioned in article 58 of the LOSC.[279] The drafters of the Convention were aware that there are matters that are not mentioned in either provision and have prescribed the basis on which conflicts in that regard must be resolved,[280] taking into account that the EEZ is a *sui generis* zone,[281] which has neither a residual high-seas character[282] nor a residual territorial-sea character.[283] The EEZ matured into customary international law before the LOSC came into force[284] and, for that reason, Eez jurisdiction is opposable to all States.[285]

4.6.1.2 Article 56(1)(a) matters

The first category of matters that are undoubtedly within the EezL jurisdiction, the EezE jurisdiction and the EezA jurisdiction of coastal States are the matters

278 See e.g., *In the Matter of the South China Sea Arbitration (Philippines v. China)*, award of 12 July 2016, XXXIII RIAA 153 § 249.

279 See e.g., *Alleged Violations* (n. 203) § 62. See further e.g., *Territorial and Maritime Dispute (Nicaragua v. Colombia)*, judgment of 19 November 2012, 2012 ICJ Reports 624 § 222, recalled in *Maritime Delimitation in the Indian Ocean (Somalia v. Kenya)*, judgment of 12 October 2021, ICJ Case No 161 § 158.

280 See article 59 of the LOSC.

281 See e.g., Churchill, Lowe & Sander (n. 82) 262.

282 *Ibid.* If the EEZ had a residual high-seas character, it would mean that matters not explicitly mentioned in article 56 would be excluded from Eez jurisdiction.

283 See e.g., Churchill, Lowe & Sander (n. 82) 262. If the EEZ had a residual territorial-sea character, it would mean that matters not explicitly mentioned in article 58 would be within the scope of Eez jurisdiction.

284 See e.g., Rothwell & Stephens (n. 131) 87.

285 At the same time, the extent of EEZ jurisdiction is contested. In that regard, see e.g., Brown (n. 100) 238; I Townsend-Gault "The 'territorialisation' of the exclusive economic zone: A requiem for the remnants of the freedoms of the seas?' in Schofield, Lee & Kwon (n. 113) 65–76 at 76; Kaye (n. 113) 333–334.

mentioned in article 56(1)(a).[286] Because the coastal States have sovereign rights for those purposes,[287] Eez jurisdiction is all-encompassing as far as those matters are concerned.[288] There are however limitations to the nature of the steps that coastal States may take in the exercise of EezE jurisdiction with regard to the resources of the EEZ.[289] For instance, while article 73 of the LOSC confirms that a coastal State may "take such measures, including boarding, inspection [and] arrest [...], as may be necessary to ensure compliance with the laws and regulations adopted by it in conformity with" the LOSC regarding its living resources,[290] it also stresses that, in the case of foreign vessels, the "[a]rrested vessels and their crews shall be promptly released upon the posting of reasonable bond or other security".[291] In that case, the coastal State may also not, in the exercise of its EezA jurisdiction, impose penalties that "include imprisonment, in the absence of agreements to the contrary by the States concerned, or any other form of corporal punishment".[292] Artificial resources do not fall within the article 56(1)(a) category.[293] This means, for instance, that coastal States have no Eez jurisdiction over wrecks. Any jurisdiction that might exist would flow from an international agreement in effect conferring that jurisdiction.[294] That agreement can be, for instance, a bilateral agreement regarding a specific wreck[295] or a multilateral agreement such as the 2007 Nairobi International Convention on the Removal of Wrecks (ICRW).[296]

4.6.1.3 Article 56(1)(b) matters

(A) INTRODUCTION

The second category of matters that are undoubtedly within the Eez jurisdiction of coastal States are the matters mentioned in article 56(1)(b), which divides those matters into three subcategories.

286 Article 56(1)(a) of the LOSC.
287 See A Proelss "Article 56" in Proelss (n. 25) 424.
288 See e.g., Vincent (n. 78) 105; *M/V "Virginia G" (Panama v. Guinea-Bissau)*, judgment of 14 April 2014, 2014 ITLOS Reports 4 §§ 211, 212 and 215; *Sub-Regional Fisheries Commission Advisory Opinion*, advisory opinion of 2 April 2015, 2015 ITLOS Reports 37 §§ 98 and 100.
289 See e.g., *The "Arctic Sunrise" Arbitration* (n. 54) § 168.
290 Article 73(1). See also article 73(4). See further e.g., *M/V "Virginia G"* (n. 288) § 211; *The "Arctic Sunrise" Arbitration* (n. 54) §§ 281, 284 and 324.
291 Article 73(2).
292 Article 73(3). See further e.g., J Harrison "Safeguards against excessive enforcement measures in the exclusive economic zone – Law and practice" in Ringbom (n. 5) 217–248 at 248.
293 See Churchill, Lowe & Sander (n. 82) 240.
294 *Ibid.*
295 See e.g., the 1995 Agreement between Estonia, Finland and Sweden regarding the *M/S Estonia* ((1996) 31 LOSB 62).
296 (2007) 46 ILM 697, (2008) 67 LOSB 45. Adopted: 18 May 2007; EIF: 14 April 2015. See article 1(1) especially.

(B) ARTICLE 56(1)(B)(I) MATTERS

The first subcategory consists of matters relating to "the establishment and use of artificial islands, installations and structures".[297] These three terms are not defined in the LOSC but, although installations and structures could be understood as types of artificial islands, "the three terms are distinct categories that do not overlap".[298] The reason is that the right of the coastal State "to construct and to authorize and regulate the construction, operation and use of" artificial islands is not limited to any specific purposes,[299] while the same right with regard to installations and structures is limited to "the purposes provided for in article 56 and other economic purposes"[300] and to "installations and structures which may interfere with the exercise of the rights of the coastal State in the zone".[301] There does not appear to be any limitation to the scope of the EezL jurisdiction of the coastal States in regard to those artificial features. There is no doubt that it includes "jurisdiction with regard to customs, fiscal, health, safety and immigration laws and regulations".[302] Linked to the Eez jurisdiction regarding the establishment and use of artificial islands, installations and structures is the Eez jurisdiction: (a) to give due notice of their construction and warning of their presence;[303] (b) to remove all installations and structures which are abandoned or disused;[304] (c) to "establish reasonable safety zones around such artificial islands, installations and structures";[305] (d) to determine their breadth;[306] and (e) to take, within those zones, "appropriate measures to ensure the safety both of navigation and of the artificial islands, installations and structures".[307]

(C) ARTICLE 56(1)(B)(II) MATTERS

The second subcategory among the matters mentioned in article 56(1)(b) consists of matters relating to "marine scientific research".[308] Eez jurisdiction in that regard includes "the right to regulate, authorize and conduct marine scientific research".[309]

297 Article 56(1)(b)(i).
298 Churchill, Lowe & Sander (n. 82) 267.
299 Article 60(1)(a).
300 Article 60(1)(b).
301 Article 60(1)(c).
302 Article 60(2). See e.g., *The M/V "Saiga" (No 2)* (n. 54) § 127.
303 Article 60(3).
304 *Ibid.*
305 Article 60(4). See further article 60(7). On safety zones around vessels engaged in oil and/or gas exploration or exploitation, see e.g., J Mossop "Protests against oil exploration at sea: Lessons from the *Arctic Sunrise* arbitration" (2016) 31 IJMCL 60–87 at 78–80.
306 Article 60(5).
307 Article 60(4). See also article 60(6). See further e.g., *The "Arctic Sunrise" Arbitration* (n. 54) § 211.
308 Article 56(1)(b)(ii).
309 Article 246(1). See S Huh & K Nishimoto "Article 246" in Proelss (n. 25) 1649–1664 at 1655. In the exercise of that right, coastal States must act consistently with the general principles for the conduct of marine scientific research listed in art. 240 of the LOSC.

The extent of the jurisdiction is not entirely clear in view of the lack of a definition of the term "marine scientific research" in the LOSC. It seems well established, nevertheless, that, in order to qualify as marine scientific research, an activity must both "meet the purpose to increase knowledge on the marine environment" and "be conducted with scientific methods".[310] If these are the only two requirements that an activity must meet to qualify as marine scientific research, any activity involving the gathering of information on the oceans, including military and hydrographic surveys as well as operational-oceanography activities,[311] would qualify as marine scientific research, on the assumption that the information is only worthy of being relied upon when it has been gathered by means of an appropriate scientific method.[312] However, the LOSC explicitly distinguishes between "marine scientific research and hydrographic surveys".[313] In addition, the obligation "to make available by publication and dissemination through appropriate channels [...] knowledge resulting from marine scientific research"[314] appears to exclude military surveys from the latter because "information concerning [those] surveys is confidential, and the results of such surveys, in general, are not disclosed".[315]

(D) ARTICLE 56(1)(B)(III) MATTERS

The third subcategory among the matters mentioned in article 56(1)(b) consists of matters relating to "the protection and preservation of the marine environment".[316] The words "protection" and "preservation" indicate the comprehensive nature of this aspect of Eez jurisdiction, "which goes far beyond the prevention of substantive pollution".[317] Indeed, it also requires "the prevention of suspected negative changes of the marine environment through its use, as well as taking active measures to preserve the ocean as an ecosystem and to minimise pollution".[318] That jurisdiction includes:

(a) the EezL jurisdiction, the EezE jurisdiction and the EezA jurisdiction to "permit, regulate and control" dumping;[319]
(b) the EezL jurisdiction, the EezE jurisdiction and the EezA jurisdiction to "prevent, reduce and control pollution of the marine environment arising from or

310 N Matz-Lück "Article 238" in Proelss (n. 25) 1605–1614 at 1609–1610.
311 See further Huh & Nishimoto (n. 309) 1656–1657.
312 See T Stephens & DR Rothwell "Marine scientific research" in DR Rothwell *et al.* (eds) *Oxford Handbook of the Law of the Sea* (2015) 571.
313 Article 21(1)(g). See also article 19(2)(j) and 40.
314 Article 244(1) of the LOSC.
315 Huh & Nishimoto (n. 309) 1656.
316 Article 56(1)(b)(iii).
317 D Czybulka "Article 192" in Proelss (n. 25) 1277–1287 at 1286.
318 *Ibid.*
319 Articles 210(5) and 216(1)(a) of the LOSC. "Dumping" is defined in article 1(1)(5).

in connection with seabed activities subject to [the State's] jurisdiction and from artificial islands, installations and structures under" its jurisdiction;[320]

(c) the EezL jurisdiction, the EezE jurisdiction and the EezA jurisdiction to prevent, reduce and control pollution from land-based sources to the extent that it reaches the EEZ;[321] and

(d) a limited EezL jurisdiction (in respect of ice-covered areas[322] and areas "where the adoption of special mandatory measures for the prevention of pollution from vessels is required for recognized technical reasons in relation to [their] oceanographical and ecological conditions, as well as [their] utilization or the protection of [their] resources and the particular character of [their] traffic"),[323] a wide EezE jurisdiction[324] and a limited EzA jurisdiction to prevent, reduce and control pollution from vessels other than by dumping.[325]

4.6.1.4 Extent ratione loci

The scope of Eez jurisdiction is not only limited *ratione materiae*, but also limited *ratione loci*. As in the case of Cz jurisdiction, provided that a coastal State has claimed an EEZ,[326] its Eez jurisdiction is, in principle, limited to the extent of that zone. The latter is located beyond the territorial sea and may "not extend beyond 200 nautical miles from the baselines from which the breadth of the territorial sea is measured".[327] As pointed out in the previous chapter, the breadth of each EEZ is determined by the coastal State, in the exercise of its inchoate EezL jurisdiction, by means of a legislative act producing a legislative instrument containing a constitutive provision to that effect.[328] There is an additional limitation *ratione loci* in that the article 56(1)(b)(i) jurisdiction is limited to the objects referred to in that provision as well as to the abovementioned jurisdiction regarding safety zones, which are clearly not part of the territory of the coastal State.[329]

In contrast to the archipelagic waters, the territorial sea and the continental shelf,[330] the LOSC does not state explicitly that the EEZ includes its bed and subsoil. However, article 56(1)(a) speaks of the seabed and its subsoil "in the exclusive economic zone" and article 58(1) speaks of the laying of submarine cables and pipelines "in the exclusive economic zone". Thus, while the coastal State's rights set out in article 56 must be exercised with respect to the seabed and subsoil "in

320 Articles 208(1)–(2) and 214 of the LOSC.
321 Articles 207(1)–(2) and 213 of the LOSC.
322 See article 234 of the LOSC.
323 Article 211(6)(a) read with article 211(5) of the LOSC.
324 See article 220(3)–(5) of the LOSC.
325 See article 220(6)–(7) of the LOSC. See also e.g., *The "Arctic Sunrise" Arbitration* (n. 54) §§ 290–292.
326 See Chapter 3 section 3.3.3.2.
327 Article 57 of the LOSC.
328 See Chapter 3 section 3.3.3.2.
329 See article 60(8) of the LOSC. See further A Proelss "Article 60" in Proelss (n. 25) 464–480 at 473.
330 See articles 49(2), 2(2) and 76(1) of the LOSC respectively.

accordance with Part VI" of the LOSC,[331] there is little doubt that the EEZ does indeed include its bed and subsoil.[332]

As in the case of T jurisdiction and Cz jurisdiction, the scope of Eez jurisdiction *ratione loci* extends exceptionally beyond the limits of the EEZ when the State exercises its EezE jurisdiction in the exercise of its right of hot pursuit, in which case the same requirements have to be met *mutatis mutandis* as in the case of TE jurisdiction.[333] In addition, there is a second exception in that the State may start taking steps in the exercise of its EezE jurisdiction within its own territory.[334]

4.6.2 Relationship between exclusive economic zone jurisdictions

Because the scope of Eez jurisdiction is, in principle, all-encompassing *ratione personae* and *ratione navis*, there is overlap in those regards. There is also a material overlap because all Eez jurisdictions have the same limited scope *ratione materiae*. By contrast, the EEZ of one State cannot spatially overlap the EEZ of another State, except while a delimitation dispute is pending.[335] In that case, article 74(3) of the LOSC provides that "the States concerned, in a spirit of understanding and cooperation, shall make every effort to enter into provisional arrangements of a practical nature and, during this transitional period, not to jeopardize or hamper the reaching of the final agreement".[336] This provision does not appear to prohibit the concurrent exercise of their respective Eez jurisdictions by the States claiming the disputed area. However, the nature and extent of that exercise is limited by the requirement that the States take into account that the area is disputed and do not act in any way that does have a negative impact on the settlement of the dispute.[337] Irrespective of any delimitation dispute, the exercise of the right of hot pursuit creates a spatial overlap of EezE jurisdictions. Indeed, in contrast to T jurisdiction and like Cz jurisdiction, EezE jurisdiction is not spatially exclusive in that an organ of one State may exercise the State's EezE jurisdiction, while in hot pursuit, within the EEZ of another State.[338] In such a case, there is nevertheless no concurrence of EezL jurisdictions and EezA jurisdictions because their scope *ratione loci* is limited to the respective EEZs.[339]

331 Article 56(3) of the LOSC.

332 See further e.g. Proelss (n. 287) 436–437; Churchill, Lowe & Sander (n. 82) 258–260.

333 See section 4.3.1.

334 This is confirmed by article 27(5) of the LOSC. See Barnes (n. 118) 237.

335 See article 74(1) of the LOSC.

336 See e.g., R Churchill "International law obligations of States in undelimited maritime frontier areas" in Barnes & Long (n. 47) 141–170.

337 Nordquist (n. 140) 815 § 74.11(d). See further e.g., V Becker-Weinberg *Joint Development of Hydrocarbon Deposits in the Law of the Sea* (2014).

338 As indicated earlier in section 4.3.1, article 111 of the LOSC makes it clear that the right of hot pursuit only ceases, as far as its geographical application is concerned, when the vessel "pursued enters the territorial sea of its own State or of a third State".

339 See section 4.6.1.4.

4.6.3 Relationship between exclusive economic zone jurisdiction and flag State jurisdiction

4.6.3.1 Introduction

When a vessel has a legal relationship of nationality with the State in the EEZ zone of which it finds itself, that State has both F jurisdiction and Eez jurisdiction. As a result, no issue of attribution of competence arises as far as international law is concerned. By contrast, the position is complex in cases where the flag State is not the same as the coastal State.

There is a spatial overlap of F jurisdiction and Eez jurisdiction in that, although Eez jurisdiction is limited *ratione loci*,[340] F jurisdiction is, in principle, all-encompassing *ratione loci*.[341] There is also a personal overlap in that both Eez jurisdiction and F jurisdiction are, in principle, all-encompassing *ratione personae*.[342] There is a potential for material overlap in that, while Eez jurisdiction is limited *ratione materiae*,[343] F jurisdiction is a form of primary jurisdiction and, in principle, all-encompassing *ratione materiae*.[344] In order to ascertain to what extent there is concurrence of F jurisdiction and Eez jurisdiction, one needs to distinguish between the different categories of Eez jurisdiction, keeping in mind that article 92 of the LOSC "applies to the exclusive economic zone by virtue of" article 58(2),[345] as does article 97.[346]

4.6.3.2 Article 56(1)(a) jurisdiction

As far as the article 56(1)(a) jurisdiction is concerned, the term "sovereign rights" is not defined in the LOSC. It would appear that those rights are exclusive in principle[347] in that the only jurisdictions that may be exercised for the purpose of governing the resources and activities with regard to which the coastal State holds sovereign rights are the State's EezL jurisdiction, EezE jurisdiction and EezA jurisdiction.[348] This does not mean, however, that other States never have FL jurisdiction, FE jurisdiction and FA jurisdiction with regard to those resources and activities. Indeed, for instance, a coastal State is either free or obliged to give access to its living resources to the vessels of one or more other States, when it cannot,[349] or

340 See section 4.6.1.
341 See section 4.2.1.
342 See sections 4.2.1 and 4.6.1.
343 See section 4.6.1.
344 See e.g., *The "Arctic Sunrise" Arbitration* (n. 54) § 231. See further section 4.2.1.
345 *The "Enrica Lexie" Incident* (n. 5) § 523.
346 *Ibid.* § 635.
347 See e.g., Proelss (n. 287) 424; *The "Enrica Lexie" Incident* (n. 5) § 953.
348 See e.g., *Alleged Violations* (n. 203) § 134. With regard to other matters, the flag State retains its exclusive FE jurisdiction (see *Advisory Opinion* (n. 288) § 115.
349 See articles 62(2) and 69–70 of the LOSC. See also e.g., the Fisheries (Conservation and Management) Ordinance, 1991, of the British Indian Ocean Territory Commissioner as well as the British-Mauritian Fisheries Commission established in 1994.

when it does not want to, harvest them itself. In addition, nothing appears to stand in the way of organs of a State deciding to exercise: (a) the State's FL jurisdiction for the limited purpose of requiring that the vessels with which it has a legal relationship of nationality comply, when in the EEZ of a coastal State, with the legal regime determined by that State in the exercise of its EezL jurisdiction;[350] (b) its FE jurisdiction to apply, monitor compliance with, and enforce that requirement; and (c) its FA jurisdiction to settle any dispute in this regard.[351] In fact, the widespread taking of such steps would contribute to better ocean governance by indirectly extending the EezE jurisdiction and the EezA jurisdiction of coastal States through the exercise of FE jurisdiction and FA jurisdiction when EezE jurisdiction and EezA jurisdiction cannot or may not be exercised.

4.6.3.3 Article 56(1)(b)(i) jurisdiction

As far as the article 56(1)(b)(i) jurisdiction is concerned (i.e., jurisdiction with regard to "the establishment and use of artificial islands, installations and structures"), the word "jurisdiction", instead of the term "sovereign rights", is used in the LOSC. It is unclear whether this difference in terminology reflects "a difference in terms of quality".[352] However, article 60(1) of the LOSC makes it clear that a coastal State has, in its EEZ,

> the exclusive right to construct and to authorize and regulate the construction, operation and use of:
>
> (a) artificial islands;
> (b) installations and structures for the purposes provided for in article 56 and other economic purposes;
> (c) installations and structures which may interfere with the exercise of the rights of the coastal State in the zone.

This provision distinguishes between artificial islands, on the one hand, and installations and structures that either are constructed, operated or used for the purposes provided for in article 56 of the LOSC or other economic purposes, or may interfere with the exercise of the rights of the coastal State in its EEZ, on the other.[353] In other words, while article 60(1) applies to all artificial islands located within a coastal State's EEZ, it only applies to specific installations and structures located in that zone.[354] The effect of the provision is that, should a State have a legal relationship of nationality with an artificial island, or an installation or structure to which article 60 apply, which is located in the EEZ of another State, the F jurisdiction of

350 See e.g., *Advisory Opinion* (n. 288) § 102.
351 *Ibid.* §§ 108, 111–112 and 119. See also *South China Sea Arbitration* (n. 278) § 249.
352 See Proelss (n. 287) 429.
353 See e.g., Proelss (n. 329) 471–472.
354 A coastal State may not rely on article 60 if it has not claimed an EEZ (see e.g., Proelss (n. 329) 472).

the flag State is excluded within that EEZ by the article 56(1)(b)(i) jurisdiction of the coastal State.[355] However, nothing appears to stand in the way of organs of a State deciding to exercise: (a) its FL jurisdiction for the limited purpose of requiring that the artificial island, installation or structure complies with the legal regime determined by the coastal State in the exercise of its EezL jurisdiction; (b) its FE jurisdiction to apply, monitor compliance with, and enforce that requirement with the consent of the coastal State; and (c) its FA jurisdiction to settle any dispute in this regard.

The position is different with regard to vessels, especially "supply ships or other vessels flying the flag of a State other than the coastal State which call at one of the objects referred to" in article 60.[356] Indeed, the waters around those objects, including their safety zones, are not part of the territory of the coastal State.[357] As a result, there is no basis for excluding F jurisdiction. In addition, there is, within any safety zone that the coastal State might establish,[358] an overlap *ratione materiae* of EeZ jurisdiction and F jurisdiction only with regard to what is required "to ensure the safety both of navigation and of the artificial islands, installations and structures".[359] To that limited extent,[360] the flag State has concurrent F jurisdiction at least insofar as it must ensure that the vessels with which it has a legal relationship of nationality "respect [the] safety zones and [...] comply with generally accepted international standards regarding navigation in the vicinity of artificial islands, installations, structures and safety zones".[361]

The position is also different with regard to installations or structures to which article 60 does not apply, such as submarine cables and pipelines laid across the EEZ from a point outside the EEZ to another point outside the EEZ.[362] In their case, there is concurrence of EEZ jurisdiction and F jurisdiction, the exercise of which is circumscribed by several provisions aimed at striking the appropriate balance.[363]

4.6.3.4 Article 56(1)(b)(ii) jurisdiction

As far as the article 56(1)(b)(ii) jurisdiction is concerned (i.e., jurisdiction with regard to "marine scientific research"), there is little doubt that a State has F

355 See e.g., *South China Sea Arbitration* (n. 278) § 1035.
356 See Proelss (n. 329) 473.
357 In terms of article 60(8) of the LOSC.
358 See further article 60(5) of the LOSC.
359 Article 60(4) of the LOSC. See e.g., *The "Arctic Sunrise" Arbitration* (n. 54) § 278.
360 See *The "Arctic Sunrise" Arbitration* (n. 54) § 244; Proelss (n. 329) 473.
361 Article 60(6) of the LOSC.
362 In the exercise of the "freedom to lay submarine cables and pipelines" (article 87(1)(c) of the LOSC read with article 58(1) (see e.g., *The "Enrica Lexie" Incident* (n. 5) § 464). See e.g. MM Roggenkamp "Petroleum pipelines in the North Sea: Questions of jurisdiction and practical solutions" (1998) 16 *Journal of Energy & Natural Resources Law* 92–109 at 96–108, who approaches the issues from the perspective that, in the case of petroleum pipelines, one is dealing with P jurisdiction, not F jurisdiction.
363 See e.g., articles 58(1) and 79 of the LOSC. See further e.g., Roggenkamp (n. 362) 95.

jurisdiction over vessels and other artificial features used for the purpose of marine scientific research in the EEZ of another State, provided that the connecting factor can be established.[364] That jurisdiction is however subject to the Eez jurisdiction of the coastal State, the consent of which is needed in order to conduct marine scientific research in the EEZ,[365] and to the duty not to "unjustifiably interfere with activities undertaken by [the] coastal [State] in the exercise of [its] sovereign rights and jurisdiction provided for in" the LOSC.[366]

4.6.3.5 Article 56(1)(b)(iii) jurisdiction

As far as the article 56(1)(b)(iii) jurisdiction is concerned (i.e., jurisdiction with regard to "the protection and the preservation of the marine environment"), there is little doubt that a State has F jurisdiction over dumping and pollution from vessels in the EEZ of another State. Flag States have a duty to "adopt laws and regulations to prevent, reduce and control pollution of the marine environment by dumping"[367] and "from vessels flying their flag or of their registry".[368] There is no basis for limiting that duty to areas where the coastal States do not have one or the other form of coastal zone jurisdiction. FL jurisdiction is however limited, for instance, to the extent that dumping within the EEZ of another State may not take place "without the express prior approval of the [...] State"[369] and, it would appear, flag States have a correlative duty to exercise their FL jurisdiction by prohibiting dumping in the EEZ of another State without the express prior approval of that State.[370] At the same time, nothing appears to stand in the way of FL jurisdiction being exercised within the permissible scope and in such a way that the relevant normative provisions offer a higher protection of the marine environment than the norms adopted by a coastal State in the exercise of its EezL jurisdiction.

Flag States also have duties of enforcement with regard to pollution and there is no basis, in that regard, for excluding the EEZs.[371] Within the latter, and in contrast to the maritime territories of coastal States,[372] EezE jurisdiction and FE jurisdiction are concurrent, when they overlap *ratione materiae*, because neither EezE jurisdiction nor FE jurisdiction is exclusive within the relevant EEZ.[373]

364 See Churchill, Lowe & Sander (n. 82) 804, with regard to FL jurisdiction.
365 See article 246(2) of the LOSC. See further article 246(3)–(7).
366 Article 246(8) of the LOSC.
367 Article 210(1) of the LOSC. See further F Wacht "Article 210" in Proelss (n. 25) 1407–1418 at 1412.
368 Article 211(2) of the LOSC.
369 Article 210(5) of the LOSC.
370 See Wacht (n. 367) 1417.
371 See article 217(1) of the LOSC. See also article 217(4). See further K Bartenstein "Article 217" in Proelss (n. 25) 1474–1487 at 1483.
372 See section 4.3.3.
373 See e.g., *Alleged Violations* (n. 203) § 95; *Advisory Opinion* (n. 288) § 120.

4.6.4 Relationship between exclusive economic zone jurisdiction and territorial jurisdiction

There is a personal overlap in that both Eez jurisdiction and T jurisdiction are, in principle, all-encompassing *ratione personae*.[374] There is also a vessel overlap in that both Eez jurisdiction and T jurisdiction are, in principle, all-encompassing *ratione navis*.[375] In addition, there is material overlap in that, although Eez jurisdiction is limited *ratione materiae*,[376] T jurisdiction is a form of primary jurisdiction and, in principle, all-encompassing *ratione materiae*.[377] However, there is, in principle, no spatial overlap because both T jurisdiction and Eez jurisdiction are limited *ratione loci* and the respective geographical areas are separate.[378] The exception is the case of hot pursuit where, as in the case of Cz jurisdiction, T jurisdiction prevails over Eez jurisdiction in that TE jurisdiction may also be exercised in another State's EEZ, but EezE jurisdiction may not be exercised in another State's territorial sea.[379]

4.6.5 Relationship between exclusive economic zone jurisdiction and personal jurisdiction

When a person is within an EEZ and the person has the nationality of the coastal State, the latter has both P jurisdiction and Eez jurisdiction and no issue of attribution of competence arises as far as international law is concerned. By contrast, the position is complex in cases where the personal State is not the same as the coastal State.

There is a spatial overlap in that, although Eez jurisdiction is limited *ratione loci*,[380] P jurisdiction is, in principle, all-encompassing *ratione loci*.[381] There is also a personal overlap in that, although P jurisdiction is limited *ratione personae*,[382] Eez jurisdiction is, in principle, all-encompassing *ratione personae*.[383] In addition, there is also a vessel overlap in that both Eez jurisdiction and P jurisdiction are, in principle, all-encompassing *ratione navis*.[384] There is a material overlap in that, although Eez jurisdiction is limited *ratione materiae*,[385] P jurisdiction is a form of primary jurisdiction and, in principle, all-encompassing *ratione materiae*.[386] As in

374 See sections 4.3.1 and 4.6.1.
375 See sections 4.3.1 and 4.6.1.
376 See section 4.6.1.
377 See section 4.3.1.
378 See sections 4.3.1 and 4.6.1.
379 See section 4.5.4.
380 See section 4.6.1.
381 See section 4.4.1.
382 See section 4.4.1.
383 See section 4.6.1.
384 See sections 4.4.1 and 4.6.1.
385 See section 4.6.1.
386 See section 4.4.1.

the case of F jurisdiction, one needs to distinguish between the different categories of Eez jurisdiction in order to ascertain to what extent concurrence is possible.

As far as the article 56(1)(a) jurisdiction is concerned, nothing appears to stand in the way of organs of a State deciding to exercise: (a) the latter's PL jurisdiction for the limited purpose of requiring that, when the connecting factor exists, a person complies, when in the EEZ of a foreign coastal State, with the legal regime determined by that State in the exercise of its EezL jurisdiction; (b) its PE jurisdiction to apply, monitor compliance with, and enforce that requirement; and (c) its PA jurisdiction to settle any dispute in this regard. In fact, the widespread taking of such steps would contribute to better ocean governance by indirectly extending the EezE jurisdiction and the EezA jurisdiction of coastal States through the exercise of PE jurisdiction and PA jurisdiction where EezE jurisdiction and EezA jurisdiction cannot or may not be exercised.

As far as the article 56(1)(b)(i) jurisdiction is concerned, the position is the same as in the case of F jurisdiction[387] in that P jurisdiction is excluded by the article 56(1)(b)(i) jurisdiction of the coastal State, although nothing appears to stand in the way of organs of a State deciding to exercise: (a) its PL jurisdiction for the limited purpose of requiring that persons operate and use artificial islands, installations or structures in compliance with the legal regime determined by the coastal State in the exercise of its EezL jurisdiction; (b) its PE jurisdiction to apply, monitor compliance with, and enforce that requirement; and (c) its PA jurisdiction to settle any dispute in this regard. With regard to persons on vessels near artificial islands, installations or structures, the position is the same as in the case of F jurisdiction,[388] taking into account the relationship between P jurisdiction and F jurisdiction.[389]

As far as the article 56(1)(b)(ii) jurisdiction is concerned, there does not appear to be any reason why States should not have P jurisdiction over persons engaged in marine scientific research in the EEZ of another State, provided that the connecting factor can be established.[390] As in the case of F jurisdiction, that jurisdiction is however subject to the Eez jurisdiction of the coastal State, the consent of which is needed in order to conduct marine scientific research in the EEZ[391] and to the duty not to "unjustifiably interfere with activities undertaken by [the] coastal [State] in the exercise of [its] sovereign rights and jurisdiction provided for in" the LOSC.[392]

As far as the article 56(1)(b)(iii) jurisdiction is concerned, there does not appear to be any reason why the duty of States "to protect and preserve the marine environment"[393] does not include the duty to make use of their P jurisdiction to that end. As in the case of F jurisdiction,[394] there is no basis for excluding the

387 See section 4.6.3.3.
388 See section 4.6.3.3.
389 See section 4.4.3.
390 See Churchill, Lowe & Sander (n. 82) 804, with regard to FL jurisdiction.
391 See article 246(2) of the LOSC. See further article 246(3)–(7).
392 Article 246(8) of the LOSC.
393 Article 192 of the LOSC.
394 See section 4.6.3.

EEZs from the spatial scope of that duty. PL jurisdiction is however limited, for instance, to the extent that dumping within the EEZ of another State may not take place "without the express prior approval of the […] State"[395] and, it would appear, personal States have a correlative duty to exercise their PL jurisdiction by prohibiting dumping in the EEZ of another State without the express prior approval of that State.[396] At the same time, nothing appears to stand in the way of PL jurisdiction being exercised within the permissible scope and in such a way that the relevant normative provisions offer a higher protection of the marine environment than the norms adopted in the exercise of EezL jurisdiction.

4.6.6 Relationship between exclusive economic zone jurisdiction and contiguous zone jurisdiction

Because the contiguous zone of a State overlaps its EEZ, there is always a spatial overlap between Eez jurisdiction and Cz jurisdiction when the coastal State has claimed both zones. Since, in that case, the same State has both jurisdictions, there is no issue of attribution of competence as far as international law is concerned. By contrast, the EEZ of one State does not normally overlap the contiguous zone of another State,[397] except while a delimitation dispute is pending. In that case, the position regarding spatial overlaps between Eez jurisdiction and Cz jurisdiction appears to be the same *mutatis mutandis* as in the case of an overlap of Eez jurisdictions.[398] Where there is no unresolved delimitation issue, the EezE jurisdiction of one State spatially overlaps the CzE jurisdiction of another State only in cases where the right of hot pursuit is exercised by one of those States. In those cases, neither CzE jurisdiction nor EezE jurisdiction prevails in that CzE jurisdiction may also be exercised in another State's EEZ and EezE jurisdiction may also be exercised in another State's contiguous zone.

There are personal and vessel overlaps between the two jurisdictions because they are both all-encompassing *ratione personae* and *ratione navis*.[399] By contrast, there is no material overlap between Eez jurisdiction and Cz jurisdiction because both sets of jurisdictions are of a secondary nature and their scopes *ratione materiae* do not intersect.[400]

4.6.7 Summary

Coastal States have authority to perform acts in the exercise of their Eez jurisdiction in a range of matters within their respective EEZs. That jurisdiction prevails over, but does not always exclude the exercise of other jurisdictions. EezE

395 Article 210(5) of the LOSC.
396 See Wacht (n. 367) 1417.
397 See e.g., *Alleged Violations* (n. 203) § 160.
398 See section 4.6.2.
399 See sections 4.5.1 and 4.6.1.
400 See e.g., *Alleged Violations* (n. 203) § 161. See further sections 4.5.1 and 4.6.1.

jurisdiction may be exercised beyond the EEZ in case of hot pursuit, except within the marine component of the territory of another State.

4.7 Continental shelf jurisdiction

4.7.1 Extent of continental shelf jurisdiction

Like Cz jurisdiction and Eez jurisdiction, Cs jurisdiction is a secondary form of State ocean jurisdiction in that it only confers authority on States with regard to a limited range of matters.[401] Those matters fall into two categories. The first category consists of the matters relating to artificial islands, installations and structures, with regard to which the position is the same *mutatis mutandis* as in the case of Eez jurisdiction.[402] The second category consists of the matters relating to the exploration and exploitation of the natural resources of the continental shelf.[403] Whether a specific living resource meets the requirement has given rise to disputes in the past[404] and it is an issue that has become relevant again with regard to bioprospecting activities especially.[405] Artificial resources are clearly not included in the definition[406] and the position is similar in this regard as in the case of Eez jurisdiction.[407]

Like the other forms of coastal zone jurisdiction, the scope of Cs jurisdiction is also limited *ratione loci*. By contrast, however, a coastal State does not have, in the exercise of its CsL jurisdiction, to perform a legislative act producing a legislative instrument containing a constitutive provision setting the breadth of its continental shelf. Indeed, article 76(1) of the LOSC sets that breadth, by default, at "200 nautical miles from the baselines from which the breadth of the territorial sea is measured". It is only when a coastal State wishes to extend its continental shelf further, and within the parameters set by the LOSC,[408] that it is expected to take steps in the exercise of its CsE jurisdiction to have its claim examined by the CLCS, only after which it may perform a legislative act producing a legislative instrument containing a constitutive provision setting a breadth wider than 200 NM.[409] Cs jurisdiction is restricted to a limited portion of the seabed and its subsoil not only with regard to the resources over which it may be exercised, but also with regard to the artificial islands, installations and structures relied upon to explore and exploit those resources, in that they "must be on the continental shelf, meaning attached

401 See Khan (n. 202) 264.
402 See article 80 of the LOSC.
403 See article 77(1) of the LOSC. See e.g., *Dispute Concerning Delimitation of the Maritime Boundary between Ghana and Côte d'Ivoire in the Atlantic Ocean (Ghana v. Côte d'Ivoire)*, order of 25 April 2015, 2015 ITLOS Reports 146 § 94. See further article 77(4) of the LOSC.
404 See Churchill, Lowe & Sander (n. 82) 240.
405 See e.g., J Mossop "Regulating uses of marine biodiversity on the outer continental shelf" in D Vidas (ed) *Law, Technology and Science for Oceans in Globalisation* (2010) 319–337.
406 See Churchill, Lowe & Sander (n. 82) 240.
407 See section 4.6.1. The "Convention area" is defined in article 1(1) of the ICRW.
408 See article 76(2)–(7) of the LOSC. See also article 76(9)–(10).
409 See article 76(8).

to the seabed".[410] At the same time, Cs jurisdiction extends above the seabed to exploration and exploitation activities that do not take place on an artificial island, installation or structure, such as seismic surveys from surface vessels.[411]

As is also the case of the other forms of coastal zone jurisdiction, the scope of Cs jurisdiction is, in principle, all-encompassing *ratione personae* and *ratione navis*. The continental shelf regime matured into customary international law even before the EEZ did so and, for that reason, Cs jurisdiction is opposable to all States.[412]

4.7.2 Relationship between continental shelf jurisdictions

The extent of the actual material overlaps of Cs jurisdictions depends on the extent to which the coastal States have exercised their respective jurisdictions. By contrast, the continental shelf of one State does not spatially overlap the continental shelf of another State, except while a delimitation dispute is pending.[413] In that case, article 83(3) of the LOSC, mirroring article 74(3), provides that "the States concerned, in a spirit of understanding and cooperation, shall make every effort to enter into provisional arrangements of a practical nature and, during this transitional period, not to jeopardize or hamper the reaching of the final agreement". This provision does not appear to prohibit the exercise of their respective Cs jurisdictions by the States claiming the disputed area. However, the nature and extent of that exercise is limited by the requirement that the States take into account that the area is disputed and do not act in any way that does have a negative impact on the settlement of the dispute.[414] Irrespective of any delimitation dispute, the exercise of the right of hot pursuit creates a spatial overlap of Cs jurisdictions. Indeed, in contrast to TE jurisdiction and like CzE jurisdiction and EezE jurisdiction, CsE jurisdiction is not spatially exclusive in that an organ of one State may exercise the State's CsE jurisdiction, while in hot pursuit, on the continental shelf of another State.[415]

4.7.3 Relationship between continental shelf jurisdiction and flag State jurisdiction

F jurisdiction and Cs jurisdiction overlap potentially on or above the continental shelf. When the vessel or other artificial feature has a legal relationship of nationality with the State on the continental shelf of which it finds itself, that State has both

410 See AR Maggio "Article 80" in Proelss (n. 25) 628–633 at 632.
411 See e.g., Mossop (n. 405) 329–335.
412 See e.g., Churchill, Lowe & Sander (n. 82) 226–227.
413 See article 83(1) of the LOSC.
414 See e.g., Nordquist (n. 140) 815 § 74.11(d); *Delimitation of the Maritime Boundary in the Atlantic Ocean*, judgment of 23 September 2017, 2017 ITLOS Reports 4 § 591.
415 As indicated earlier in section 4.3.2, article 111(3) of the LOSC makes it clear that the right of hot pursuit only ceases, as far as its geographical application is concerned, when the vessel "pursued enters the territorial sea of its own State or of a third State".

F jurisdiction and Cs jurisdiction. As a result, no issue of attribution of competence arises as far as international law is concerned. The position is, in cases where the flag State is not the same as the coastal State, the same, *mutatis mutandis*, as in the case of overlap of Eez jurisdiction and F jurisdiction.[416]

This means, for instance, that, while the rights of a coastal State over the resources of its continental shelf are exclusive,[417] in that the only legislative, executive and adjudicative jurisdictions that may be exercised for the purpose of governing those resources are CsL jurisdiction, CsE jurisdiction and CsA jurisdiction, it is possible for other States to exercise FL jurisdiction, FE jurisdiction and FA jurisdiction with regard to those resources. Indeed, for instance, a coastal State is either free to give access to its resources to the vessels of one or more other States, when it cannot or when it does not want to harvest them itself. In addition, nothing appears to stand in the way of organs of a State deciding to exercise: (a) the State's FL jurisdiction for the limited purpose of requiring that the vessels with which it has a legal relationship of nationality comply, when over the continental shelf of a coastal State, with the legal regime determined by that State in the exercise of its CsL jurisdiction; (b) its FE jurisdiction to apply, monitor compliance with, and enforce that requirement; and (c) its FA jurisdiction to settle any dispute in this regard. In fact, the widespread taking of such steps would contribute to better ocean governance by indirectly extending the CsE jurisdiction and the CsA jurisdiction of coastal States through the exercise of FE jurisdiction and FA jurisdiction when CsE jurisdiction and CsA jurisdiction cannot or may not be exercised.

4.7.4 Relationship between continental shelf jurisdiction and territorial jurisdiction

There is a personal overlap in that both Cs jurisdiction and T jurisdiction are, in principle, all-encompassing *ratione personae*.[418] There is also a vessel overlap in that both Cs jurisdiction and T jurisdiction are, in principle, all-encompassing *ratione navis*.[419] In addition, there is material overlap in that, although Cs jurisdiction is limited *ratione materiae*,[420] T jurisdiction is a form of primary jurisdiction and, in principle, all-encompassing *ratione materiae*.[421] However, there is, in principle, no spatial overlap because both T jurisdiction and Cs jurisdiction are limited *ratione loci* and the respective geographical areas are separate.[422] The exception is the case of hot pursuit where, as in the case of Cz jurisdiction and Eez jurisdiction, T jurisdiction prevails over Cs jurisdiction in that TE jurisdiction may also be

416 See section 4.6.3.
417 See article 77(2) of the LOSC. See further e.g., *South China Sea Arbitration* (n. 278) § 244.
418 See sections 4.3.1 and 4.7.1.
419 See sections 4.3.1 and 4.7.1.
420 See section 4.7.1.
421 See section 4.3.1.
422 See sections 4.3.1 and 4.7.1.

exercised over another State's continental shelf, but CsE jurisdiction may not be exercised in another State's territorial sea.[423]

4.7.5 Relationship between continental shelf jurisdiction and personal jurisdiction

When a person is involved in activities relating to the resources of a continental shelf and the person has the nationality of the coastal State, the latter has both P jurisdiction and Cs jurisdiction and no issue of attribution of competence arises as far as international law is concerned. By contrast, the position is complex in cases where the personal State is not the same as the coastal State.

There is a spatial overlap in that, although Cs jurisdiction is limited *ratione loci*,[424] P jurisdiction is, in principle, all-encompassing *ratione loci*.[425] There is also a personal overlap in that, although P jurisdiction is limited *ratione personae*,[426] Cs jurisdiction is, in principle, all-encompassing *ratione personae*.[427] In addition, there is also a vessel overlap in that both Cs jurisdiction and P jurisdiction are, in principle, all-encompassing *ratione navis*.[428] There is a material overlap in that, although Cs jurisdiction is limited *ratione materiae*,[429] P jurisdiction is a form of primary jurisdiction and, in principle, all-encompassing *ratione materiae*.[430]

While, as already indicated above,[431] the rights of a coastal State over the resources of its continental shelf are exclusive,[432] in that the only legislative, executive and adjudicative jurisdictions that may be exercised for the purpose of governing those resources are CsL jurisdiction, CsE jurisdiction and CsA jurisdiction, it is possible for other States to exercise PL jurisdiction and PA jurisdiction over individuals involved in activities relating to those resources for the limited purpose of: (a) requiring that, when the connecting factor exists, a person complies, when involved in those activities, with the legal regime determined by that State in the exercise of its CsL jurisdiction; and (b) settling any dispute in this regard. In fact, as in the case of F jurisdiction,[433] the widespread taking of such steps would contribute to better ocean governance by indirectly extending the CsE jurisdiction and the CsA jurisdiction of coastal States through the exercise of PE jurisdiction and PA jurisdiction where CsE jurisdiction and CsA jurisdiction cannot or may not be exercised.

423 See sections 4.5.4 and 4.6.4.
424 See section 4.6.1.
425 See section 4.4.1.
426 See section 4.4.1.
427 See section 4.6.1.
428 See sections 4.4.1 and 4.6.1.
429 See section 4.6.1.
430 See section 4.4.1.
431 See section 4.7.3.
432 See article 77(2) of the LOSC.
433 See section 4.7.3.

4.7.6 Relationship between continental shelf jurisdiction and contiguous zone jurisdiction

There are personal and vessel overlaps between the Cs jurisdiction and Cz jurisdiction because they are both all-encompassing *ratione personae* and *ratione navis*.[434] The waters of which the contiguous zone of a State consists[435] are above, and separate from, its continental shelf. However, many activities and objects relating to the continental shelf, such as exploration vessels and exploitation installations, take place, or are, within the waters above the shelf. It is to that extent that there is a spatial overlap of Cs jurisdiction and Cz jurisdiction when the coastal State has claimed a contiguous zone. In that case, the same State has both jurisdictions and there is no issue of attribution of competence as far as international law is concerned.

The continental shelf of one State can overlap the contiguous zone of another State while a delimitation dispute is pending. In that case, the position regarding spatial overlaps between Cs jurisdiction and Cz jurisdiction is the same *mutatis mutandis* as in the case of an overlap of Eez jurisdictions.[436] Where there is no unresolved delimitation issue, the Cs jurisdiction of one State spatially overlaps the Cz jurisdiction of another State only in cases where the right of hot pursuit is exercised by one of those States. In those cases, neither Cz jurisdiction nor Cs jurisdiction prevails in that CzE jurisdiction may also be exercised above another State's continental shelf and CsE jurisdiction may also be exercised in another State's contiguous zone. There is, however, no material overlap between Cs jurisdiction and Cz jurisdiction because both sets of jurisdictions are of a secondary nature and their scopes *ratione materiae* do not intersect.[437]

4.7.7 Relationship between continental shelf jurisdiction and exclusive economic zone jurisdiction

There is always a spatial overlap between Cs jurisdiction and Eez jurisdiction when the coastal State has claimed an EEZ,[438] to the geographical extent of that EEZ.[439] Because, in that case, the same State has both jurisdictions, there is no issue of attribution of competence as far as international law is concerned. By contrast, the continental shelf of one State does not normally overlap the EEZ of another State,[440] except while a delimitation dispute is pending. In that case, the position

434 See sections 4.5.1 and 4.6.1.

435 See Khan (n. 202) 263.

436 See section 4.6.2.

437 See sections 4.5.1 and 4.6.1.

438 See section 4.6.1.

439 As indicated above, the continental shelf of a coastal State may extend beyond the outer limit of its EEZ (see section 4.7.1).

440 An exception exists, for instance, within the Torres Strait, where part of the zone in which Papua New Guinea has fisheries jurisdiction is above an area of the seabed and subsoil over which Australia has seabed jurisdiction (see article 4 of the 1978 Treaty between Australia and the Independ-

regarding spatial overlaps between Cs jurisdiction and Eez jurisdiction is the same *mutatis mutandis* as in the case of an overlap of Eez jurisdictions.[441] Where there is no unresolved delimitation issue, the Cs jurisdiction of one State spatially overlaps the Eez jurisdiction of another State only in cases where the right of hot pursuit is exercised by one of those States. In those cases, neither Eez jurisdiction nor Cs jurisdiction prevails in that EezE jurisdiction may also be exercised above another State's continental shelf and CsE jurisdiction may also be exercised in another State's EEZ.

There are personal and vessel overlaps between the two jurisdictions because they are both all-encompassing *ratione personae* and *ratione navis*.[442] There is also a potential material overlap between CsL jurisdiction and EezL jurisdiction, on the one hand, and CsA jurisdiction and EezA jurisdiction, on the other, because the scope of Cs jurisdiction *ratione materiae* falls entirely within the scope of Eez jurisdiction *ratione materiae*.[443] There is only concurrence of jurisdictions up to the outer limit of the EEZ because the scope of Eez jurisdiction *ratione loci* does not extent beyond that limit.[444]

4.7.8 Summary

Coastal States have authority to perform acts in the exercise of their Cs jurisdiction with regard to the natural resources within their respective continental shelves, that jurisdiction prevailing over, but not always excluding the exercise of other jurisdictions. CsE jurisdiction may be exercised beyond the continental shelf in case of hot pursuit, except within the marine component of the territory of another State.

4.8 Universal jurisdictions

4.8.1 Extent of the universal jurisdictions

4.8.1.1 Introduction

While the scopes of the universal jurisdictions are similar in most respects,[445] a particular feature of the universal jurisdictions is that they differ in that they do not all include legislative and adjudicative jurisdictions.

ent State of Papua New Guinea Concerning Sovereignty and Maritime Boundaries in the Area between the Two Countries, Including the Area known as Torres Strait, and Related Matters (1985 ATS No 4; adopted: 18 December 1978; EIF: 15 February 1985)).

441 See section 4.6.2.

442 See sections 4.5.1 and 4.6.1.

443 See sections 4.6.1 and 4.7.1.

444 See sections 4.6.1.4 and 4.7.1.

445 See section 4.8.2.

4.8.1.2 Extent of piracy jurisdiction

Article 100 of the LOSC states that all States must "cooperate to the fullest possible extent in the repression of piracy on the high seas or in any other place outside the jurisdiction of any State".[446] It is unclear whether this provision refers only to PiE jurisdiction, but there is no doubt that Pi jurisdiction includes also PiL jurisdiction and PiA jurisdiction.[447] Indeed, with regard to PiA jurisdiction, article 105 confirms that "[t]he courts of the State which carried out the seizure may decide upon the penalties to be imposed, and may also determine the action to be taken with regard to the ships, aircraft or property, subject to the rights of third parties acting in good faith".[448] In turn, PiA jurisdiction presupposes the existence and exercise of PiL jurisdiction.[449]

PiE jurisdiction is an exception to the principle that FE jurisdiction excludes other executive jurisdictions outside the territories of the coastal States.[450] For that reason, PiE jurisdiction is limited in several ways. Indeed, the seizure of a vessel or aircraft on account of piracy "may be carried out only by warships or military aircraft, or other ships or aircraft clearly marked and identifiable as being on government service and authorized to that effect".[451] Seizure must take place on adequate grounds[452] and, in order to avoid incurring that liability, the course of action to follow consists in boarding the vessel when "there is reasonable ground for suspecting that [...] the ship is engaged in piracy".[453] This is done by sending "a boat under the command of an officer to the suspected ship".[454] Once on board, the officer is expected to first check the vessels' documents and, should the suspicion remain thereafter, the boarding party "may proceed to a further examination on board the ship, which must be carried out with all possible consideration".[455]

446 See e.g., *The "Enrica Lexie" Incident* (n. 5) § 722, § 723 (quoting D Guilfoyle "Article 100" in Proelss (n. 25) 733–737 at 734)) and § 727.

447 See further e.g., P-M Dupuy & C Hoss "La chasse aux pirates par la communauté internationale. Le cas de la Somalie" in SE Bedjaoui *et al.* (eds) *L'Afrique et le Droit International: Variations sur l'Organisation Internationale* (2013) 135–146 at 138; R Beckman "Jurisdiction over pirates and maritime terrorists" in Schofield, Lee & Kwon (n. 113) 349–371 at 355.

448 See further e.g., *In re Piracy Jure Gentium* [1934] AC 586 at 589; Beckman (n. 447) 356; D Kritsiotis "The establishment, change, and expansion of jurisdiction through treaties" in Allen *et al.* (n. 5) 251–299 at 274.

449 See Guilfoyle (n. 446) 734. See further e.g., section 74 of the Criminal Code, 1985, of Canada, section 328N and 328O of the Criminal Code, 1854, of Malta, section 1 of the Suppression of Piracy and Other Maritime Offences Act, 2019, of Nigeria and the Prevention and Suppression of Piracy Act, 1991, of Thailand.

450 See section 4.2.2. See further section 4.8.3.

451 See section 4.8.3.

452 See article 106 of the LOSC.

453 Article 110(1)(a) of the LOSC. See also article 110(3).

454 Article 110(2) of the LOSC. The officer must be attached to a warship (article 110(1)), a military aircraft (article 110(4)) or "any other duly authorized ships or aircraft clearly marked and identifiable as being on government service" (article 110(5)).

455 Article 110(2) of the LOSC.

Further enforcement steps may then be taken either in the exercise of PiE jurisdiction, in the exercise of delegated FE jurisdiction[456] or a granted jurisdiction.

Piracy jurisdiction is one of the oldest forms of universal jurisdiction.[457] There is no doubt that it has matured into customary international law and that it is opposable to all States.[458]

4.8.1.3 Extent of slave trade jurisdiction

Article 99 of the LOSC mirrors the corresponding customary international law rule[459] when it states that "[e]very State shall take effective measures to prevent and punish the transport of slaves in ships", but the latter are only those "authorized to fly its flag".[460] This provision, therefore, does not refer to Sl jurisdiction, but to F jurisdiction. Indeed, Sl jurisdiction is limited to SlE jurisdiction in the form of boarding a foreign vessel when "there is reasonable ground for suspecting that [...] the ship is engaged in the slave trade".[461] As in the case of PiE jurisdiction, this is done by sending "a boat under the command of an officer to the suspected ship".[462] Once on board, the officer is expected to first check the vessels' documents and, should the suspicion remain thereafter, the boarding party "may proceed to a further examination on board the ship, which must be carried out with all possible consideration".[463] By contrast to PiE jurisdiction, no further enforcement steps may be taken thereafter in the exercise of SlE jurisdiction.[464] Such steps may only be taken in the exercise of delegated FE jurisdiction[465] or a collective jurisdiction.[466]

4.8.1.4 Extent of statelessness jurisdiction

Like Sl jurisdiction, St jurisdiction appears to be limited to StE jurisdiction in the form of boarding a vessel, a step which, in the case of St jurisdiction, is only allowed when "there is reasonable ground for suspecting that [...] the ship is without nationality".[467] As in the case of Sl jurisdiction, this is done by sending "a boat

456 See Guilfoyle (n. 31) 770.
457 See e.g., E Kontorovich & S Art "An empirical examination of universal jurisdiction for piracy" (2010) 104 AJIL 436–453 at 437.
458 See e.g., M Gagain "Neglected waters: Territorial maritime piracy and developing States: Somalia, Nigeria and Indonesia" (2010) 16 *New England Journal of International & Comparative Law* 169–196 at 179–180.
459 See article 4 of the UDHR; article 3(2)(a) of the SCAS; ILC (n. 60) 281–282; MH Nordquist *United Nations Convention on the Law of the Sea 1982: A Commentary* (ed) III 180 § 99.6(a).
460 See further article 99.
461 Article 110(1)(b) of the LOSC. See also article 110(3).
462 Article 110(2) of the LOSC. See also article 110(1) and (4)–(5).
463 Article 110(2) of the LOSC.
464 See e.g., Brown (n. 100) 310; D Guilfoyle "Article 99" in Proelss (n. 25) 731.
465 See section 4.10.
466 See section 4.11.
467 Article 110(1)(b) of the LOSC. See also article 110(3).

under the command of an officer to the suspected ship".[468] Once on board, the officer is expected to first check the vessels' documents and, should the suspicion remain thereafter, the boarding party "may proceed to a further examination on board the ship, which must be carried out with all possible consideration".[469] The LOSC is silent on whether further enforcement steps may be taken thereafter in the exercise of StE jurisdiction.[470] It is clear that it is not possible to take any further step in the exercise of any delegated FE jurisdiction when the vessel turns out to be indeed without nationality because FE jurisdiction is grounded on nationality.[471] As a result, it may be argued that steps may only be taken in the exercise of either PE jurisdiction (when the flag State of the boarding vessel is also the personal State),[472] delegated PE jurisdiction or a collective jurisdiction.[473]

There is, however, domestic case-law and doctrinal support for the view that a stateless vessel may be arrested by any State and, actually, that the arresting State has StL jurisdiction and StA jurisdiction over both the vessel and the individuals on board.[474] This approach does raise concerns regarding overreach, especially by States with substantial enforcement capabilities. These concerns are, however, to a large extent addressed by the existence of the right of diplomatic protection by the State(s) with which the individuals on board a boarded vessel have the necessary legal relationship.[475] The approach also has the benefit of reducing the room for successful challenges to public order at sea which, it will be recalled, is the purpose of the universal jurisdictions.[476]

4.8.2 Relationship between universal jurisdictions

Pi jurisdiction, Sl jurisdiction and St jurisdiction overlap spatially because their scopes *ratione loci* are identical, i.e., the marine areas outside the territories of the coastal States.[477] They also overlap materially in the cases where the three connect-

468 Article 110(2) of the LOSC. See also article 110(1) and (4)–(5).
469 Article 110(2) of the LOSC.
470 See e.g., E Papastavridis *The Interception of Vessels on the High Seas – Contemporary Challenges to the Legal Order of the Oceans* (2013) 265; S Bouwhuis "South Africa: The *Samudera Pasific* and the exercise of jurisdiction over stateless vessels on the high seas" (2014) 29 IJMCL 363–372.
471 See Chapter 3 section 3.2.2.
472 See section 4.8.5.
473 See e.g., Guilfoyle (n. 23) 264.
474 See e.g., *Naim Molvan v. Attorney General for Palestine (The "Asya")* 81 Lloyds Law Reports 277 at 284; *United States v. Marino-Garcia* 679 F.2d 1373 (1982) 1382; Jennings & Watts (n. 83) 731; US Navy *The Commander's Handbook on the Law of Naval Operations* (2017) 3.11.2.3; McDougal & Burke (n. 91) 1084–1085; Bouwhuis (n. 470) at 368; Rob McLaughlin "Article 110 of the Law of the Sea Convention 1982 and jurisdiction over vessels without nationality" (2019) 51 *George Washington International Law Review* 373–406 at 404; Pancracio (n. 23) 330; A Murdoch "Ships without nationality: Interdiction on the high seas" in MD Evans & S Galani (eds) *Maritime Security and the Law of the Sea* (2020) 157–179 at 172.
475 See Churchill, Lowe & Sander (n. 82) 404.
476 See Chapter 3 section 3.5.1.
477 See article 110(1) and 58(2) of the LOSC.

ing factors can be established with regard to the same vessel.[478] In addition, there is a personal overlap because the three jurisdictions are, in principle, all-encompassing *ratione personae*.[479] There is, by contrast, a somewhat limited vessel overlap in that, while Pi jurisdiction and Sl jurisdiction are all-encompassing *ratione navis*, St jurisdiction is limited in that regard.[480] In case of concurrence, there does not appear to be any basis for one form of universal jurisdiction to prevail over another.

4.8.3 Relationship between the universal jurisdictions and flag State jurisdiction

Pi jurisdiction and F jurisdiction overlap materially and spatially because, while Pi jurisdiction is limited *ratione materiae* and *ratione loci*,[481] F jurisdiction is all-encompassing *ratione materiae* and *ratione loci*.[482] There is also a personal overlap because both jurisdictions are all-encompassing *ratione personae*.[483] In addition, there is a vessel overlap because, while F jurisdiction is limited *ratione navis*, Pi jurisdiction is all-encompassing *ratione navis*.[484] In light of the above, there is no need for a State to rely on its Pi jurisdiction when it has F jurisdiction. In the case of two different States, Pi jurisdiction does not exclude F jurisdiction and F jurisdiction does not exclude Pi jurisdiction.[485] There is therefore concurrence of F jurisdiction and Pi jurisdiction.

The position is, regarding the overlap of SlE jurisdiction and FE jurisdiction, the same *mutatis mutandis* as in the case of the overlap of Pi jurisdiction and F jurisdiction.

There cannot be any overlap of St jurisdiction and F jurisdiction *ratione navis* in the case of stateless vessels because the connecting factor of St jurisdiction consists in that no State has F jurisdiction over the vessel.[486] The position is the same in the case of vessels with more than one nationality because, as indicated earlier, in those cases only States other than those having F jurisdiction have St jurisdiction.[487]

4.8.4 Relationship between the universal jurisdictions and territorial jurisdiction

In principle, there cannot be a spatial overlap of Pi jurisdiction, Sl jurisdiction or St jurisdiction, on the one hand, and T jurisdiction, on the other, because their respective scopes *ratione loci* are limited and separate.[488] Spatial overlaps only exist with regard to executive jurisdiction when a coastal State exercises its right of

478 See Chapter 3 sections 3.5.2, 3.5.3 and 3.5.4.1.
479 See section 4.8.1.
480 See Chapter 3 section 3.5.4.
481 See section 4.8.1.2.
482 See section 4.2.1.
483 See sections 4.2.1 and 4.8.1.2.
484 *Ibid.*
485 See e.g., Guilfoyle (n. 25) 703.
486 See Chapter 3 section 3.5.4.2.
487 See Chapter 3 section 3.5.4.3.
488 See sections 4.3.1 and 4.8.2.

hot pursuit.[489] In that case, there is overlap also in other respects because, as already indicated, T jurisdiction is all-encompassing *ratione navis*, *ratione personae* and *ratione materiae*.[490]

4.8.5 Relationship between the universal jurisdictions and personal jurisdiction

The universal jurisdictions and P jurisdiction overlap materially and spatially because, while the universal jurisdictions are limited *ratione materiae* and *ratione loci*,[491] P jurisdiction is all-encompassing *ratione materiae* and *ratione loci*.[492] There is also a personal overlap because, while the scope of P jurisdiction is limited *ratione personae*,[493] the universal jurisdictions are all-encompassing *ratione personae*.[494] In addition, there is a vessel overlap because, while the scope of the universal jurisdictions *ratione navis* varies, P jurisdiction is all-encompassing in that regard.[495] In cases of concurrence, there does not appear to be any basis for the universal jurisdictions to prevail over P jurisdiction or for the latter to prevail over any of the universal jurisdictions either.[496]

4.8.6 Relationship between the universal jurisdictions and the extraterritorial coastal zone jurisdictions

There are personal and vessel overlaps of the universal jurisdictions, on the one hand, and the extraterritorial coastal zone jurisdictions, on the other. This is because all those jurisdictions are all-encompassing *ratione personae* and, while the scope of the universal jurisdictions *ratione navis* varies, the extraterritorial coastal zone jurisdictions are all-encompassing in that regard.[497] There is a spatial overlap because, while the scope of the universal jurisdictions *ratione loci* is limited, the scopes of the extraterritorial coastal zone jurisdictions *ratione loci* are also limited, but to a greater extent and within the scope *ratione loci* of the universal jurisdictions.[498] In addition, the spatial overlap increases when organs of States exercise the right of hot pursuit.[499] However, there is no material overlap because the scopes of the jurisdictions *ratione materiae* are limited and distinct.[500]

489 See section 4.3.1.
490 See section 4.3.1.
491 See section 4.8.1.
492 See section 4.4.1.
493 See section 4.4.1.
494 See section 4.8.1.
495 See sections 4.4.1 and 4.8.1.
496 See e.g., JM Goodwin (n. 176) 1005; A Montas "L'ordre publique en mer à l'épreuve de la piraterie maritime" in A Cudennec (ed) *Ordre Public et Mer* (2012) 235–245 at 238.
497 See sections 4.5.1, 4.6.1, 4.7.1 and 4.8.1.
498 Compare sections 4.5.1, 4.6.1, 4.7.1 and section 4.8.1.
499 See sections 4.5.1, 4.6.1 and 4.7.1.
500 Compare sections 4.5.1, 4.6.1, 4.7.1 and section 4.8.1. See e.g., Beckman (n. 447) 351.

4.8.7 Summary

While the scopes of the universal jurisdictions are similar in most respects, they differ in that they do not all include legislative and adjudicative jurisdictions. The positions in case of overlap are also different in some cases, while identical in others.

4.9 Port State jurisdiction

4.9.1 Extent of port State jurisdiction

4.9.1.1 Introduction

As explained in the previous chapter, the connecting factor that is the ground of Pt jurisdiction is the voluntary presence of a vessel within a port of the State wishing to exercise that jurisdiction.[501] While that connecting factor suggests a wide scope of Pt jurisdiction, the scope is actually narrow, due to the supplementary function of Pt jurisdiction.[502] Indeed, it is limited to very specific matters relating to either environmental protection[503] or fisheries.[504]

4.9.1.2 Supplementary function

While the definition of the term "port State jurisdiction" as "the term given to the jurisdiction a state may exercise over vessels visiting its ports" is useful in pointing to the spatial element of the connecting factor of Pt jurisdiction,[505] it is too broad in that it does not assist in adequately distinguishing Pt jurisdiction from T jurisdiction, F jurisdiction and P jurisdiction.

Ports are located landward of the outer limit of the territorial sea and, for that reason, coastal States have TL jurisdiction, TE jurisdiction and TA jurisdiction over the matters relating to, or the incidents all or part of the facts of which arise within, their ports to the same extent as anywhere else within the marine components of their territories. This means that, as far as those matters and incidents are concerned, no analytical contribution to the understanding of State ocean jurisdiction is made by distinguishing instances of exercise of T jurisdiction relating to, or taking place within, ports from instances of exercise of T jurisdiction relating to, or taking place within, other parts of the marine component of the territory of a coastal State. Likewise, the scopes of F jurisdiction and P jurisdiction do not differ in instances relating to, or taking place within, ports from instances that do not relate to, or do not take place within, ports.[506] This means that, as in the case of T

501 The term "port" being understood broadly. See Chapter 3 section 3.6.
502 See section 4.9.1.2.
503 See section 4.9.1.3.
504 See section 4.9.1.4.
505 See Chapter 3 section 3.6.
506 See sections 4.2.1 and 4.4.1, respectively.

jurisdiction, no analytical contribution to the understanding of F jurisdiction or P jurisdiction is made by distinguishing between those two categories of instances.

The above is not meant to suggest that vessels and the individuals on board are not subject to a specific combination of jurisdictions while they are in a port. Indeed, State jurisdiction in ports is different from State jurisdiction outside ports in that the port State not only has T jurisdiction (as well as, possibly, other forms of coastal zone jurisdiction, F jurisdiction and P jurisdiction),[507] but also port State jurisdiction correctly understood as a supplementary ground of jurisdiction on which a port State may rely when it is unable to rely on another ground of jurisdiction.[508] That is the case when the coastal State is not able to exercise its authority over the matter on any other ground, such as the fact that: (i) the vessel has the nationality of the State; (ii) the persons concerned have the nationality of the State or reside in the State; or (iii) the matter relates to, or all or part of the incident arose within, an area where the coastal State has any form of coastal zone jurisdiction,[509] as in the case of port State control.[510]

4.9.1.3 Environmental protection

A provision conferring Pt jurisdiction on a port State is article 218(1) of the LOSC, which authorises the State to

> undertake investigations and, where the evidence so warrants, institute proceedings in respect of any discharge from that vessel outside the internal waters, territorial sea or exclusive economic zone of that State in violation of applicable international rules and standards established through the competent international organization or general diplomatic conference.

The term "discharge" is not defined in the LOSC. However, article 218(1) refers to a discharge "in violation of applicable international rules and standards established through the competent international organization or general diplomatic conference".[511] Those rules and standards are at least those set by the

507 Because most ports are in the internal waters or the territorial sea of a coastal State, a port State is also a coastal State. The exception is "the case of an inland port of a landlocked State, accessible to sea-going vessels (such as Basel, Switzerland)" (MH Nordquist (ed) *United Nations Convention on the Law of the Sea 1982: A Commentary* (2002) IV 261 § 218.1).

508 R Rayfuse *Non-Flag State Enforcement in High Seas Fisheries* (2004) 60–61. See also Nordquist (n. 507) 261 § 218.1. *Contra* B Marten *Port State Jurisdiction and the Regulation of International Shipping* (2014) 3.

509 See e.g., D König "Article 218" in Proelss (n. 25) 1487–1496 at 1493.

510 In that case, "the port state is only enforcing domestic legislation which just happens to incorporate internationally agreed standards in respect of breaches of that legislation committed by non-nationals that have occurred within its territory" (R Rayfuse "The role of port States" in Warner & Kaye (n. 23) 71–85 at 77).

511 König (n. 509) 1493–1494.

1973 International Convention for the Prevention of Pollution from Ships,[512] as amended by its 1978 Protocol[513] (MARPOL), and its Annexes I to IV.[514] For purposes of MARPOL, the word "discharge" is defined as any release of "harmful substances or effluents containing such substances [...] howsoever caused from a ship and includes any escape, disposal, spilling, leaking, pumping, emitting or emptying".[515] The term does not refer to: (a) dumping within the meaning of the 1972 Convention on the Prevention of Marine Pollution by Dumping of Wastes and Other Matter (LC 1972);[516] (b) the "release of harmful substances directly arising from the exploration, exploitation and associated offshore processing of seabed mineral resources";[517] and (c) the "release of harmful substances for purposes of legitimate scientific research into pollution abatement and control".[518] Article 218(1) states that the international rules and standards must be "applicable". This is understood to mean that the States involved in a specific exercise of PtE jurisdiction, including the port State and the flag State, must be parties to the instrument setting the rules and standards concerned in that instance.[519]

Article 218(1) grants PtE jurisdiction in relation to the undertaking of investigations.[520] It includes, for instance, boarding, inspection as well as "[d]etention until standards are complied with, e.g., repairs to meet technical standards",[521] subject to the safeguards provided for in section 7 of Part XII of the LOSC[522] as well as the prompt release procedure in article 292. That jurisdiction is all-encompassing *ratione personae* and *ratione navis*, but it is limited *ratione loci* to the port or offshore terminal within which the vessel concerned finds itself.[523] It is also limited *ratione materiae* to investigations relating to the discharges taking place in the geographical area described in the provision.

In addition, article 218(1) expressly grants PtA jurisdiction in respect of those discharges "before administrative, civil and/or criminal courts, depending on the

512 1340 UNTS 184, (1973) 12 ILM 1319. Adopted: 2 November 1973; EIF: 10 February 1983.
513 1340 UNTS 61, (1978) 17 ILM 546. Adopted: 17 February 1978; EIF: 2 October 1983.
514 See Nordquist (n. 507) 271 § 218.9(a); König (n. 509) 1493.
515 Article 2(3)(a). The definition "encompasses operational as well as accidental discharges" (König (n. 509) 1493). The term "harmful substance" is defined article 2(2).
516 1046 UNTS 138, (1972) 11 ILM 1294. Adopted: 29 December 1972; EIF: 30 August 1975. See article 2(3)(b)(i). The definition in article III(1) of the Convention was taken over *verbatim* in article 1(1)(5) of the LOSC. Compare the definition in article 1(4) of the 1996 Protocol to the 1972 Convention ((1997) 36 ILM 1, (1997) 34 LOSB 71; adopted: 17 November 1996; EIF: 24 March 2006).
517 Article 2(3)(b)(ii).
518 Article 2(3)(b)(iii).
519 As indicated above, MARPOL is likely to be that instrument in most instances. However, the instrument can be a regional, local or bilateral treaty setting more stringent rules and standards when all the States concerned are parties to it (see König (n. 509) 1494).
520 See König (n. 509) 1494.
521 EJ Molenaar "Port State jurisdiction" (2014) MPEPIL § 22.
522 See, in particular, article 226, 228 and 230–232.
523 See Chapter 3 section 3.6.

seriousness of the violation and the port State's national legal system".[524] That jurisdiction appears to be limited to discharge violations on the high seas. This is because a coastal State's jurisdiction in respect of a discharge violation in the internal waters, territorial sea or EEZ of another State" is arguably best understood as either: (a) a delegated jurisdiction, when it is subject to a request by "that State, the flag State, or a State damaged or threatened by the discharge violation";[525] (b) TA jurisdiction, when the violation has caused, or is likely to cause, pollution in the internal waters, archipelagic waters and/or territorial sea of the coastal State;[526] or (c) EezA jurisdiction, when the violation has caused, or is likely to cause, pollution in the EEZ of the coastal State.[527]

PtA jurisdiction is based on the implied PtL jurisdiction to perform legislative acts producing legislative instruments containing normative provisions incorporating into domestic law the "applicable international rules and standards" referred to in the provision.[528] The scope of that jurisdiction is limited *ratione materiae* to the abovementioned discharges. It appears to be also limited *ratione loci* in that it only relates to the high seas. By contrast and like PtE jurisdiction, it is all-encompassing *ratione personae* and *ratione navis*.

Article 218 is a "carefully structured compromise" and a "generally acceptable package in which proper balance was maintained".[529] It is also "truly innovatory"[530] and it is not entirely clear whether its provisions have matured into customary international law and they are opposable to the States that are not parties to the LOSC.

4.9.1.4 Fisheries

In terms of article 23(1) of the Fish Stocks Agreement, "[a] port State has the right and the duty to take measures, in accordance with international law, to promote the effectiveness of subregional, regional and global conservation and management measures". Those measures include the "measures to conserve and manage one or more species of [straddling fish stocks and highly migratory fish stocks] that are adopted and applied consistent with the relevant rules of international law as reflected in the [LOSC] and th[e] Agreement".[531] To the extent that those stocks are located within areas where a coastal State has one or other form of coastal zone

524 See König (n. 509) 1494.
525 Article 218(2) of the LOSC. See Chapter 3 section 3.7. See also König (n. 509) 1495.
526 Article 218(2) of the LOSC. See section 4.3.1.
527 Article 218(2) of the LOSC. See section 4.6.1.
528 See H-S Bang "Port State jurisdiction and article 218 of the UN Convention on the Law of the Sea" (2009) 40 JMLC 291; König (n. 509) 1495; TL McDorman "Port State enforcement: A comment on article 218 of the 1982 Law of the Sea Convention" (1997) 28 JMLC 315.
529 UNCLOS III "Memorandum by the President of the Conference on Document A/CONF.62/WP.10", UN Doc. A/CONF.62/WP.10/ADD.1 (1977) in (1977) VIII *UNCLOS III Official Records* 65 at 69. See further e.g., Rothwell & Stephens (n. 131) 383.
530 RR Churchill & AV Lowe *The Law of the Sea* (1999) 350.
531 Article 1(1)(b) read with article 3(1) of the Fish Stocks Agreement.

jurisdiction, there does not appear to exist any reason why any exercise of jurisdiction by the State over a vessel in one of its ports should not be understood as the exercise of that coastal zone jurisdiction.

As far as the stocks located in areas where coastal States do not have any form of coastal zone jurisdiction, although no States have such jurisdiction, they nevertheless have the duty to "cooperate with each other in the conservation and management of [those] living resources [...]".[532] This general duty is fulfilled primarily by States fulfilling their more specific "duty to take, or to cooperate with other States in taking, such measures for their respective nationals as may be necessary for the conservation of the living resources of the high seas", i.e., in the exercise of their P jurisdiction.[533] However, where a State within a port of which a vessel finds itself voluntarily does not have F jurisdiction or P jurisdiction, that State is unable to exercise its authority unless the matter falls within the scope of Pt jurisdiction. It is to this extent that article 23(1) has an impact on the scope of Pt jurisdiction.

In terms of article 23(2), "[a] port State may, inter alia, inspect documents, fishing gear and catch on board fishing vessels [...]",[534] steps that fall within the PtE jurisdiction of the port State. As far as article 23(3) is concerned, it makes it clear that States have the PtL jurisdiction to

> adopt regulations empowering the relevant national authorities to prohibit landings and transshipments where it has been established that the catch has been taken in a manner which undermines the effectiveness of subregional, regional or global conservation and management measures on the high seas.

As far as PtA jurisdiction is concerned, it would appear to be limited to disputes related to PtL jurisdiction or PtE jurisdiction as circumscribed above. The Fish Stocks Agreement has not received overwhelming support yet[535] and it is doubtful that article 23 reflects general customary international law.[536]

Another global instrument that has an impact on Pt jurisdiction in fisheries-related matters is the 2009 Agreement on Port State Measures to Prevent, Deter and Eliminate Illegal, Unreported and Unregulated Fishing (PSMA).[537] It is important to keep in mind, however, that, although the objective of the PSMA is "to prevent, deter and eliminate IUU fishing through the implementation of

532 Article 118 of the LOSC. See e.g., R Rayfuse "Article 118" in Proelss (n. 25) 817–830 at 823–824. There is little doubt that this duty is also part of customary international law (see *Fisheries Jurisdiction Case (Great Britain v. Iceland)*, judgment of 25 July 1974, 1974 ICJ Reports 3 § 72; *Fisheries Jurisdiction Case (Germany v. Iceland)*, judgment of 25 July 1974, 1974 ICJ Reports 175 § 64).

533 Article 117 of the LOSC. See section 4.4.1.

534 Article 23(2).

535 At the end of 2021, only 95 States were parties to the Agreement.

536 This is illustrated by the fact that "[n]o RFMO scheme goes so far as to provide for port state enforcement" (Rayfuse (n. 510) 80).

537 (2016) 55 ILM 1159. Adopted: 22 November 2009; EIF: 5 June 2016. The connecting factor exists to the extent that "[n]othing in th[e] Agreement affects the entry of vessels to port in accordance with international law for reasons of force majeure or distress [...]" (article 10).

effective port State measures, and thereby to ensure the long-term conservation and sustainable use of living marine resources and marine ecosystems",[538] its provisions do not exclusively relate to Pt jurisdiction. Indeed, its application is not limited to fishing on the high seas.[539] As a result, the PSMA applies also to IUU fishing and to "fishing related activities in support of such fishing"[540] that occur in areas over which coastal States have one or the other form of coastal zone jurisdiction. With regard to those activities taking place within its relevant zone, any authority taken in one of its ports by a coastal State is taken in the exercise of that jurisdiction, not Pt jurisdiction.[541] In relation to those cases, it is confirmed expressly in the PSMA that the latter does not affect both "the sovereignty of Parties over their internal, archipelagic and territorial waters or their sovereign rights over their continental shelf and in their exclusive economic zones"[542] and "the exercise by Parties of their sovereignty over ports in their territory in accordance with international law".[543]

To the extent that the PSMA applies, in cases where the port State does not have F jurisdiction and/or P jurisdiction, in marine areas where no State has any coastal zone jurisdiction, the Agreement constitutes the legal basis for taking a range of steps in the exercise of PtE jurisdiction[544] or PtL jurisdiction.[545] As far as PtA jurisdiction is concerned, it is limited to adjudicative recourses available to the owner, operator, master or representative of a vessel in relation to port State measures taken by that party regarding port entry, authorisation or denial, the use of a port, the conduct of inspections and/or follow-up actions as well as "any right to seek compensation [...] in the event of any loss or damage suffered as a consequence of any alleged unlawful action by the" port State.[546]

The PSMA has not received overwhelming support yet[547] and it is doubtful that its provisions reflect general customary international law.[548]

538 Article 2. The term "IUU fishing" is defined by reference in article 1(e).

539 See article 3(3). See e.g., FAO *A Guide to the Background and Implementation of the 2009 FAO Agreement on Port State Measures to Prevent, Deter and Eliminate Illegal, Unreported and Unregulated Fishing* (2012) 39.

540 See article 3(3).

541 See also e.g., article 3(2), which relates to vessels chartered for fishing in areas under the "national jurisdiction" of the State "and operating under its authority therein". In such cases, State authority is exercised on a ground of coastal zone jurisdiction.

542 Article 4(1)(a).

543 Article 4(1)(b).

544 See e.g., article 7(1).

545 See e.g., article 8(1).

546 Article 19(1). See further article 18(1). Article 18(3) confirms that, while the port State has very limited PtA jurisdiction, nothing in the Agreement stands in the way of the State exercising delegated FA jurisdiction.

547 At the end of 2021, only 70 States were parties to the Agreement.

548 See e.g., Rayfuse (n. 510) 78.

4.9.2 Relationship between the port State jurisdictions

Because any State may exercise its Pt jurisdiction once the connection has been established by the voluntary presence of the relevant vessel within a port of that State, the PtL jurisdictions of all the coastal States overlap each other. Indeed, they overlap *ratione personae*, *ratione navis* and *ratione materiae*. They also overlap *ratione loci* on the high seas. By contrast, overlaps in the exercise of PtE jurisdiction are not possible at any given time because the scope of that jurisdiction *ratione loci* is limited to the ports and offshore installations of the State where a vessel finds itself voluntarily. As far as they are concerned, overlaps in the performance of adjudicative acts in the exercise of PtA jurisdiction are only possible when two or more States exercise their PtE jurisdictions one after the other in respect of the same discharge violation.

4.9.3 Relationship between port State jurisdiction and flag State jurisdiction

Because F jurisdiction is all-encompassing *ratione materiae* and *ratione loci*,[549] there are spatial and material overlaps of Pt jurisdiction and F jurisdiction. When the ship has the nationality of the State in a port of which it has called, that State has both jurisdictions and no issue of attribution of competence arises as far as international law is concerned. The position is more complex in cases where the flag State is not the same as the port State.

The FL jurisdiction of one State overlaps the PtL jurisdiction of another State. Indeed, the principle of non-intervention by a State in the internal affairs of another State does not apply because, as explained earlier, PtL jurisdiction is not exercised by a State in respect of its own maritime zones.[550] That is not the case with regard to PtE jurisdiction and FE jurisdiction. Indeed, as in the case of overlap of F jurisdiction and T jurisdiction, although the two jurisdictions do potentially overlap, the principle of exclusive executive jurisdiction of a State within its territory results in the exclusion of FE jurisdiction. In contrast, there is no basis for the exclusion of FA jurisdiction, the exercise of which is, however, affected by the fact that executive steps may only be taken by, or with the consent of, the port State while the vessel is within the latter's territory.

4.9.4 Relationship between port State jurisdiction and territorial jurisdiction

Pt jurisdiction differs from T jurisdiction in that PtL jurisdiction confers authority upon the coastal State to take legislative and adjudicative steps in matters arising outside the marine component of the State's territory.[551] In other words, TL jurisdiction is a territorial jurisdiction while PtL jurisdiction is an extraterritorial

549 See section 4.2.2.1. The fact that the flag State has F jurisdiction with regard to discharge violations occurring anywhere is confirmed by article 218(2) of the LOSC.

550 See section 4.9.1.

551 Compare sections 4.2.3.1 and 4.9.1.

jurisdiction. In contrast, Pt jurisdiction has in common with T jurisdiction that PtE jurisdiction is exercised in a coastal State's ports and off-shore terminals, that is to say in areas where TE jurisdiction is also exercised by the coastal State.

However, while there is a spatial overlap between PtE jurisdiction and TE jurisdiction, there is no material overlap between the two jurisdictions because, as it has just been pointed out, Pt jurisdiction confers authority upon a coastal State over matters that do not fall within the T jurisdiction of the State. In other words, although PtE jurisdiction is exercised in a geographical area where a coastal State exercises primarily its TE jurisdiction, the taking of executive steps in a port in the exercise of PtE jurisdiction does not alter the fact that the coastal State does not have TE jurisdiction over the matters over which it has PtE jurisdiction.

There is no concurrence of the PtL jurisdiction of one State and the TL jurisdiction of another State. Indeed, while the two jurisdictions have the same scope *ratione materiae*, *ratione personae* and *ratione navis*, it has already been explained earlier that the scope of PtL jurisdiction *ratione loci* is limited to discharge violations on the high seas,[552] while TL jurisdiction is limited *ratione loci* to discharge violations landward of the outer limit of the State's territorial sea.[553] That is also the case with regard to PtE jurisdiction and TE jurisdiction. Indeed, as in the case of overlap of T jurisdictions, the principle of exclusive executive jurisdiction of a State within its territory results in the exclusion of the TE jurisdiction of another State.[554] In the absence of concurrence of legislative jurisdictions and executive jurisdictions, there is no room for concurrence of adjudicative jurisdictions.

4.9.5 Relationship between port State jurisdiction and personal jurisdiction

Because P jurisdiction is all-encompassing *ratione materiae* and *ratione loci*,[555] there is a spatial overlap and a material overlap between Pt jurisdiction and P jurisdiction. When a person is on board a vessel that has called in a port of a State and he or she has the nationality of that State, the latter has both jurisdictions and no issue of attribution of competence arises as far as international law is concerned. The position is more complex in cases where the personal State is not the same as the port State.

The law of the sea does not contain any obstacle to the concurrence of PL jurisdiction and PtL jurisdiction.[556] That is not the case with regard to PE jurisdiction and PtE jurisdiction. Indeed, the principle of exclusive executive jurisdiction of a State within its territory results, in principle, in the exclusion of the exercise of the

552 See section 4.9.1.
553 See section 4.3.1.
554 See section 4.3.2.
555 See section 4.2.4.1.
556 The fact that P jurisdiction with regard to discharge violations occurring anywhere is not confirmed by article 218 of the LOSC, in contrast to F jurisdiction and T jurisdiction, is probably best explained by the limited attention paid to P jurisdiction by the drafters of the Convention and their predecessors. See e.g., Staker (n. 39) 299.

PE jurisdiction of a foreign personal State.[557] In contrast, there is no basis for the exclusion of PA jurisdiction, the exercise of which is however affected by the fact that executive steps may only be taken by, or with the consent of, the port State while the vessel is within the latter's territory.

4.9.6 Relationship between port State jurisdiction and the extraterritorial coastal zone jurisdictions

Pt jurisdiction differs from Cz jurisdiction, Eez jurisdiction and Cs jurisdiction in that PtL jurisdiction confers authority upon the coastal State to take steps in matters arising beyond the outer limit of its EEZ.[558] In other words, CzL jurisdiction, EezL jurisdiction as well as, to a large extent, CsL jurisdiction relate to matters arising landward of the outer limit of the EEZ while PtL jurisdiction relates to matters arising beyond that limit.

At the same time, there is a spatial overlap between PtE jurisdiction, on the one hand, and CzE jurisdiction, EezE jurisdiction and CsE jurisdiction, on the other, when the coastal State exercises its extraterritorial coastal zone jurisdiction within one of its ports or off-shore terminals.[559] Even in those cases, however, it has just been pointed out that there is no material overlap between the jurisdictions because Pt jurisdiction confers authority upon a coastal State over matters that do not fall within the Cz jurisdiction, the Eez jurisdiction or the Cs jurisdiction of the State.

4.9.7 Relationship between port State jurisdiction and the universal jurisdictions

There are personal and vessel overlaps because the four jurisdictions are all-encompassing *ratione personae* and *ratione navis*.[560] There is also a spatial overlap to the extent that the limited scope *ratione loci* of PtL jurisdiction and PtA jurisdiction falls within the limited, but wider scope of the universal jurisdictions *ratione loci*.[561] However, the universal jurisdictions and Pt jurisdiction do not overlap materially because their respective scopes *ratione materiae* are limited and distinct.[562]

4.9.8 Summary

While the connecting factor of Pt jurisdiction suggests a wide scope, the latter is actually narrow, due to the supplementary function of Pt jurisdiction, which also explains the few overlaps with other jurisdictions.

557 See section 4.4.4.
558 See section 4.3.2.1. The issue of the distinction between the coastal zone jurisdictions and Pt jurisdiction obviously does not arise where the port State does not have a coast.
559 Compare sections 4.5.1, 4.6.1, 4.7.1 and 4.9.1.
560 Compare sections 4.8.1 and 4.9.1.
561 Compare sections 4.8.1 and 4.9.1.
562 Compare sections 4.8.1 and 4.9.1.

4.10 Delegated jurisdictions

4.10.1 Extent of the delegated jurisdictions

The fact that, in the case of a delegated jurisdiction, the connecting factor is the existence of a delegation of a jurisdiction by a State to another State that would not otherwise have the jurisdiction means that the extent of each delegated jurisdiction is determined by the nature of the delegation concerned. A State is not able to delegate a jurisdiction of a wider scope than it has itself. For instance, a coastal State cannot delegate its TA jurisdiction to another State for the purpose of the latter exercising that jurisdiction in respect of a discharge violation within the territorial sea of a neighbouring State because TA jurisdiction of the coastal State does not extend to disputes relating to matters arising beyond the outer limit of its territorial sea.[563] By contrast, nothing stands in the way of a State delegating a jurisdiction of a narrower scope than it has itself. For instance, a coastal State may delegate its Eez jurisdiction only to the extent that it is exercised in respect of living resources.

Prima facie, the *pacta tertiis nec nocent nec prosunt* rule appears to mean that third States do not derive rights or obligations from the delegation of a jurisdiction by means of an agreement.[564] The same would apply in the case of a delegation in the form of a unilateral act.[565] In other words, delegated jurisdictions appear not to be opposable to third States. It is important in this respect to have regard to the relevant legal instrument. The delegation might indeed take place in terms of an earlier agreement making provision for the delegation. In such a case, the only States that are in the position of third States are the States that are neither parties to the delegation nor parties to the agreement. For instance, the delegated TA jurisdiction of a State made by another State in terms of article 218(2) of the LOSC is opposable to the flag State of a vessel that is alleged to have committed a discharge violation when the flag State is a party to the LOSC, but it is not opposable to the flag State when the latter is not a party to the Convention.[566] This means that the impact of a delegated jurisdiction depends on the number of States that are parties either to the delegation instrument or the instrument providing for the delegation.

However, it would seem that, unless their terms point to a different conclusion, delegated jurisdictions are opposable to third States. Indeed, it has already been pointed out that a State cannot delegate to another State a jurisdiction of a wider scope than it has itself. This means that the delegation of a jurisdiction does not increase or limit the rights or obligations of third States. For instance, should State A delegate its EezE jurisdiction to State B, the rights and obligations of a third State C as a flag State with regard to the EEZ of State A, are neither increased

563 See sections 4.3.1 and 4.9.1.

564 See article 34 of the 1969 Vienna Convention on the Law of Treaties (1155 UNTS 332, (1969) 8 ILM 679; adopted: 23 May 1969; EIF: 27 January 1980; VCLT).

565 See principle 9 of the Guiding Principles Applicable to Unilateral Declarations of States Capable of Creating Legal Obligations adopted by the ILC in 2006 ((2006) II YILC 159–166 at 161).

566 The flag State is unlikely to be a party to the delegation because, should it wish the port State to have jurisdiction, it is likely to delegate its own (FA) jurisdiction.

nor limited. In other words, the delegation does not affect the legal relationship between the EezE jurisdiction of State A and the FE jurisdiction of State C.[567] The impact is at the practical level in that, in addition to the organs of State A, the organs of State B also have EezE jurisdiction now, thereby increasing the likelihood of EezE jurisdiction being exercised. It is difficult to envisage a valid reason why State C would object to such a result.

4.10.2 Relationship between the delegated jurisdictions and the other jurisdictions

In most cases, a delegated jurisdiction is concurrent with at least one jurisdiction: the jurisdiction that the delegating State delegated. This is because a State is unlikely to be willing, or be allowed, to divest itself from its jurisdiction when delegating it to another State. In other words, the delegation of a jurisdiction is not a transfer of that jurisdiction, but rather a sharing of that jurisdiction.[568] Provided that it is opposable,[569] a delegated jurisdiction is concurrent with jurisdictions other than the jurisdiction that has been delegated to the same extent as the latter does.

4.11 Collective jurisdictions

4.11.1 Extent of the collective jurisdictions

As in the case of delegated jurisdiction, the fact that, in the case of a collective jurisdiction, the connecting factor consists in the decision taken by an international organisation with the capacity to confer to States authority to be involved in a specific matter, in terms of which that body does confer that authority, means that the extent of each collective jurisdiction is determined by the nature of the conferral concerned. For instance, the UNSC gave to the United Kingdom, in 1966, the authority "to prevent, by the use of force if necessary, the arrival at Beira of vessels reasonably believed to be carrying oil destined for Southern Rhodesia [...]".[570] The conferring of a collective jurisdiction is *ultra vires* when the organisation does not have the legal power to confer that jurisdiction. For instance, the European Union does not have any legal power with regard to the management of the living resources of the African maritime domain. The *pacta tertiis nec nocent nec prosunt* rule means that third States do not derive rights or obligations from the conferring of a collective jurisdiction in terms of the treaty establishing the organisation concerned.[571] In other words, a collective jurisdiction is not opposable to a State that is not a member of the organisation.

567 See section 4.6.3.

568 This is subject to the principle *ne bis in idem* as far as adjudicative jurisdiction is concerned. See n. 6.

569 See section 4.10.1.

570 Paragraph 5 of UNSC Resolution 221 (9 April 1966).

571 See article 34 of the VCLT.

4.11.2 Relationship between the collective jurisdictions and the other jurisdictions

The possibility and nature of overlap of a collective jurisdiction, on the one hand, and one or more other jurisdictions, on the other, depend on the extent of that collective jurisdiction. Examples are many of the UNSC resolutions regarding piracy in the waters off the coast of Somalia adopted since 2008. In those resolutions, the UNSC conferred upon States cooperating with the Transitional Federal Government of Somalia the collective jurisdiction to "[e]nter the territorial waters of Somalia for the purpose of repressing acts of piracy and armed robbery at sea, in a manner consistent with such action permitted on the high seas with respect to piracy under relevant international law"[572] and to "[u]se, within the territorial waters of Somalia, in a manner consistent with action permitted on the high seas with respect to piracy under relevant international law, all necessary means to repress acts of piracy and armed robbery".[573] This executive collective jurisdiction is concurrent with the TE jurisdiction of Somalia. By contrast, the former is not concurrent with PiE jurisdiction because the two jurisdictions do not overlap *ratione loci*, the executive collective jurisdiction being exercised landward of the outer limits of the territorial sea of Somalia while PiE jurisdiction may only be exercised seaward of those limits.[574]

4.12 Protective jurisdictions

4.12.1 Extent of the protective jurisdictions

4.12.1.1 Introduction

Ps jurisdiction and Pe jurisdiction have in common that there does not appear to be any basis for limiting the scopes of the jurisdictions *ratione personae* or *ratione navis*. As far as the scopes *ratione loci* are concerned, they do not include the marine component of the territory of a coastal State relying on the ground of Ps jurisdiction or Pe jurisdiction because the State would be able to rely on its undisputable and all-encompassing T jurisdiction. Beyond the territories of the coastal States, the scope *ratione loci* varies depending on whether the matter concerned falls within the scope *ratione materiae* of one or more of the extraterritorial coastal zone jurisdictions. When it does, a coastal State would be able to rely on that undisputable jurisdiction. Where Ps jurisdiction and Pe jurisdiction differ is with regard to their respective scopes *ratione materiae*.

4.12.1.2 Protective jurisdiction exercised for State security purposes

The scope of Ps jurisdiction is limited by the fact that the matter with regard to which the State wants to exercise its jurisdiction must constitute a threat to the security of the State that is seen as sufficiently serious by the community of States for the latter to allow

572 Paragraph 7(a) of UNSC Resolution 1816 (2 June 2008).
573 Paragraph 7(b).
574 See section 4.8.1.2.

organs of that State to act in the exercise of that ground of jurisdiction. In that regard, "[i]t has long been recognized that when essential interests of the State are at stake States need to, and will, act in order to preserve themselves".[575] When those actions are taken in the exercise of F jurisdiction, a coastal zone jurisdiction or P jurisdiction, they are less likely to give rise to any objection by other States because the respective connecting factors of those jurisdictions do not include any protective element. This is well illustrated in the case of unauthorised broadcasting[576] from the high seas when the LOSC confirms that a State has adjudicative jurisdiction when, for instance: (a) the State is "the flag State of the ship"[577] (FA jurisdiction); (b) the State is "the State of which the person is a national"[578] (PA jurisdiction); and/or (c) the transmission can be received in the territory of the State[579] or "authorized radio communication is suffering interference" in that territory[580] (ToA jurisdiction).[581]

By contrast, "there is unmistakably a danger that States might abuse the protective principle".[582] "The pressure to expand the use of th[e] [protective] principle, and the danger of unshackling it from the protection of truly *vital* interests and of permitting its use for the convenient advancement of important interests, is clear"[583] and requires some form of control. One way of doing so is to require a "direct and substantial connection between the state exercising [Ps] jurisdiction and the matter in relation to which jurisdiction is exercised".[584]

One area where protection is required is marine pollution. The latter's definition, for purposes of the LOSC,[585] makes it clear that pollution exists even when there has been no "deleterious effects" yet. All that is required is that such effects be "likely to result" from the introduction by humans of a substance or energy.[586]

575 Staker (n. 39) 301. See also e.g., Simma & Müller (n. 14) 143.

576 Unauthorised broadcasting is defined for the purposes of the LOSC as "the transmission of sound radio or television broadcasts from a ship or installation [...] intended for reception by the general public contrary to international regulations, but excluding the transmission of distress calls" (article 109(2)).

577 Article 109(3)(a) of the LOSC.

578 Article 109(3)(c).

579 Article 109(3)(d).

580 Article 109(3)(e).

581 The position is the same with regard to legislative jurisdiction. The position is different with regard to executive jurisdiction because it is either limited *ratione loci* (in the case of the coastal zone executive jurisdictions (see sections 4.3.1, 4.5.1, 4.6.1 and 4.7.1) or excluded by another jurisdiction (in the case of FE jurisdiction (see sections 4.2.2 and 3.3) and PE jurisdiction (see sections 4.4.3 and 4.4.4)).

582 Ryngaert (n. 6) 115.

583 Staker (n. 39) 302.

584 Jennings & Watts (n. 83) 468.

585 See article 1(1)(4). See e.g., Churchill, Lowe & Sander (n. 82) 620–622; Rothwell & Stephens (n. 131) 366–369; Tanaka (n. 47) 324–329.

586 See e.g., Y Tanaka "Article 1" in Proelss (n. 25) 17–26 at 23; C Ha "Criminal jurisdiction for ship collision and marine pollution in high seas – Focused on the 2015 judgement on M/V *Ernest Hemingway* case" (2020) 4 *Journal of International Maritime Safety, Environmental Affairs and Shipping* 8–15 at 13.

This means that a mere threat is sufficient for there to be pollution and the presence of that threat is sufficient to establish the Ps jurisdiction of a coastal State. This is confirmed by article 221(1) of the LOSC.[587]

Another area where control is required is the illicit traffic in narcotic drugs or psychotropic substances, an activity "regarded as constituting a grave threat to States targeted for" importation.[588] For that reason, several States have asserted jurisdiction in related instances. For instance, in *US v. Gonzalez*,[589] the Court held that,

> the United States could prosecute foreign nationals on foreign vessels under the "protective principle" of international law, which permits a nation to assert jurisdiction over a person whose conduct outside the nation's security or could potentially interfere with the operation of its governmental functions.[590]

On that basis, the Court asserted that PsE jurisdiction could be exercised "to such an extent and to so great a distance as is reasonable and necessary to protect itself and its citizens from injury".[591] Without "any other limiting criterion *ratione loci* or *ratione materiae*", such a wide claim has "enormous potential scope, capable of subsuming and considerably extending not only the rules on the contiguous zone, but also the rules on visit and search on the high seas".[592] This appears to be the reason why the LOSC does not recognise that claim.[593] Indeed, the illicit traffic in narcotic drugs or psychotropic substances is not a ground of universal jurisdiction and there is no general right of visit over suspect vessels. Instead, article 108 requires cooperation and flag State control by means of bilateral and multilateral conventions.[594] One of those instruments is the 1988 UN Convention against Illicit Traffic in Narcotic Drugs and Psychotropic Substances,[595] which does not provide any evidence of the existence of a protective jurisdiction.

587 See further article 221(2). See also the 1969 International Convention Relating to Intervention on the High Seas in Cases of Oil Pollution Casualties (970 UNTS 212, (1969) 9 ILM 24; adopted: 29 November 1969; EIF: 6 May 1975). See further e.g., *The "Arctic Sunrise" Arbitration* (n. 54) § 308; Churchill, Lowe & Sander (n. 82) 658.

588 Churchill, Lowe & Sander (n. 82) 405.

589 776 F.2d 931 (1985).

590 At 938, relying on *US v. Romero-Galue* 757 F.2d 1147 (1985) at 1154. In such cases, the United States has neither P jurisdiction (because the cases involve foreign nationals) nor F jurisdiction (because the individuals concerned are on foreign vessels).

591 At 939. This assertion is necessary when executive authority is to be exercised beyond the scope *ratione loci* of the coastal zone jurisdictions.

592 Churchill & Lowe (n. 530) 218.

593 See e.g., Oxman (n. 145) 829; Nordquist (n. 459) 226 § 108.4.

594 See e.g., Churchill, Lowe & Sander (n. 82) 400–403; D Guilfoyle "Article 108" in Proelss (n. 25) 759–763 at 760 and 762.

595 1582 UNTS 165, (1989) 28 ILM 493. Adopted: 20 December 1988; EIF: 11 November 1990.

A similar approach has been adopted with regard to migration control at sea. Indeed, in practice, migration-related measures taken in cases where the State concerned may not rely on the ground of F jurisdiction, T jurisdiction or Cz jurisdiction, "are taken on the basis either of bilateral or multilateral treaties".[596] Two examples are the PSM,[597] at the global level, and the 2008 CARICOM Maritime and Airspace Security Co-operation Agreement,[598] at the regional level.[599]

A somewhat different approach has been followed to combat the threat constituted by the transfer at sea of materials related to weapons of mass destruction (WMD).[600] One of the concrete steps taken to that end is the Proliferation Security Initiative (PSI) launched in 2003.[601] Led by the United States and endorsed by more than a hundred States, the PSI is not legally binding and, therefore, cannot constitute a valid basis for Ps jurisdiction.[602] Instead, the legal basis for measures is found either in bilateral treaties[603] or in the 2005 Protocol amending the SUA Convention,[604] all of which address the concern that "a unilateral interdiction at sea may be used to promote the strategic interests of a particular State on the pretext of maritime terrorism and the transfer of WMD-related materials at sea".[605]

Ps jurisdiction is often seen as "deriving from a State's inherent right of self-defense".[606] The existence of the right of self-defence was already assumed by Great Britain and the United States in *Caroline*.[607] The incident occurred in 1837 during the uprising against the British Crown in the Province of Upper Canada. One of the two defences raised by Great Britain when the United States angrily reacted

596 Tanaka (n. 47) 210.
597 2241 UNTS 480, (2001) 40 ILM 384. Adopted: 15 November 2000; EIF: 28 January 2004.
598 (2008) 68 LOSB 20. Adopted: 4 July 2008; EIF: article 27.
599 On the legal arrangements within the European Union, see e.g., E Papastavridis "'Fortress Europe' and FRONTEX: Within or without international law?" (2010) 79 NJIL 75–111.
600 See e.g., R Geiß & CJ Tams "Non-flag States as guardians of the maritime order: Creeping jurisdiction of a different kind?" in Ringbom (n. 5) 19–49 at 43–48.
601 See e.g., M Byers "Policing the high seas: The PSI" (2004) 98 AJIL 526–545.
602 See e.g., F Spadi "Bolstering the Proliferation Security Initiative at sea: A comparative analysis of ship-boarding as a bilateral and multilateral implementing mechanism" (2006) 75 NJIL 249–278 at 251.
603 *Ibid.* 256–268; H Jessen "United States' bilateral shipboarding agreements – Upholding law of the sea principles while updating State practice" in Ringbom (n. 5) 50–81; Bateman (n. 100) 47.
604 See e.g., Spadi (n. 602) 268–276.
605 Tanaka (n. 47) 469. The relevant UNSC resolutions do not constitute a separate ground of (collective) jurisdiction regarding WMD. What the resolutions often do, instead, is to render a jurisdiction the exercise of which is, or might be, otherwise only discretionary, obligatory. See e.g., UNSC Resolution 1716 (14 October 2006).
606 Ryngaert (n. 6) 114.
607 RY Jennings "The *Caroline* and McLeod cases" (1938) 32 AJIL 82–99. The right was later acknowledged by Spain in *Virginius* (see section 4.2.5.2(d)) and relied on by France, half a century ago, in *Duizar* (*Société Ignazio Messina et Cie v. l'Etat (Ministre des Armées "Marine")*, Tribunal administratif of Paris judgment of 22 October 1962 reproduced and discussed in L Lucchini "Un aspect des mesures de surveillance maritime au cours des opérations d'Algérie" (1962) 8 AFDI 920–928.

to the incident was "[s]elf-defence and self-preservation".[608] In the process of settling the dispute, four years later, the United States challenged Great Britain to show a "necessity of self-defence, instant, overwhelming, leaving no choice of means, and no moment for deliberation".[609] "These requirements for self-defence are commonly accepted as constituting the [...] customary law of self-defence" as it stood at the beginning of the Second World War.[610] Since then, the UNC stresses that nothing in the Charter "shall impair the inherent right of individual or collective self-defence if an armed attack occurs against a Member of the United Nations, until the Security Council has taken the measures necessary to maintain international peace and security".[611] In other words, the Charter only confirms expressly the existence of the right of self-defence in cases where an armed attack has occurred.[612] With regard to the latter, the ICJ stressed in *Nicaragua*[613] that it is "necessary to distinguish the most grave [sic] forms of the use of force (those constituting an armed attack) from other less grave forms".[614] The Court then found that there appeared

> to be general agreement on the nature of the acts which can be treated as constituting armed attacks. In particular, it may be considered to be agreed that an armed attack must be understood as including not merely action by regular armed forces across an international border, but also "the sending by or on behalf of a State of armed bands, groups, irregulars or mercenaries, which carry out acts of armed force against another State of such gravity as to amount to" (*inter alia*) an actual armed attack conducted by regular forces, "or its substantial involvement therein". [...] The Court [saw] no reason to deny that, in customary law, the prohibition of armed attacks may apply to the sending by a State of armed bands to the territory of another State, if such an operation, because of its scale and effects, would have been classified as an armed attack rather than as a mere frontier incident had it been carried out by regular armed forces. But the Court [did] not believe that the concept of "armed attack" includes not only acts by armed bands where such acts occur on a significant scale but also assistance to rebels in the form of the provision of weapons or logistical or other support.[615]

608 Jennings (n. 607) 85. The two other defences were "[t]he 'piratical character of the vessel'" and that fact that "[t]he ordinary laws of the United States were not being enforced at the material time and their authority was publicly overborne". They are discussed at 85–87.

609 Jennings (n. 607) 89, quoting the US Secretary of State.

610 H Strydom & L Juma "Maintaining international peace and security: The enforcement of international law" in H Strydom (ed) *International Law* (2020) 185–262 at 234.

611 Article 51.

612 See further *Case Concerning Military and Paramilitary Activities in and against Nicaragua (Nicaragua v. United States of America)*, judgment of 27 June 1986, 1986 ICJ Reports 14 § 179.

613 See n. 612.

614 *Ibid.* § 191.

615 *Ibid.* § 195. The Court quoted article 3(g) of the Definition of Aggression annexed to UNGA Resolution 3314 (XXIX) (UN Doc. A/RES/3314(XXIX) of 14 December 1974), which it took as

In other words, in the latter cases, the use of force is unlawful because the "wrongful act is not an armed attack".[616]

In *Oil Platforms*,[617] the facts related to ramifications of the war between Iran and Iraq within the Persian Gulf "in the period between 1984 and 1988".[618]

> Two specific attacks on shipping [were] of particular relevance in th[e] case. On 16 October 1987, the Kuwaiti tanker *Sea Isle City*, reflagged to the United States, was hit by a missile near Kuwait harbour. The United States attributed this attack to Iran, and three days later, on 19 October 1987, it attacked Iranian offshore oil production installations, claiming to be acting in self-defence.[619]

On the basis of the evidence before it,[620] the Court ruled that, even when taking the attack and related incidents cumulatively, they did "not seem to the Court to constitute an armed attack on the United States, of the kind that [is] qualified as a 'most grave' form of the use of force".[621] At the same time, the Court stressed that it did "not exclude the possibility that the mining of a single military vessel might be sufficient to bring into play the 'inherent right of self-defence'".[622]

Because article 51 requires that an attack has occurred before a State may act in self-defence, the issue whether a State has Ps jurisdiction before an attack occurs (i.e., in anticipatory self-defence)[623] remains controversial to the extent that it rests on an assessment of customary international law.[624] It would appear that, in terms of the latter, "a threatened State [...] can take military action as long as the threatened attack is imminent, no other means would deflect it and the action is proportionate".[625] By contrast, in cases where the threat is not imminent, the route to follow is to put good arguments for action, "with good evidence to support them,

reflecting customary international law.

616 *Ibid*,, § 211.

617 *Case Concerning Oil Platforms (Iran v. United States of America)*, judgment of 6 November 2003, 2003 ICJ Reports 161 § 51.

618 *Ibid.* § 23.

619 *Ibid.* § 25.

620 *Ibid.* § 57 (where the Court confirmed that the burden of proof of the facts showing the existence of an armed attack rests on the State alleging that it has been the victim of such an attack).

621 *Ibid.* § 64.

622 *Ibid.* § 72. See further e.g., T Ruys *"Armed Attack" and Article 51 of the UN Charter: Evolutions in Customary Law and Practice* (2010).

623 In such a case, the State may not rely on the ground of F jurisdiction or T jurisdiction because the connecting factor does not exist (yet).

624 In *Nicaragua* (n. 612), the ICJ was careful to stress that "the issue of the lawfulness of a response to the imminent threat of armed attack ha[d] not been raised. Accordingly the Court expresse[d] no view on that issue" (§ 194). See e.g. KT Szabó *Anticipatory Action in Self-Defence* (2011) 1–3; F Grimal "Missile defence shields: Automated and anticipatory self-defence" (2014) 19 *Journal of Conflict and Security Law* 317–339 at 327; C Gray "The use of force and the international legal order" in Evans (n. 39) 601–632 at 614.

625 UN *A More Secure World: Our Shared Responsibility* (report of the High-level Panel on Threats, Challenges and Change) UN Doc. A/59/565 (2004) 54 § 188.

[…] to the Security Council, which can authorize such action if it chooses to".[626] The main issue appears therefore to revolve around imminence, a concept made more and more acute by rapid technological developments.[627]

It is unclear whether State practice accepts self-defence being invoked against non-state actors and, if so, under which circumstances. When the question arose, during the debates of the ILC on the right to visit on the high seas,

> whether the right to board a vessel should be recognized also in the event of a ship being suspected of committing acts hostile to the State to which the warship belongs, at a time of imminent danger to the security of that State[,]

the Commission decided not to include such a provision.[628] It did so because it was concerned by "the vagueness of terms like 'imminent danger' and 'hostile acts', which leaves them open to abuse".[629]

4.12.1.3 Protective jurisdiction exercised for economic purposes

It was already explained that the answer to the question whether a State has To jurisdiction depends to a large extent on how the matter concerned is defined.[630] Indeed, the definition determines the elements of the matter and, by implication, assists in determining whether any of those elements are located within the territory of the State.[631] As a result, Pe jurisdiction only plays a role, as an additional ground of jurisdiction distinct from To jurisdiction, when, in the absence of any element located within the territory of the State, the latter is only able to rely on a more tenuous link in the form of an effect or impact within that territory.[632]

The controversial nature of Pe jurisdiction flows from the fact that the concepts of "effect" or "impact" are difficult to define and their meaning can be stretched to

626 *Ibid.* § 190.

627 See e.g., SR Shahriar "The issue of imminence: Can the threat of cyber-attack invoke the right to anticipatory self-defence under international law?" (2020) 9 *UCL Journal of Law and Jurisprudence* 55–84 at 73–79.

628 (1956) II YILC 284.

629 *Ibid.* On self-defence against acts of terrorism committed against non-State actors, see e.g., the third preambular paragraph of UNGA Resolution 1368 (UN Doc. S/RES/1368 (2001) (12 September 2001)) and the fourth preambular paragraph of UNGA Resolution 1373 (UN Doc. S/RES/1373 (2001) (28 September 2001)); CA Ward "Building capacity to combat international terrorism: The role of the United Nations Security Council" (2003) 8 *Journal of Conflict and Security Law* 289–306; Gray (n. 624) 615–617; D Tladi "The use of force in self-defence against non-State actors, decline of collective security and the rise of unilateralism: Wither international law?" in ME O'Connell, CJ Tams & D Tladi (eds) *Self-Defence against Non-State Actors* (2019) 14–89.

630 See Chapter 3 section 3.3.2.4.

631 See e.g., *The "Enrica Lexie" Incident* (n. 5) § 840; B Cartoon "*The Westinghouse Case*: Collective response to the extraterritorial enforcement of United States anti-trust laws" (1983) 100 SALJ 731–741 at 734; AV Lowe "The problems of extraterritorial jurisdiction: Economic sovereignty and the search for a solution" (1985) 34 ICLQ 724–746 at 735.

632 See e.g., § 409 comment (a) *Restatement of the Law (Fourth)* (n. 12).

such an extent that Pe jurisdiction would allow a State to exercise its authority with regard to economic activities that do not have a sufficiently close connection with that State.[633] In that regard, there seems to be little doubt that the effect or impact must be substantial for Pe jurisdiction to exist.[634] It is also argued that there must be concurrent (il)legality. In other words, the existence of Pe jurisdiction is likely to be objected to when the normative provisions adopted by the State claiming Pe jurisdiction have no equivalent in the other State(s) concerned.[635]

In contrast to Ps jurisdiction, while Pe jurisdiction entails PeL jurisdiction and PeA jurisdiction that extends *ratione loci* beyond the territory of the State, there does not appear to be any evidence that PeE jurisdiction extends *ratione loci* beyond the borders of the State.[636]

4.12.2 Relationship between the protective jurisdictions

It is possible for a matter to constitute a threat to the security of two or more States. In such a case, each State has the same Ps jurisdiction, with all the Ps jurisdictions being concurrent. The position is the same with regard to Pe jurisdiction when an activity taking place outside the territory of two or more States has an actual or intended economic effect or impact in the territories of those States. The respective scopes *ratione materiae* make it unlikely that the same matter or activity would constitute a ground for both Ps jurisdiction and Pe jurisdiction.

4.12.3 Relationship between the protective jurisdictions and flag State jurisdiction

One expects a flag State to exercise its F jurisdiction to ensure that no matter or activity linked to a vessel with which it has a legal relationship of nationality constitutes a threat to the security of the State or has a negative actual or intended economic effect or impact in the territory of the State. In cases where one State has a ground to exercise a protective jurisdiction and another State has a ground to exercise F jurisdiction, there is overlap *ratione personae* and *ratione materiae* because F jurisdiction is all-encompassing in those regards.[637] There does not appear to exist any basis for PsL jurisdiction or PeL jurisdiction to exclude the FL jurisdiction of the State with which the vessel concerned has a relationship of nationality, and vice versa. Likewise, there does not seem to be any basis for the position to differ with regard to PsA jurisdiction, PeA jurisdiction and FA

633 See e.g., Simma & Müller (n. 14) 140–141. With regard to the United States anti-trust legislation (primarily the 1890 Sherman Act (15 USC § 1–7)), see e.g. B Cartoon (n. 631). See further e.g., § 409 comment (b) *Restatement of the Law (Fourth)* (n. 12).

634 See e.g., § 409 comment (a) *Restatement of the Law (Fourth)* (n. 12).

635 See e.g., Lowe (n. 631) 739; J Dugard, M du Plessis & E Cohen "Jurisdiction and international crimes" in J Dugard, M du Plessis, T Maluwa & D Tladi (eds) *Dugard's International Law* (2018) 210–244 at 217. In addition, retaliatory legislation might be adopted (see e.g., Cartoon (n. 631) 735–741).

636 See e.g., J Crawford *Brownlie's Principles of Public International Law* (2012) 479.

637 See section 4.2.1.

jurisdiction. As far as it is concerned, PsE jurisdiction is undoubtedly not excluded by FE jurisdiction.[638] PeE jurisdiction is not concurrent with FE jurisdiction to the extent that the latter is excluded, in principle, within the marine component of the territories of the coastal States.[639]

4.12.4 Relationship between the protective jurisdictions and territorial jurisdiction

As in the case of F jurisdiction, one expects a coastal State to exercise its T jurisdiction to ensure that no matter or activity linked to its territory constitutes a threat to its security or has a negative actual or intended economic effect or impact in its territory.[640] In cases where one State has a ground to exercise a protective jurisdiction and another State has a ground to exercise T jurisdiction, there is overlap *ratione personae* and *ratione navis* because T jurisdiction is all-encompassing in those regards.[641] *Ratione loci*, respect for the territorial integrity of a coastal State would appear to exclude the exercise of PsE jurisdiction within the marine component of the territory of a foreign State.[642] However, it can be argued that PsE jurisdiction may be exercised landward of the outer limits of the territorial sea of another State.[643] Beyond the territories of coastal States, there is no spatial overlap of PsE jurisdiction or PeE jurisdiction, on the one hand, and TE jurisdiction, on the other, except in case of hot pursuit.[644] However, in such a case, there is only a material overlap in the specific case where the matter or activity with regard to which the coastal State, an organ of which is in hot pursuit, exercises its T jurisdiction falls within the scope of Ps jurisdiction or Pe jurisdiction *ratione materiae*.[645]

4.12.5 Relationship between the protective jurisdictions and personal jurisdiction

One expects a personal State to exercise its P jurisdiction to ensure that no matter or activity linked to a person with whom it has the relevant legal relationship constitutes a threat to the security of the State or has an actual or intended negative economic effect or impact in the territory of the State.[646] As far as other persons are concerned, P jurisdiction and the protective jurisdictions overlap *ratione materiae*

638 As indicated above, article 221(1) of the LOSC confirms the existence of the international-law right of States "to take and enforce measures [...] proportionate to the actual or threatened damage to protect their coastline or related interests". See further e.g., Churchill, Lowe & Sander (n. 82) 409 and 658.

639 See section 4.3.3.3.

640 See section 4.12.3.

641 See section 4.3.1.

642 See section 4.3.2.

643 See e.g., K Bartenstein "Article 221" in Proelss (n. 25) 1512–1521 at 1518.

644 See section 4.3.1.

645 See section 4.12.1.

646 See e.g., Staker (n. 39) 301.

because P jurisdiction is all-encompassing in that regard.[647] In addition, all three jurisdictions are all-encompassing *ratione navis*.[648] By contrast, while the three legislative jurisdictions and the three adjudicative jurisdictions overlap fully, that is not the case for the executive jurisdictions because PE jurisdiction is excluded, in principle, within the maritime component of the territory of another State exercising either PsE jurisdiction or PeE jurisdiction, and vice versa.[649]

4.12.6 Relationship between the protective jurisdictions and the extraterritorial coastal zone jurisdictions

Once again, one expects a coastal State to exercise its extraterritorial coastal zone jurisdictions to ensure that no matter or activity linked to the relevant maritime zones constitutes a threat to its security or has a negative actual or intended economic effect or impact in its territory. Beyond the maritime zones of coastal States, there is no spatial overlap of Ps jurisdiction or Pe jurisdiction of one State and the extraterritorial coastal zone jurisdictions of another State, except in case of hot pursuit. However, in such a case, while all the jurisdictions are all-encompassing *ratione personae* and *ratione navis*, there is only a material overlap in the specific case where the matter or activity with regard to which the coastal State, an organ of which is in hot pursuit, exercises its extraterritorial coastal zone jurisdiction constitutes a ground for Ps jurisdiction or Pe jurisdiction.[650] Within the extraterritorial maritime zones of coastal States, the PsE jurisdiction of one State overlaps the executive extraterritorial coastal zone jurisdictions of another State and the exercise of the former jurisdiction might affect the sovereign rights of the latter State. In such a case, it can nevertheless be argued, especially if it is accepted that the exercise of PsE jurisdiction is not excluded within the marine component of the territories of the coastal States,[651] that it is not excluded within the extraterritorial maritime zones of those States.[652]

4.12.7 Relationship between the protective jurisdictions and the universal jurisdictions

The protective jurisdictions and the universal jurisdictions are all-encompassing *ratione personae* and *ratione navis*. In addition, their respective scopes *ratione loci* largely overlap beyond the territories of the coastal States. While the universal jurisdictions aim at collective protection and the protective jurisdictions at individual (State) protection, it is possible for the jurisdictions to overlap *ratione materiae*. This is the case, for instance, of a vessel used to engage in the trade of slaves,

647 See section 4.4.1.
648 See sections 4.4.1 and 4.12.1.
649 See sections 4.4.4 and 4.12.4.
650 Compare sections 4.5.1, 4.6.1, 4.7.1 and 4.12.1.
651 See section 4.12.4.
652 See e.g., Bartenstein (n. 643) 1518.

in migrant smuggling and/or in human trafficking.[653] In such a case, it would appear that there is no basis for Sl jurisdiction to exclude Ps jurisdiction and vice versa. In practice, it is unlikely that a State would choose to rely on Ps jurisdiction to exercise authority over a vessel over which another State has F jurisdiction when the requirements for the exercise of Sl jurisdiction are met. This is because the existence of the latter[654] is not open to dispute while the exercise of the former is more likely to give rise to a dispute.[655] At the same time, however, one must take into account that, as explained in the previous chapter, the conditions for the existence of the connecting factor establishing Sl jurisdiction are narrower than those for the existence of the connecting factor establishing Ps jurisdiction.[656] In addition, it has been shown earlier in this chapter that the scope of Ps jurisdiction is broader than the scope of Sl jurisdiction.[657] It is thus possible that, after having taken the three factors into account, one State might chose to rely on Ps jurisdiction while another State chooses to rely on Sl jurisdiction.

4.12.8 Relationship between the protective jurisdictions and port State jurisdiction

There are personal and vessel overlaps because the three jurisdictions are all-encompassing *ratione personae* and *ratione navis*.[658] There is also a material overlap because the limited scope of Pt jurisdiction *ratione materiae* falls within the wider scope of the protective jurisdictions *ratione materiae*.[659] In addition, there is a spatial overlap for the reason that the limited scope of Pt jurisdiction *ratione loci* falls within the wider scope of protective jurisdictions *ratione loci*.[660] However, a State may not exercise its PsE jurisdiction where another State may exercise its PtE jurisdiction because to do so would probably violate unjustifiably the territorial integrity of the latter State.[661] At the same time, the PeE jurisdiction of one State cannot overlap the PtE jurisdiction of another State because there are each limited to the whole or part of the territory of the State concerned.[662]

653 On the relationship between slavery, migrant smuggling and human trafficking, see Chapter 3 section 3.5.3.

654 And the exercise of the SlE jurisdiction that it confers (see section 4.8.1.3).

655 See section 4.12.1.2. When two States contemplate exercising Sl jurisdiction over a vessel over which a third State has F jurisdiction, the relationship is then a relationship between universal jurisdictions (see section 4.8.2).

656 Compare Chapter 3 sections 3.5.3 and 3.9.

657 Compare sections 4.8.1.3 and 4.12.1.

658 Compare sections 4.8.1 and 4.12.1.

659 Compare sections 4.8.1 and 4.12.1.

660 Compare sections 4.8.1 and 4.12.1.

661 See section 4.12.4.

662 Compare sections 4.8.1 and 4.12.1.3.

4.12.9 Summary

Ps jurisdiction and Pe jurisdiction differ with regard to their respective scopes *ratione materiae*, which are quite narrow and, to a large extent, controversial. As a result, the relationship between the two jurisdictions and the other jurisdictions is sometimes uncertain.

4.13 Conclusion

This chapter confirmed what was already argued earlier in this book,[663] that is, F jurisdiction plays a central role in the State ocean jurisdiction architecture. It is all-encompassing *ratione materiae*, *ratione personae* and *ratione loci*, with only the principle of equality of States and the latter's sovereignty and sovereign rights constraining it. However, those constraints are not rigid and nothing stands in the way of a flag State choosing not to exclude the exercise by one or more States of their respective FE jurisdictions over the vessels with which it has a link of nationality. Likewise, it appears that, at the very least, nothing stands in the way of a flag State exercising its FL jurisdiction and its FA jurisdiction to support a coastal State in the management of its resources and the protection of its national interests, in all likelihood on a reciprocal basis.

T jurisdiction plays a role similar to that of F jurisdiction, but only close to the shores of the coastal States, where it is all-encompassing *ratione materiae*, *ratione personae* and *ratione navis*. In this case, far from constraining T jurisdiction, the principle of equality of States and the latter's sovereignty are the basis for excluding the jurisdiction of other States. However, while this exclusion is strongest with regard to the exercise of executive jurisdiction, it is not absolute and there is a complex array of exceptions of general application that are often complemented by bilateral arrangements, at least.

P jurisdiction is the third element of the triad of primary jurisdictions, with its all-encompassing scope *ratione materiae*, *ratione navis* and *ratione loci*. It is very widely overlooked because PE jurisdiction is excluded by FE jurisdiction and, when it is not, it is in most cases excluded by the executive coastal zone jurisdictions. Probably for that reason, PL jurisdiction and PA jurisdiction are clearly perceived as less invasive and, as a result, they have nevertheless a powerful jurisdictional potential, provided that the link between the State and the person with which it has the required legal relationship ensures that the State has regular opportunities to exercise its PE jurisdiction.

Over and above these three grounds of jurisdiction, the jurisdictional setup is complemented by a number of grounds of much more limited scopes. When its exists, Cz jurisdiction has a relatively limited scope, primarily within the confines of executive jurisdiction. Eez jurisdiction, again when it exists, has a much wider scope with regard to all its three forms. The sovereign rights that constitute its

663 See Chapter 3 section 3.1.

foundation, together with the principle of equality of States, leads, in principle, to the exclusion of the jurisdiction of other States within the scope of Eez jurisdiction *ratione materiae*. As a result, that scope is contested, in a largely erratic manner, as Eez jurisdiction competes with F jurisdiction. By contrast, the process of ascertaining the potentially more problematic aspect of Cs jurisdiction, i.e., its scope *ratione loci*, is more structured. In both cases, exclusion is a feature aimed at protecting the rights of the coastal States. Nothing stands in the way of a coastal State deciding that any of its rights does not need to be protected or that it would best be protected through a cooperative arrangement(s) allowing one or more other States to exercise F jurisdiction that would otherwise be excluded.

As far as the universal jurisdictions are concerned, they are either only concurrent with F jurisdiction or may be relied upon when no State has either T jurisdiction or F jurisdiction. Their scopes vary, with Pi jurisdiction at the one end and Sl jurisdiction at the other end. They do not in any way place any additional limit on the scope of any other jurisdiction. This is also the case of Pt jurisdiction.

In the same way that a State may decide not to rely on the exclusion of the jurisdiction of another State by allowing the latter to exercise its jurisdiction when it would otherwise not have been allowed to do so, a State may decide to delegate one of its jurisdictions to one or more other States, to whichever extent it may decide. While jurisdiction is most likely to be conferred in these two cases on a reciprocal basis, it is also possible for jurisdiction to be conferred on a collective basis, a step well suited to deal with exceptional situations and less open to contestation than the protective jurisdictions, which play a residual role.

In light of the above, it is possible to take a further step in unravelling the sometimes-puzzling dicta of adjudicative bodies. Starting with the *Lotus* case, once it is accepted that neither France nor Turkey had T jurisdiction, because the matter arose on the high seas,[664] but that each of them had F jurisdiction with regard to the vessel flying its flag as well as either Fo jurisdiction or Fs jurisdiction with regard to the other vessel,[665] the only remaining step is to establish the scope of the FL jurisdiction, the FE jurisdiction and the FA jurisdiction of both States. The fact that "a ship on the high seas is assimilated to the territory of the State the flag of which it flies […]"[666] speaks to the fact that FL jurisdiction, FE jurisdiction and FA jurisdiction are, in principle, all-encompassing *ratione personae* and *ratione materiae*.[667] It also speaks to the fact that FE jurisdiction is limited, outside of the territory of the flag State, to the vessels flying the flag of the State.[668] This means that, in cases where a flag State exercises its Fo jurisdiction or Fs jurisdiction (i.e., where the State cannot rely on the "full" connecting factor), it is only in a position to exercise

664 And neither State could rely on either Ts jurisdiction or To jurisdiction. See Chapter 3 sections 3.3.2.1 and 3.3.2.4.

665 See Chapter 3 section 3.2.2.

666 *The 'Lotus' Case (France v. Turkey)*, judgment of 7 September 1927, 1927 PCIJ Reports, Series A No 10 at 25.

667 See section 4.2.1.

668 See section 4.2.2.

its FoE jurisdiction or FsE jurisdiction when the vessel that does not fly its flag is within its territory, provided that, even in that instance, the exercise of executive jurisdiction has not been excluded.

One of those exclusions is confirmed in article 97 of the LOSC, which was relied upon by Italy in *Enrica Lexie*. As mentioned earlier,[669] in that case, neither India nor Italy had T jurisdiction, because the matter arose in India's contiguous zone.[670] By contrast, each of them had F jurisdiction with regard to the vessel flying its flag as well as either Fo jurisdiction or Fs jurisdiction with regard to the other vessel. Italy argued that India exercised a FoE jurisdiction that it did not have beyond the marine component of its territory. The Tribunal held, however, that "Italy ha[d] not discharged its burden of proving that the Indian Coast Guard, by 'interdicting' and 'escorting' the 'Enrica Lexie', exercised enforcement jurisdiction".[671] Once the *Enrica Lexie* entered the maritime component of India's territory, the exclusion of India's FoE jurisdiction over the vessel no longer applied. Faced with this situation, Italy was unable, by relying on article 97, to oppose the exercise by India of its FoE jurisdiction because no collision nor any "'incident of navigation' ha[d] occurred that would trigger the application of" that provision.[672]

Shortly before, in *Norstar*, Panama, which had F jurisdiction because the vessel was flying its flag,[673] had not relied on article 97 when opposing the exercise by Italy, in some cases itself and in other cases by a third State on its behalf, of executive and adjudicative jurisdiction within its own territory or the territory of the other coastal State concerned.[674] Unlike in *Lotus* and *Enrica Lexie*, Italy could not claim F jurisdiction, including Fo jurisdiction or Fs jurisdiction, because the required connection with the *M/V "Norstar"* did not exist. In contrast, while the connection required to establish T jurisdiction did not exist with regard to one of the elements of the matter (i.e., the bunkering by the *M/V "Norstar"* of "mega yachts outside the territorial sea of Italy"), the connection existed with regard to the other two elements of the matter: (a) "[m]arine gasoil was purchased exempt from taxes in Italian port and boarded on the *M/V 'Norstar'*"; and (b) after the bunkering had taken place, "[t]he mega yachts returned to Italian port without declaring the possession of the product".[675] As indicated above, T jurisdiction is, in principle, all-encompassing *ratione materiae* and *ratione personae*.[676] By contrast, T jurisdiction is limited *ratione loci*, but there is no doubt that it may be exercised within the marine component of the territory of the coastal State, including its ports where T

669 See Chapter 3 section 3.10.
670 And neither State could rely on either Ts jurisdiction or To jurisdiction. See Chapter 3 sections 3.3.2.1 and 3.3.2.4.
671 *The "Enrica Lexie" Incident* (n. 5) § 535.
672 *Ibid.* § 656. As a result, Italy was left with the avenue of arguing that its nationals enjoyed immunity (see §§ 732–874).
673 *The M/V "Norstar" Case* (n. 167) § 69.
674 *Ibid.* §§ 70–71 and 74–86.
675 *Ibid.* § 166. See Chapter 3 sections 3.3.2.1 and 3.3.2.4.
676 See section 4.3.1.

jurisdiction is, in principle, all-encompassing *ratione navis*.[677] There appears thus to be little doubt that Italy had TL jurisdiction, TE jurisdiction and TA jurisdiction over the *M/V "Norstar"* within its territory with regard to the latter two elements of the matter mentioned above. At the same time, Italy did not have T jurisdiction with regard to the third element because it fell outside of its scope *ratione loci*. It is clearly for those two reasons that "[i]t was only the [two other] elements [...] that were targeted and prosecuted by Italy".[678] Nevertheless, ITLOS found that "the evidence show[ed] that the bunkering activities of the *M/V 'Norstar'* on the high seas [...] constitute[d] not only an integral part, but also a central element, of the activities targeted [...]".[679] For that reason, ITLOS "conclude[d] that article 87 of the [LOSC] may be applicable [...]" and it applied its mind to the question whether the provision was "applicable and ha[d] been breached", a question the answer to which depended, according to the Tribunal, *inter alia* "on how the freedom of navigation provided for in article 87 [was] to be interpreted and applied in the [...] case".[680]

Read with jurisdictional lenses, this statement may be interpreted to mean that: (a) ITLOS considered that Italy had exercised its jurisdiction beyond the outer limits of its territorial sea; and (b) it was necessary to establish whether the exercise of that jurisdiction was lawful. With regard to the first aspect, ITLOS could not have been reasoning in terms of executive jurisdiction because at no stage did Italy exercise that jurisdiction outside of its territory. ITLOS was thus focusing only on legislative jurisdiction and adjudicative jurisdiction. Assuming that Italy did indeed exercise those jurisdictions, it would have had a ground to do so because, again assuming that the bunkering constituted a "central element" of the activities, that bunkering constituted the connecting factor required to establish To jurisdiction.[681] Turning to the second aspect, as already indicated earlier in this chapter, in such a case the rationale for the existence of To jurisdiction arguably requires that a coastal State may exercise its ToL jurisdiction and ToA jurisdiction although that element occurred outside the Italian territory.[682] There would then be concurrence of Italy's ToL jurisdiction and ToA jurisdiction and Panama's FL jurisdiction and FA jurisdiction, the latter not excluding the former according to most authorities,[683] but against the view of the majority of the members of ITLOS.[684] The latter reached their conclusion after they had elevated above the others one of the elements that

677 See sections 4.3.1 and 4.3.3.
678 Joint dissenting opinion of judges Cot, Pawlak, Yanai, Hoffmann, Kolodkin and Lijnzaad and judge *ad hoc* Treves § 26.
679 *The M/V "Norstar" Case* (n. 167) § 186.
680 *Ibid.* § 187.
681 See Chapter 3 section 3.3.2.4.
682 See section 4.3.3.5.
683 See section 4.2.2 and *The M/V "Norstar" Case* (n. 167), joint dissenting opinion of judges Cot, Pawlak, Yanai, Hoffmann, Kolodkin and Lijnzaad and judge *ad hoc* Treves § 36.
684 See *The M/V "Norstar" Case* (n. 167) § 225, restated in *The "Enrica Lexie" Incident* (n. 5) § 527.

States have to take into account when exercising their ocean jurisdiction.[685] This is the fourth and last facet of State ocean jurisdiction – its purpose – which is the focus of the next chapter.

685 The *ius communicationis*. See e.g., *The M/V "Norstar" Case* (n. 167) § 222.

5 The purpose of State ocean jurisdiction

5.1 Introduction

It is helpful, when approaching the purposive aspects of the exercise of State ocean jurisdiction in a specific instance, to have regard to the historical process that led to the complex regime described in the previous chapters.[1] In the course of reviewing that process, a number of principles that point towards the lawful purpose of State ocean jurisdiction can be identified.[2] Light can also be shed on the parameters within which the purpose for which State ocean jurisdiction is exercised is to be lawfully achieved.[3] One must, however, first dwell on the premise on which the exercise of State ocean jurisdiction is based (i.e., the sovereign equality of States and the independence that it entails).[4]

5.2 Sovereign equality of States

In *Lotus*, the ICJ held that a State's "title to exercise jurisdiction rests in its sovereignty",[5] a statement which is consistent with the view that State sovereignty is "the basic constitutional doctrine of the law of nations".[6] However, it has already been pointed out at the

1 In this regard, see S Wittich "Immanuel Kant and jurisdiction in international law" in S Allen *et al.* (eds) *The Oxford Handbook of Jurisdiction in International Law* (2019) 81–96, who cautions that, "[w]hile jurisdiction is, to be sure, a time-honoured institution, it not only is based on completely different structural, political, legal and other premises today than those that existed in the [past], but it has also been subject to significant change and progressive development in detail over the last decades" (at 82). See further section 5.3.
2 See section 5.4.
3 See section 5.5.
4 See section 5.2.
5 *The "Lotus" Case (France v. Turkey)*, judgment of 7 September 1927, 1927 PCIJ Reports, Series A No 10 at 19. See also e.g., S Allen *et al.* "Defining State jurisdiction and jurisdiction in international law" in Allen *et al.* (n. 1) 3–22 at 5; D Costelloe "Conceptions of State jurisdiction in the jurisprudence of the International Court of Justice and the Permanent Court of International Justice" in Allen *et al.* (n. 1) 455–480 at 456.
6 J Crawford *Brownlie's Principles of Public International Law* (2012) 448. See also e.g., S Besson "Sovereignty" 2011 MPEPIL § 2; C Ryngaert "Cosmopolitan jurisdiction and the national interest" in Allen *et al.* (n. 1) 209–227 at 210.

DOI: 10.4324/9781003383871-5

beginning of this book[7] that "[j]urisdiction is not coextensive with state sovereignty"[8] in that, on the one hand, States do have jurisdiction in certain cases where they do not have sovereignty[9] and, on the other, States do not have jurisdiction in certain cases where they do have sovereignty.[10] What has not been pointed out yet is that basing jurisdiction on sovereignty raises a number of difficulties revolving around the term "sovereignty", which is a "greatly contested term".[11] The concept is preeminent in the State-centered traditional international law, which allowed States

> to do whatever was not expressly prohibited by international law. And since not much was prohibited, there was a great deal states could do. They could wage war without restriction. They could commit genocide against their own populations. They could torture detainees.[12]

Although "the traditional state-centered model of international law is still alive and well",[13] it is increasingly tempered by the infusion of values which fetter sovereignty. As a result, it is today more accurate to refer to qualified versions of the concept, such as, for instance, "responsible sovereignty", which stresses that "sovereignty entails obligations and duties to one's own citizens and to other sovereign states",[14] and "custodial sovereignty", which stresses that States are the custodians of the renewable natural resources located in their territories, but which are needed and enjoyed by the whole of humankind.[15]

The above illustrates that sovereignty

> does not define, but is defined by, the legal powers of a state within an international society of states. It does not exist prior to law, but as a set of attributes of the legal construct that is the state, existing as a consequence of law.[16]

7 See Chapter 1 section 1.4.
8 R Jennings & A Watts (eds) *Oppenheim's International Law* (1992) I 457.
9 For instance, the exclusive jurisdiction of the flag State on the high seas (see articles 89 and 92(1) of the LOSC) is meant precisely to counter claims of sovereignty in that area (see e.g., *The M/V "Norstar" Case (Panama v. Italy)*, judgment of 10 April 2019, (2019) 58 ILM 673 § 218).
10 For instance, warships and other government ships operated for non-commercial purposes enjoy immunity to a certain extent in the territorial sea (see article 32 of the LOSC).
11 A Mills "Rethinking jurisdiction in international law" (2014) 84 BYIL 187–239 at 192. See also e.g., J Crawford "Sovereignty as a legal value" in J Crawford & M Koskenniemi (eds) *The Cambridge Companion to International Law* (2012) 117–133 at 118.
12 P Sands "Lawless world: The cultures of international law" (2006) 41 TILJ 387–398 at 388.
13 D Tladi "Security Council, the use of force and regime change: Libya and Côte d'Ivoire" (2012) 37 SAYIL 22–45 at 29.
14 B Jones, C Pascual and SJ Stedman *Power and Responsibility* (2009) 9. See further e.g., International Commission on Intervention and State Sovereignty *The Responsibility to Protect* (2001) available at <http://responsibilitytoprotect.org/ICISS%20Report.pdf>.
15 See e.g., W Scholtz "The reconciliation of transnational, social and cultural human rights *via* the common interest" (2012) 37 SAYIL 232–248 at 237. See also e.g., AA Cançado Trindade "International law for humankind: Towards a new *jus gentium*" (2005) 316 RCADI 9–440 at 325.
16 Mills (n. 11) 193. See also e.g., Crawford (n. 11) 122.

For that reason, sovereignty cannot be the *basis* of State jurisdiction. Rather, sovereignty is an evolving and still very important *feature* of the allocation to States and other international-law entities of the legal authority to be involved in factual matters.

One element of sovereignty is the principle of sovereign equality of States, "a fundamental axiomatic premise of the international legal order"[17] entrenched in article 2(1) of the UNC.[18] The principle implies that States are independent of each other in that the legal authority held by the highest organs of a State is the highest authority lawfully exercised in the territory of that State.[19] It implies also "a condition of reciprocity in the sense that it would offend against the principle of equality if State A were to assume a jurisdiction it was not prepared to concede to State B".[20] That independence has three implications.

The first one is that the exercise of authority in the territory of a State by an organ which is not an organ of the State, or under the authority of the State, is only lawful if it is authorised by the State. In other words, the State is, in most instances, the only entity exercising authority in a specific area of land, a fact on which is based the principle that the State is involved on an exclusive basis in matters arising in its territory.[21] In practice, a State other than the territorial State must therefore be considered not to have authority in the territory of the latter State until a valid legal ground for that authority has been established and that authority is not excluded by the authority of the territorial State.

The second implication of the independent exercise of authority by a State in its territory flows from the first one. Indeed, the fact that a State exercises authority in its territory on an exclusive basis implies that the State must be able to exercise that authority over all matters that require State involvement because, otherwise, some matters would fall beyond the reach of any State. The authority of a State in its territory is thus all-encompassing or "full".[22] It is in that sense, as a feature of

17 J Kokott "States, sovereign equality" 2011 MPEPIL § 1. See also e.g., *Norwegian Shipowners' Claims (Norway v. United States of America)*, award of 13 October 1922, I RIAA 307 at 338; *Jurisdictional Immunities of the State (Germany v. Italy, Greece intervening)*, judgment of 3 February 2012, 2012 ICJ Reports 99 § 57.

18 "The Organization is based on the principle of the sovereign equality of all its Members". See further e.g., B Kapossy & R Whatmore (eds) *E de Vattel "The Law of Nations"* (2008) Preliminaries § 18; *Reparations for Injuries Suffered in the Service of the United Nations*, advisory opinion of 11 April 1949, 1949 ICJ Reports 174 at 177; Crawford (n. 11) 119.

19 See e.g., *Island of Palmas Case (Netherlands v. United States of America)*, award of 4 April 1928, II RIAA 829 at 838; 2002 ILA New Delhi Declaration of Principles of International Law Relating to Sustainable Development (UN Doc. A/57/329 of 31 August 2002) § 1.1.

20 DW Bowett "Jurisdiction: Changing patterns of authority over activities and resources" (1982) 53 BYIL 1–26 at 16.

21 See e.g., *Island of Palmas Case* (n. 19) 838; Crawford (n. 11) 120–121.

22 See e.g., *Jurisdictional Immunities* (n. 17) § 57. See further Chapter 4 section 4.3.1.

State jurisdiction referring to the exclusive and all-encompassing authority of a State in its territory,[23] that the term "sovereignty" is used in article 2 of the LOSC.[24]

The third implication is the principle of non-intervention in the internal or external affairs of other States, proclaimed in article 2(7) of the UNC.[25] This principle requires a balance between "each State's interest in exercising jurisdiction to advance its own policies [and] each State's interest in avoiding interference with its policies resulting from the exercise of jurisdiction by foreign States".[26] This balance is so important that the principle

> has acquired the fundamental value of a solid and indispensable "bridge" between the traditional, sovereignty-oriented structure of the international community and the "new" attitude of States, based on more intense social intercourse and closer co-operation. The principle currently plays the role of a necessary shield behind which States can shelter in the knowledge that more intense international relations will not affect their most vital and delicate domestic interests.[27]

Those interests have played a central role in the centuries-old tensions between the *mare clausum* principle and the *mare liberum* principle as well as the adoption of the package deal that the LOSC contains.

5.3 *Mare clausum, mare liberum* and the package deal

The legal regime of the oceans has undergone a long and complex evolution during which the Western worldview and interests have prevailed over other worldviews and interests when they differed.[28] In the Mediterranean Sea, some ancient powerful polities appear to have exerted control over surrounding maritime areas.[29] "Nevertheless, the first individuals to develop legal thought about the nature of the

23 See e.g., G Gidel *Le Droit International Public de la Mer* (1934) III 181–186; Y Tanaka *The International Law of the Sea* (2019) 9.

24 See e.g., RA Barnes "Article 2" in A Proelss (ed) *United Nations Convention on the Law of the Sea – A Commentary* (2017) 27–34 at 32–33.

25 See e.g., NL Dobson "Reflections on 'reasonableness' in the Restatement (Fourth) of US Foreign Relations Law" (2019) 62 *Questions of International Law* 19–33 at 26.

26 BH Oxman "Jurisdiction of States" 2007 MPEPIL § 9. See also e.g., Bowett (n. 20) 16.

27 A Cassese *International Law* (2005) 54. See also e.g., Crawford (n. 11) 119; JL Cohen *Globalization and Sovereignty* (2012) 15.

28 See e.g., A Kirchner "Law of the sea, history of" 2007 MPEPIL § 3; DJ Bederman "The sea" in D Fassbender *et al.* (eds) *The Oxford Handbook of the History of International Law* (2012) 359–379 at 360.

29 Many Greek thinkers propounded the view that "the development of civilization may be measured by the effort to control the sea" and "the myth of the Minoan thalassocracy became a commonplace of ancient thought" (CG Starr "The myth of the Minoan thalassocracy" (1955) 3 *Historia* 282–291 at 291). See also WF Newton "Inexhaustibility as a law of the sea determinant" (1981) 16 TILJ 369–432 at 370.

sea were [...] Roman jurists".[30] In Roman law, the sea had a communal nature as *res communis omnium*.[31] At the same time, it was already mentioned in Chapter 1 that, for international-law purposes, the Romans considered the Mediterranean Sea as theirs.[32] After the Viking Age from the ninth century to the eleventh century,[33] a number of claims were made regarding the waters adjacent to the land territory of new maritime powers.[34]

Those claims, the nature and extent of which varied,[35] were confined to the relatively limited areas around Europe where important maritime trade and fisheries took place. This changed dramatically at the end of the fifteenth century when, with the establishment of the sea routes to America in 1492 and to India in 1498, "Europe became fascinated by the potential of far-away lands".[36] The geographical ambits of the competing claims of the two States involved, Portugal and Spain,[37] were defined by Pope Alexandre VI in its Bull *Inter Caetera* of 4 May 1493.[38] A year later, the line drawn by the Pope was moved westwards in one of the treaties of Tordesillas,[39] by means of which the two States agreed on their respective spheres of control in order to secure a balance of power.[40] "After 1580, when both countries came to be ruled by the King of Spain in personal union, the arrangement lost its practical value and Spain/Portugal seemed to have a firm grip on the non-European world and on the seas by which to reach it".[41]

No polity was able to concretely challenge the closure of the oceans by Portugal and Spain until, in 1588, an English fleet "defeated the Great Spanish Armada and

30 Kirchner (n. 28) § 5. See also Newton (n. 29) 376.
31 See e.g., Newton (n. 29) 381–382.
32 See e.g., JPA Francois *Report on the Regime of the High Seas* ILC Doc. A/CN.4/17 (1950) in (1950) 2 YILC 36 § 1; WP Gormley "The development and subsequent influence of the Roman legal norm of freedom of the seas" (1963) 40 *University of Detroit Law Journal* 561–596 at 562; K Tuori "The beginnings of State jurisdiction in international law until 1648" in Allen *et al.* (n. 1) 25–39 at 30.
33 See e.g., JH Barrett & SJ Gibbon (eds) *Maritime Societies of the Viking and Medieval World* (2015).
34 See e.g., G Gidel *Droit international public de la mer* (1932) I 129–131; TW Fulton *The Sovereignty of the Sea* (1911) 4; Bederman (n. 28) 364; K Bangert "Belts and Sound" 2018 MPEPIL § 6; A Raestad *La Mer territoriale. Etudes historiques et juridiques* (1913) 58 and 61; Kirchner (n. 28) § 8.
35 See e.g., Francois (n. 32) § 2.
36 K Zemanek "Was Hugo Grotius really in favour of the freedom of the seas?" (1999) 1 *Journal of the History of International Law* 48–60 at 48.
37 See e.g., R Crowley *Conquerors – How Portugal Forged the First Global Empire* (2015).
38 See further e.g., FG Davenport (ed) *European Treaties Bearing on the History of the United States and its Dependencies to 1648* (1917) I 76; Francois (n. 32) § 3 with a footnote referring to A Geouffre de Lapradelle *La Mer* (1934) 153.
39 See e.g. Davenport (n. 38) 84. See further e.g., T Duve "Treaty of Tordesillas" 2013 MPEPIL. Portugal and Spain had earlier settled their dispute over the islands in the eastern Atlantic when they concluded the 1479 Treaty of Alcacovas (see e.g., Davenport (n. 38) 33).
40 See e.g., Duve (n. 39) § 21. The line was moved further westwards in the 1579 Peace Treaty (see Zemanek (n. 36) 48), half a century after the dividing line in the Pacific Ocean had been agreed in the 1529 Treaty of Zaragoza (see e.g., P Borschberg "Introduction" in PH Kratoska (ed) *South East Asia – Colonial History* (2001) I 3–4).
41 Zemanek (n. 36) 48.

England emerged as a new sea power to enter into competition with the old".[42] This was a decade after the northern provinces of the Low Countries had constituted themselves, by the Union of Utrecht,[43] into an independent republic. It is in the employ of the latter's semi-official United East India Company (VOC)[44] that Admiral van Heemskerk was when, in 1603, he seized "in the vicinity of present-day Singapore" the Portuguese carrack *Santa Catarina* and its cargo, which fetched a "stunning sum" when auctioned.[45] "[T]he incident alarmed the Portuguese about the reality of successful Dutch penetration into the commercial world of Southeast Asia".[46] It also had an impact on the relationship between, on the one hand, the Netherlands, which were still engaged in the Eighty Years War to secure their independence from Spain,[47] and, on the other, England, Denmark/Norway and Scotland, which asserted control over fishing grounds in the surrounding waters.[48]

In contrast to that of its neighbours, England's position was new. During the reign of Elizabeth I, England had consistently opposed, in its struggle against Portugal and Spain, any attempt at asserting exclusive control over maritime areas.[49] This was in line with a long tradition regarding the fishing grounds off the English coast.[50] However, the king of Scotland, James VI, succeeded to the queen as James I of England and imposed the Scottish approach to fisheries.[51] It is James' son, Charles I, who, in 1635, gave the go-ahead to the publication by the English jurist John Selden (1584–1654) of his *Mare Clausum sire de dominio maris libri II*,[52] which aimed at buttressing his country's claims and let "the genie [...] out of the bottle: there was no influential counter to Selden's innovative justification of private dominion over the seas"[53] until the 1830s.[54] Selden's work had been prompted a quarter of a century earlier by the publication by the Dutch jurist Hugo de Groot or Grotius (1583–1645) of a chapter of his *De Jure Praedae Commentarius*[55] under

42 *Ibid.*
43 See e.g., LM Salmon *The Union of Utrecht* (1894).
44 The Vereenigde Oostindische Compagnie in Dutch. See further e.g., Zemanek (n. 36) 48–49.
45 P Borschberg "The seizure of the *Santa Catarina* revisited: The Portuguese empire in Asia, VOC politics and the origins of the Dutch-Johor alliance (1602 c1616)" (2002) 33(1) *Journal of South east Asian Studies* 31–62 at 32.
46 *Ibid.* 33.
47 See e.g., P Groen (ed) *The Eighty Years War: From Revolt to Regular War 1568–1648* (2020).
48 See e.g., Kirchner (n. 28) § 12.
49 See e.g., T Treves "Historical development of the law of the sea" in DR Rothwell *et al.* (eds) *The Oxford Handbook of the Law of the Sea* (2017) 1–23 at 3.
50 See e.g., Gidel (n. 34) 151.
51 *Ibid.* See also Bederman (n. 28) 368–369.
52 See e.g., J Howell (ed) *John Selden "Mare Clausum: The Right and Dominion of the Sea in Two Books"* (1663). See further e.g., M Somos "Selden's *Mare Clausum*: The secularisation of international law and the rise of soft imperialism" (2012) 14 *Journal of the History of International Law* 287–330 at 293.
53 Somos (n. 52) 295. See also Zemanek (n. 36) 52.
54 See further e.g., Fulton (n. 34).
55 See e.g., Zemanek (n. 36) 50.

the title *Mare liberum sive de jure quod Batavis competit ad Indicana commercia dissertatio.*[56] It was published at the insistence of the VOC to oppose the attempt by

> the Spanish king on behalf of his Portuguese kingdom [...] to obtain from [the Dutch] a guarantee to respect Portugal's exclusive commercial and political connections with India, the Indonesian Archipelago and the Far East, and to refrain from any direct contacts with these parts of the world

during negotiations that ended in the Armistice of Antwerp which was concluded in April 1609.[57]

It is not necessary, for present purposes, to discuss in detail the works of de Groot and Selden.[58] Suffice it to point out that, while their arguments were based to a large extent on higher authorities and sought to provide rational support for their authors' respective positions,[59] they were used selectively in practice.[60] It is also important to keep in mind that, at the beginning of the seventeenth century,

> the controversy over the freedom of the seas had, in reality, only marginally to do with the prohibition to establish sovereignty (*dominium*) over parts of it, a sovereignty which would have been fictious [sic] anyway considering the means existing in the 16th or 17th century to enforce it. It had more to do with the free use of the seas for commercial purposes and with the refusal to accept trading monopolies in the guise of the exclusive use of parts of the sea, whether claimed as a legal right or simply established by naval force, which certain powers tried to impose in certain regions of the world. It was, therefore, inherently linked to the idea of free trade. The 17th century was, however, not a propitious time for the propagation of liberal overseas trade.[61]

Indeed, "[t]he 17th and 18th centuries were marked by [...] endless wars among the European powers, each struggling to prevail over the others".[62] Nevertheless, the law of the sea progressively "emerged into a period of great stability and

56 See JB Scott (ed) *Grotius "Mare Liberum" (1633)* (1916).

57 Zemanek (n. 36) 51.

58 See e.g., RP Anand *Origin and Development of the Law of the Sea* (1982) 72–123; DP O'Connell *The International Law of the Sea* (1982) I 1–18.

59 Pufendorf (1632–1694) lamented that "many of the disputants hold their zeal for their own country before their eyes rather than the truth" (S Pufendorf (translated by CH Oldfather & WA Oldfather) *De Iure Naturae et Gentium Libri Octo* (1934) 560). See also e.g., H Djalal "The developing countries and the Law of the Sea Conference" (1980) 15 *Columbia Journal of World Business* 22–29 at 22; Newton (n. 29) 392.

60 See e.g., Zemanek (n. 36) 58–59; Bederman (n. 28) 367.

61 Zemanek (n. 36) 52. See also e.g., M Vœlckel *Rien que la Mer* (1981) 62 ("[l]e 'principe' de la liberté des mers est, en effet, de ne pas avoir de principe. A quoi bon. La mer est la chose de tous et la chose de personne"); D Momtaz "La haute mer" in R-J Dupuy & D Vignes (eds) *Traité du Nouveau Droit de la Mer* (1985) 337–374 at 338.

62 Kirchner (n. 28) § 15.

coherence"[63] that saw, in the nineteenth century, "the creation of colonial empires, the outbreak of the industrial revolution in Europe, and the need for free trade of goods and raw materials".[64] In this context, it was undoubtedly "in the interest of the European countries to keep the sea open to trade and navigation and Grotius's [sic] freedom of the high seas [was] a celebrated principle of international law".[65] That principle was formally accepted in the 1882 Convention for Regulating the Police of the North Sea Fisheries[66] and it is a fundamental feature of the CHS[67] as well as the LOSC.[68]

The scope of the principle has progressively been limited during the twentieth century to give way to two sets of competing claims: those of the international community as a whole and those of the coastal States. The latter hinged mainly around the breadth of the territorial sea – the existence of which had not been challenged by de Groot[69] – until the geographical extent of the claims became so large that they could only be accepted in a limited substantive form (i.e., the contiguous zone, the continental shelf and the EEZ).[70] As far as they are concerned, over and above the protection and preservation of the marine environment as well as the development of marine scientific research and marine technology, for instance, the claims of the international community as a whole translated into the seabed and ocean floor beyond the continental shelves, as well as the subsoil thereof, becoming, together with their mineral resources, the common heritage of mankind.[71] This was part of the package deal reflected in the LOSC and fine-tuned by the Part XI Agreement and the Fish Stocks Agreement.[72]

5.4 Teleological principles

5.4.1 Introduction

Several arguments have been put forward since the sixteenth century to support the principle of freedom of the high seas, to justify its limitations and to transcend the tensions between *mare liberum* and *mare clausum* through a collective and

63 Bederman (n. 28) 370.

64 Kirchner (n. 28) § 19. See also e.g., Zemanek (n. 36) 59–60; TO Akintoba *African States and Contemporary International Law* (1996) 57; A Anghie *Imperialism, Sovereignty and the Making of International Law* (2004). For a comparison with land territory, see e.g., N Yahaya "The European concept of jurisdiction in the colonies" in Allen *et al.* (n. 1) 59–80.

65 Kirchner (n. 28) § 19. See further e.g., R-J Dupuy *L'Océan Partagé* (1979) 11; Anand (n. 58) 230.

66 (1882) 73 *British and Foreign State Papers* 39. Adopted: 6 May 1882; EIF: 15 May 1884. See article 2 *a contrario*.

67 See article 2.

68 See article 87.

69 See e.g., JB Scott (ed) *Grotius "De Jure Belli ac Pacis Libri Tres" (1646)* (1913) I 130.

70 See Chapter 4 sections 4.5.1, 4.6.1 and 4.7.1, respectively.

71 See article 136 read with article 1(1)(1) of the LOSC as well as article 133(a).

72 See e.g., E Franckx "*Pacta tertiis* and the Agreement for the Implementation of the Straddling and Highly Migratory Fish Stocks Provisions of the United Nations Convention on the Law of the Sea" (2000) 8 *Tulane Journal of International and Comparative Law* 49–82 at 50–52.

intergenerational approach. Distilling those arguments reveals at least four jurisdictional elements, which one may arguably refer to as "teleological principles": the protection of the *ius communicationis*;[73] the avoidance of harm to States, individuals as well as the cultural and natural environment;[74] the pursuit of equity;[75] and integrative cooperation.[76]

5.4.2 Protection of the ius communicationis

The Spanish jurist Francisco de Vitoria (c1483–1546) posited that "it was permissible from the beginning of the world (when everything was in common) for any one [sic] to set forth and travel wheresoever he would".[77] For that reason, there cannot be any doubt as to the existence of the *ius communicationis.*[78] Relying also on this argument, de Groot cited Plutarch, who had contended that

> [t]he element of water has given a social form to our life which would otherwise be almost savage and without intercourse, in that through mutual help it completes what we lack, creating human society and friendship by means of the exchange of goods.[79]

By the beginning of the nineteenth century, the right had been accepted as a "fundamental" principle.[80] The fact that the freedom of navigation is part of the legal regime of the EEZ[81] and that a right of passage exists not only in the territorial sea,[82] but also in newly enclosed internal waters[83] as well as in archipelagic waters[84] confirms that the *ius communicationis* continues to be a fundamental factor in the contemporary law of the sea.[85] This is hardly surprising because the oceans are the common highways of all the nations.[86]

73 See section 5.4.2.
74 See section 5.4.3.
75 See section 5.4.4.
76 See section 5.4.5.
77 E Nys (ed) *F de Vitoria "De Indis et de Iure Belli Relectiones"* (1917) 151. See also e.g., C Barcia Trelles "Francisco De Vitoria et l'école moderne du droit international" (1927) 17 RCADI 109–342 at 198–199; R Lapidoth "Freedom of navigation – Its legal history and its normative basis" (1975) 6 JMLC 259–272 at 263.
78 See Nys (n. 77) 152. See further e.g., Barcia Trelles (n. 77) 202 and 205.
79 M Diesselhorst "Hugo Grotius and the freedom of the seas" (1982) 3 *Grotiana* 11–26 at 20. See also e.g. Gidel (n. 34) 211.
80 Newton (n. 29) 407. See also e.g., *The Marianna Flora* 11 Wheaton 1 (1826) 43.
81 See article 58(1) of the LOSC. See further Chapter 4 section 4.6.1.
82 See article 17 of the LOSC.
83 See article 8(2) of the LOSC.
84 See articles 52–53 of the LOSC. See further Chapter 4 section 4.3.3.
85 See e.g., Vœlckel (n. 61) 144; BH Oxman "The rule of law and the United Nations Convention on the Law of the Sea" (1996) 7 *European Journal of International Law* 353–371 at 365.
86 See e.g., P Fauchille *Traité du Droit International Public* (1925) I(2) 11; J de Louter *Le Droit International Public Positif* (1920) 379.

5.4.3 Avoidance of harm

5.4.3.1 Introduction

As the requirements for its exercise within the marine component of the territories of the coastal States illustrates, the main principle that affects the scope of the *ius communicationis* is the principle of avoidance of harm to States, individuals as well as the natural and cultural environment.

5.4.3.2 Harm to States

Article 301 of the LOSC requires that,

> [i]n exercising their rights and performing their duties under th[e] Convention, States Parties [...] refrain from any threat or use of force against the territorial integrity or political independence of any State, or in any other manner inconsistent with the principles of international law embodied in the Charter of the United Nations.[87]

Harm to States was relied upon by de Groot himself to justify the right of the coastal States to exercise exclusive control over coastal waters.[88] De Groot also argued that the extent to which coastal States could impose their will by force was the determining factor in defining the breadth of the territorial sea.[89]

87 See also e.g., article 2(4) of the UNC; UNGA Declaration on Principles of International Law Concerning Friendly Relations and Co-operation among States in accordance with the Charter of the United Nations (Resolution 2625 (XXV) of 24 October 1970); the 1963 Treaty Banning Nuclear Weapon Tests in the Atmosphere, in Outer Space and under Water (480 UNTS 45, (1963) 2 ILM 889; adopted: 5 August 1963; EIF: 10 October 1963); the 1971 Treaty on the Prohibition of the Emplacement of Nuclear Weapons and Other Weapons of Mass Destruction on the Seabed and Ocean Floor and in the Subsoil Thereof (955 UNTS 115, (1971) 10 ILM 145; adopted: 11 February 1971; EIF: 18 May 1972); the 1996 Comprehensive Nuclear-Test-Ban Treaty ((1996) 35 ILM 1439, adopted. 10 September 1996; EIF: not yet); the 2017 Treaty on the Prohibition of Nuclear Weapons (adopted: 7 July 2017; EIF: 22 January 2021); and the 1985 Treaty of Rarotonga on the South Pacific Nuclear-Free Zone (1445 UNTS 177, (1985) 24 ILM 1440; adopted: 6 August 1985; EIF: 11 December 1986). See further e.g., *The "Enrica Lexie" Incident (Italy v. India)*, award of 21 May 2020, (2021) 60 ILM 180 § 1071; BA Boczek "Peaceful purposes provisions of the United Nations Convention on the Law of the Sea" (1989) 20 ODIL 359–390 at 370; S Kaye "Freedom of navigation in a post 9/11 world: Security and creeping jurisdiction" in D Freestone, R Barnes & D Ong (eds) *The Law of the Sea: Progress and Prospects* (2006) 347–364 at 353; R Pedrozo "Military activities in the exclusive economic zone: East Asia focus" (2014) 90 *International Law Studies* 514–543 at 532–536.

88 See JB Scott (ed) *H Grotius "De Jure Praedae"* (1950) 238–239. See also e.g., C Dupuis "Liberté des voies de communication. Relations internationales" (1924) 2 RCADI 125–444 at 132; JB Scott (ed) *E de Vattel "Le Droit des Gens, ou Principes de la Loi Naturelle, Appliqués à la Conduite et aux Affaires des Nations et des Souverains" (1758)* (1916) 243–244.

89 See Scott (n. 69) I 130. See further e.g., R Churchill, V Lowe & A Sander *The Law of the Sea* (2022) 136–137. See also e.g., Gidel (n. 23) 38.

The doctrine was consolidated during the eighteenth century[90] and, towards the end of that century, it started morphing into a three-mile rule applied along the whole coast.[91] However, the distance not only lost any relation to the increasing range of weapons,[92] as illustrated today by the opposing views on military activities in the EEZ,[93] but became irrelevant, for instance, in matters relating to customs, fiscal, sanitary and immigration matters (with regard to which coastal States claimed control over a wider area, the contiguous zone)[94] and in case of pollution.[95] A State is also harmed outside of the abovementioned zones when steps are taken that affect the immunity of its warships.[96]

The harm to States can be less direct than in the cases mentioned above. An example is the development of the resources of the Area. Indeed, during UNCLOS III, land producers, especially in the so-called "developing States", were concerned by the negative economic impact of an "increased availability of the minerals derived from the Area [...]".[97] To address that concern, article 150 of the LOSC requires that the activities in the Area

> be carried out in such a manner as to [protect] developing countries from adverse effects on their economies or on their export earnings resulting from a reduction in the price of an affected mineral, or in the volume of exports of that mineral, to the extent that such reduction is caused by activities in the Area, as provided in article 151 [...].[98]

90 See e.g., T Scovazzi "The frontier in the historical development of the international law of the sea" in R Barnes & R Long (eds) *Frontiers in International Environmental Law: Oceans and Climate Challenges* (2021) 217–243 at 222–224.
91 See e.g., Treves (n. 49) 5.
92 See e.g., Gidel (n. 23) 128.
93 Compare e.g., the declaration of Brazil upon ratification of the LOSC in 1988 ((1994) 25 LOSB 11) and article 9 of Act 8617 of 4 January 1993 on the Brazilian territorial sea, the contiguous zone, the exclusive economic zone and the continental shelf and related matters ((1993) 23 LOSB 17) with the declaration of Germany upon accession in 1994 ((1995) 27 LOSB 7). See further e.g., Boczek (n. 87) 372–373; F Francioni "Peacetime use of force, military activities, and the new law of the sea" (1985) 18 *Cornell International Law Journal* 203–226 at 213–216; B Kwiatkowska "Military uses in the EEZ: A reply" (1987) 11 MP 249–250; AV Lowe "Some legal problems arising from the use of the seas for military purposes" (1986) 10 MP 171–184; AV Lowe "Rejoinder" (1987) 11 MP 250–252; Pedrozo (n. 87) 514–543.
94 See e.g., Gidel (n. 23) 38.
95 See further Chapter 4 section 4.12.1.2.
96 See e.g., *Case Concerning the Detention of Three Ukrainian Naval Vessels (Ukraine v. Russia)*, order of 25 May 2019, 2018–2019 ITLOS Reports 283, (2019) 58 ILM 1147 § 110. See further Chapter 4 section 4.3.3.3(c).
97 Article 150(e) of the LOSC. See e.g., JP Levy "Le cadre de l'exploitation" in R-J Dupuy & D Vignes (eds) *Traité du Nouveau Droit de la Mer* (1985) 507–550 at 541.
98 Paragraphs (f) and (h). See e.g., J Siegfried "Article 150" in Proelss (n. 24) 1058–1066 at 1064.

The latter has been made almost completely inapplicable by the Part XI Agreement,[99] but article 151 still requires that,

> [u]pon the recommendation of the Council [of the ISA] on the basis of advice from the [ISA] Economic Planning Commission, the [ISA] Assembly shall establish a system of compensation or take other measures of economic adjustment assistance including cooperation with specialized agencies and other international organizations to assist developing countries which suffer serious adverse effects on their export earnings or economies resulting from a reduction in the price of an affected mineral or in the volume of exports of that mineral, to the extent that such reduction is caused by activities in the Area [...].[100]

In addition, the agreement requires that,

> [b]etween the entry into force of the Convention and the approval of the first plan of work for exploitation, the Authority [...] concentrate on [the] [s]tudy of the potential impact of mineral production from the Area on the economies of developing land-based producers of those minerals which are likely to be most seriously affected, with a view to minimizing their difficulties and assisting them in their economic adjustment, taking into account the work done in this regard by the Preparatory Commission.[101]

Ultimately, harms to States are harms to the individuals under the authority of States.[102]

5.4.3.3 Harm to individuals

There is no doubt that "[t]he law of the sea is a State-centred regime, in which it is States that have the rights (and obligations) while people may at most be considered as the beneficiaries".[103] Nevertheless, "[t]he Law of the Sea and the law of

99 See section 6 § 7 of the Annex to the Agreement.
100 Paragraph 10. See e.g., J Siegfried "Article 151" in Proelss (n. 24) 1066–1074 at 1074.
101 Section 1 § 5(e).
102 See e.g., BH Oxman "Human rights and the United Nations Convention on the Law of the Sea" (1997) 36 *Columbia Journal of Transnational Law* 399–429 at 402.
103 I Papanicolopulu "Human rights and the law of the sea" in DJ Attard *et al. IMLI Manual on International Maritime Law* (2014) I 509–532 at 510. See also e.g., G Bastid-Burdeau "Migrations clandestines et droit de la mer" in V Coussirat-Coustère *et al.* (eds) *La Mer et Son Droit* (2003) 57–66 at 58; I Papanicolopulu "The Law of the Sea Convention: No place for persons?" (2012) 27 IJMCL 867–874 at 868; I Papanicolopulu 'A missing part of the Law of the Sea Convention: Addressing issues of State jurisdiction over persons at sea' in M Kwon, C Schofield and S Lee (eds) *The Limits of Maritime Jurisdiction* (2014) 387–404; I Papanicolopulu "International law and the protection of fishers" in A del Vecchio (ed) *International Law of the Sea* (2014) 317–328. Oxman (n. 102) 399–429 at 399. See further B Vukas "Droit de la mer et droits de l'Homme' in B Vukas (ed) *The Law of the Sea: Selected Writings* (2004) 71.

human rights are not separate planets rotating in different orbits. Instead, they meet in many situations".[104] They do so to such an extent that "human rights concerns are now inextricably intertwined with the concerns of the Law of the Sea".[105]

The LOSC recognises the imperative of protecting individuals at sea from the greatest harm, the loss of their lives, by confirming that all States must exercise their FL jurisdiction so as to require the masters of vessels flying their flags "to render assistance to any person found at sea in danger of being lost".[106] It is not entirely clear whether that rule has been part of the law of the sea for as long as it is often thought.[107] At the same time, it is clear that the rule is not absolute. Indeed, the LOSC does not expect States to place a duty on masters to act when to do so would put their vessels, crew or passengers in "serious danger".[108] In addition, the LOSC only expects States to place a duty on masters to proceed to the rescue of "persons in distress" when such action "may reasonably be expected of him" or her.[109] Moreover, the LOSC only places a duty on States to "*promote* the establishment, operation and maintenance of an adequate and effective search and rescue service regarding safety on and over the sea",[110] a weakness which is however

104 T Treves "Human rights and the law of the sea" (2010) 28 *Berkeley Journal of International Law* 1–14 at 12. See also e.g., C McLachlan "The principle of systemic integration and article 31(3)(c) of the Vienna Convention" (2005) 54 ICLQ 279–320.

105 Treves (n. 104) 5 and 13–14. See further e.g., *Corfu Channel Case (United Kingdom v. Albania)*, judgment of 9 April 1949, 1949 ICJ Reports 4 at 22; *M/V* Saiga *(No. 2) (Saint Vincent and the Grenadines v. Guinea)* 1999 ITLOS Reports 10 § 155, restated in *The "Enrica Lexie" Incident (Italy v. India)*, order of 24 August 2015, 2015 ITLOS Reports 182 § 133 and *The "Enrica Lexie" Incident (Italy v. India)*, order of 29 April 2016, PCA Case No 2015-28 § 104; *The 'Juno Trader' Case (Saint Vincent and the Grenadines v. Guinea-Bissau)*, judgment of 18 December 2004, 2004 ITLOS Reports 17 § 77; *M/V "Louisa" (Saint Vincent and the Grenadines v. Spain)*, judgment of 28 May 2013, 2013 ITLOS Reports 4 § 155; *The "Arctic Sunrise" Arbitration (Netherlands v. Russia)*, award of 14 August 2015, XXXII RIAA 205 § 227; Papanicolopulu (n. 103) 874; E De Wet & J Vidmar "Conflicts between international paradigms: Hierarchy versus systemic integration" (2013) 2(2) *Global Constitutionalism* 196–217 at 216; I Mann *Humanity at Sea* (2016) 215; B Wilson "Human rights and maritime law enforcement" (2016) 52 *Stanford Journal of International Law* 243–319 at 245; the 2022 Geneva Declaration on Human Rights at Sea.

106 Article 98(1)(a). See also article 98(1)(c). See further e.g., S Cacciaguidi-Fahy "The law of the sea and human rights" (2007) 19 *Sri Lanka Journal of International Law* 85–108 at 90 and 94.

107 The earliest global treaty provisions are article XI of the 1910 Brussels Convention for the Unification of Certain Rules of Law Respecting Assistance and Salvage at Sea (1913 UKTS 4; adopted: 23 September 1910; EIF: 1 March 1913) and article 8 of the 1910 Convention for the Unification of Certain Rules of Law with respect to Collisions between Vessels (1930 ATS 14; adopted: 23 September 1910; EIF: 1 March 1913). See further e.g., R Barnes "Refugee law at sea" (2004) 53 ICLQ 47–77 at 49; Cacciaguidi-Fahy (n. 106) 90; TM Ndiaye "Human rights at sea and the law of the sea" (2019) 10 *Beijing Law Review* 261–277 at 269; MH Nordquist (ed) *United Nations Convention on the Law of the Sea 1982 – A Commentary* (1995) III 171 § 98.1. See, however, D Guilfoyle "Article 98" in Proelss (n. 24) 725–730 at 726; WH Smith "The duty to render assistance at sea: Is it effective or adrift" (1971) 2 CWILJ 146–163 at 146.

108 Article 98(1).

109 Article 98(1)(b).

110 Article 98(2) (own emphasis).

addressed in the 1979 Convention on Maritime Search and Rescue,[111] for instance. Finally, while there is a customary international law right of vessels in distress to enter internal waters "to shelter in order to preserve human life",[112] the duty of masters to rescue is not complemented in the LOSC by a duty of States to allow the disembarkation of the individuals who have been rescued,[113] an issue that is only addressed, to some extent, by the amended 1979 Convention on Maritime Search and Rescue,[114] for instance.[115]

The LOSC is less cautious regarding the steps to be taken to prevent human lives finding themselves in danger of being lost. For instance, the Convention requires that every State "take such measures for ships flying its flag as are necessary to ensure safety at sea [...]"[116] and that "the necessary measures [...] be taken to ensure effective protection of human life" in the course of the activities in the Area".[117] The generally accepted international rules in this regard are contained primarily in the 1966 International Convention on Load Lines,[118] the 1972 International Convention for the Prevention of Collisions at Sea,[119] the 1974 International Convention for the Safety of Life at Sea[120] and the

111 1405 UNTS 97. Adopted: 27 April 1979; EIF: 22 June 1985. See § 2.1.1 of the Annex to the Convention.

112 Churchill, Lowe & Sander (n. 89) 115. See further Chapter 4 section 4.3.3.3(d).

113 See Barnes (n. 107) 49; Cacciaguidi-Fahy (n. 106) 98–101.

114 2004 amendments (IMO Doc. MSC.155(78)); adopted: 20 May 2004; EIF: 1 July 2006. See § 3.1.9 of the Annex to the Convention.

115 See also e.g., reg. 33(1.1) of chapter V of the Annex to SOLAS 1974, article 16 of the PSM, the 2004 IMO Guidelines on the Treatment of Persons Rescued at Sea (IMO Resolution MSC.167(78) of 20 May 2004) and Regulation No 656/2014 of the European Parliament and of Council of 15 May 2014 establishing rules for the surveillance of the external sea borders in the context of operational cooperation coordinated by the European Agency for the Management of Operational Cooperation at the External Borders of the Member States of the European Union [2014] OJ 189/93. See, however, Council Decision (CFSP) 2015/778 of 18 May 2015 on a European Union military operation in the Southern Central Mediterranean (EUNAVFOR MED) [2015] OJ 122/31. See further e.g., M Davies "Obligations and implications for ships encountering persons in need of assistance at sea" (2003) 12 PRLPJ 109–142; GS Goodwin-Gill "Refugees and responsibility in the twenty-first century: More lessons learned from the South Pacific" (2003) 12 PRLPJ 23–48; X Hinrichs "Measures against smuggling of migrants at sea: A law of the sea-related perspective" (2003) 36 *Belgian Review of International Law* 413–451; I Khan "Trading in human misery: A human rights perspective on the Tampa Incident" (2003) 12 PRLPJ 9–22; A Fischer-Lescano, T Löhr & T Tohidipur "Border controls at sea: Requirements under international human rights and refugee law" (2009) 21 *International Journal of Refugee Law* 256–296; Guilfoyle (n. 107) 729–730; M Ratcovich *International Law and the Rescue of Refugees at Sea* (2019).

116 Article 94(3).

117 Article 146. See also e.g., articles 21(1)(a), 22(1), 39(2)(a), 39(3)(a), 42(1)(a), 60(2), 194(3)(b)–(d) and 225.

118 640 UNTS 133. Adopted: 5 April 1966; EIF: 21 July 1968.

119 1050 UNTS 18, (1973) 12 ILM 734. Adopted: 20 October 1972; EIF: 15 July 1977.

120 1184 UNTS 278, (1975) 14 ILM 959. Adopted: 1 November 1974; EIF: 25 May 1980.

1978 International Convention on Standards of Training, Certification and Watchkeeping of Seafarers.[121]

While there is thus a well-established and very detailed legal regime aimed at ensuring the safety of life at sea, the regime governing conditions of work at sea is still maturing, with major steps being the adoption of the 2006 Maritime Labour Convention[122] and the adoption of the 2007 Work in Fishing Convention.[123] That is also the case regarding persons who are the objects of, or affected by, enforcement procedures and adjudicatory proceedings. For instance, SUA requires that, when a State party takes measures to prevent and suppress unlawful acts covered by the Convention, it ensures that "all persons on board are treated in a manner which preserves their basic human dignity, and in compliance with the applicable provisions of international law, including international human rights law".[124] The State must also ensure that searches are "conducted in accordance with applicable international law".[125] In addition, SUA requires that

> [a]ny person who is taken into custody, or regarding whom any other measures are taken or proceedings are being carried out pursuant to th[e] Convention, [...] be guaranteed fair treatment, including enjoyment of all rights and guarantees in conformity with the law of the State in the territory of which that person is present and applicable provisions of international law, including international human rights law.[126]

This requirement broadens, with regard to the conduct of proceedings, the LOSC's requirement that "recognized rights of the accused [...] be observed" when the alleged violations are violations of national laws and regulations or applicable international rules and standards for the prevention, reduction and control of pollution of the marine environment.[127] As far as sentencing is concerned, the arguably odd position is that, in the case of fisheries violations, the LOSC completely prohibits corporal punishment and permits imprisonment conditionally,[128] while "many fisheries access agreements explicitly prohibit imprisonment as a penalty for fisheries offences".[129] By contrast, the Convention does not prohibit imprisonment for violations that are not directly related to fisheries,[130] except "with respect

121 1361 UNTS 2. Adopted: 7 July 1978; EIF: 28 April 1984.

122 2952 UNTS 3, (2014) 53 ILM 937. Adopted: 23 February 2006; EIF: 20 August 2013. The Convention does not apply to "ships engaged in fishing or in similar pursuits" (article II(4)).

123 Adopted: 14 June 2007; EIF: 16 November 2017.

124 Article 8bis(10)(a)(ii).

125 Article 8bis(10)(a)(iii).

126 Article 10(2).

127 Article 230(3). See Oxman (n. 102) 426.

128 See article 73(3). The condition is that there be agreement of "the States concerned".

129 J Harrison "Article 73" in Proelss (n. 24) 556–563 at 561.

130 See e.g., DH Anderson "Investigation, detention and release of foreign vessels under the UN Convention on the Law of the Sea of 1982 and other international agreements" (1996) 11 IJMCL 165–178 at 170; Harrison (n. 129) 556–563 at 561.

to violations of national laws and regulations or applicable international rules and standards for the prevention, reduction and control of pollution of the marine environment",[131] provided that a violation did not take the form of "a wilful and serious act of pollution in the territorial sea".[132]

Article 2*bis*(1) of SUA stresses that nothing in the Convention affects "other rights, obligations and responsibilities of States and individuals under international law, in particular the purposes and principles of the Charter of the United Nations and international human rights, refugee and humanitarian law". This provision is an illustration of an approach similar to that adopted in the LOSC, where article 293(1) provides that "[a] court or tribunal having jurisdiction [...] shall apply th[e] Convention and other rules of international law not incompatible with th[e] Convention", while article 311(2) provides that the LOSC does not alter "the rights and obligations of States Parties which arise from other agreements compatible with this Convention and which do not affect the enjoyment by other States Parties of their rights or the performance of their obligations under th[e] Convention".[133] Articles 293(1) and 311(2) differ from article 2*bis*(1) in that the former allows for the "application of rights and obligations derived from other international treaties only if and insofar as they are compatible with the Convention and do not infringe upon [the] rights and obligations of other parties to" the LOSC.[134] However, against the background of this supremacy clause, the fact that the LOSC makes very limited forays into human rights law turns out to be one of its strengths in that there is little room for inconsistencies. In other words, the main issue regarding the protection of human rights in ocean-related matters does not lie in the LOSC, but in the application of human rights law to acts or omissions of organs of States outside the territories of the respective States and/or relating to individuals outside those territories.[135]

The spatial scope of application of human rights instruments varies. For instance, article 2(1) of the 1966 International Covenant on Civil and Political Rights (ICCPR)[136] provides that "[e]ach State Party [...] undertakes to respect and to ensure to all individuals within its territory and subject to its jurisdiction the rights recognized in the [...] Covenant". Read literally, this provision does not

131 Article 230(1).
132 Article 230(2).
133 See also article 31(3)(c) of the VCLT; A Rachovitsa "The principle of systemic integration in human rights law" (2017) 66 ICLQ 557–588.
134 N Matz-Lück "Article 311" in Proelss (n. 24) 2009–2019 at 2015.
135 See e.g., B Simma "The ICJ and common goods: The case of human rights" in F Lenzerini & AF Vrdoljak (eds) *International Law for Common Goods* (2014) 11–39 at 37; W Vandenhole "The 'J' word" in Allen *et al.* (n. 1) 413–430 at 415 and 416. Expulsion and extradition cases are not cases of extraterritorial application of human rights law when the individuals to be expelled or extradited are within the territories of the States concerned at the time of the relevant acts or omissions of the organs of State involved (see e.g., *Banković & Others v. Belgium & Others*, ECHR Application No. 52207/99, judgment of 12 December 2001 § 68).
136 999 UNTS 171. Adopted: 16 December 1966; EIF: 23 March 1976.

state that the States parties undertook to respect and to ensure that the rights of individuals are recognised outside their territories.[137] However, this is not the interpretation adopted by the ICJ in *Legal Consequences of the Construction of a Wall in the Occupied Palestinian Territory*.[138] Indeed, in its advisory opinion, the ICJ observed that,

> while the jurisdiction of States is primarily territorial, it may sometimes be exercised outside the national territory. Considering the object and purpose of the [...] Covenant [...], it would seem natural that, even when such is the case, States parties to the Covenant should be bound to comply with its provisions.[139]

The Court also pointed out that this interpretation is consistent with the one adopted by the Human Rights Committee.[140] Interpreted accordingly, article 2(1) means that the States parties must also respect and ensure to all individuals the rights recognised in the Covenant outside their territories in cases where they have extra-territorial jurisdiction.

This is also the position held, in Europe, regarding the 1950 Convention for the Protection of Human Rights and Fundamental Freedoms (ECHR),[141] article 1 of which provides that "[t]he High Contracting Parties shall secure to everyone within their jurisdiction the rights and freedoms defined in Section I of th[e] Convention". In that regard, the European Court of Human Rights (ECtHR) recalled in *Banković*[142] that,

> [i]n keeping with the essentially territorial notion of jurisdiction, the Court ha[d] accepted only in exceptional cases that acts of the Contracting States performed, or producing effects, outside their territories can constitute an exercise of jurisdiction by them within the meaning of Article 1 of the Convention.[143]

137 See e.g., N Wenzel "Human rights, treaties, extraterritorial application and effects" 2008 MPEPIL § 4.
138 Advisory opinion of 9 July 2004; 2004 ICJ Reports 136, (2004) 43 ILM 1009.
139 Paragraph 109.
140 See Human Rights Committee "General comment 31: Nature of the general legal obligation on States parties to the Covenant" (UN Doc. CCPR.C.21.Rev.1.Add.13 of 29 March 2004) 10. The ICJ was of the view that the interpretation is confirmed by the *travaux préparatoires*, but the latter are not entirely clear in this regard (see Commission on Human Rights "Summary record of the hundred and ninety-fourth meeting" (UN Doc. E/CN.4/SR.194 of 25 May 1950) and UN Secretary-General "Annotations on the text of the draft International Covenants on Human Rights" (UN Doc. A/2929 of 1 July 1955) part II ch V § 4).
141 213 UNTS 222. Adopted: 4 November 1950; EIF: 3 September 1953.
142 *Banković* (n. 135).
143 Paragraph 67. See also § 71.

This pronouncement must be understood in the context of the ECtHR's broad understanding of the extent of a coastal State's territory. Indeed, the Court has repeatedly overlooked the difference between, on the one hand, the sovereignty of a State over the waters up to the outer limit of its territorial sea and, on the other, its sovereign rights over the resources in the adjacent waters.[144] On that basis, it is likely that, given the opportunity to do so, the ECtHR will confirm that the ECHR applies, for instance, when a State party to the Convention exercises its EezE jurisdiction on exploration and exploitation platforms.[145] A decade later, the ECtHR added in *Medvedyev* that

> the special nature of the maritime environment [...] cannot justify an area outside the law where ships' crews are covered by no legal system capable of affording them enjoyment of the rights and guarantees protected by the Convention which the States have undertaken to secure to everyone within their jurisdiction [...].[146]

For that reason, it is clear that the ECHR applies also to the organs of a State party when they act at sea beyond the State's maritime zones, not only in the exercise of the State's FE jurisdiction,[147] but also in the case of a vessel without nationality.[148]

The above supports the view that States remain bound by the whole range of ICCPR obligations they have regarding their territories, in the case of their acts or omissions beyond the outer limits of their respective territorial seas as well as their acts or omissions within their territories that relate to and/or have effects at sea. The result is that, for instance, irrespective of the persons or entities to whom States owe a duty to render assistance to persons in danger of being lost in terms of article 198(1) of the LOSC, that duty appears to be complemented by a duty owed directly to individuals in terms of the applicable human-rights instruments entrenching the right to life.[149]

The position is not as clear with regard to the rights on which the 1966 International Covenant on Economic, Social and Cultural Rights (ICESCR)[150] focuses.[151] One of the reasons is that the ICESCR does not contain any provision relating to its

144 See e.g., Cacciaguidi-Fahy (n. 106) 103.

145 See, in this regard, Papanicolopulu (n. 103) 873.

146 *Medvedyev and Others v. France*, ECHR Application No 3394/03, judgment of 29 March 2010 § 81. In this case, a French special-forces team boarded in waters off Cabo Verde a Cambodia-registered vessel suspected of being used for drug-trafficking purposes (see § 9–13). For an earlier case with similar facts, see *Rigopoulos v. Spain*, ECHR Application No 37388/97, judgment of 12 January 1999. See further e.g., P Tavernier "La Cour européenne des droits de l'Homme et la mer" in Coussirat-Coustère *et al.* (n. 103) 575–589 at 577.

147 See e.g., *Banković* (n. 135) § 73.

148 See e.g., Oxman (n. 102) 428. See further Chapter 4 section 4.8.1.4.

149 See e.g., article 6 of the ICCPR. With regard to the rights of arrested, detained and accused persons, see articles 9–10 of the ICCPR. Regarding working conditions, see article 7 of the ICESCR.

150 999 UNTS 3. Adopted: 16 December 1966; EIF: 3 January 1976.

151 See e.g., E Askin "Economic and social rights, extraterritorial application" 2019 MPEPIL § 7.

territorial applicability and the Committee on Economic, Social and Cultural Rights[152] has not, to date, issued a General Comment document on the issue. Such a document would probably answer the question whether a State remains bound by its ICESCR duties in the case of its "acts and omissions [...], within or beyond its territory, that have effects on the enjoyment of [...] rights outside of that State's territory"[153] (i.e., beyond the outer limit of its territorial sea). In this regard, the LOSC offers limited support when, in contrast to the position adopted in 1974 by the ICJ in *Fisheries Jurisdiction (Federal Republic of Germany v. Iceland)*,[154] article 62(3) requires that a coastal State merely "take into account [...] the need to minimize economic dislocation in States whose nationals have habitually fished in the zone or which have made substantial efforts in research and identification of stocks" when giving access to the surplus of the allowable catch in its EEZ to other States.[155] In addition, there is "a general rule of customary international law that States must not permit their nationals to discharge into the sea matter that could cause harm to the nationals of other States".[156]

That issue must be approached, in the case of the environmental rights for instance, not only from the perspective of the harm to individuals,[157] but also the harm to the cultural and natural environment.[158]

5.4.3.4 Harm to the cultural and natural environment

As far as the natural environment and ocean resources are concerned, article 192 of the LOSC confirms that "States have the obligation to protect and preserve the

152 The Committee assists the UN Economic and Social Council in the performance of the monitoring functions assigned to it in terms of Part V of the Covenant (see the Council's Resolution 1985/17 of 28 May 1985).

153 Principle 8(a) of the 2011 Maastricht Principles on Extraterritorial Obligations of States in the Area of Economic, Social and Cultural Rights. See further e.g., O De Schutter *et al.* "Commentary to the Maastricht Principles on Extraterritorial Obligations of States in the Area of Economic, Social and Cultural Rights" (2012) 34 *Human Rights Quarterly* 1084–1169 at 1101–1103.

154 Judgment of 25 July 1974, 1974 ICJ Reports 175 § 61.

155 See *Award in the Matter of the South China Sea Arbitration (Philippines v. China)*, award of 12 July 2016, XXXIII RIAA 153 § 243. See also §§ 800–804 for a comparison between the position in the EEZ and the position landward of the outer limit of the territorial sea. See further J Harrison & E Morgera "Article 62" in Proelss (n. 24) 493–506 at 500. See, however, *Award of the Arbitral Tribunal in the Second Stage of the Proceedings (Maritime Delimitation) (Eritrea v. Yemen)*, award of 17 December 1999, XXII RIAA 335 § 109.

156 RR Churchill & AV Lowe *The Law of the Sea* (1999) 332. See e.g., the *Trail Smelter Case (United States v. Canada)*, award of 11 March 1941, III RIAA 1905 at 1965; *Corfu Channel Case* (n. 105) 23.

157 See e.g., Askin (n. 151) § 14–42.

158 See e.g., article 116(a) of the LOSC. See further e.g., R Rayfuse "Article 116" in Proelss (n. 24) 791–803 at 799.

marine environment".[159] Buttressed by a wide range of treaties,[160] the rule undoubtedly reflects an important factor in the scope of State ocean jurisdiction.[161] The rule also plays an important role in the exercise of that jurisdiction, for instance when it places a responsibility on States "to ensure that activities within their jurisdiction or control do not cause significant damage to the environment of other States or of areas beyond the limits of national jurisdiction".[162] In addition, article 61(2) of the LOSC compels coastal States to ensure that "the maintenance of the living resources in the [EEZ] is not endangered by over-exploitation", while articles 117 and 118 place a similar duty on all States regarding the living resources of the high seas.[163]

States not only have a duty not to actually harm the natural environment, but they also have a duty to follow a precautionary approach, principle or process aimed at avoiding taking the risk of causing significant harm to the natural environment.[164] There is little doubt that, if precaution is not a general rule of law yet, it is a legally binding rule in an increasing number of specific areas.[165] An example

159 See also e.g., *South China Sea Arbitration* (n. 155) §§ 941 and 956; *Alleged Violations of Sovereign Rights and Maritime Spaces in the Caribbean Sea (Nicaragua v. Colombia)*, judgment of 21 April 2022, ICJ Case No 155 § 62; R Churchill "The LOSC regime for protection of the marine environment – Fit for the twenty-first century?" in R Rayfuse (ed) *Research Handbook on International Marine Environmental Law* (2015) 3–30 at 30.

160 See e.g., the LC 1972; 1992 Convention on Biological Diversity (CBD; 1760 UNTS 79, (1992) 31 ILM 818; adopted: 5 June 1992; EIF: 29 December 1993); 1992 United Nations Framework Convention on Climate Change (FCCC; 1771 UNTS 107, (1992) 31 ILM 849; adopted: 9 June 1992; EIF: 21 March 1994).

161 See e.g., Oxman (n. 85) 364; P Chaumette (ed) *Le Droit de l'Océan Transformé par l'Exigence de Conservation de l'Environnement Marin* (2019); P Verlaan "The interface of science and law" in Barnes & Long (n. 90) 409–429.

162 New Delhi Declaration (n. 19). See also *Legality of the Threat or Use of Nuclear Weapons*, advisory opinion of 8 July 1996, 1996 ICJ Reports 226 § 29, restated in *Dispute Concerning Delimitation of the Maritime Boundary between Ghana and Côte d'Ivoire in the Atlantic Ocean (Ghana v. Côte d'Ivoire)*, order of 25 April 2015, 2015 ITLOS Reports 146 § 71.

163 See e.g., *Southern Bluefin Tuna Cases (New Zealand* v. *Japan; Australia* v. *Japan)*, order of 27 August 1999, 1999 ITLOS Reports 295 § 70, restated in *Alleged Violations* (n. 159) § 95).

164 See e.g *Responsibilities and Obligations of States Sponsoring Persons and Entities with respect to Activities in the Area*, advisory opinion of 1 February 2011, 2011 ITLOS Reports 10 § 131; P-M Dupuy "Le principe de précaution et le droit international de la mer" in Coussirat-Coustère *et al.* (n. 103) 205–220; J Peel "Precaution – A matter of principle, approach or process?" (2004) 5 *Melbourne Journal of International Law* 483–501; P Taylor "The future of the common heritage of mankind: Intersections with the public trust doctrine" in L Westra, P Taylor & A Michelot (eds) *Confronting Ecological and Economic Collapse* (2013) 32–46 at 39.

165 See e.g., *Activities in the Area* (n. 164) §§ 127 and 135. See also e.g., article 4(3)(a) of the 1976 Convention for the Protection of the Marine Environment and the Coastal Region of the Mediterranean as amended ((1996) 31 LOSB 65; adopted: 10 June 1995; EIF: 9 July 2004); article 6 and 8 of the 1991 Protocol on Environmental Protection to the Antarctic Treaty ((1991) 30 ILM 1455; adopted: 4 October 1991; EIF: 14 January 1998); and article 6 of the Fish Stocks Agreement. See further e.g., D French "From the depths: Rich pickings of principles of sustainable development and general international law on the ocean floor – The Seabed Disputes Chamber's 2011 Advisory Opinion" (2011) 26 IJMCL 525–568 at 547–555.

is the requirement, in terms of article 206 of the LOSC, to undertake an environmental impact assessment "when States have reasonable grounds for believing that planned activities under their jurisdiction or control may cause substantial pollution of or significant and harmful changes to the marine environment [...]".[166]

As alluded to in *Southern Bluefin Tuna*,[167] the impact of harm is compounded when the resources concerned can be exhausted. De Groot appears to have been the first to rely on inexhaustibility when he posited that

> all that which has been so constituted by nature that although serving some one person it still suffices for the common use of all other persons, is today and ought in perpetuity to remain in the same condition as when it was first created by nature,[168]

that is to say in common. While he relied on this argument to defend both the freedom of navigation and the freedom of fishing, he was aware that it did not have the same force in both cases when he asserted that, "if it were possible to prohibit [...] fishing, for in a way it can be maintained that fish are exhaustible, still it would not be possible to prohibit navigation, for the sea is not exhausted by that use".[169]

Inexhaustibility has played a major role "as a presupposition in evolving regimes governing uses of the oceans",[170] but, even with regard to navigation, it has turned out not to be true in some locations where, while navigation is not in most instances prohibited, it may nevertheless be controlled.[171] This is a relatively recent development,[172] which appears to have only been implicitly acknowledged in the CTSCZ.[173] However, the need for regulation increased very quickly thereafter and led to the adoption of the 1972 Collisions Convention[174] as well as provisions in the LOSC regarding sea lanes and traffic separation schemes in the territorial sea,[175] in straits used for international navigation[176] and in archipelagic waters.[177]

166 See e.g., *Case Concerning Pulp Mills on the River Uruguay (Argentina v. Uruguay)*, judgment of 20 April 2010, 2010 ICJ Reports 14 § 204; *Activities in the Area* (n. 164) § 145. See further e.g., French (n. 165) 542–544; W Gullett "The contribution of the precautionary principle to marine environmental protection" in Barnes & Long (n. 90) 368–406.
167 *Southern Bluefin Tuna Cases* (n. 163) § 71.
168 Scott (n. 56) 27. See also Scott (n. 88) 247.
169 Scott (n. 56) 43.
170 Newton (n. 29) 370. See also e.g., Dupuy (n. 65) 25; Vœlckel (n. 61) 132.
171 See RA Barnes "Article 22" in Proelss (n. 24) 208–213 at 211.
172 See e.g., DR Rothwell "Sea lanes" 2009 MPEPIL §§ 2 and 4.
173 516 UNTS 206. Adopted: 29 April 1958; EIF: 10 September 1964. See article 17 and Barnes (n. 171) 210.
174 See n. 118.
175 See article 22.
176 See article 41.
177 See article 53(6) and (11).

The German jurist Samuel von Pufendorf (1632–1694) alluded to the fact that the finiteness of resources is a relative concept in a physical sense.[178] For instance, for a first category of individuals, who are unable to venture further than a few nautical miles from the shore, it does not matter that there are abundant fisheries hundreds of nautical miles away. For them, those resources are inaccessible and, for all practical purposes, inexistent. In other words, the only resources that matter are those that are accessible to them and the only issue is whether those specific resources can be exhausted.[179] At the same time, for a second category of individuals, who might be able to sail thousands of nautical miles,[180] many more resources are accessible, including those that are the only ones that the first category of individuals can access. For the latter, resources might be depleted in a specific area, but they are not exhausted for the former because those individuals can access resources in other areas. The same applies at the economic level, a fact already pointed out by Selden.[181] For instance, even when local fishers are able to fish far away from their coast, participation of foreign fishers in the coastal fisheries may reduce the size of the catches of the local fishers, thereby reducing their profits and their ability to contribute to meeting the nutritional needs of the coastal population to which they belong. It may also compel them to increase their costs as a result of them having to fish further away from their coast than they would otherwise have done.[182]

The finiteness of resources becomes more and more an objective concept as one zooms in on a specific kind of resources. An early illustration is the 1893 *Fur Seal Arbitration*,[183] during which the arbitrators adopted regulations aimed at ensuring "the proper protection and preservation of the fur-seal in, or habitually resorting to, the Behring Sea".[184] Since then, more and more fisheries are under threat[185] and the need to preserve the resources has attained the status of a global legal imperative. A confirmation of this development is found in the 1958 Convention on Fishing and Conservation of the Living Resources of the High Seas (CLRHS),[186] which already contained provisions limiting the freedom of fishing for the purpose of "conserva-

178 See Pufendorf (n. 59) 562.

179 See e.g., F Berkes "Alternatives to conventional management: Lessons from small-scale fisheries" (2003) 31(1) *Environments* 5–19.

180 Possibly because, having exhausted the resources near their shores, they had no choice but to develop the means to do so.

181 Selden challenged the assumption of inexhaustibility on the ground that "the sea itself, by reason of other men's Fishing, Navigation, and Commerce, becomes the worse for him that owns it, and others that enjoy it in his right; So that less profit ariseth, than might otherwise be received thereby" (J Selden (translated by M Nedham) *Mare Clausum seu De Dominio Maris* (1652) 141).

182 Newton (n. 29) 395.

183 *Rights of Jurisdiction of the United States in the Bering's Sea and the Preservation of Fur Seals (United States of America v. United Kingdom)*, award of 15 August 1893, XXVIII RIAA 263.

184 *Ibid.* 267 and 270–271. For other examples of conservation efforts at the turn of the twentieth century, see Newton (n. 29) 410.

185 See e.g., FAO *The State of World Fisheries and Aquaculture 2020 – Sustainability in Action* (2020) 47–55.

186 599 UNTS 285. Adopted: 29 April 1958; EIF: 20 March 1966.

tion of the living resources of the high seas".[187] Almost two decades later, the ICJ explained in *Fisheries Jurisdiction Case (Great Britain v. Iceland)* that

> [i]t is one of the advances in maritime international law, resulting from the intensification of fishing, that the former *laissez-faire* treatment of the living resources of the sea in the high seas has been replaced by a recognition of […] the needs of conservation for the benefit of all.[188]

Avoiding harm to the tangible and intangible cultural elements of the ocean environment is a much more recent concern,[189] but nevertheless imperative.[190] This is the case not only for coastal communities,[191] but also for the whole of humankind.[192] Article 303(1) of the LOSC makes it clear that "States have the duty to protect objects of an archaeological and historical nature found at sea [...]". This means, at least, that

> [a] State which knowingly allows the destruction of objects belonging to [the] underwater cultural heritage or a State which persistently rejects any request by other States to cooperate in the protection of such heritage would be [...] responsible for an internationally wrongful act.[193]

The limited provisions of the LOSC[194] are complemented by those of several other instruments, including the CPUCH.[195]

The protection of the *ius communicationis* and the avoidance of harm contribute to the pursuit of equity.

5.4.4 Pursuit of equity

In 1817,

> Sir Walter Scott (later Lord Stowell) writing [...] in the case of *Le Louis*, countered arguments for dominion of the oceans, observing that [one of the]

187 Article 1(1). It was already pointed out above that the expression "conservation of the living resources of the high seas" does not merely refer to avoiding the depletion of the resources but to securing a maximum supply of food and other marine products (see section 5.3.3).

188 Judgment of 25 July 1974, 1974 ICJ Reports 3 § 72.

189 See e.g., T Scovazzi "Article 303" in Proelss (n. 24) 1950–1961 at 1951.

190 See e.g., R Caddell & S Esterling "The cultural rights imperative" (2011) 42 *Cambrian Law Review* 7–10 at 9.

191 See e.g., S Claesson "The value and valuation of maritime cultural heritage" (2011) 18 *International Journal of Cultural Property* 61–80.

192 See e.g., the third preambular paragraph of the 1972 UNESCO Convention for the Protection of the World Cultural and Natural Heritage (CCNH; 1037 UNTS 151, (1972) 11 ILM 1358; adopted: 16 November 1972; EIF: 17 December 1975).

193 Scovazzi (n. 189) 1953.

194 See e.g., article 149. See further Chapter 4 section 4.5.1.

195 See further e.g., S Dromgoole *Underwater Cultural Heritage and International Law* (2013); AF Vrdoljak "Human rights and cultural heritage in international law" in Lenzerini & Vrdoljak (n. 135) 139–173.

"two principles of public law [...] generally recognized as fundamental [...] is the perfect equality and entire independence of all distinct states".[196]

However, sovereign equality remains today "a formal legal concept" that seldom reflects reality.[197] This is confirmed in the UNC itself[198] as well as many other instruments,[199] including the LOSC. Indeed, while article 157(3) confirms that the ISA "is based on the principle of the sovereign equality of all its members" and other provisions forbid discrimination,[200] the LOSC takes into account that States are not all equal when it requires that equality be transcended by equity.[201] In doing so, "the Convention follows a general trend in international law for differential instead of formally equal treatment of States".[202]

In that sense,[203] equity plays a fundamental role in the LOSC,[204] in the same way as it does in other global instruments.[205] The manner in which the LOSC fosters geographical equity in the spatial allocation of jurisdiction has been alluded to in

196 See Newton (n. 29) 407 quoting from 165 Eng. Rep. 1464, 1475 (1817). For a similar statement, see the opinion of Mr Justice Story in *The Marianna Flora* (n. 80) 43.

197 Kokott (n. 17) § 2 (see also § 43). See also e.g., Vœlckel (n. 61) 63; LJ Kotzé & W Muzangaza "International environmental law and the Anthropocene's energy dilemma" (2018) 36 *Review of European, Comparative and International Environmental Law* 278–292.

198 See e.g., article 23(1), which distinguishes between the permanent members and the non-permanent members of the Security Council.

199 See e.g., the 1970 Declaration on Principles (n. 87).

200 See articles 25(3), 26(2), 42(2), 52(2), 119(3), 140(2), 141, 151(1)(c), 152(1), 227 and 234, articles 6(3), 6(5), 7(2), 7(5), 13(1)(d), 13(14) and 17(1)(c)(i) of Annex III as well as articles 12(3)(b)(i), 12(5), 13(4)(b) of Annex IV. See also section 1 § 6(a)(iii) and 15(c) and section 8 § 1(e) of the Annex to the 1994 Agreement as well as articles 8(3), 21(2) and 23(1) of the 1995 Agreement.

201 See F Francioni "Equity in international law" 2013 MPEPIL § 23.

202 S Vönecky & A Höfelmeier "Article 140" in Proelss (n. 24) 980. See also e.g., the New Delhi Declaration (n. 19) § 3.1; P Cullet "Differential treatment in international law: Towards a new paradigm of inter-State relations" (1999) 10 EJIL 549–582 at 551; N Kofele-Kale "The principle of preferential treatment in the law of GATT: Towards achieving the objective of an equitable world trading system" (1988) 18 CWILJ 291–333 at 333; WD Verwey "The principle of preferential treatment for developing countries" (1983) 23 *Indian Journal of International Law* 343–500.

203 Akin to that of "substantive equality" "understood as a multidimensional concept, pursuing four complementary and interrelated objectives [...]: redressing disadvantage (the redistributive dimension); addressing stigma, stereotyping, prejudice and violence (the recognition dimension); facilitating participation (the participatory dimension); and accommodating difference, including through structural change (the transformative dimensions)" (S Fredman "Emerging from the shadows: Substantive equality and article 14 of the European Convention on Human Rights" (2016) 16 *Human Rights Law Review* 273–302 at 282). See also L Pereira "The role of substantive equality in finding sustainable development pathways in South Africa" (2014) 10(2) *McGill International Journal of Sustainable Development Law and Policy* 147–178 at 154.

204 See e.g., Vœlckel (n. 61) 144.

205 See e.g., articles 1, 8, 15 and 19 of the CBD and articles 3, 4 and 11 of the FCCC. See further Francioni (n. 201) § 25.

the previous chapter.[206] In addition, the LOSC takes geographical inequalities into account, for instance, when it allows all States to claim a 200 NM legal continental shelf irrespective of the topography of their geological continental shelves[207] and when it makes special provisions for landlocked States[208] and geographically disadvantaged States.[209] At the systemic level, the preamble to the LOSC explains that its States parties recognised "the desirability of establishing through th[e] Convention, with due regard for the sovereignty of all States, a legal order for the seas and oceans which [would] promote [...] the equitable and efficient utilization of their resources [...]"[210] as a contribution "to the realization of a just and equitable international economic order which takes into account the interests and needs of mankind as a whole and, in particular, the special interests and needs of developing countries, whether coastal or land-locked".[211] It is not clear whether the phrase "just and equitable international economic order" refers to the new international economic order called for in the 1974 Declaration for the Establishment of a New International Economic Order[212] and the establishment of which the 1974 Charter of Economic Rights and Duties of States[213] had as one of its purposes to promote.[214]

206 See Chapter 4 sections 4.6.1.1, 4.6.2 and 4.7.2. Equity was not discussed in the preceding chapters in order to avoid "confusing the allocation to states of governmental powers over resources with the wise utilization of those powers by governments for economic or other ends, including maximization and distribution of wealth" (Oxman (n. 102) 411).

207 See article 76(1).

208 Article 124(1)(a) confirms that the term "'land-locked State' means a State which has no sea-coast". See further e.g., articles 69, 82(4), 124–132, 160(2)(k), 161(2)(a) and 254.

209 For purposes of Part V of the LOSC, the term "'geographically disadvantaged States' means coastal States, including States bordering enclosed or semi-enclosed seas, whose geographical situation makes them dependent upon the exploitation of the living resources of the exclusive economic zones of other States in the subregion or region for adequate supplies of fish for the nutritional purposes of their populations or parts thereof, and coastal States which can claim no exclusive economic zones of their own" (article 70(2)). See also e.g., articles 70(1) and (3)–(6); 160(2)(k), 161(2)(a) and 254. States which have claimed the status of "geographically disadvantaged State" in their declarations made under article 310 of the LOSC include Germany ((1995) 27 LOSB 7), Romania ((1997) 33 LOSB 9), Slovenia ((1995) 28 LOSB 5) and Ukraine ((1999) 41 LOSB 14). See further e.g., J-F Pulvenis "La notion de l'Etat géographiquement désavantagé et le nouveau droit de la mer" (1976) 22 AFDI 678–719 at 717; LM Alexander "The 'disadvantaged States' and the law of the sea" (1981) 5 MP 185–193; L Caflisch "What is a geographically disadvantaged State?" (1987) 18 ODIL 641–663 at 643; SC Vasciannie *Land-locked and Geographically Disadvantaged States in the International Law of the Sea* (1990).

210 Paragraph 4.

211 Paragraph 5. This is one of the reasons why the coming into effect of the LOSC was brought about primarily through the support of developing States (see e.g., SP Jagota "Developments in the law of the sea between 1970 and 1998: A historical perspective" (2000) 2 *Journal of the History of International Law* 91–119 at 105; P Vrancken "UNCLOS at 30: Africa at 50" in G Xue & A White (eds) *30 Years of UNCLOS (1982-2012): Progress and Prospects* (2013) 96–114).

212 UNGA Resolution 3201 (XXIX) of 1 May 1974.

213 UNGA Resolution 3281 (XXIX) of 12 December 1974.

214 Fourth preambular paragraph. See e.g., E Mann Borgese "The new international economic order and the law of the sea" (1977) 14 *San Diego Law Review* 584–596 at 585; L Juda "UNCLOS III and the new international economic order" (1979) 7 ODIL 221–256 at 249; M Hope-Thompson

Nevertheless, the need to give preferential treatment to the so-called "developing States"[215] is given legal effect through several provisions of the LOSC.[216]

The link between equity and development was made when it was suggested that,

> in keeping with the object and purpose of the [LOSC], it may be possible to distribute the [article 82] payments and contributions in kind through established programmes and funds to help developing States meet agreed targets under commitments such as the Millennium Development Goals and other sustainable development goals.[217]

When, in 1986, the UN General Assembly adopted the Declaration on the Right to Development,[218] it did so "[a]ware that efforts at the international level to promote and protect human rights should be accompanied by efforts to establish a new international economic order"[219] and to confirm that "the right to development is an inalienable human right and that equality of opportunity for development is a prerogative both of nations and of individuals who make up nations".[220] The Declaration proclaims that "[t]he human person is the central subject of development and should be the active participant and beneficiary of the right to development"[221] at the same time that it stresses that "[a]ll human beings have a responsibility for development, individually and collectively [...] and they should therefore promote and protect an appropriate political, social and economic order

---

"The Third World and the law of the sea: The attitude of the Group of 77 toward the continental shelf" (1980) 1 *Boston College Third World Law Journal* 37–70 at 39; RC Ogley "The law of the sea draft convention and the new international economic order" (1981) 5(3) MP 240–251; RJ Payne & JR Nassar "The new international economic order at sea" (1982) 17 *Journal of Developing Areas* 31–50 at 45–46; BA Boczek "Ideology and the law of the sea: The challenge of the new international economic order" (1984) 7 *Boston College International and Comparative Law Review* 1–30 at 30; JN Moore "The law of the sea and the new international economic order" (1984) 3A *Public Law Forum* 13–28 at 21.

215 On the meaning of the term "developing State", see e.g., M Hirsch "Developing countries" 2017 MPEPIL, who cautions that "[t]here is no single indicator to classify countries as developing or developed" (§ 3); MH Nordquist *United Nations Convention on the Law of the Sea 1982 – A Commentary* (1990) IV 104 § 202.6(b); G Verdirame "The definition of developing countries under GATT and other international law" (1996) 39 GYIL 164–197 at 196. See further *Activities in the Area* (n. 164) § 162; French (n. 165) 558.

216 See e.g., articles 61(3), 62, 69(3), 70(4), 82(1), 82(4), 119(1)(a), 148, 150, 194(1), 202, 203, 207(4), 244(2), 266(2) and 276.

217 ISA "Outcomes of the International Workshop on Further Consideration of the Implementation of Article 82 of the United Nations Convention on the Law of the Sea" (ISBA Doc. ISBA/19/A/4 of 6 May 2013) § 4(h).

218 UNGA Resolution 41/128 of 4 December 1986.

219 Fifteenth preambular paragraph. See also articles 3(3) and 4(2).

220 Sixteenth preambular paragraph. See also article 1(1).

221 Article 2(1).

for development".[222] The following year, the intergenerational-equity imperative,[223] which was missing in the Declaration, became a central tenet of the developmental agenda when the World Commission on Environment and Development described "sustainable development" as seeking "to meet the needs and aspirations of the present without compromising the ability of to meet those of the future".[224] At the same time, the Commission posited that,

> [f]ar from requiring the cessation of economic growth, [sustainable development] recognizes that the problems of poverty and underdevelopment cannot be solved unless we have a new era of growth in which developing countries play a large role and reap large benefits.[225]

Since then, "[t]he notion of 'sustainable development' and a variety of sub-notions that are derived from it, such as 'sustainable use', 'sustainable utilization', 'maximum sustainable yield', or 'sustainable management', have been included in almost all important [...] instruments".[226] Among them are the 2000 UN Millennium Declaration,[227] in which the oceans are absent,[228] and the 2030 Agenda for Sustainable Development adopted by the UN General Assembly in 2015.[229] One of the Agenda's sustainable development goals (SDGs)[230] is SDG 14, which is to "conserve and sustainably use the oceans, seas and marine resources for

222 Article 2(2). See also the New Delhi Declaration (n. 19) § 2.4.

223 See the New Delhi Declaration (n. 19) § 2.2; E Brown Weiss "Intergenerational equity" 2013 MPEPIL § 6.

224 World Commission on Environment and Development *Our Common Future* (1987) 49. See Pereira (n. 203) 149.

225 *Our Common Future* (n. 224) 49. For an outline of the six main development theories, see Hirsch (n. 215) § 8–27. On the concept "development", see e.g., JE Stiglitz, J-P Fitoussi & M Durand *Beyond GDP – Measuring What Counts for Economic and Social Performance* (OECD 2018); RH Wade "What strategies are viable for developing countries today? The World Trade Organization and the shrinking of 'development space"' (2003) 10(4) *Review of International Political Economy* 621–644 at 639.

226 U Beyerlin "Sustainable development" 2013 MPEPIL § 1. Sustainability was already a priority for the drafters of article 2 of the CLRHS and of the LOSC (see articles 61(3) and 119(1)(a)). See further e.g., the Fish Stocks Agreement, the objective of which is "to ensure the long-term conservation and sustainable use of straddling fish stocks and highly migratory fish stocks [...]" (article 2).

227 UNGA Resolution 55/2 of 8 September 2000.

228 However, two years later, the Plan of Implementation of the 2002 World Summit on Sustainable Development (UN Doc. A/CONF.199/20 (2002) 8–72) acknowledged that the "[o]ceans, seas, islands and coastal areas form an integrated and essential component of the Earth's ecosystem and are critical for global food security and for sustaining economic prosperity and the well-being of many national economies, particularly in developing countries" (§ 30).

229 UNGA Resolution 70/1 of 25 September 2015. See also the outcome document of the UN Conference on Sustainable Development entitled "The future we want", which was endorsed by the UN General Assembly by means of Resolution 66/288 of 27 July 2012.

230 See e.g., D French & LJ Kotzé *Sustainable Development Goals: Law, Theory and Implementation* (2018).

sustainable development".[231] The weaknesses of SDG 14[232] are compensated by the fact that "[t]he Sustainable Development Goals and targets are integrated and indivisible",[233] although that fact is not reflected by the overall level of integration in the Agenda, which is "far lower than justified from a science perspective and far lower than discussed in the [...] preparation process".[234] In other words, SDG 14 is expected to make a contribution to SDGs such as SDG 1 (ending poverty), SDG 2 (ending hunger), SDG 5 (achieving gender equality),[235] SDG 8 (promoting full and productive employment) and SDG 9 (fostering innovation). At the same time, a contribution to SDG 14 will be made by SDGs such as SDG 10 (reduce inequality within and among countries), SDG 13 (take urgent action to combat climate change and its impacts)[236] and SDG 16 (promote peaceful and inclusive societies for sustainable development, provide access to justice for all and build effective, accountable and inclusive institutions at all levels). That is also the case of SDG 17, which is to "strengthen the means of implementation and revitalise the global partnership for sustainable development".

5.4.5 Integrative cooperation

Integrative cooperation reflects the core spirit of the law of the sea. The preamble to the LOSC confirms that the States parties to the Convention are "[c]onscious that the problems of ocean space are closely interrelated and need to be considered as a whole"[237] "in a spirit of mutual understanding and cooperation".[238] In other words, the States parties acknowledge that the law of the sea, like the whole of contem-

231 See e.g., MH Nordquist, JN Moore & R Long (eds) *The Marine Environment and United Nations Sustainable Development Goal 14* (2018); L Recuero Virto "A preliminary assessment of the indicators for sustainable development goal (SDG) 14 'Conserve and sustainably use the oceans, seas and marine resources for sustainable development'" (2018) 98 MP 47–57; W Huck (ed) *Sustainable Development Goals* (2022) 520–553.

232 See e.g., M Ntona & E Morgera "Connecting SDG 14 with the other sustainable development goals through marine spatial planning" (2018) 93 MP 214–222 at 215; P Vrancken "Life below water" in K De Feyter, GE Türkelli & S de Moerloose (eds) *Encyclopedia of Law and Development* (2021) 184–186.

233 Paragraph 55 of UNGA Resolution 70/1 of 25 September 2015.

234 M Nilsson & R Costanza "Overall framework for the sustainable development goals" in ICSU & ISSC *Review of the Sustainable Development Goals: The Science Perspective* (2015) 9.

235 See e.g., I Papanicolopulu (ed) *Gender and the Law of the Sea* (2019).

236 See e.g., A Boyle "Climate change, ocean governance and UNCLOS" in J Barrett & R Barnes (eds) *Law of the Sea* (2016) 211–230.

237 Third preambular paragraph. See e.g., JM Sobrino Heredia "La tensión entre la gobernanza zonal y la gobernanza global en la conservación y gestión de los recursos pesqueros" in JM Sobrino Heredia (ed) *The Contribution of the United Nations Convention on the Law of the Sea to Good Governance of the Oceans and Seas* (2014) II 455–483 at 455.

238 First preambular paragraph. See e.g., L Brilmayer & N Klein "Land and sea: Two sovereignty regimes in search of a common denominator" (2001) 33 *New York University Journal of International Law and Politics* 703–768 at 705; DR Rothwell & T Stephens *The International Law of the Sea* (2016) 521.

porary public international law, reflects the coexistence of the Westphalian paradigm, characterised by "co-operation and regulated intercourse among States, each pursuing its own interests", and the commons paradigm "based on a universalist or cosmopolitan outlook"[239] focusing "on the international community that shares common values or interests" requiring "a more holistic or integrated management approach".[240] The commons paradigm is often described as reflecting a new pattern in public international law,[241] but it was shown above that, as far as the law of the sea is concerned, communality has always been a fundamental element, admittedly to a varying degree.[242]

We will probably never know whether there ever existed an "original communality of property"[243] and what exactly it entailed legally. However, the premise of an original common state,[244] together with an assumed impossibility of effective occupation,[245] has led to viewing ocean waters as *res communis* "open to use by all members of the community"[246] and over which "no nation can claim exclusive rights or sovereignty [...]".[247] In that sense,[248] this is still the legal nature of the high seas[249] and the basis of the legal regime of the Area and its resources,[250] although the concept of the common heritage of mankind in the form it takes in the LOSC is "much more than the *res communis*

239 Cassese (n. 27) 21.

240 Tanaka (n. 23) 5. See also e.g., S Villalpando "The legal dimension of the international community: How community interests are protected in international law" (2010) 21 EJIL 387–419 at 388; O McIntyre "The principle of 'integration' in international law relating to sustainable development" in Westra, Taylor & Michelot (n. 164) 104–119 at 104; S Bateman "Sovereignty as an obstacle to effective oceans governance and maritime boundary making – The case of the South China Sea" in Kwon, Schofield and Lee (n. 103) 201–223 at 201.

241 Cassese (n. 27) 21.

242 See section 5.2 above.

243 Somos (n. 52) 298.

244 Selden challenged that premise on the ground that "the Law of God, or the Divine Oracles of holy Scriptures, do allow a private Dominion of the Sea" (Selden (n. 181) 27). See further e.g., Newton (n. 29) 389; Somos (n. 52) 296–302.

245 See e.g., Momtaz (n. 61) 342; H Grotius (translated by R Magoffin) *The Freedom of the Seas* (1916) 27; Selden (n. 181) 138; Pufendorf (n. 59) 559); C van Bynkershoek (translated by R Magoffin) *De Dominio Maris Dissertatio* (1923) 32–33 and 77.

246 GJH van Hoof "Legal status of the concept of the common heritage of mankind" (1986) 7 *Grotiana* 49–79 at 54.

247 J Van Dyke & C Yuen "'Common heritage' v. 'freedom of the high seas': Which governs the seabed?" (1982) 19 *San Diego Law Review* 493–551 at 515–516. See however SJ Burton "Freedom of the seas: International law applicable to deep seabed mining claims" (1977) 29 *Stanford Law Review* 1135–1180 at 1159–1161.

248 See Francois (n. 32) § 9. See also e.g., Gidel (n. 34) 213.

249 See articles 87 and 89 of the LOSC. See also e.g., DW Arrow "The customary norm process and the deep seabed" (1981) 9 ODIL 1–59 at 12.

250 See e.g., J Logue "The revenge of John Selden: The draft Convention on the Law of the Sea in the light of Hugo Grotius' *Mare Liberum*" (1982) 3 *Grotiana* 27–56 at 37.

omnium"[251] because it requires "that the management of the area be undertaken by community political organs".[252]

The concept of community ocean management has deep historical roots. In 1832, the Latin American jurist Andrés Bello (1781–1865) "argued that the seas are the undivided heritage of mankind".[253] At the end of that century, the French jurist Albert Geouffre de Lapradelle (1871–1955) argued, in an attempt to refute the arguments in support of the sovereignty of a coastal State over the waters adjacent to its coast, that both the territorial sea[254] and "the high seas are the common property of the whole of humankind"[255] and, therefore, a part of the "estate of humankind",[256] "a juristic person consisting of the international community of States".[257]

While these views contributed to weakening the theory that ocean resources are *res nullius* in the sense that they belong to no one and are acquired by whoever first takes possession of them,[258] they did not succeed in addressing the concerns of coastal States over the resources off their shores being appropriated by nationals of other States.[259] After "[t]he question of [...] property rights over marine resources [had been] proposed for examination by the Hague conference, but not discussed by that conference",[260] States took the matter in their own hands. A major role was played in this regard by the USA when it was proclaimed in 1945 that: (a) "the United States regard[ed] it as proper to establish explicitly bounded conservation zones [in the high seas] in which fishing activities shall be subject to the regulation and control of the United States";[261] and (b) the USA regarded "the natural resources of the subsoil and sea bed of the continental shelf beneath the

251 A Kiss "The common heritage of mankind: Utopia or reality?" (1985) 40 *International Journal* 423–441 at 425.

252 MW Zacher & JG McConnell "Down to the sea with stakes: The evolving law of the sea and the future of the deep seabed regime" (1990) 21 ODIL 71–103 at 76. See also e.g., L Torreh-Bayouth "UNCLOS III: The remaining obstacles to consensus on the deep sea mining regime" (1981) 16 TILJ 79–115 at 99.

253 K Baslar *The Concept of the Common Heritage of Mankind in International Law* (1997) 87.

254 A Geouffre de Lapradelle "Le droit de l'Etat riverain sur la mer territoriale" (1898) 5 RGDIP 264 284 and 309 347 at 309.

255 *Ibid.* 274.

256 *Ibid.* 321.

257 *Ibid.* 283.

258 See Newton (n. 29) 379. See also e.g., M Chemillier-Gendreau "Retour sur une question controversée: La notion de *terra nullius* à l'origine des conquêtes coloniales et ses résonances contemporaines" in SE Bedjaoui *et al.* (eds) *L'Afrique et le Droit International: Variations sur l'Organisation Internationale* (2013) 461–470; A Fitzmaurice *Sovereignty, Property and Empire, 1500–2000* (2014) 256–270.

259 See e.g., Rayfuse (n. 158) 793. Those concerns were not new. Indeed, Selden challenged the assumption of inexhaustibility on the ground that "the sea itself, by reason of other men's Fishing, Navigation, and Commerce, becomes the worse for him that owns it, and others that enjoy it in his right; So that less profit ariseth, than might otherwise be received thereby" (Selden (n. 181) 141).

260 Churchill, Lowe & Sander (n. 89) 224.

261 Presidential Proclamation No 2668 of 29 September 1945 on the Policy of the United States with respect to coastal fisheries in certain areas of the high seas.

high seas but contiguous to the coasts of the United States, subject to [its] jurisdiction and control".[262] Similar claims were later made by about twenty States before UNCLOS I. During the latter, the participating States confirmed the State practice when they adopted the 1958 Convention on the Continental Shelf,[263] in which it is stated that "[t]he coastal State exercises over the continental shelf sovereign rights for the purpose of exploring it and exploiting its natural resources".[264]

By contrast, faced with more contentious claims over the waters above the continental shelf and their resources, the States were only prepared to acknowledge in the CLRHS[265] that coastal States had "a special interest in the maintenance of the productivity of the living resources in any area of the high seas adjacent to [their] territorial sea[s]".[266] Nevertheless, the process gained momentum during the preparations for UNCLOS III[267] and coalesced into the EEZ,[268] together with an explicit recognition of the interests of coastal States in adjacent high-seas area with regard to straddling stocks and highly migratory species[269] as well as anadromous stocks[270] and catadromous stocks.[271]

The above means that the only resources that arguably still have the status of *res nullius* are the resources of the high seas.[272] That status does not mean that their appropriation is unregulated. Indeed, over and above complying with all their treaty obligations and taking into account the rights, duties and interests of the

262 Presidential Proclamation No 2667 of 28 September 1945 on the Policy of the United States with respect to the natural resources of the subsoil and sea bed of the continental shelf.

263 499 UNTS 311. Adopted: 29 April 1958; EIF: 10 June 1964.

264 Article 2(1).

265 See n. 186. See article 2.

266 Article 6(1). See also article 1(1)(b). See further ILC "Report of the International Law Commission to the General Assembly" UN Doc. A/3159 (1956) in (1956) II YILC 286–288.

267 See *Fisheries Jurisdiction Case* (n. 188) 52.

268 See further Chapter 4 section 4.6.1.

269 See articles 63–64 of the LOSC. See also the Fish Stocks Agreement; the 1966 International Convention for the Conservation of Atlantic Tunas (673 UNTS 64, (1967) 6 ILM 293; adopted: 14 May 1966; EIF: 21 March 1969); the 2000 Convention on the Conservation and Management of Highly Migratory Fish Stocks in the Western and Central Pacific Ocean (2275 UNTS 43; adopted: 5 September 2000; EIF: 19 June 2004).

270 See article 66 of the LOSC. See also the 1982 Convention for the Protection of Salmon in the North Atlantic Ocean (1338 UNTS 33; adopted: 2 March 1982; EIF: 1 October 1983) and the 1992 Convention for the Conservation of Anadromous Stocks in the North Pacific Ocean (TIAS 11465; adopted: 11 February 1992; EIF: 16 February 1993). See further e.g., WT Burke "Anadromous species and the new international law of the sea" (1991) 22 ODIL 95–131.

271 See article 67 of the LOSC. See further e.g., the 2014 Hamilton Declaration on Collaboration for the Conservation of the Sargasso Sea; D Freestone & KK Morrison "The Sargasso Sea Alliance: Seeking to protect the Sargasso Sea" (2012) 27 IJMCL 647–655.

272 See e.g., Rayfuse (n. 158) 793.

neighbouring coastal States,[273] the LOSC requires that States take steps to conserve the living resources of the high seas,[274] including cooperating "to establish subregional or regional fisheries organizations" to manage those resources ("the RFMOs").[275]

The RFMOs, together with a wide range of other bodies,[276] including the International Seabed Authority, which is the organisation through which the States parties to the LOSC "organize and control activities in the Area, particularly with a view to administering the resources of the Area",[277] are the progenies of a century-long history of efforts towards the collective management of the oceans.[278] In 1910, the Dutch jurist Cornelis van Vollenhoven (1874–1933) proposed the establishment of "a naval force under international command that would have consisted of contingents from the individual states".[279]

After the First World War, the Greek jurist Nicolas Politis (1872–1942) asserted that the need for international control of all activities at sea was reflected more and more in the habits and conscience of the peoples.[280] He was not alone in holding this view. The International Law Association proposed the establishment of an international commission composed of State representatives from the various continents responsible for checking whether the applicable regulations were

273 See article 116(a)–(b) of the LOSC. See also e.g., Y Takei *Filling Regulatory Gaps in High Seas Fisheries* (2013) 42–48; Rayfuse (n. 158) 796. See further, with regard to Chile's claim to a "mar presencial", e.g., TA Clingan "*Mar presencial* (the presential sea): *Deja vu* all over again? A response to Francisco Orrego Vicuña" (1993) 24 ODIL 93–97; JG Dalton "The Chilean mar presencial: A harmless concept or a dangerous precedent?" (1993) 8 IJMCL 397–418; JA de Yturriaga *The International Regime of Fisheries: From UNCLOS 1982 to the Presential Sea* (1997) 228–237; CC Joyner & PN de Cola "Chile's presential sea proposal: Implications for straddling stocks and the international law of fisheries" (1993) 24 ODIL 99–121; PS Kibel "Alone at sea: Chile's presencial ocean policy" (2000) 12 *Journal of Environmental Law* 43–63; F Orrego Vicuña "The presential sea: Defining coastal States' special interests in high seas fisheries and other activities" (1992) 35 GYIL 264–292; F Orrego Vicuña "Toward an effective management of high seas fisheries and the settlement of the pending issues of the law of the sea" (1993) 24 ODIL 81–92; F Orrego Vicuña "Coastal States' competences over high seas fisheries and the changing role of international law" (1995) 55 *Zeitschrift für ausländisches öffentliches Recht und Völkerrecht* 520–535.

274 See e.g., article 117 and 119–120 of the LOSC.

275 See article 118 of the LOSC. For an assessment of early examples of RFMOs, see e.g., R Rayfuse *Non-Flag State Enforcement in High Seas Fisheries* (2004) 17–49. See further e.g., J Ellis "Fisheries conservation in an anarchical system: A comparison of rational choice and constructivist perspectives" (2007) 3(2) *Journal of International Law and International Relations* 1–40; T Henriksen "Revisiting the freedom of fishing and legal obligations on States not party to regional fisheries management organizations" (2009) 40 ODIL 80–96; S Borg *Conservation on the High Seas* (2012); CM Brooks *et al.* "Challenging the 'right to fish' in a fast-changing ocean" (2014) 33(3) *Stanford Environmental Law Journal* 289–324.

276 See Chapter 1 section 1.3.

277 See article 157(1) of the LOSC.

278 See also article 123 of the LOSC regarding cooperation of States bordering enclosed and semi-enclosed seas.

279 F Bodendiek "Walther Schücking and the idea of 'international organization'" (2011) 22 EJIL 741–754 at 749.

280 (1925) 31 AIDI 526–527.

complied with.[281] It is along the lines of a proposal by the German jurist Walther Schücking (1875–1935) in the League of Nations' Committee of Experts for the Progressive Codification of International Law[282] that the German jurist Karl Strupp (1886–1940) proposed at the Institute of International Law that an "international water office" composed of 15 members elected by States, at least half of whom had to be international-law experts, be established.[283] That proposal was supported by the Chilean jurist Alejandro Alvarez (1868–1960), who requested the constitution of a committee to examine it.[284] At the same time, the French jurist Gilbert Gidel (1880–1958) called for the creation of an "international ocean bureau" with more limited functions, but a wider geographical reach.[285] Geouffre de Lapradelle was much more ambitious when he called for the establishment of an international organisation bringing together coastal and landlocked States, all having equal rights in the resources of the sea.[286] The French jurist Charles Dupuis had however resigned himself to considering the establishment of an international body to be impossible at that stage.[287]

After the Second World War, the French jurist Georges Scelle (1878–1961) argued at the ILC that, "if coastal States were not to exercise unlimited sovereignty over the continental shelf they must be subject to the control of some supranational authority to ensure that the natural resources of the sea-bed were not lost to the international community".[288] He also explained that he regretted

> that a specialized agency of the United Nations had not been given responsibility for determining what governments or undertakings might be permitted to apply for and be granted concessions for the exploration and exploitation of the bed of the high seas, and for controlling the use made of such concessions.[289]

Failure to take such a step was bound to substantially increase the inequality between States that are able to exploit their resources and those that are not.[290] This is a major factor that contributed to the LOSC, a mere 24 years after the Geneva Conventions, making "a fundamental shift to multilateralism from unilateralism in the development of the law of the sea".[291] It is undoubtedly the general support for that approach that made possible the adoption of the

281 *Ibid.* 521.
282 (1929) 35(1) AIDI 200.
283 (1928) 34 AIDI 674–675. See also (1929) 35(1) AIDI 197.
284 (1928) 34 AIDI 733.
285 (1929) 35(1) AIDI 199–212.
286 Geouffre de Lapradelle (n. 38) 380.
287 (1927) 34(1) AIDI 114.
288 UN Doc. A/CN.4/SR.197 § 75 in (1953) 1 YILC 84.
289 UN Doc. A/CN.4/SR.234 § 70 in (1953) 1 YILC 343. See also e.g., Vœlckel (n. 61) 95.
290 G Scelle "Plateau continental et droit international" (1955) 58 RGDIP 5–62 at 11.
291 Oxman (n. 85) 356 and 361.

Part XI Agreement and the Fish Stocks Agreement.[292] Within this framework, increased human activity at sea has compelled States "to increase their ability to deter illegal activity [by] cooperat[ing] with other States in potentially all aspects of law enforcement, from intelligence gathering and security patrols through to arrest and prosecution activities"[293] using "a growing number of technology applications".[294]

The shift from division to cooperation has been accompanied by a shift from disaggregation to integration,[295] illustrated by the ecosystem paradigm of which the large marine ecosystem approach,[296] the concept of marine protected areas,[297] the world heritage sites at sea[298] as well as the MARPOL special areas[299] and particularly sensitive sea areas[300] are good examples.[301] In addition, the shift has given rise to new concepts and disciplines, such as the rights of nature,[302] integrated coastal zone management,[303] comprehensive ocean zoning[304] and marine spatial planning. The latter "is about managing the distribution of human activities in space and time to achieve ecological, economic and social objectives and outcomes" through pro-

292 *Ibid.* 361.

293 W Gullett & Y Shi "Cooperative maritime surveillance and enforcement" in R Warner & S Kaye (eds) *Routledge Handbook of Maritime Regulation and Enforcement* (2016) 378–393 at 378. See further e.g., D Guilfoyle "Transnational crime" in Warner & Kaye (*ibid.*) 262–276.

294 C Rahman "Use of technology in maritime regulation and enforcement" in Warner & Kaye (n. 293) 363.

295 See e.g., New Delhi Declaration (n. 19) § 7.1.

296 See e.g., P Vrancken "The 2050 Africa's Integrated Maritime Strategy: The combined exclusive maritime zone of Africa as an instrument of sustainable development of the African large marine ecosystems" (2020) 36 *Environmental Development* 100557.

297 See e.g., Y Tanaka "The institutional application of the law of *dedoublement fonctionnel* in marine environmental protection: A critical assessment of regional regimes" (2014) 57 GYIL 143–180 at 152–167; *Chagos Marine Protected Area Arbitration (Mauritius v. United Kingdom)*, award of 18 March 2015, PCA Case No 2011–03 § 298.

298 See the CCNH.

299 See reg. 1(10) I MARPOL. An example is the designation, in 2006 by the Marine Environment Protection Committee of the IMO, of the waters off southern Africa as a special area "to protect wildlife and the marine environment in an ecologically important region used intensively by shipping" (IMO Briefing 38/2006 reporting on the 55th session of IMO's Marine Environment Protection Committee (MEPC) – 9–13 October 2006).

300 See e.g., A Chircop "The designation of particularly sensitive sea areas: A new layer in the regime for marine protection from international shipping" in A Chircop *et al.* (eds) *The Future of Ocean Regime-Building* (2009) 573–608; MJ Kachel *Particularly Sensitive Sea Areas* (2008); J Kraska "Particularly sensitive sea areas and the law of the sea" in MH Nordquist (ed) *Freedom of Seas, Passage Rights and the 1982 Law of the Sea Convention* (2009) 511–572.

301 See also e.g., *MOX Plant (Ireland v. United Kingdom)*, order of 3 December 2001, 2001 ITLOS Reports 95 § 82, restated in *Sub-Regional Fisheries Commission Advisory Opinion*, advisory opinion of 2 April 2015, 2015 ITLOS Reports 404 § 140 (with regard to IUU fishing activities) and *Maritime Boundary in the Atlantic Ocean* (n. 162) § 73.

302 See e.g., MK Vierros & H Harden-Davies "Is there a role for rights of nature in the blue economy debate?" (2022) 38 OY 48–70.

303 See e.g., Y Tanaka *A Dual Approach to Ocean Governance* (2008).

304 See e.g., T Agardy *Ocean Zoning* (2015) 13.

cesses "informed by both the natural and social sciences"[305] that "provide a basis for marine use that takes account of current uses, while being future oriented".[306] When those processes are transparent and participatory,[307] they constitute powerful instruments of sustainable ocean governance[308] at the national and regional levels[309] allowing, among others, the linking of SDG 14 with the other SDGs.[310]

5.5 Purposive parameters

5.5.1 Introduction

In contrast to the teleological principles, which point towards the lawful purposes for which the State ocean jurisdictions are to be exercised, one may possibly refer as "purposive parameters" the jurisdictional elements that act as guide posts within

305 C Ehler, J Zaucha & K Gee "Maritime/marine spatial planning at the interface of research and practice" in J Zaucha & K Gee (eds) *Maritime Spatial Planning – Past, Present and Future* (2019) 1–21 at 1. See further e.g., F Maes "The international legal framework for marine spatial planning" (2008) 32 MP 797–810; C Ehler & F Douvere *Marine Spatial Planning: A Step-by-Step Approach toward Ecosystem-Based Management* (2009); D Pyć "The role of the law of the sea in marine spatial planning" in Zaucha & Gee (*ibid.*) 375–395.

306 FP Saunders, M Gilek & R Tafon "Adding people to the sea: Conceptualizing social sustainability in maritime spatial planning" in Zaucha & Gee (n. 305) 175–199 at 187. See also e.g., D Kitsiou & M Karydis (eds) *Marine Spatial Planning* (2017).

307 See e.g., with regard to the domestic level, Principle 10 of the 1992 Rio Declaration and, with regard to the international level, the 1998 (Aarhus) Convention on Access to Information, Public Participation in Decision-Making and Access to Justice in Environmental Matters (2161 UNTS 447; adopted: 25 June 1998; EIF: 30 October 2001), relied upon in *Dispute Concerning Access to Information under Article 9 of the OSPAR Convention (Ireland v. United Kingdom)*, award of 2 July 2003, (2003) 42 ILM 1118, and the 2018 Regional Agreement on Access to Information, Public Participation and Justice in Environmental Matters in Latin America and the Caribbean (adopted: 4 March 2018; EIF: 22 April 2021). See also e.g., B Queffelec *et al.* "Marine spatial planning and the risk of ocean grabbing in the tropical Atlantic" (2021) 78(4) *ICES Journal of Marine Science* 1196–1208; S Guggisberg, A Jaeckel & T Stephens "Transparency in fisheries governance: Achievements to date and challenges ahead" (2022) 136 MP 104639.

308 See e.g., N Soininen & D Hassan "Marine spatial planning as an instrument of sustainable ocean governance" in D Hassan, T Kuokkanen & N Soininen (eds) *Transboundary Marine Spatial Planning and International Law* (2015) 3–20.

309 See e.g., Directive 2014/89/EU of the European Parliament and of the Council of 23 July 2014 establishing a framework for maritime spatial planning (*Official Journal* L 257 of 28 August 2014 at 135–145). See further e.g., R Long "Principles and normative trends in EU ocean governance" in Kwon, Schofield and Lee (n. 103) 699–726; A Zervaki "The legalization of maritime spatial planning in the European Union and its implications for maritime governance" (2016) 30 OY 32–52; C Le Lièvre & AM O'Hagan "Legal frameworks for marine spatial planning" in Kitsiou & Karydis (n. 306) 37–69 at 53–63; A Schultz-Zehden, B Weig & I Lukic "Maritime spatial planning and the EU's Blue Growth Policy: Past, present and future perspectives" in Zaucha & Gee (n. 305) 121–149.

310 See e.g., Ntona & Morgera (n. 232) 214–222. See also section 5.3.4.

which the purposes are to be achieved. The main parameters are, arguably, good faith,[311] abuse of rights[312] and reasonableness.[313]

5.5.2 Good faith

Article 300 of the LOSC requires that States parties "fulfil in good faith the obligations assumed under th[e] Convention" and, in doing so, mirrors article 2(2) of the UNC.[314] There is no doubt that, not only with regard to the law of treaties,[315] but in international law as a whole, the fulfilment by States of their obligations in good faith is a "universally recognized" principle[316] "of the greatest importance for the maintenance of international peace and security and for the implementation of the other purposes of the United Nations".[317] While it has been argued that good faith is a general principle that can create obligations on its own,[318] the ICJ reiterated in *Land and Maritime Boundary between Cameroon and Nigeria* that, "although the principle of good faith is 'one of the basic principles governing the creation and performance of legal obligations[, …] it is not in itself a source of obligation where none would otherwise exist'".[319] This is also the position adopted by ITLOS.[320]

"General notions such as good faith cannot be entirely grasped by abstract definitions",[321] especially in view of the fact that "good faith is invoked in three rather different settings and functions": in a subjective sense, as an open-ended legal standard and as a general principle of law.[322] In the latter case, the main element of good faith is the requirement that legitimate expectations be respected.[323] In ocean-related matters, it would appear that whether expectations are legitimate and whether a State has acted up to those expectations depend on whether those expectations and actions are consistent with the teleological principles discussed

311 See section 5.5.2.
312 See section 5.5.3.
313 See section 5.5.4.
314 See also articles 18, 26 and 31(1) of the 1969 Vienna Convention on the Law of Treaties (n. 133).
315 See e.g., M Kotzur "Good faith (bona fide)" 2009 MPEPIL § 19.
316 Third preambular paragraph of the 1969 Vienna Convention on the Law of Treaties (n. 133).
317 Fifth preambular paragraph of the 1970 Declaration on Principles (n. 87).
318 See e.g., R Kolb "Principles as sources of international law (with special reference to good faith)" (2006) 53 *Netherlands International Law Review* 1–36 at 27–36.
319 *Land and Maritime Boundary between Cameroon and Nigeria (Cameroon v. Nigeria, Equatorial Guinea intervening)*, judgment of 11 June 1998, 1998 ICJ Reports 275 § 39, quoting *Border and Transborder Armed Actions (Nicaragua v. Honduras)*, judgment of 20 December 1988, 1988 ICJ Reports 105 § 94, itself quoting *Nuclear Tests (Australia v. France)*, judgment of 20 December 1974, 1974 ICJ Reports 253 § 46 and *Nuclear Tests (New Zealand v. France)*, judgment of 20 December 1974, 1974 ICJ Reports 457 § 49.
320 See *The M/V "Virginia G" Case (Panama v. Guinea Bissau)*, judgment of 14 April 2014, 2014 ITLOS Reports 4 § 398; *M/V "Louisa"* (n. 105) § 137, reiterated in *The M/V "Norstar" Case* (n. 9) § 131.
321 Kolb (n. 318) 13.
322 *Ibid.* 14–20.
323 *Ibid.* 17.

above.[324] This is what the tribunal implied in *North Atlantic Fisheries* when it decided that, because the fisheries regulations the United Kingdom made were,

> (1) appropriate or necessary for the protection and preservation of such fisheries, or (2) desirable or necessary on grounds of public order and morals without unnecessarily interfering with the fishery itself, and in both cases equitable and fair as between local and American fishermen, and not so framed as to give unfairly an advantage to the former over the latter class,

they were "not inconsistent with the obligation to execute the Treaty in good faith [...]".[325] In addition, ITLOS pointed out in *Sub-Regional Fisheries Commission* that good faith required that States make substantial efforts aimed at taking meaningful steps to fulfil their duties.[326]

5.5.3 Abuse of rights

Article 300 of the LOSC refers to good faith with regard to the fulfilment of the States' obligations while an abuse of right can take place in the exercise of "the rights, jurisdiction and freedoms recognised in" the LOSC.[327] While abuse of rights "is closely related to good faith",[328] it is hardly surprising that the abuse of rights is so clearly distinguished from good faith when one keeps in mind that "[t]he international law of the sea is especially susceptible to rights being exercised in a manner which amount[s] to an abuse".[329] For instance, "the possibility of abuse would seem to be inherent in the very concept of the freedom of the high seas".[330] While good faith requires, at least, that enough be done and for the right ends,[331] abuse of rights relates to cases where too much is done and/or where what is done is done for the wrong ends.

A State does too much when it "exercises its rights in such a way that another State is hindered in the exercise of its own rights and, as a consequence, suffers injury".[332] For instance, a State would abuse its freedom of fishing on the high seas were it not to do so "with due regard for the interests of other States in their exercise of" that freedom.[333] It is on "the understanding that the concept of abuse of rights was to be interpreted relative to the rights of other States" that article

324 On the 1843 *Port of Portendick* case between France and the United Kingdom, see A Geouffre de Lapradelle & N Politis *Recueil des Arbitrages Internationaux* (1905) I 512.
325 *North Atlantic Fisheries (Great Britain v. United States of America)*, award of 7 September 1910, XI RIAA 173 at 189.
326 *Sub-Regional Fisheries Commission* (n. 301) § 210.
327 The distinction is also made in article 34 of the 1995 Fish Stocks Agreement.
328 *The M/V "Norstar" Case* (n. 9) § 303.
329 K O'Brien "Article 300" in Proelss (n. 24) 1937–1943 at 1942.
330 *Ibid.*
331 See section 5.4.2.
332 A Kiss "Abuse of rights" 2006 MPEPIL § 4.
333 Article 87(2) of the LOSC.

300 was accepted.[334] However, it could be argued that the harm that is the symptom of a possible abuse should not be limited to a harm to a State, but include also a harm to an individual(s) or to the environment.[335] In that case, for instance, it would be sufficient to provide adequate evidence that the exercise by a State of its freedom of fishing is threatening a fish stock, for that State to be found to be abusing that freedom, irrespective of whether evidence is available that one or more States suffered injury as a result.[336]

A State acts for a wrong end when it exercises a right, jurisdiction or freedom "intentionally for an end which is different from that for which the right", jurisdiction or freedom has been created.[337] For instance, a State would appear to be abusing its right to establish reasonable safety zones around the artificial islands, installations and structures in its EEZ should it do so in order to take measures in those zones for any other purpose than "to ensure the safety both of navigation and of the artificial islands, installations and structures".[338]

5.5.4 Reasonableness

5.5.4.1 Introduction

Reasonableness is perhaps best understood as the coin of which good faith and abuse of rights are the two sides. "States include the term 'reasonable' in legal instruments in order to introduce a degree of flexibility".[339] The latter is required for "the law-applier to weigh up a series of contextual aspects: teleological aspects (policy reasons), efficacy, reasons of the rule and nature of things, equity *intra legem*, *effet utile*, practicability, consideration of the consequences of a course taken",[340] necessity and proportionality,[341] for instance.[342] In view of the nature of

334 O'Brien (n. 329) 1939; MH Nordquist (ed) *United Nations Convention on the Law of the Sea 1982 – A Commentary* (1989) V 150–151 § 300.1.

335 See sections 5.3.3.3 and 5.3.3.4.

336 O'Brien (n. 329) 1942.

337 Kiss (n. 332) § 5.

338 Article 60(4) of the LOSC. See further *M/V* "Saiga" *(No 2)* (n. 105) § 127; MH Nordquist (ed) *United Nations Convention on the Law of the Sea 1982 – A Commentary* (1993) II 586 § 60.15(g); A Proelss "The law of the exclusive economic zone in perspective: Legal status and resolution of user conflicts revisited" (2012) 26 OY 87–112 at 107; A Proelss "Article 60" in Proelss (n. 24) 464–480 at 476; Rothwell & Stephens (n. 238) 95.

339 O Corten "Reasonableness in international law" 2013 MPEPIL § 6.

340 See Kolb (n. 318) 16.

341 See e.g., *Legality of the Threat or Use of Nuclear Weapons* (n. 162) § 41; *Case Concerning Oil Platforms (Iran v. United States of America)*, judgment of 6 November 2003, 2003 ICJ Reports 161 § 76; *The "Duzgit Integrity" Arbitration (Malta v. São Tomé and Príncipe)*, award of 5 September 2016, PCA Case No. 2014–07 § 209. *Contra* e.g., *The "Arctic Sunrise" Arbitration* (n. 105) § 326.

342 See further e.g., MS McDougal & WT Burke "Crisis in the law of the sea: Community perspectives versus national egoism" (1958) 67 *Yale Law Journal* 539–589 at 565; E Franckx "Reasonable bond in the practice of the International Tribunal for the Law of the Sea" (2002) 32 CWILJ 303–342 at 323.

the marine environment and the complexity of State relations at sea, it is hardly surprising that reasonableness permeates the law of the sea. It does so both when it acts as a parameter in the exercise of a specific State ocean jurisdiction (in which case one may arguably refer to it as "performative reasonableness")[343] and in the case of concurrent jurisdictions (in which case one may arguably refer to it as "intersective reasonableness").[344]

5.5.4.2 Performative reasonableness

Performative reasonableness compels a State, when it exercises each of its ocean jurisdictions to take into account one or more interests other than its own, irrespective of whether there is one or more concurrent jurisdictions in the situation where the jurisdiction is exercised. An example is article 73(2) of the LOSC, which states that "[a]rrested vessels and their crews shall be promptly released upon the posting of reasonable bond or other security".[345] That requirement must be read in the light of the fact that "[t]he genesis of Article 73 makes it clear that States originally had quite divergent opinions on which State was competent to prosecute violations of the coastal State's sovereign rights in its EEZ".[346] Thanks to the prompt release procedure spelt out in article 292, with its own adjudicative-body jurisdictional requirements,[347] there have been many opportunities for gaining greater clarity regarding this requirement. For instance, it has been explained that

> Article 73 identifies two interests, the interest of the coastal State to take appropriate measures as may be necessary to ensure compliance with the laws and regulations adopted by it on the one hand and the interest of the flag State in securing prompt release of its vessels and their crews from detention on the other. It strikes a fair balance between the two interests. It provides for release of the vessel and its crew upon the posting of a bond or other security, thus protecting the interests of the flag State and of other persons affected by the detention of the vessel and its crew.[348]

343 See section 5.4.4.2.

344 See section 5.4.4.3.

345 Compare article 226(1)(b). See e.g., DJ Devine "Relevant factors in establishing a reasonable bond for prompt release of a vessel under article 292(1) of the United Nations Convention on the Law of the Sea 1982" (2002) 27 SAYIL 140–149 at 140.

346 Franckx (n. 342) 307.

347 See e.g., article 292(2). See further e.g., *The M/V* Saiga *(Saint Vincent and the Grenadines v. Guinea)*, judgment of 4 December 1997, 1997 ITLOS Reports 16 § 44; *The "Camouco" Case (Panama v. France)*, judgment of 7 February 2000, 2000 ITLOS Reports 10 § 46; *The "Monte Confurco" Case (Seychelles v. France)*, judgment of 18 December 2000, 2000 ITLOS Reports 86 § 58; *The "Grand Prince" Case (Belize v. France)*, judgment of 20 April 2001, 2001 ITLOS Reports 17 § 66–93; T Treves "Article 292" in Proelss (n. 24) 1881–1892.

348 *The "Monte Confurco" Case* (n. 347) § 70. See also e.g., *The 'Juno Trader' Case* (n. 105) § 77; *The M/V "Virginia G" Case* (n. 320) § 270; Devine (n. 345) 143.

Many other relevant provisions of the LOSC have received less attention. For instance, article 60(4) states that safety zones around artificial islands, installations and structures must be "reasonable". It is not entirely clear what this means, but the coastal States' discretion is limited by the requirement that their design must take into account "the nature and function of the artificial islands, installations or structures".[349] When the duty "to proceed with all possible speed to the rescue of persons in distress" is qualified by the fact that such a step "reasonably be expected",[350] this is understood to mean that "a master must make a discretionary judgement based on all the relevant circumstances of the case".[351] As far as it is concerned, the duty of the coastal States not to impede the laying or maintenance of submarine cables and pipelines on their continental shelves is counterbalanced by their right, confirmed in article 79(2), "to take reasonable measures for the exploration of the continental shelf, the exploitation of its natural resources and the prevention, reduction and control of pollution from pipelines". The ILC was unwilling to propose a more specific wording,[352] but a measure will arguably be unreasonable if it results "in the impossibility of laying a submarine cable, or if the costs would increase disproportionally".[353]

As the LOSC illustration of the "requirement under general international law to undertake an environmental impact assessment",[354] article 206 only requires that States assess the potential effects of "planned activities under their jurisdiction or control" on the marine environment when they "have reasonable grounds for believing that [those] activities […] may cause substantial pollution of[,] or significant and harmful changes to[,] the marine environment". The phrase "reasonable grounds for believing" suggests a more subjective assessment than the phrase "likely to have", which is used in many environmental-law instruments.[355] Nevertheless, the discretion must be exercised in the fulfilment of the States' general "obligation to protect and preserve the marine environment",[356] their duty to take measures "necessary to prevent […] pollution of the marine environment"[357] and, arguably, the precautionary principle.[358] The phrase

349 Article 60(5). See also article 260.

350 Article 98(1)(b).

351 Guilfoyle (n. 107) 727.

352 See § 20 of the Statement by Mr François in UNCLOS I "Summary records of the 13th meeting of the Second Committee" (UN Doc. A/AC.13/C.4/SR.13 (1958) in (1958) IV *UNCLOS I Official Records* 33–34).

353 W Heintschel von Heinegg "Protecting critical submarine cyber infrastructure: Legal status and protection of submarine communications cables under international law" in K Ziolkowski (ed) *Peacetime Regime for State Activities in Cyberspace* (2013) 291–318 at 306.

354 *Case Concerning Pulp Mills on the River Uruguay* (n. 166) § 204. See further L Kong "Environmental impact assessment under the United Nations Convention on the Law of the Sea" (2011) 10 *Chinese Journal of International Law* 651–670 at 658.

355 See e.g., article 14(1)(a)–(b) of the CBD. See further e.g., Kong (n. 354) 659.

356 Article 192.

357 Article 194(1).

358 See e.g., *Southern Bluefin Tuna Cases* (n. 163) § 77; *Case Concerning Land Reclamation in and around the Straits of Johor (Malaysia v. Singapore)*, order of 8 October 2003, 2003 ITLOS Reports 10 § 99. See further *Indus Waters Kishenganga Arbitration (Pakistan v. India)*, award of

"reasonable grounds for believing" is used also in article 211(6)(a) regarding the adoption of special mandatory measures for the prevention of pollution from vessels in "a particular, clearly defined area" of an EEZ. In this case, the coastal State's discretion is limited by the requirement that the special measure must be "required for recognized technical reasons in relation to its oceanographical and ecological conditions, as well as its utilization or the protection of its resources and the particular character of its traffic".[359]

Article 225 requires that, when the organs of States exercise the latter's "powers of enforcement", they do not "expose the marine environment to an unreasonable risk". This requires both a prior assessment of the environmental impact that enforcement measures might have and an assessment in each case "taking into account the specificities of the situation".[360] Article 226(1)(c) allows a State to refuse, or make "conditional upon proceeding to the nearest appropriate repair yard", the release of a vessel that "would present an unreasonable threat of damage to the marine environment" were it to be released. "The assessment of reasonableness of the threat of damage [...] is subject to a case-by-case analysis".[361] When article 246(3) requires that coastal States establish rules and procedures ensuring that their consent to marine scientific research and their EEZs and on their continental shelves "will not be delayed or denied unreasonably", it does so "to ensure the effectiveness of the consent regime".[362] Likewise, article 255 requires that the "rules, regulations and procedures to promote and facilitate marine scientific research [...]", which States must "endeavour to adopt", be "reasonable", "a notion that is particularly relevant with respect to the content of any documents and the timeliness of the application and response".[363]

Article 266(1) requires that States cooperate "to promote actively the development and transfer of marine science and marine technology on fair and reasonable terms and conditions", while article 269(b) requires that States "promote favourable conditions for the conclusion of agreements, contracts and other similar arrangements, under equitable and reasonable conditions".

> Neither the *raison d'être* of the words "equitable and reasonable conditions" nor its meaning are entirely clear. As a consequence, an attempt at interpretation may be made in the sense both of strengthening the purpose of

---

18 February 2013, XXXI RIAA 55 § 452; W Gullett "Environmental impact assessment and the precautionary principle: Legislating caution in environmental protection" (1998) 5(3) *Australian Journal of Environmental Management* 146–158 at 148.

359 See K Bartenstein "Article 211" in Proelss (n. 24) 1419–1443 at 1439.

360 V Becker-Weinberg "Article 225" in Proelss (n. 24) 1534–1537 at 1536. See further e.g., *The M/V "Virginia G" Case* (n. 320) § 373.

361 V Becker-Weinberg "Article 226" in Proelss (n. 24) 1537–1544 at 1543.

362 S Huh & K Nishimoto "Article 246" in Proelss (n. 24) 1649–1664 at 1660. See further article 246(6).

363 S Huh & K Nishimoto "Article 255" in Proelss (n. 24) 1713–1716 at 1716.

> technology transfer, by emphasizing the word "equitable", and of weakening it, by emphasizing the word "reasonable".[364]

As far as it is concerned, article 147 requires that activities in the Area be carried out "with reasonable regard for other activities in the marine environment"[365] and the latter be conducted "with reasonable regard for activities in the Area".[366] The term "reasonable regard" is not defined in the LOSC and it is not used in any other respect. It was used in the CHS,[367] with regard to which it would appear to refer to the requirement that

> a State which is contemplating a particular use of the high seas [considers] the interest of other States in their own use of the high seas and [adjusts] or [qualifies] its activity (whether in method or manner or in point of place or time) so as to avoid or minimize unnecessary interference with others.[368]

There seems to be no reason why the same would not apply with regard to the Area.[369] The term "reasonable regard" was replaced by the term "due regard" in article 87(2) of the LOSC, which requires that the freedoms of the high seas be exercised by all States "with due regard for the rights under th[e] Convention with respect to activities in the Area".[370] Reading articles 87(2) and 147 together, it appears that "the term 'reasonable regard' essentially describes the same standard as that of 'due regard'".[371] As a result, the difference between the two terms is "purely semantic and the test remains in essence one of reasonableness".[372]

Relatedly, article 110(1) confirms that the right of visit on the high seas is subject to the existence of a "reasonable ground for suspecting" specific activities or facts. Weight is added to that requirement by the fact that, "[i]f the suspicions prove to be unfounded, and provided that the ship boarded has not committed any act justifying them, it shall be compensated for any loss or damage that may have been sustained".[373] The severe penalty of this strict liability is "justified in order to prevent the right of visit being abused".[374]

364 K Bartenstein "Article 269" in Proelss (n. 24) 1783–1788 at 1787.
365 Article 147(1) of the LOSC. See also Annex III article 17(1)(b)(ix).
366 Article 147(3) of the LOSC.
367 See article 2.
368 D Anderson "The principle of reasonableness in the law of the sea" in HP Hestermeyer *et al.* (eds) *Coexistence, Cooperation and Solidarity* (2012) 657–669 at 660.
369 See S Vöneky & F Beck "Article 147" in Proelss (n. 24) 1035–1045 at 1040–1041.
370 See further e.g., *The "Enrica Lexie" Incident* (n. 87) § 973; Nordquist (n. 107) 86 § 87.9(l).
371 Vöneky & Beck (n. 369) 1041. See also e.g., J Kraska *Maritime Power and the Law of the Sea* (2011) 262.
372 Anderson (n. 368) 662.
373 Article 110(3).
374 ILC (n. 266) 284.

Performative reasonableness applies even when the parameter is not mentioned explicitly in the LOSC. This was made clear in *M/V "Saiga" (No 2)*, when ITLOS stated that,

> [a]lthough the Convention does not contain express provisions on the use of force in the arrest of ships, international law, which is applicable by virtue of article 293 of the Convention, requires that the use of force must be avoided as far as possible and, where force is unavoidable, it must not go beyond what is reasonable and necessary in the circumstances.[375]

This principle was confirmed in the Fish Stocks Agreement, which requires that inspecting States ensure that their duly authorised inspectors "avoid the use of force except when and to the degree necessary to ensure the safety of the inspectors and where the inspectors are obstructed in the execution of their duties" and that "[t]he degree of force used shall not exceed that reasonably required in the circumstances".[376] In the process of reaching the conclusion that an unreasonable use of force had been made in *M/V "Saiga" (No 2)*, ITLOS took into account that,

> [h]aving boarded the ship without resistance, and although there is no evidence of the use or threat of force from the crew, [the Guinean officers] fired indiscriminately while on the deck and used gunfire to stop the engine of the ship. In using firearms in this way, the Guinean officers appeared to have attached little or no importance to the safety of the ship and the persons on board. In the process, considerable damage was done to the ship and to vital equipment in the engine and radio rooms. And, more seriously, the indiscriminate use of gunfire caused severe injuries to two of the persons on board.[377]

5.5.4.3 Intersective reasonableness

It was explained, in Chapter 4, how sovereignty and sovereign rights have the effect, directly or by implication, of excluding many overlaps of State ocean jurisdiction by limiting the scope of potentially intersecting jurisdictions.[378] Nevertheless, there remain a number of situations in which different States may have a jurisdictional ground to be involved at the same time. In those situations, the question arises whether reasonableness has any role to play in the case of conflicting exercises by States of their concurrent jurisdictions. The answer to that question is important because there does not appear to be any basis for *a priori* prioritising one ground ahead of another, although State practice may lead to considering one ground of

375 *M/V "Saiga" (No 2)* (n. 105) § 155.
376 Article 22(1)(f).
377 *M/V "Saiga" (No 2)* (n. 105) § 158.
378 Or concurrent jurisdictions.

jurisdiction as normal and another one as exceptional in any given situation.[379] This is, for instance, the case of personal jurisdiction, the ocean-governance contribution of which is often underestimated due to the comparatively small scope of PE jurisdiction.

The avoidance of conflicting exercises of jurisdiction appears not to be as important a concern in the law of the sea as it is in other fields, such as economic law.[380] One of the reasons is that many problematic conflicts have been eliminated by conventional provisions. For instance, it was already pointed out in the previous chapter that TL jurisdiction regarding innocent passage is limited by article 21(2) of the LOSC in that the laws and regulations adopted in the exercise of that jurisdiction may "not apply to the design, construction, manning or equipment of foreign ships unless they are giving effect to generally accepted international rules or standards".[381] This limitation of TL jurisdiction contributes to the protection of the *ius communicationis* in that it "removes the risk of divergent design, construction, manning and equipment standards [adopted by coastal States], to which ships cannot adjust during a voyage".[382] At the same time, it contributes to the avoidance of harm to States, individuals and the environment, both by confirming the TL jurisdiction to adopt normative provisions containing requirements up to the generally accepted international rules or standards, and by not limiting the FL jurisdiction to adopt normative provisions containing requirements higher than those rules or standards. In the process, article 21(2) strikes the balance between TL jurisdiction and FL jurisdiction that is required to take into account as many of the teleological principles as possible.

A second reason why the avoidance of conflicting exercises of jurisdiction is a relatively less important concern in the law of the sea flows from the polymorphic extent of the scopes of State ocean jurisdiction. Using once again personal jurisdiction as an example, PL jurisdiction is all-encompassing *ratione materiae* and *ratione loci*, but PE jurisdiction is excluded by the TE jurisdiction and the FE jurisdiction of other States. Together with the fact that PL jurisdiction does not exclude other legislative jurisdictions, this position explains why the exercise of PL jurisdiction does not usually give rise to much concern by other States.

Against the background of a conflict-avoidance approach being of little assistance in giving meaning to intersective reasonableness, comity is also of little assistance, irrespective of whether it is part of public international law or whether it is

379 See e.g., *The "Enrica Lexie" Incident* (n. 87) § 973; § 407 comment (d) *Restatement of the Law (Fourth): The Foreign Relations Law of the United States* (2018); Bowett (n. 20) 14–15; B Simma & AT Müller "Exercise and limits of jurisdiction" in Crawford & Koskenniemi (n. 11) 134–157 at 151; C Ryngaert *Jurisdiction in International Law* (2015) 143–144, who appears to attribute that situation to the fact that "[t]he classical doctrine of international jurisdiction [...] is not concerned with exclusivity of jurisdiction [...]").

380 See Ryngaert (n. 379) 146.

381 See Chapter 4 section 4.3.3.2.

382 Churchill, Lowe & Sander (n. 89) 158.

synonymous to international law.[383] For jurisdictional purposes, "comity means that States limit the reach of their laws, and defer to other States that may have a stronger, often territorial, nexus to a situation".[384] However, there is little evidence in the ocean governance context that deference is a policy consideration, let alone a legal duty, in cases of overlapping jurisdictions. The reason is that, in cases where precedence is required, the possibility of overlap has been explicitly excluded, as is the case, for instance, of TE jurisdiction. This goes a long way towards removing concerns of intervention in the domestic affairs of coastal States when flag States and personal States exercise their respective legislative jurisdictions by adopting normative provisions applicable within the internal waters and territorial seas of foreign States.[385] Such an exclusion also has the effect of significantly restricting the exercise of FA jurisdiction and PA jurisdiction to the extent that the exercise of FE jurisdiction or PE jurisdiction is required to bring the persons concerned within the jurisdiction of the courts.

A purposive approach is a more compelling avenue to follow. In that approach, a first step entails recognising that overlaps of jurisdictions should not be viewed with suspicion, but rather be seen as important assets for ocean governance.[386] There are two main reasons for this. The first one is that most activities at sea take place outside the territorial limits of States. In that extraterritorial space, there is no equivalent to the monopolistic claim of territory-based jurisdiction. The second reason is that, in practice, many ocean activities involve persons and objects connected to different States. In that state of affairs, the principle of equality of States militates against treating jurisdictional assertions differently.[387]

At the same time, placing the entire jurisdictional burden on one State is probably logistically unrealistic for any State, let alone States confronted with relatively high-capacity challenges, thereby doing little to take into account the factor of equity. To do so would also unnecessarily reduce the jurisdictional arsenal available to take into account other factors, such as the prevention of harm to persons, for instance.

A second step involves acknowledging that it is not unreasonable for States to make use of their jurisdictions to replicate the normative provisions of foreign States that apply in the extraterritorial ocean space, and thereby empower their courts to adjudicate on related disputes. For instance, there appears to be no basis for objecting to a State exercising its PL jurisdiction by adopting a normative provision forbidding its nationals to fish in the EEZ of a foreign State in violation of the latter's fisheries legislation. Indeed, in doing so, the personal State is not arrogating to itself the sovereign rights of the foreign State by making any independent

383 See JA Kämmerer "Comity" 2006 MPEPIL § 1. See also e.g., M Akehurst "Jurisdiction in international law" (1972–1973) 46 BYIL 145–257 at 214–216.

384 Ryngaert (n. 379) 148.

385 See Chapter 4 section 4.4.3.

386 See e.g., *The "Enrica Lexie" Incident* (n. 87) § 975.

387 See e.g., *The "Arctic Sunrise" Arbitration* (n. 105) § 328; J Mossop "Protests against oil exploration at sea: Lessons from the *Arctic Sunrise* Arbitration" (2016) 31 IJMCL 60–87.

decision relating to the exploration, exploitation, conservation and management of the living resources in the EEZ of the foreign State. In fact, and this is the third step, one should arguably accept that it is reasonable to expect States to make use of their legislative jurisdictions and adjudicative jurisdictions for replicative purposes.[388] The additional burden on States would indeed be little compared to the contribution such a requirement would make towards goals such as the prevention of harm to the environment and equity, for instance.

A fourth step entails recognising that, while it is probably unreasonable to expect States to go beyond replication in order to act in a manner that, in their own assessment, conforms better to the teleological principles, it is also not *a priori* unreasonable for them to do so. For instance, it appears at first glance reasonable for a State to exercise its PL jurisdiction for conservation purposes by adopting a normative provision forbidding its nationals to be involved in specific fishing activities even where such activities are lawful in the domestic law of the coastal State concerned. One must however guard against the pursuit of one goal running against another goal. For instance, in a case where the fishing activities are heavily dependent on the involvement of the nationals of the personal State, the prohibition might result in a considerable reduction of those activities, with less fish available for consumption and the resulting harm to individuals. In such a case, the exercise by the State of its PL jurisdiction might be found to be unreasonable at the end of a balancing exercise.

At the same time, one must guard against assuming that the exercise of a concurrent jurisdiction in order to achieve a national goal is inevitably unreasonable. For instance, a State might exercise its PL jurisdiction to combat what it considers to be unfair competition in the shipping industry by adopting a normative provision forbidding its nationals from being employed on vessels that do not comply with the generally accepted international regulations, procedures and practices. Such a step falls short of imposing those regulations, procedures and practices on vessels flying the flags of foreign States. In addition, even though it might harm some individuals by reducing their opportunities of employment, it might be found to be reasonable in view of its contribution to the prevention of other harm to those same individuals, such as injury and inhumane working conditions, as well as the prevention of harm to the environment, for instance.

5.6 Conclusion

The purpose of State ocean jurisdiction is less circumscribed by international law than its form, ground and scope. This is to be expected in view of the principle of sovereign equality of States and the independence that it entails. Thus, the purpose of State ocean jurisdiction remains primarily for each State to pursue its own interests in ocean-related matters through the exercise of whichever jurisdiction, and to whatever extent, it deems appropriate in any specific instance. That freedom has

388 See Ryngaert (n. 379) 190.

however never been absolute. It is limited by an ever-increasing number of specific duties which, taking into account the ever-increasing interdependence of States, contribute to ensuring that "effective jurisdiction exists to achieve certain common objectives of States".[389] In addition, as the history of the international law of the sea and the numerous relevant international instruments presently in force demonstrate, the freedom is limited also by teleological principles that point towards the lawful purpose of State ocean jurisdiction as well as purposive parameters within which the purpose for which State ocean jurisdiction is exercised is to be lawfully achieved.

While the protection of the *ius communicationis* remains an important teleological principle because it constitutes one of the pillars on which the present globalised economic order rests, the scale of contemporary shipping, together with the ever-growing multiplicity of ocean uses and actors as well as the ever more sophisticated technologies available, contribute to the continued relevance of the need to avoid harm to States, to the growing urgency of avoiding harm to the cultural and natural environment and to the (strikingly only recent) recognition that avoidance of harm to individuals is at least an equally weighty imperative. It is that recognition that opened the door to the realisation that the two most important teleological principles are arguably the pursuit of equity, both at the intragenerational level and the intergenerational level, and integrative cooperation.

In turn, the pursuit of equity and integrative cooperation offer arguably the soundest foundations on which to base the purposive parameters of good faith, abuse of right and reasonableness. In other words, the three parameters are arguably best seen as being aimed at ensuring that equity and integrative cooperation are not only taken into account by States when they determine the purpose for which they want to exercise their State ocean jurisdiction, but also when they determine the manner in which they intend to exercise that jurisdiction. Equity and integrative cooperation demand that States respect and protect other States, the cultural and natural environment as well as individuals by acting within the parameters of good faith, abuse of rights and performative reasonableness. They also demand that States promote and fulfil humankind's needs and interests by acting within the parameter of intersective reasonableness.

389 Oxman (n. 26) § 9.

6 Conclusion

In the same way as light and sound are both related aspects of the same physical reality, territoriality and jurisdiction are both related aspects of the same legal reality. At the same time, while light travels faster and further outside water than in water, sound travels faster and further in water than outside water.[1] It can be argued that, likewise, territoriality plays the predominant role on land, while jurisdiction plays the predominant role at sea. Like light, territoriality (and its companion, extraterritoriality) has been, and will probably remain, the primary lens for understanding the allocation of authority between States on land. For that reason, it is likely that space will continue to play a major role in our approach to the allocation of authority between States at sea and in our attempts at tackling the ocean-governance challenges to which we are faced. Arguably, the jurisdictional approach adopted in this study shows that a weakness of the territorial or spatial approach is that it opens the door to a truncated understanding of State ocean jurisdiction, with negative effects on our collective ability to improve our management of the oceans and to imagine sustainable ocean futures for the benefit of all ocean stakeholders.

While territoriality is suited to an almost exclusively two-dimensional and sedentary land environment, it is an ill-suited starting point in the predominantly four-dimensional and mobile ocean environment.[2] In addition, the significantly limited jurisdiction of the coastal States *ratione loci* is at the same time multidimensional. As a result, the concept "coastal State jurisdiction" is arguably too imprecise to make it possible to analyse with sufficient accuracy both the scope of that jurisdiction and its relationship with other grounds of jurisdiction. While this is the main reason why the concept was disaggregated in this study, an analytical and systematic study of State ocean jurisdiction provides a different lens with which to engage with the international-law-of-the-sea regime. That lens makes it possible to approach the regime not as a combination of juxtaposed and largely monolithic maritime-zone regimes, as the separate 1958 Geneva conventions and the structure of the LOSC suggest, but as the manifestation of an ocean-wide web of jurisdictions interacting with each other at different levels and in different ways spatially.

1 See e.g., S Dosso & J Dettmer "Studying the sea with sound" (2013) 19 *Acoustical Society of America – Proceedings of Meetings on Acoustics* 032001.

2 See e.g., KA Alexander *Conflicts over Marine and Coastal Common Resources* (2020) 18.

DOI: 10.4324/9781003383871-6

This has the effect of shedding a different light on the relationships between the jurisdictions as well as on the substantive and procedural aspects of the exercise of each jurisdiction.

In the first regard, the study highlighted that each of the coastal State jurisdictions as well as port State jurisdiction carry a relatively lighter weight in the overall scheme of allocation of ocean jurisdiction among States than one would expect from a land perspective. This has the effect of bringing into sharper focus the extent to which P jurisdiction and F jurisdiction need to play a role in any sustainable ocean-governance regime. In turn, this points to the fact that the (temptingly straightforward) dichotomy between *mare clausum* and *mare liberum* was arguably never about a blunt distinction between (quasi-)territoriality and extraterritoriality, between areas within "national jurisdiction" and areas beyond "national jurisdiction" (ABNJ). It was rather about the relationship between, on the one hand, the spatially bound jurisdictions and, on the other hand, the ocean-wide mobile jurisdictions exercised both in the areas within the scope *ratione loci* of the coastal jurisdictions and in the areas beyond the coastal jurisdictions (ABCJs).

The dichotomy between *mare clausum* and *mare liberum* was arguably also never meant to reflect a distinction between the existence of full jurisdiction, on the one hand, and the complete absence of jurisdiction, on the other. When the allocation of authority between States is approached with a jurisdictional lens rather than a spatial lens, it becomes clearer that sovereignty, sovereign rights and the freedom of the high seas are not *cartes blanches* for succumbing to "unilateralist impulse[s] often born of narrow agendas, impatience, frustration, or political and bureaucratic ambition".[3] Instead, they constitute yardsticks on which to rely when establishing the default balance between the different State ocean jurisdictions, a balance that States are always free to agree among themselves to alter for the purpose of better protecting the *ius communicationis*, avoiding harm to States, individuals and the environment, and pursuing equity through integrative cooperation within the bounds of reasonableness.

In the same way that sound has different frequencies which affect human and other beings differently, State ocean jurisdictions take different forms which affect States differently. Legislative flag State jurisdiction and legislative personal jurisdiction have the widest scope *ratione loci*. This means that the flag State and the personal State always have legislative authority *ratione loci* over the vessels and persons with which they have the necessary link. At the same time, legislative flag State jurisdiction and legislative personal jurisdiction are all-encompassing *ratione materiae*, being only limited by the principle of non-intervention in the internal or external affairs of other States. In the latter regard, it has been shown in this study that a flag State or a personal State does not violate the principle when it requires vessels or persons over which it has jurisdiction, that they comply with the norms adopted by a coastal State in the exercise of one of its legislative coastal jurisdictions when they are within the relevant maritime zone of the coastal State.

3 BH Oxman "The territorial temptation: A siren song at sea" (2006) 100 AJIL 830–851 at 851.

Obviously, the principle is also not violated when States agree with each other at the normative level.

The scope of executive flag State jurisdiction and executive personal jurisdiction is potentially as wide as the respective legislative jurisdictions, being only limited, in the case of enforcement acts, when there is a lack of consent by either a flag State or a coastal State having executive territorial jurisdiction. In other words, the very limited extent of executive personal jurisdiction at sea and the limitations of executive flag State jurisdiction are arguably not a structural, but a "conjunctural" feature of the State ocean jurisdiction regime. This means that the limitations of executive flag State jurisdiction and executive personal jurisdiction are not insurmountable, as many examples already confirm. It also means that those limitations only remain in existence as long as States are unwilling or unable to remove them and as long as other States are unwilling or unable to extend their jurisdictions once the limitations have been removed.

A jurisdictional lens also allows us to cross more easily the divide between the sea and the land, where the polities remain based. Indeed, when one appreciates more accurately both the complex relationship between the various forms of jurisdictions and the fact that, while a substantial part of the acts performed by States in the exercise of their ocean jurisdictions are performed at sea, many others are performed on land, it becomes unavoidable to acknowledge and take into account the symbiotic relationship, both at the substantive and procedural levels, between ocean governance and land governance.

At the substantive level, a jurisdictional lens reminds us that the role of the LOSC, like many constitutions, is, on the one hand, to allocate jurisdiction and, on the other hand, to regulate its exercise with regard to the substantive and procedural aspects which are considered the most important at the time of its adoption. In other words, the LOSC was never intended to provide a comprehensive detailed normative regime governing all activities at sea. This means that nothing in the LOSC stands in the way of a State exercising its legislative jurisdiction in any matter *as long as*, when it does so, it does not arrogate to itself a jurisdiction which it does not have, or violate one of its international obligations. With the same proviso, this also means that, when there is no rational basis for a distinction to be made, nothing in the LOSC stands in the way of a State ensuring that the normative regime that governs persons and activities under its territorial jurisdiction on land, including the human-rights and environment components of that regime, governs also persons and activities under its jurisdictions at sea.

Likewise, at the procedural level, a jurisdictional lens reminds us that, in addition to the forms of exercise of authority on which the international-law-of-the-sea regime focuses (e.g., the enforcement acts performed in the exercise of executive jurisdiction), there is a range of related acts left to be governed by the domestic laws of States. This, in turn, alerts us to the fact that the standards of international ocean governance cannot be divorced from the standards of domestic (land) governance. It alerts us also to the possibility that acts related to ocean matters might be governed by different (possibly less stringent) procedural requirements than acts related to land matters in cases where there is no rational basis for a distinction to be made. This ought to be a serious jurisdictional concern, particularly in view of the (often huge) economic interests at stake, the continuously increasing complexity of natural and human interactions at sea as well as the wide range of unequally powerful stakeholders involved. If humankind is to have any chance of tackling successfully the existential challenges to which it is faced, that concern needs to be addressed by means of fully inclusive domestic processes leading to decisions which are based on the best disciplinary and transdisciplinary knowledge, and the primary goal of which is to contribute to the common good. This requires that domestic-governance standards be improved, if necessary, that capacity and knowledge inequalities between and within States be addressed wherever they exist, and that States be prepared to make their respective contributions to the international-law-of-the-sea regime and how it is applied. This study has hopefully made a useful contribution at least in the latter respect.

Index

For Product Safety Concerns and Information please contact our EU
representative GPSR@taylorandfrancis.com
Taylor & Francis Verlag GmbH, Kaufingerstraße 24, 80331 München, Germany

www.ingramcontent.com/pod-product-compliance
Ingram Content Group UK Ltd.
Pitfield, Milton Keynes, MK11 3LW, UK
UKHW020152200926
475702UK00016B/2674
* 9 7 8 1 0 3 2 4 6 9 3 7 9 *